ECONOMICS

THIRD EDITION

Alan J. Carper
Roger Bradley
Brad A. Payne

bju press®
Greenville, South Carolina

Note: The fact that materials produced by other publishers may be referred to in this volume does not constitute an endorsement of the content or theological position of materials produced by such publishers. Any references and ancillary materials are listed as an aid to the student or the teacher and in an attempt to maintain the accepted academic standards of the publishing industry.

ECONOMICS
Third Edition

Alan J. Carper, MBA
Roger Bradley, PhD
Brad A. Payne, MA, MS

Coordinating Writer
Elizabeth B. Payne, MS

Contributing Writers
Pamela B. Creason, MEd
Franklin S. Hall, MA

Consultant
Sonia Johnson, EdD

Bible Integration
Wesley Barley, MDiv

Project Editor
Jill Blackstock, MEd

Concept Design
Drew Fields

Cover Design
Drew Fields

Page Layout
Jessica Johnson

Design
Josh Frederick

Permissions
Sylvia Gass
Brenda Hansen
Meg Jones
Carrie Walker

Project Manager
Benjamin Sinnamon

Illustrators
John Cunningham
Sarah Ensminger
Courtney Godbey
Preston Gravely
Cynthia Long
Dave Schuppert
Lynda Slattery
Del Thompson

Photo credits appear on page 337.

All trademarks are the registered and unregistered marks of their respective owners. BJU Press is in no way affiliated with these companies. No rights are granted by BJU Press to use such marks, whether by implication, estoppel, or otherwise.

© 2017 BJU Press
Greenville, South Carolina 29609
First Edition © 1991, 1999 BJU Press
Second Edition © 2010 BJU Press

Printed in the United States of America

All rights reserved

ISBN 978-1-60682-877-9

15 14 13 12 11 10 9 8 7 6 5

Introduction vi

UNIT 1: ECONOMICS: THE SCIENCE OF CHOICE

Chapter 1: What Is Economics? 2
Personal Finance: Budgeting *16*

Chapter 2: Economic Models 22
Personal Finance: Principles of Purchasing *38*
Personal Finance: Consumerism *41*

Chapter 3: Value and Demand 44
Personal Finance: Insuring Your Home, Auto, and Life *58*

Chapter 4: Supply and Prices 64
Personal Finance: The Christian and Debt *80*

UNIT 2: ECONOMICS OF THE NATIONS

Chapter 5: What Is the Economic Problem? 86
Personal Finance: The Consumer and Debt *102*

Chapter 6: Economic Systems 106
Personal Finance: Types of Consumer Credit *122*

UNIT 3: ECONOMICS OF THE BUSINESS FIRM

Chapter 7: Forms of Business Ownership 128
Personal Finance: Sources of Consumer Credit *142*

Chapter 8: The Stock Market 146
Personal Finance: Creditworthiness *160*

Chapter 9: Market Structure and Competition 164
Personal Finance: Cash Management *180*

UNIT 4: ECONOMICS OF THE FINANCIAL MARKET

Chapter 10: Money and the Financial Market 186
Personal Finance: Opening and Maintaining a Transaction Account ... *202*

Chapter 11: Central Banking 208
Personal Finance: Ways to Save *228*

UNIT 5: ECONOMICS OF THE GOVERNMENT

Chapter 12: Measuring the Wealth of the Nation 234
Personal Finance: Understanding How Interest Works *252*

Chapter 13: The Business Cycle and Unemployment **256**
    Personal Finance: Savings Instruments *274*

Chapter 14: Inflation **278**
    Personal Finance: Estate Planning *294*

Chapter 15: Fiscal Policy **300**
    Personal Finance: Retirement Planning *318*

Glossary **322**

Index **331**

Photograph Credits **337**

⁶But godliness with contentment is great gain.

⁷For we brought nothing into this world, and it is certain we can carry nothing out.

⁸And having food and raiment let us be therewith content.

⁹But they that will be rich fall into temptation and a snare, and into many foolish and hurtful lusts, which drown men in destruction and perdition.

¹⁰For the love of money is the root of all evil: which while some coveted after, they have erred from the faith, and pierced themselves through with many sorrows.

¹¹But thou, O man of God, flee these things; and follow after righteousness, godliness, faith, love, patience, meekness.

1 TIMOTHY 6:6-11

INTRODUCTION

Choices and consequences—each day you make choices, and each one has consequences. Many of those choices, and their consequences, seem rather insignificant. Others, though, even some you may have judged of little importance, can have considerable immediate and future impact—sometimes far more than you could have anticipated. The study of the short- and long-term effects of people's choices is a part of economics: the science of how and why people make the choices they do.

The purpose of this textbook is to provide you with a working knowledge of basic economic principles and to introduce you to factors that economists have identified as influences on your choices. This knowledge will assist you in understanding current economic issues and will help prepare you for the economic questions and challenges you will face on whatever path God leads you. This book takes a conservative approach to economic philosophy. It is not intended to be an exhaustive study of classical capitalist economics, but rather, its design is to give you the basic tools, the "nuts and bolts," of economics, such as fundamental laws and models. Your study will include such basic concepts as utility, opportunity benefit, opportunity cost, subjective value, and the laws of demand and supply. You will learn about economic systems, seeing both their strengths and weaknesses. You will be exposed to the economic workings of business firms and financial markets and to the business cycle. And by studying the concepts of GDP, unemployment, trade, inflation, and taxation, you will learn how an economy functions in today's world and how it affects you as an individual in that economy.

As you learn these concepts, you will be challenged to look at them from a biblical worldview. This will often require that you evaluate your own choices and assess their consequences. People are made in the image of God. The choices they make are not neutral. Economics is full of things that are good and bad, right and wrong, just and unjust. Being a Christian who glorifies God in all areas of his life means being someone who can apply the Bible to all kinds of economic realities in order to choose what is good, right, and just.

The Bible has a lot to say about economics. While it doesn't use most of the economic terms discussed in this textbook, it does tell us that "the eyes of man are never satisfied" (Prov. 27:20). It tells us about the basic nature of man. It tells us what we should and should not pursue (Luke 12:30, 31). The Bible also has a lot to say about money—where it comes from, how we should use it, and even how we should feel about it. Some ideas in economics contradict Scripture or encourage people to act unbiblically. You need to be able to recognize these and avoid them. Whatever your economic positions, you are a Christian first of all. To that end we have tried to consistently direct you to the Bible and biblical thinking.

Regardless of whether they are accountants, entrepreneurs, plumbers, teachers, or surgeons, Christians need to understand basic economic principles. In the United States we operate mainly under principles of free-market capitalism. While we support this system, we must also recognize its weaknesses. Although it works best when unregulated, because of man's sin nature, regulations are necessary. Balance resulting from sound judgment is the key.

Christians must also take heed that they live the economic principles they espouse. While opposing governmental interventions and efforts to redistribute the nation's wealth, they must not ignore their personal responsibility to help those in need. Showing love through giving manifests the character of God (John 3:16). Christians ought to be known as caring, generous people.

Luke 12:48 teaches that "unto whomsoever much is given, of him shall be much required." As you are exposed to a biblically based approach to economics, you will become accountable to appropriate what you learn. The real test will be if and how your choices change.

AT THE MARGIN

In economics the term *margin* refers to "value added." Economists often use the phrase *at* (or *on*) *the margin*. In keeping with this economic phraseology, this book contains material at the margin that is intended to add value to your understanding of the concepts and principles it presents. Such material includes definitions, explanatory notes, and biblical applications.

UNIT ONE

UNIT ONE

ECONOMICS: THE SCIENCE OF CHOICE

CHAPTER 1
What Is Economics? — 2

Personal Finance: Budgeting —16

CHAPTER 2
Economic Models — 22

Personal Finance: Principles of Purchasing — 38
Personal Finance: Consumerism — 41

CHAPTER 3
Value and Demand — 44

Personal Finance: Insuring Your Home, Auto, and Life — 58

CHAPTER 4
Supply and Prices — 64

Personal Finance: The Christian and Debt — 80

CHAPTER ONE
WHAT IS ECONOMICS?

1A THE SCIENCE OF CHOICE — 02

1B THE COST OF CHOICE — 07

1C THE SCOPE AND PURPOSE OF CHOICE — 12

1A THE SCIENCE OF CHOICE

What comes to mind when you hear the word *economics*? Perhaps you think of a business reporter on an evening news program describing the stock market action, economic indicators, or unemployment figures. Perhaps you think of a college classroom full of business majors listening to a professor explaining theoretical equations and monetary policies. Or perhaps you think of yourself and your weekly paycheck, spending habits, and savings account.

Each of these thoughts would be correct. All these ideas fall within the sphere of economics. You may be tempted to think then that economics is too broad or difficult a subject for you to understand. But economics is a part of our God-created world and the processes He set in motion in Genesis 1. Therefore, we glorify God when we learn to make wise use of the economic resources that He has given us dominion over (Gen. 1:26). And economics is not nearly as difficult a subject as you might imagine. In fact, you probably know a lot more about economics than you think because it plays a part in everyone's life.

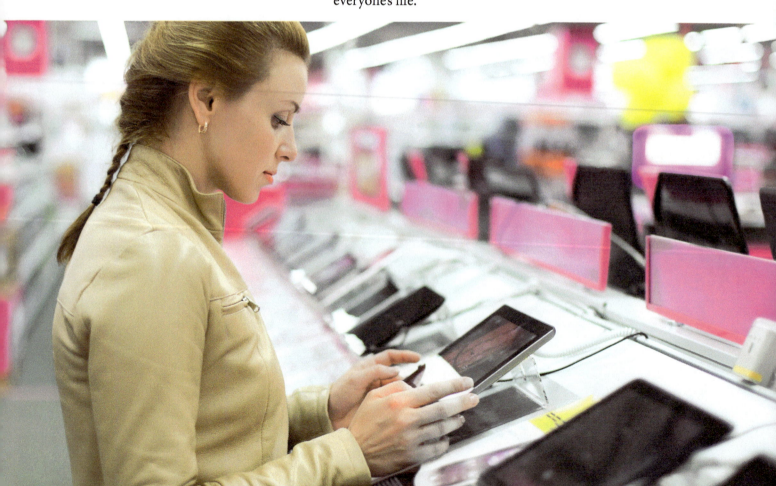

THE SCIENCE OF ECONOMICS

What, then, is economics? **Economics** is the common-sense science of how and why people, businesses, and governments make the choices they do. Economics is as much a science as biology, chemistry, or physics for the following reasons:

- Science always begins with observation. The economist observes how and why choices are made.
- Scientists use their observations as a basis to predict future cause-and-effect relationships. Economists observe trends of the economy and use those observations to predict the future choices of households, business firms, and governments.
- In many cases scientists go one step further by attempting to control future events through altering important variables. Some economists attempt to control the economy by manipulating key variables involved in economic choices (lowering unemployment, lowering prices, etc.).

HOW AND WHY WE MAKE CHOICES

Most students do not realize that they make a multitude of economic choices every day. Should I get out of bed or sleep just a few more minutes? Do I want oatmeal or pizza for breakfast? Should I drink milk or orange juice? How will I get to school—walk, drive, or take the bus? Our lives consist of millions of small economic choices. Each choice, no matter how insignificant it appears, acts like an individual link that joins with other links to form a chain. As the quality of each link determines the quality of the chain, so the quality of each choice a person makes determines the quality of his life.

The Bible has much to say about the choices we make each day. Scripture tells us that our choices are driven by what we love. If we love God, the pattern of our choices will demonstrate that (John 14:23). If we love ourselves, our choices will prove that as well (James 3:16). Christians must seek "the kingdom of God, and his righteousness" (Matt. 6:33) and "set [their] affection on things above, not on things on the earth" (Col. 3:2). They must face the challenge of loving God more than themselves so that God's priorities become their priorities and they make excellent choices. To understand how to make right choices, then, is to understand how to show love for God, and to understand economics is to understand much about making choices. A first step in understanding economics is to learn why choices are necessary.

Choices are necessary because two ideas pull you in opposite directions, making it impossible for you to satisfy both. You, like everyone else, are caught in the struggle between these two ideas: unlimited wants and limited resources.

Everyone has unlimited wants. If you were to write down everything you could possibly desire, the list would illustrate this idea. How long would it take

CHAPTER ONE

Unlimited wants lead people to desire more—perhaps another pair of shoes.

for you to complete your list? An hour? A day? A year? Fifty years?

Consider the things that might go on your list. You might first list basic needs, such as food, shelter, and clothing, but you would quickly begin listing your wants. What kinds of foods would you want? This part of the list alone could take considerable time to complete. What about shelter? Would you really be content with basic shelter when you could have a mansion? Would you be happy with just one mansion when you could have one at the lake and one in the mountains? How about one (or several) in each major city of the world? Next is clothing. No sooner would you finish your immense clothing list than it would require rewriting because tastes, preferences, and styles change.

Add to your list cars, electronics, jewelry, books, music, tools, and thousands of other things, and you will come to the conclusion that your desires are infinite. That our desires are limitless is not a newly discovered truth. Nearly three thousand years ago God gave us this truth in Proverbs 27:20, which states that "the eyes of man are never satisfied," and in Ecclesiastes 5:10, which declares that "he that loveth silver shall not be satisfied with silver; nor he that loveth abundance with increase."

Pursuing the acquisition of things or material gains will shift your focus away from Christ and bring you grief. This is a trap of Satan into which many Christians have fallen. The warning from 1 Timothy 6:9–10 is clear:

> But they that will be rich fall into temptation and a snare, and into many foolish and hurtful lusts, which drown men in destruction and *perdition*. For the love of money is the root of all evil: which while some coveted after, they have erred from the faith, and pierced themselves through with many sorrows.

Everyone also has to deal with limited resources, or **scarcity**. To the economist, scarcity does not mean that everything is in short supply. Instead, it means that everything is finite, or limited in quantity. Only God is truly infinite. There are only so many hours in a day, so many dollars in circulation, so many tasks that one may perform at any given time, and so many barrels of oil in the earth. We say, therefore, that time, money, labor, and natural resources are scarce, or limited in quantity.

The problem, as stated previously, is that our wants are not limited. In fact, we live in a world that defines happiness as the satisfaction

---

Did your list of wants include wisdom? Note what God says about His wisdom: "For wisdom is better than rubies; and all the things that may be desired are not to be compared to it" (Prov. 8:11).

perdition: loss of the soul, eternal damnation, hell

of all wants. Scarcity prevents us from obtaining everything we want, yet we seek to maximize our happiness and devote our energies and activities to an endless cycle of desiring, seeking, acquiring, and consuming those things we believe will bring us satisfaction. God points out the emptiness of such efforts through Solomon's relation of his own experience in this cycle: "And whatsoever mine eyes desired I kept not from them, I withheld not my heart from any joy; for my heart rejoiced in all my labour: and this was my portion of all my labour. Then I looked on all the works that my hands had wrought, and on the labour that I had laboured to do: and, behold, all was vanity and vexation of spirit, and there was no profit under the sun" (Eccles. 2:10–11). No matter how long we search or how hard we try, we can never achieve total satisfaction or peace apart from receiving Jesus Christ as Savior.

Because of the conflict between unlimited wants and limited resources, choices become necessary. Since your time is limited, you must choose which of the many desirable time-consuming activities you will perform. Since your money is scarce, you must choose what you will buy. Although choosing is not always a pleasant experience, if you are a child of God, it need not be a frustrating one. Yes, you still face the struggle between your unlimited wants and your scarce resources, but you know that your God is in control of all things. You also know that He has given you the Holy Spirit and the Scriptures to guide you and that He has promised to give you the wisdom you need to make right choices (James 1:5).

CONTENTMENT

Curbing Unlimited Wants and Living with Limited Resources

Let your conversation be without covetousness; and be content with such things as ye have: for he hath said, I will never leave thee, nor forsake thee.

Hebrews 13:5

In the verse above you see that God commands you to be content. But what does it mean to be content?

If you were to define contentment, what words would you choose? Which words come first to your mind? More than likely you think of phrases such as *having enough*, *being satisfied*, or *not wanting more*.

Contentment can be difficult in a world where there are not enough resources to satisfy everybody's wants. Yet if you are a Christian, you can be content when you live in the truth that God is enough. His grace is always sufficient, no matter what your need may be (2 Cor. 12:9). Colossians 2:10 teaches that a Christian is complete in Christ. If you are complete, then you need nothing more, nothing else. When you find your satisfaction in your relationship with Jesus Christ, you discover that your list of wants noticeably shortens. You realize that you already have all you really need in Christ, and being satisfied with what God provides frees you from much of the scarcity struggle.

You may be wondering what living as a contented Christian with unlimited wants looks like practically. First, being content means that our economic choices themselves will be pleasing to God. You won't want all the same things ungodly people want. Being content also means you won't cheat people when you buy or sell. Finally, you are making progress in contentment when you are able to genuinely thank God for the clothes or electronics that you do have instead of constantly thinking about all the things that you don't have.

The consequences of being content are many. Freedom from a desire for material things means you won't always be caught up in the latest fads or fashions. You will be able to save and even invest your money. It means you won't feel compelled to complain when your wages or benefits do not increase as much or as fast as you would like. It also means you won't define success simply as climbing the corporate ladder or getting more money.

True contentment is possible only because of Christ. He is the only source of real joy, peace, and satisfaction. The more we come to realize that, the more desire we have for Him and the greater need we feel to look to Him.

CHAPTER ONE

STEWARDSHIP

Using Wisely and Well What God Has Given You

Luke 12:42–43 shows the connection between the terms *economics* and *steward*. The steward, or economist, oversees the profitable use of his master's resources, demonstrating wisdom and, most important, faithfulness. The master trusts the steward to do what is right and best with the resources placed under his management.

Paul describes the role of the apostles with these words: "stewards of the mysteries of God" (1 Cor. 4:1). Because Paul was a steward, his primary responsibility was not to please man but to be faithful (1 Cor. 4:2). Although you are not an apostle, it is proper to think of yourself as a steward. You not only have been shown truths about and from God that the unsaved cannot see ("the mysteries of God"), but you have also been given the grace of God (Eph. 4:7, 1 Pet. 4:10). In addition to these benefits, Scripture teaches that every good gift you enjoy has come from God (James 1:17). Consider some of the good gifts God has given you.

God entrusts His stewards with some of His financial resources. For some He provides money through a job; for others He sends financial resources through generous gifts. You may say, "Neither of those applies to me," and you may think God has not entrusted much to you. However, you likely have some money, and you have important decisions to make regarding its use. Do you hide it somewhere in your room (the sock drawer?), save it for college, invest it, or spend it on the latest clothes or electronic gadgets? When making financial decisions, do you seek your Master's wisdom, or do your personal desires determine the choice?

How about time—the twenty-four hours in a day? Everyone has the same amount, the same resource from God. How do you spend yours? You cannot save time; you can only spend it. Nevertheless, you can invest your time by spending it wisely. When you use the time God gives you in wholehearted service for Him, you spend your time laying up treasures in heaven. You can make no better investment.

You are young and perhaps still at an age when you wish you could be just a little older. However, have you ever considered your youth as a resource from God? It is during your high-school and college years that you will likely have more energy and physical ability than at any other time in your life. Yes, God may grant you a long life, but not eternal youth. You have the opportunity right now to use this resource for the glory of God and the good of others.

There are many other gifts God gives: academic talent, athletic skills, and musical or artistic ability. Into each steward's care, the Master places His treasures—to some, many, and to others, few. As a steward commanded to manage well your portion of the Master's resources, you will be held accountable for the choices you make (Luke 12:48).

---

oikos (OY kahs)

nomos (NAH mahs)

Economics is the study of how people, businesses, and governments allocate their limited resources in attempts to satisfy their unlimited wants and needs.

Everyone has to make choices. But as you read in the box on contentment, choices have a new dimension for a Christian. He is not only making choices, but in his choices he is trying to glorify his heavenly Father. A believer glorifies God when he makes wise choices with the limited, or scarce, resources that God has given him. Therefore, we see the importance for the believer of these foundational themes of economics: scarcity and choice.

Even the word *economics* implies scarcity and choice; it comes from the Greek words *oikos*, which means "house," and *nomos*, which means "administration/management of." In the New Testament the Greek words for *economist* are frequently translated "steward," someone responsible for the day-to-day administration of a household. We could say, then, that a biblical economist is a believer who exercises wisdom in making all his choices with the goal of pleasing Jesus Christ: "And the Lord said, Who then is that faithful and wise steward [*oikonomos* or economist], whom his lord shall make ruler over his household, to give them their portion of meat in due season? Blessed is that servant, whom his lord when he cometh shall find so doing" (Luke 12:42–43).

SECTION REVIEW 1A

1. What is economics?
2. What two contradictory ideas result in the necessity of choice?
3. What character quality is essential for a Christian response to scarcity? Why?

1B THE COST OF CHOICE

Everything is scarce, but all things are not equally desirable and therefore not equally scarce. The more desirable and scarce a good or service becomes, the higher its economic cost. **Economic cost** is the value people place on a good or service, and that value, in turn, helps to determine the price of the good or service.

But what exactly is a good or a service? A **good** is any tangible (physical) thing that has a measurable life span. This textbook is a good in that it is a physical thing and its life may be measured. Your shoes, clothing, car keys, eyeglasses, and goldfish are all goods. **Services**, on the other hand, are intangible items. Services include the labor of the accountant, the performance of the singer, and the work of the teacher.

Those goods and services that bear a positive economic cost (a price tag higher than zero) are known as **economic goods** and **economic services**. Goods that a consumer pays to have removed are said to bear a negative economic cost and are called **nuisance goods**. Some examples are discarded cardboard containers, used paper towels, broken toys, empty bottles, dirty motor oil, other garbage, toxic waste, and sewage. Some firms make significant profits by providing the service of turning various nuisance goods into economic goods, a process called **recycling**. Recycling is an application of the stewardship principle. It shows good management of the natural resources God has given to man and plays an important role in caring for the earth and minimizing the costs of further production of economic goods.

Goods and services with a price tag of zero are called **free goods** and **free services**. Free services include the service provided by the wind on a windmill, a rushing stream on a water wheel, and

Economic goods and services are those that have a positive economic cost.

Garbage is a nuisance good that bears a negative economic cost.

Recycling is an example of good economic stewardship.

geothermal steam on an electrical power generator. Free goods, such as air and water, are gifts from God. As free goods become more scarce, they become economic goods. For example, the free air that the farmer in the country enjoys may be an economic good to the citizen of the large polluted city. If the city dweller wants to breathe pure air, he must either pay higher taxes to have the polluted air cleaned or pay to move to the country. Another example is the growth of the bottled water industry. Millions of Americans now pay for a drink of water.

Harnessing a free good (the wind) to produce an economic good (electricity)

Water has transformed from a free good to an economic good.

INTRINSIC VERSUS SUBJECTIVE VALUE

What has more economic value: a handful of diamonds or a single glass of water? Keep in mind that the phrase *economic value* means the value of a good or service in dollars.

Before 1871 this economic riddle, known as the **diamond-water paradox**, had not been solved. The obvious reply was that diamonds, of course, were more valuable, but this answer was incorrect when one considered that a wealthy person dying of thirst would give every diamond he possessed for one glass of water. The riddle appeared to have no correct answer because the "obvious" solution depended on the principle of **intrinsic value**. This principle holds that a thing is valuable because of the nature of the product, such as its scarcity or the amount of labor and natural resources that goes into its production. Diamonds, therefore, would be extremely valuable because they are scarce and require much human labor to extract from the ground. Water, on the other hand, would have little or no value since it is free.

An Austrian economist named Carl Menger put the riddle to rest in his book *Principles of Economics*, published in 1871. In it he argued that there is not just one economic value for every good. The value of an object is not determined by the object itself, but rather by the subject, the person buying the good or service. Therefore, every good's value differs from person to person. The answer to the question of what is more valuable (a handful of diamonds or a glass of water) is that it depends on the state of mind of the one answering the riddle—there is no wrong answer! Menger called his new idea the principle of **subjective value**, which states that it is an object's usefulness to the buyer that determines its worth. Economists have another word for usefulness—**utility**. An important component of utility is the amount of satisfaction the good or service provides the buyer. Utility, of course, varies from person to person. For a person living beside a stream, diamonds would provide far more utility and be far more valuable than the glass of water, while for the man dying of thirst in the desert, diamonds would hold little or no utility relative to the value of the water.

You must keep in mind this idea of subjective value, or you may easily fall into the intrinsic value trap. For example, a pilot of a jumbo jet may believe that his labor is worth $500,000 per year because of the stress involved, the years of study endured, and the responsibility of having several hundred lives in his care while he flies. Economically speaking, however, the pilot's service is worth whatever his passengers are willing to pay. If he were the only pilot of jumbo jets in the world, they might be willing to pay him $500,000. However, if there were 200 million jumbo-jet pilots, his relative value would decrease, resulting in lower pay.

Carl Menger published a solution to the diamond-water paradox in 1871.

OPPORTUNITY COST IS THE BASIS OF CHOICE

For you to apply Menger's principle of subjective value, it is critical that you understand the twin concepts of **opportunity benefit** and **opportunity cost**. Opportunity benefit is the satisfaction you receive from the choice you make. Opportunity cost, on the other hand, is the satisfaction you give up or the regret you experience for not choosing differently.

Suppose you are behind the steering wheel cruising happily down the street. You have $30 in your pocket, and you are on your way to your favorite restaurant for a long-awaited dinner. As you drive by an electronics store, this sign in the window grabs your attention:

You are now forced to make a choice because you are being pulled between unlimited wants and scarcity. You want the dinner and the upgrades, but you do not have the money for both.

THE BROKEN WINDOW FALLACY

Most people assume that the cost of something is limited to its listed price. In his book *Economics in One Lesson*, Henry Hazlitt points out that there are hidden opportunity costs lurking behind every decision. He illustrates this principle with the following story.

A young hoodlum, say, heaves a brick through the window of a baker's shop. The shopkeeper runs out furious, but the boy is gone. A crowd gathers, and begins to stare with quiet satisfaction at the gaping hole in the window and the shattered glass over the bread and pies. After a while the crowd feels the need for philosophic reflection. And several of its members are almost certain to remind each other or the baker that, after all, this misfortune has its bright side. It will make business for some glazier. As they begin to think of this they elaborate upon it. How much does a new plate glass window cost? Two hundred and fifty dollars? That will be quite a sum. After all, if windows were never broken, what would happen to the glass business? Then, of course, the thing is endless. The glazier will have $250 more to spend with other merchants, and these in turn will have $250 more to spend with still other merchants, and so ad infinitum. The smashed window will go on providing money and employment in ever-widening circles. The logical conclusion from all this would be, if the crowd drew it, that the little hoodlum who threw the brick, far from being a public menace, was a public benefactor.

Now let us take another look. The crowd is at least right in its first conclusion. This little act of vandalism will in the first instance mean more business for some glazier. The glazier will be no more unhappy to learn of the incident than an undertaker to learn of a death. But the shopkeeper will be out $250 that he was planning to spend for a new suit. Because he has had to replace a window, he will have to go without the suit (or some equivalent need or luxury). Instead of having a window and $250 he now has merely a window. Or, as he was planning to buy the suit that very afternoon, instead of having both a window and a suit he must be content with the window and no suit. If we think of him as part of the community, the community has lost a new suit that might otherwise have come into being, and is just that much poorer.

The glazier's gain of business, in short, is merely the tailor's loss of business. No new "employment" has been added. The people in the crowd were thinking only of two parties to the transaction, the baker and the glazier. They had forgotten the potential third party involved, the tailor. They forgot him precisely because he will not now enter the scene. They will see the new window in the next day or two. They will never see the extra suit, precisely because it will never be made. They see only what is immediately visible to the eye.

Hazlitt therefore concludes,

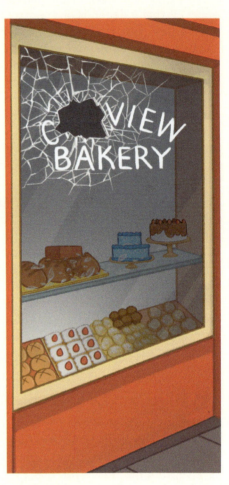

The whole of economics can be reduced to a single lesson, and that lesson can be reduced to a single sentence. *The art of economics consists in looking not merely at the immediate but at the longer effects of any act or policy; it consists in tracing the consequences of that policy not merely for one group but for all groups.*

Excerpts from ECONOMICS IN ONE LESSON: THE SHORTEST AND SUREST WAY TO UNDERSTAND BASIC ECONOMICS by Henry Hazlitt, copyright © 1946 by Henry Hazlitt. Copyright renewed © 1974 by Henry Hazlitt. Copyright © 1962, 1979 by Henry Hazlitt. Used by permission of Crown Books, an imprint of the Crown Publishing Group, a division of Penguin Random House LLC. All rights reserved. Any third party use of this material, outside of this publication, is prohibited. Interested parties must apply directly to Penguin Random House LLC for permission.

Immediately your mind begins calculating opportunity benefits and opportunity costs. If you choose to ignore the upgrades and keep on driving, you will enjoy the utility (satisfaction) that your favorite dinner will afford, but you will also experience a degree of opportunity cost (regret) for not purchasing the upgrades.

A rational person will make his decision by determining which choice's anticipated satisfaction most exceeds the probable regret. Suppose that before you left home to go to the restaurant, an economist attached to your brain a meter that has the ability to measure satisfaction. Imagining the delicious dinner that awaits you, the meter jumps to ten utils. **Util** is an economic term for an imaginary unit of satisfaction.

While considering the upgrades and imagining their benefits, you notice that the meter registers nine utils. If you choose to buy the upgrades, you will receive nine utils of opportunity benefit, or satisfaction, but you will also experience ten utils of opportunity cost, or regret, for not buying your favorite dinner, for a net utility of negative one util. If you purchase the dinner, however, you will experience a positive one util of overall satisfaction.

Under these circumstances a rational person would choose to purchase the dinner, but it is not a happy choice. Had you never passed the electronics store, you would have enjoyed the dinner in the amount of ten utils, but now that satisfaction has evaporated to one util. Your satisfaction is diminished because, while you eat your dinner, you will be thinking of what you gave up. You would have been better off had you never passed that store!

Every decision has opportunity benefits and opportunity costs. When people spend money on one good, they must necessarily give up the satisfaction that a different good would have provided. When a business chooses to produce shoes, it must forego the profit it could have made on purses. When the government creates a job and hires a person to fill it, someone else in the economy may lose the opportunity for a job. The money the potential employer would have been willing to pay his new employee has been reduced by increased taxes to pay for the government program. This lost potential job is the hidden cost of the government's decision. Prior to making a decision, the wise consumer always asks himself, "What is the hidden cost of making this decision?"

This concept of opportunity cost is one reason that some people in the world dislike the study of economics. For them, it truly is a *dismal science*. Every decision brings with it some degree of regret, and that regret varies according to the subjective value placed on the opportunity costs. As a Christian grows more and more to have the values that God has, though, he finds that he looks at the opportunity cost and benefit of choices differently than other people. The believer examines the subjective value of his life's choices in the light of the principles of God's Word. Making godly choices helps Christians minimize regret because they know they made the right choice. Your choices speak of the value system that underlies your priorities. When you allow the Holy Spirit to renew your mind by seeking God's wisdom in His Word, you can become truly capable of making godly choices.

util (YOO till)

Fig. 1-1	Dinner/Upgrades Utils	
	Purchase the dinner; forgo the upgrades	Purchase the upgrades; forgo the dinner
Opportunity benefit	10 utils	9 utils
Opportunity cost	-9 utils	-10 utils
Net utility	1 util	-1 util

You will recognize the truth in the words of Christ found in Matthew 6:20–21, "But lay up for yourselves treasures in heaven, where neither moth nor rust doth corrupt, and where thieves do not break through nor steal. For where your treasure is, there will your heart be also." You can be satisfied knowing that your choices please God.

SECTION REVIEW 1B

1. What is the difference between an economic cost and an opportunity cost?
2. What is the difference between intrinsic value and subjective value?
3. Explain and give an example of any three of the following: good, service, free good, nuisance good, economic good, economic service, and free service.
4. You must choose between going to bed at your regular time and staying up late to study. What would be the opportunity costs and benefits of your decision?

1C THE SCOPE AND PURPOSE OF CHOICE

Economists study the choices people make, the impact of those choices, and the need for new economic policies or changes in existing ones based on those choices. Their study of these items ranges from the individuals within a nation to the nation itself, and the uses of their findings range from predicting economic events to making value judgments.

MICROECONOMICS VERSUS MACROECONOMICS

Economists study their subject on two levels. The first is **microeconomics**, which deals with choices made by individual units: individual people, individual households, or individual business firms. What causes a person to save money? How does one business firm set its prices? How will the closing of a factory affect the individual community?

The second level of economic study is **macroeconomics**, which examines large-scale economic choices and issues. What causes bank interest rates to rise and fall? What causes widespread national unemployment? Why does China sell more goods to the United States than the United States sells to China?

POSITIVE ECONOMICS VERSUS NORMATIVE ECONOMICS

The approach of observing economic choices and predicting economic events is referred to as **positive economics**. For example, an economist might study the daily stock market reports of two businesses. From his observations he might state that a small chain called Tug's Ice Cream Parlor and Groceries will soon become a nationwide chain, while Ethel's Mart might go bankrupt within the year.

CARL MENGER (1840-1921)
Founder of the Austrian School of Economics

Carl Menger was born on February 23, 1840, in Neu-Sandec, Galicia. (At that time Galicia was a part of Austria, but today it lies within Poland.) Menger was one of three brothers who distinguished themselves in various ways. Carl Menger became famous in the field of economics, while his brothers gained their fame in law and politics. Menger was educated in law at universities in Prague and Vienna and later studied economics at the Jagiellonian University in Krakow, where he received a PhD in 1867.

In that same year the liberals (at that time the word *liberal* referred to a person who desired individual freedom) persuaded the Austrian emperor to draw up a new constitution promoting the ideas of free trade, equality of individuals under the law, and representative government. Menger studied in universities that were full of the nonliberal professors of the day, and he was taught that the economic affairs of individuals were best controlled by the government. Menger, however, disagreed with this teaching; he saw governmental officials as inefficient decision makers who enslave individuals to the state.

Menger then tried to determine the exact process for making efficient economic choices. In the work that resulted from his research, *Grundsätze der Volkswirtschaftslehre (Principles of Economics)*, he noted that a person makes his decisions more efficiently than the government because the individual's decisions are based on personal utility as opposed to some vague notion of the "public good." Menger explained that it is utility that gives value to anything. This idea contradicted the myth that the quality of raw materials or quantity of labor used to create the item determines its value.

In looking at the diamond-water paradox, Menger questioned whether a diamond was valuable simply because it took so much labor to get it out of the ground. If that were the case, how could a diamond found on the surface of the ground possibly sell for the same price as one that "took a thousand days' labor" to produce? As a result of his liberal ideas that advocated personal freedom, the German government barred Menger's followers from teaching in any German university.

Because his work placed so much emphasis on individual economic freedom, Carl Menger is regarded as the Father of Austrian Economics, the school of thought that stresses the free market, private ownership of property, and limited government.

Normative economics refers to making value judgments about existing or proposed economic policies. It deals with the way things should be as opposed to the way they are. "Everyone should save 10% of his income" and "The government must get our nation back to being a major producer of the world's goods" are examples of normative economic statements. Governmental leaders often make economic choices based on statements such as these. For example, the Social Security Act, which Congress passed in 1935, requires people to save for retirement. Also, Congress has passed laws forbidding certain imports in order to discourage the purchase of foreign-made goods. Governmental interventions of this kind may result in beneficial outcomes or may create problems. As was mentioned in the box about the broken window fallacy, economists must learn to look at the big picture, not just at what is immediately evident.

Economics—it is all about choices: why you must make them, what they cost you, and what the consequences are of each one. Why

must you make choices? You can answer that question by explaining the conflict between unlimited wants and scarcity. What will your choices cost you? To answer this question, you must differentiate between intrinsic and subjective value and explain the idea of a personal value system. What are the consequences of your choices? To answer this question, you need to understand the economic application of utility, opportunity benefit, and opportunity cost. If you have mastered these basic concepts and can apply appropriate biblical principles to each of them, then you are off to a good start in this foundational, Christian study of economics.

SECTION REVIEW 1C

1. What is the difference between microeconomics and macroeconomics? Give examples of each.
2. What is the difference between positive and normative economics? Give examples of each.
3. Why is Carl Menger called the Founder of the Austrian School of Economics?
4. The Austrian School emphasizes what three important economic ideas?

CHAPTER REVIEW

CONTENT QUESTIONS

1. List three reasons why economics is considered a science.
2. According to Scripture, what guides all of the choices that we make?
3. Why do unlimited wants and scarcity necessitate choice?
4. From which language did the word *economics* originate, and what was its original meaning?
5. What English word that is used in Scripture comes from the same origin as the word *economics*?
6. What process discussed in the chapter is an application of the stewardship principle? Explain.
7. How is it possible for a handful of diamonds to be worth less than a single glass of water?
8. What idea did Menger propose that radically changed the way economists determine an object's value?
9. What does an economist mean when he uses the word *utility*?
10. Why do some consider economics a *dismal science*?

APPLICATION QUESTIONS

1. List three economic choices you made today. Discuss how the concepts of opportunity benefit and opportunity cost were a part of your decision making whether you were consciously aware of them or not.
2. "Because it provides employment opportunities, a natural disaster like Hurricane Sandy is good for the economy." Use the broken window fallacy to disprove this statement.

TERMS

economics	3
scarcity	4
economic cost	7
good	7
services	7
economic goods	7
economic services	7
nuisance goods	7
recycling	7
free goods	7
free services	7
diamond-water paradox	8
intrinsic value	8
subjective value	9
utility	9
opportunity benefit	9
opportunity cost	9
util	11
microeconomics	12
macroeconomics	12
positive economics	12
normative economics	13

PERSONAL FINANCE
BUDGETING

A **budget** is a tabulation of income and planned expenditures. For centuries business firms and governments have used budgets as a means of getting the most profitable use from their money. Yet financial preparation is perhaps nowhere more important than in the home. Christians who desire to honor the Lord in their homes should follow the example set by the steward in Luke 12, who was faithful in his responsibilities to manage his household. Families and individuals can and should use household and personal budgets to prioritize and allocate their resources so that they get the greatest possible good from their income.

BENEFITS OF BUDGETING

Why should you develop a personal budget? After all, it takes time and thought—not to mention a little mathematical ability—to identify the sources of your income, calculate its total, and determine your expenditures. However, the following reasons should encourage you to formulate a personal and, later, a family budget.

First, creating a budget allows you to identify your current spending patterns and helps you to establish spending priorities. Chapter 1 points out that all of us live in a world in which we cannot have everything we want. We are pulled between unlimited wants on one hand and scarcity on the other. Consequently, we must make choices about how we portion and spend our limited time, effort, and money. If we do not create a budget that provides a systematic plan for future spending, we will be vulnerable to **impulse buying**, purchasing things that we think we need at that moment or that merely strike our fancy. Such unplanned purchases may force us later to forgo purchasing something truly important. Developing a personal budget encourages you to set your priorities ahead of time, and that enables you to make more of your own choices instead of having circumstances constantly dictate them for you.

Second, a budget prevents potential conflicts with loved ones. When a husband and wife prepare a household budget that establishes mutually agreed upon family priorities, they can avoid many future tensions. The same is often true for teens who work with their parents to create a budget based on their first real job. A family that spends without regard to priorities can easily make unwise purchases that exceed its income. This overspending can force the family either to forgo purchasing some necessity or to rely on credit agencies. When this situation occurs and the family begins to feel financially stressed, the seeds of resentment and disharmony find fertile soil. On the other hand, a husband and wife often find that planning a budget together strengthens their relationship. Each now has a financial stake in the relationship; each must compromise personal needs and wants for the good of the other and the family; and each is inclined to be more willing to sacrifice in the future if their jointly created budget needs adjustment.

Third, a budget is a big first step toward a successful comprehensive **financial plan**. A budget creates a strategy for achieving financial goals; it can not only balance present needs and wants but also help plan

THE IMPULSE BUYER'S DREAM COME TRUE
ONLINE SHOPPING

toward the purchase of specific future necessities, such as an automobile or house, with a minimum of debt. A budget allows the family to provide insurance for emergencies, savings for children's college expenses, and provision for retirement.

Finally, in developing a budget the Christian is properly exercising his role as a steward. Do you recall the origin of the word *economics*?

Chapter 1 notes that *economics* originates from two Greek words that mean "management of the house." In the truest sense of the word, therefore, economics begins in the home, with the home's finances ruled by an effective budget. By developing a Christ-centered family budget, a family can provide for the Lord's work, meet the physical needs of family members, and assist others as well. By developing a personal budget, you can keep track of spending and saving and be better prepared to give an account of the funds God entrusts to you.

STRETCHING THE FAMILY BUDGET

Most families who budget agree that they could benefit from decreasing some of their expenses. But where should the decreases begin? Numerous possibilities exist in almost every household for successfully cutting corners to reduce spending. Some may be obvious, while others may require some ingenuity. Here are a few suggestions that could help a family economize.

- When shopping for groceries, always use a list. When possible, buy groceries that are on sale and use coupons for further reductions.
- Never go grocery shopping when hungry. Hunger creates a strong drive for unnecessary items.
- Prepare more meals at home from scratch instead of buying costlier prepared foods.
- Take snacks from home instead of buying candy and drinks from vending machines or convenience stores.
- Consolidate business and shopping errands into fewer driving trips and walk when possible.
- Buy versatile clothing instead of faddish garments and accessories that must be replaced frequently.
- Do not hesitate to buy only sale-priced items in a store without buying additional merchandise.
- Play games at home or visit local parks and museums instead of pursuing more expensive entertainment.
- Conserve energy by turning off all unneeded lights, running only full loads in the dishwasher and washing machine, and adjusting the thermostat to cut the use of the air conditioner or furnace.

FIXED VERSUS VARIABLE EXPENSES

The obvious purpose of a budget is to determine where money has been going and if it needs to keep going there. If so, what is the best way to allocate present funds to meet future expenses, and if not, how should the budget be reprioritized?

Families creating a budget need to consider that two kinds of expenses exist. First, there are **fixed expenses**, which do not rise or fall as the family's income increases in the short run. Families cannot immediately change fixed expenses without disrupting their financial situation. Examples of fixed expenses include rent or mortgage payments, minimum food expenses, minimum utilities, property taxes, and essential transportation costs. **Variable expenses**, on the other hand, are those costs that rise and fall as the family's income changes. If a family experiences a cut in income, it may need to reduce variable expenses and can do so with minimal harm to the family's financial situation. Examples of variable expenses include vacation expenses, gifts, entertainment, new clothes, and allowances.

ENGEL'S LAW

Ernst Engel was a German statistician who lived from 1821 to 1896. He developed the principle known as Engel's law, which observes that as a family's income goes up,

- the percentage of income spent on food declines;
- the percentage spent on clothing, rent, fuel, and electricity stays about the same;
- and the percentage spent on education and recreation increases.

BUDGET CATEGORIES

A budget contains a variety of categories to encompass the various ways in which the budgeter spends his money. The first step in creating an effective budget is to identify what those categories are. The categories a person or family uses vary according to each specific situation. This section presents fifteen suggested spending categories.

1. Scriptural Giving and Other Contributions and Gifts

A Christian's budget reflects his priorities. If his priorities are to seek first the kingdom of God (Matt. 6:33) and to honor God with the first fruits of his increase (Prov. 3:9), then his budget will start with systematic scriptural giving. In the New Testament the Apostle Paul tells the believer to give according as he may prosper (1 Cor. 16:2) and with a proper heart attitude (2 Cor. 9:7). God doesn't need our money, but He chooses to use our giving in His work.

Besides providing for the financial needs of your local church and other worthy Christian ministries, you must budget any other giving you plan to make. This category could include gifts to other charitable organizations and birthday, Christmas, anniversary, wedding, and graduation gifts. For some, it might be better to place such non-ministry-related gifts into a separate category.

2. Saving

Unfortunately, recent data indicate that Americans place a low priority on saving. Compared to the citizens of most other industrialized countries, Americans save relatively little of their income. While personal saving in the United States from 1995 to 2013 averaged around 4 percent of disposable household income, it averaged over 10 percent in France, Germany, and Switzerland. Though the abundance of material goods in the Unites States can create a temptation to spend and though some may need all of their income just to cover basic living expenses, the decision to save, as one is able, can produce great benefits for the future.

To save meaningful amounts, individuals and families must plan to save and must systematically carry out their plan. Saving becomes much easier if families recognize its importance and specifically budget a certain dollar amount or percentage of their income to deposit each month. Many financial planners suggest that a family set aside at least 10 percent of its income toward savings, but this may be too difficult a goal to achieve at first. As a family gradually reduces unnecessary spending, it may gradually increase its savings. Families also "save" by investing in the purchase of homes, contributing to private and business retirement plans, and purchasing investment insurance policies. They can adjust the 10 percent figure to suit their financial situations.

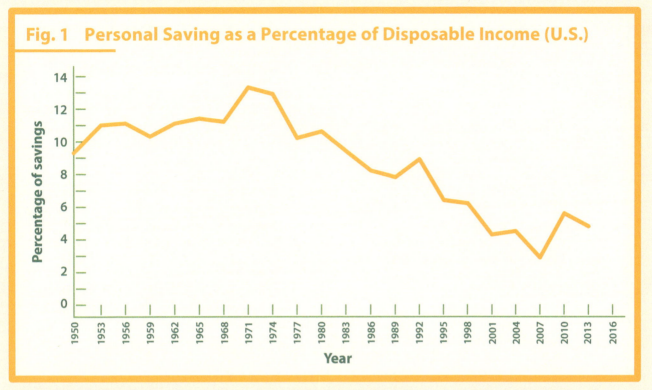

Fig. 1 Personal Saving as a Percentage of Disposable Income (U.S.)

Source: US Bureau of Economic Analysis, "Table 2.1 Personal Income and Its Disposition" (accessed September 21, 2015)

3. Food

When families budget for their food needs, they have a tendency to include only the expense of foods prepared at home. This category should also include purchases of school lunches, coffee break or snack money, and the cost of dining in restaurants.

4. Housing

Housing includes mortgage payments, property taxes, homeowner's insurance, rent, and renter's insurance. Many lending institutions provide for a home buyer to pay property taxes and property insurance through an **escrow account**. The lender determines the total of the buyer's annual obligation for property taxes and property insurance, divides the amount by twelve months, and increases the borrower's monthly payment. The lender then holds the additional money in the escrow account until the tax collector and the insurance company send the lending institution a bill. Escrow accounts permit homeowners to avoid the inconvenience of having to make large lump-sum payments yearly or every six months. Also included in the housing category are the costs of routine maintenance and repairs, such as paint and wallpaper, and of furnishings, such as carpets, furniture, appliances, and so forth. Authorities generally recommend that total monthly housing expenses account for no more than 30–35 percent of the family's monthly income.

5. Utilities

The public utilities budget should include expenses for electricity, heating oil, natural gas, telephone, Internet, water, sewage disposal or septic tank service, and garbage pickup (if not paid for by property taxes). Since phone service is a utility, families may decide to include the cost of their cell phone plan in this category.

6. Transportation

The transportation budget includes payments on automobile loans, license renewal charges, license fees, vehicle inspection charges, automobile insurance, gasoline, oil, other maintenance expenses, and parking

expenses, such as change for parking meters and fees for parking garages. This category also includes expenses for car rentals and airplane, bus, train, and subway tickets.

7. Clothing

The clothing budget includes the purchase not only of garments but also of items such as hats, purses, shoes, and billfolds, as well as dry cleaning bills, laundry expenses, alterations, and sewing supplies.

8. Health

Under this category, families should budget all health insurance, including hospital, medical, dental, and life insurance. They should also include costs for prescription drugs, especially any that one or more family members take regularly.

9. Personal

The personal budget includes items such as soaps, hair-care products, toothpaste, makeup, and self-medications, including bandages, over-the-counter medications, and aspirin.

10. Work

Some people incur expenses that are directly related to employment. For example, they must purchase uniforms; safety items such as shoes, gloves, or glasses; work-related tools; or office equipment.

11. Contingencies

A **contingency** is an uncertain event. It is unlikely that all expenses will be accurately predicted; therefore, it is wise to create a contingency category in one's budget. Contingency expenses could include those which result from unforeseen damage to one's house, higher costs related to unexpected guests, and deductibles, amounts not covered by insurance policies.

12. Entertainment and Recreation

This part of the budget should include all planned expenses related to vacations, hobbies, and sporting events. It would include such things as tickets, equipment, cameras, and babysitting fees.

13. Education

The education budget should include all items of a personal improvement nature. Such expenses consist of school tuition and fees, books, office equipment used in the home, laptops, tablets, apps, and software.

14. Allowances

Many families provide small allowances for children (and adults as well!) for which the budget details no specifically required use.

15. Miscellaneous

The miscellaneous category includes expenses that are so small or so infrequent that to create a separate category for each would be impractical. Miscellaneous expenses may include bank service charges, watch batteries, and photocopying charges.

From this list you can see why many do not create a budget. Categorizing can be intimidating, and it does mean that budgeting will take some work. However, the benefits of a budget truly outweigh the costs. A budget will allow you to keep better track of what money comes in to you and where your money is going. Doing that may result in your being better able to make ends meet and perhaps even having some leftover funds. Most of all, you will be able, as a good steward, to give a proper accounting of what you did with what your Lord gave you.

REVIEW QUESTIONS

1. Explain why having a budget is evidence of being a good steward.
2. What are the four benefits of budgeting?
3. What is the difference between a fixed expense and a variable expense?
4. According to Engel's law, in what categories does spending typically increase as a family's income rises?
5. Why would a Christian's budget start with scriptural giving? Use a scripture reference in your answer.
6. On average, Americans saved yearly approximately what percentage of their income during the last decade?
7. The housing category should be approximately what percentage of the family budget?
8. Name two examples of a public utility.

TERMS

budget	16
impulse buying	16
financial plan	16
fixed expenses	18
variable expenses	18
escrow account	19
contingency	20

CHAPTER TWO
ECONOMIC MODELS

2A MODELS: THE TOOLS OF THE ECONOMIST — 22

2B THE CIRCULAR FLOW MODEL — 27

2A MODELS: THE TOOLS OF THE ECONOMIST

Were you to visit almost any hobby store, you could easily become convinced that there are models of almost everything. The shelves of such stores are filled with models of airplanes, trains, automobiles, and ships from a variety of time periods as well as models of plants, animals, the solar system, and spacecraft. These models differ greatly not only in the things they represent but also in their complexity. Consider, for example, model trains. A child's toy train set is usually very simple. It is easy to assemble, is inexpensive, travels in a circle, and has a relatively short life expectancy. An adult's model train set, on the other hand, is usually a technological marvel. It is likely to have a whole room devoted to its permanent display; to cost several months' salary; to resemble a small country complete with rivers, mountains, roads, citizens, and army bases; and to last well beyond the life of the owner.

Why do we make models? Models are representations of objects or concepts, often in a greatly simplified form. Often the real object or concept is impractical or unavailable for study because it is too big, too expensive, too difficult to obtain, too complex, or some

combination of these. Consequently, we resort to using models. They aid our learning by allowing us to see what objects or concepts look like and how their various parts interact, even though they are not an exact or perfectly accurate replication. Sometimes, a description of what something is and how it works is not sufficient for you to understand it fully. However, if you can see it, you may be able to make sense of what before were just words. We develop models to help us understand our world. In Genesis 1:28 God instructs mankind to have dominion over all creation. In order to manage our world effectively, we have to understand it, and models facilitate that process.

WHY DO ECONOMISTS USE MODELS?

Economists seek to understand why people make the choices they do and how those choices affect others, particularly business firms. They also desire to study the actions of business and government, why each makes certain choices and how each one's decisions affect the other and the populace. Since economists cannot know exactly the what, how, and why of people, businesses, and governments making their choices, they construct models to provide data that indicate possible reasons. They construct these models using their observations of human behavior and economic principles. Basically, economic models assist economists in analyzing choices and their consequences.

While economic models may not come in a box marked "some assembly required," they serve purposes similar to their hobby store counterparts. For economists, economic models serve as simplified representations of how various factors influence our choices.

Like other professionals, economists use models for two purposes. The first is instruction. The economics teacher uses models to present abstract concepts to students in an understandable, visible way or to provide a means for them to analyze the interactions of economic variables that can set or alter a nation's economy. In a similar fashion the biology teacher finds it preferable to use a plastic model to explain the workings of a human heart. The model is more durable, less costly, and easier to use than a real human heart. But, like the plastic heart, any model is not the real thing and therefore cannot be true in every aspect to what it represents. Models are a way for our finite human minds to portray the realities of our world. Some models, like the plastic heart, are physical representations of other physical objects. Other models, such as those in economics, physically represent intangible concepts or processes. Some, such as the temple in the Old Testament, are physical representations of spiritual truths revealed by God. The arrangement of the building was to teach how God wanted sinful human beings to approach Him.

A second purpose for models is to assist economists in predicting future events. As architects use models of bridges to predict their ability to hold their designed weight capacities, so economists use models to predict the possible consequences of various economic choices or policy decisions. Economic models prove helpful for those seeking to answer such questions as, What would happen to inflation if the number of dollars in circulation increased by 25 percent? or What would happen to its budget if the government increased purchases of military hardware by $100 billion without increasing taxes to pay for the increase?

Economic models are incredibly useful for businesspersons, governmental leaders, and those who teach economics; however, they are only attempts to illustrate and explain human activities. They cannot be entirely accurate. They are the work of flawed persons relying on incomplete knowledge. As our body of knowledge increases and changes, we adjust or alter our economic models. Consequently, we may not be able to use an economic model developed a hundred years ago because the information it provides is no longer accurate.

Biblical principles should guide the models we make. For example, what the Bible teaches regarding the dangers of greed or the rewards of faithfulness has been and always will be true. When our model is related to the motives people have or the rewards they receive, we need to rely on the Bible's statements. When our fundamental beliefs line up with Scripture, the result will be a biblical *worldview*. Recognizing the role that a biblical worldview plays in economics helps you to better analyze economic models. Some economists knowingly and intentionally incorporate biblical principles into their models, while others do so without realizing they have. Whether intentional or not, those who utilize biblical principles in the development of their models produce models that are more accurate than the models of those who disregard what God has revealed. The more accurate the model, the more useful and enduring it is.

worldview: the overall perspective from which one sees and interprets the world (from *American Heritage Dictionary*)

WHAT DO ECONOMIC MODELS LOOK LIKE?

You may wonder how economists make economic models. Unlike plastic models with parts and instructions, economic models take the form of theories or explanations of how people make choices. Economists usually express these theories and explanations as tables or graphs.

The **tabular model**, also known as a **schedule**, is a popular method of explaining simple relationships between pairs of variables. For example, Figure 2-1 shows how a limited number of changes in the price of Coastal Cola alter the number of cans sold.

While tabular models help to show relationships between variables, they provide information that is limited to only a few observations. A **line graph**, on the other hand, provides significantly more data. For example, Figure 2-1 gives the number of cans that Coastal Cola sold only at 75¢, 90¢, $1.25, $1.75, and $2.25, a rather limited number of observations. A line graph, however, can tell the economist approximately how many cans will be sold at any given price that falls between 75¢ and $2.25. To construct a line graph, economists place price on the vertical axis and quantity on the horizontal axis. They then plot on the graph the limited number of observations and draw lines connecting the observed points. Figure 2-2 is an illustration of a line graph for Coastal Cola.

Another model that economists present in graphic form is a **production possibilities curve (PPC)**. The PPC enables the economist to see the maximum feasible amounts of two

Fig. 2-1 Tabular Model for Coastal Cola

Price per can	Quantity sold per month (cans)
$2.25	250,000
1.75	500,000
1.25	1,000,000
.90	2,000,000
.75	3,000,000

commodities that a business can produce when those items are competing for that business's limited resources.

Figure 2-3 illustrates the most common form of PPC. It presents the production options of a farmer who has forty acres of fertile land on which to grow corn or wheat or some combination of the two. If the farmer chooses to grow only wheat, he can produce 5,000 bushels; if only corn, he can produce 4,500 bushels. He can also choose to grow a number of different combinations of amounts of both. He can grow 2,700 bushels of corn and 3,000 bushels of wheat (point D) or 4,200 bushels of corn and 1,000 bushels of wheat (point B).

Any point on the curve represents productive efficiency in the use of his resources. That means he is producing as much as he can and is not wasting any of his resources. Any point inside the curve, such as planning to grow 1,000 bushels of wheat and 2,000 bushels of corn, represents inefficient production. He would not be maximizing the use of his land. There would be wasted resources. Any point outside the curve represents a combination of products that would be impossible for the farmer to produce. If, for example, this farmer wished to grow 2,000 bushels of corn and 4,000 bushels of wheat, he would have to obtain more land. These levels of production would not be possible on the acreage he currently possesses.

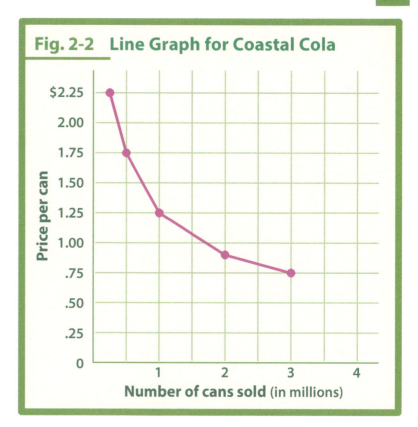

Fig. 2-2 Line Graph for Coastal Cola

Figure 2-4 is another common form of PPC. This graph depicts the possibilities for a fast-food cook who has only one deep fryer. He can produce eight batches of french fries or four batches of potato nuggets per hour. Again, any point on the curve, such as four batches of fries and two batches of nuggets, represents productive efficiency in the use of his resources. Any point inside the curve represents

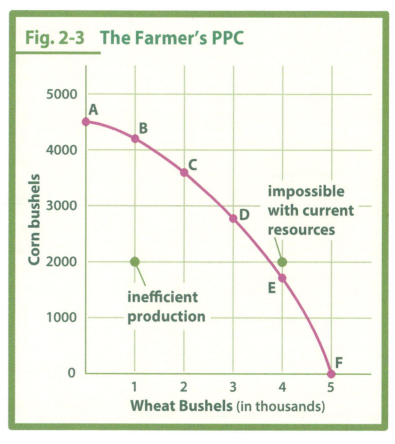

Fig. 2-3 The Farmer's PPC

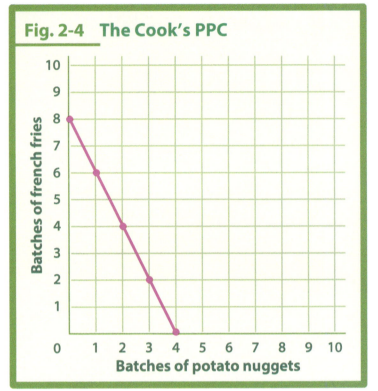

Fig. 2-4 The Cook's PPC

inefficient production, and any point outside the curve is impossible with his present resources.

Students looking at these two examples often have a question that you may be wondering about as well: Why is the curve in Figure 2-3 an actual curve, while in Figure 2-4 it is a straight line? The answer lies in the slope of the curve. Both figures are curves. Yes, Figure 2-4 looks like a straight line, but mathematically, a straight line is a curve with a constant slope. The slope of the PPC at any given point shows the rate at which one good must be reduced to produce an additional unit of the other good. For example, if the cook is currently producing all french fries and no potato nuggets (that is 8 FF and 0 PN) but wants to make one batch of potato nuggets (that is to move to 6 FF and 1 PN), he must give up two batches of fries (8 minus 6). To put that in terms you studied in Chapter 1, the opportunity cost of producing potato nuggets equals two batches of french fries.

This is true no matter where on the PPC you start, because the slope on this graph is the same everywhere. The cost of producing nuggets is always two batches of fries. In practice, this is because the resources used to produce both nuggets and fries are fairly similar. The cook can switch from french fries to potato nuggets and back again quickly and easily any time he completes a batch. Switching requires no special training, no advanced technical knowledge, and no interchange of equipment. Therefore, that curve is a straight line.

In contrast, on the graph in which the PPC is not a straight line (Fig. 2-3), the cost of wheat does depend on where you begin along the slope because it is not constant. The resources the farmer uses to produce wheat and corn are not identical. Switching from wheat to corn requires different tillage, planting schemes, fertilizing practices, spraying for disease prevention and insect pest control, and so on. Consequently, as the farmer seeks to produce more and more wheat, the slope gets steeper and the cost gets greater. The result is that the PPC bows outward. In fact, most true production processes show this pattern of costs, which economists call the *law of increasing marginal costs of production*.

SECTION REVIEW 2A

1. What are the two purposes for economic models?
2. What advantage does a line graph offer over a tabular model?
3. For an economist, what is the primary value of a production possibilities curve?

2B THE CIRCULAR FLOW MODEL

The tabular model and line graph examples in Section 2A are microeconomic models that show how the price of a single product affects the quantity sold. The PPC has micro- and macroeconomic applications, as both individual businesses and governments employ PPC models in their decision-making processes. Economists have

PERSONAL APPLICATIONS OF THE PPC

Consider the following example as a way to apply the idea of the PPC to your life. Your talents and your personal time are like the farmer's land. You have a limited amount of both. What you do with them compares to growing wheat or corn. You could devote all your time and talents to a certain activity or use them in several activities. However, to use less than all of them, whether in one activity or several, would be inefficient production. Like the farmer failing to maximize the production possibilities of his land, you would be failing to maximize your God-given talents and wasting precious time. Similarly, to involve yourself in too many activities may place you outside your curve, and you may find that you cannot do all that you would like because you just do not have sufficient talents or time. Ask God to give you wisdom to be diligent and discerning so that you might exercise productive efficiency in the use of your talents and personal time.

also created other models to illustrate the behavior of entire nations. Perhaps the best example of such models is the **circular flow model**, which provides a visual explanation of how a complete national economic system functions.

THE BASIC CIRCULAR FLOW

Business firms and households are the two basic participants of virtually every economic system. Business firms create billions of dollars in goods and services, and households are the principal purchasers of those goods and services. If you were to add up all the goods and services businesses produced and sold, you would have a figure that economists call the gross domestic product (GDP). (You will learn more about GDP in a later chapter.) On the other side of the equation, if you were to total all that households spend on those goods and services, you would have an amount that economists call **consumption expenditures**.

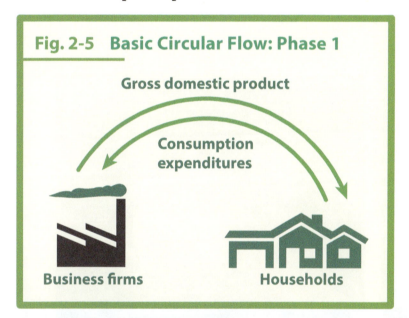

Fig. 2-5 Basic Circular Flow: Phase 1

Business firms can also be called producers.

The term households *does not refer to houses or families but is rather a synonym for* consumers.

Factors of Production

The exchange of households' expenditures for businesses' goods and services is only part of the model, however. Business firms need resources to produce their goods and services, but they cannot create those resources nor count on them to appear spontaneously. To produce their total of goods and services (the GDP), business firms obtain the resources they need from households. Economists call these necessary resources the **factors of production**, and they have identified four of them that go into the production of all goods and services.

- **Land** refers to all the natural resources that go into the production of goods. Every economic good contains some form of animal, vegetable, or mineral resource. In an automobile, for example, are glass, steel, and other materials composed

FACTORS OF PRODUCTION

LAND

LABOR

CAPITAL

ENTREPRENEURSHIP

of minerals, and the plastics and textiles in it may be formed from petroleum and other natural resources.
- **Labor** is all human effort that goes into the creation of goods or services. Labor includes the mental work of the manager as well as the physical effort of the employee.
- **Capital** is the third factor of production and refers to goods used to produce other goods. Economists divide capital into two major categories: financial and real. Financial capital is all money the household sector loans directly to business firms. Business firms then use this borrowed financial capital to purchase real capital—the tools they use to produce their goods and services.
- **Entrepreneurship** is the activity of creatively combining natural resources, human labor, and capital in unique ways to develop new and useful goods and services. Although land, labor, and capital are necessary to produce goods and services, entrepreneurship is the most important factor of production. Why? The reason is that entrepreneurship directs, organizes, and plans the production process. Without the direction entrepreneurship provides, a nation would likely fail to use extensive pockets of resources. Without its organizing function, much of the labor supply would probably remain idle. Without the planning it provides, a nation could have large amounts of financial resources remaining untapped. Individuals become entrepreneurs for a host of reasons, including personal recognition, the ability to use their talents, and a desire for financial rewards. If a nation discourages the benefits associated with entrepreneurship, it will undoubtedly see a significant reduction in its flow of new and useful products and services. Therefore, it is of great importance to the economic growth of a nation that entrepreneurs be free to use their talents and to receive the profits they have earned.

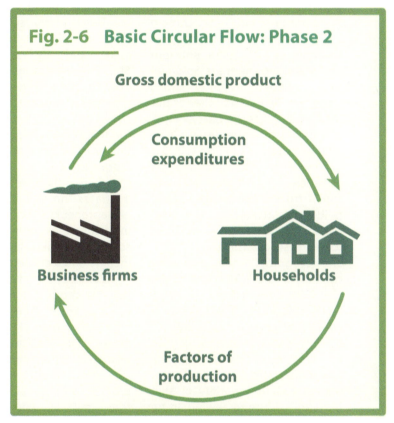

Fig. 2-6 Basic Circular Flow: Phase 2

Factor Costs

Although households provide the factors of production, they do not provide them without cost. Notice the arrow going from the business sector to the households in Figure 2-7 that represents the payments business firms make in exchange for the four factors of production. Economists know these as the **factor costs** and have identified four of them.
- **Rent** includes all payments for the use of an owner's property. Rent includes not only payments for the use of buildings and land but also payments such as royalties to authors.
- **Wages** are all payments for labor used to produce goods or services. Wages include all salaries, hourly wages, and bonuses in addition to other payments that workers do not receive directly, such as medical and dental benefits, unemployment and worker's compensation, and the employer's portion of

social security payments. Wages make up the largest portion of all the factor costs.
- **Interest** is the payment business firms make on borrowed money. One example would be the money households lend

THE PROVERBS 31 WOMAN: A MODEL ENTREPRENEUR

While you will not find the term *entrepreneur* in the Bible, there are examples in Scripture of individuals who demonstrate the qualities of successful entrepreneurs. Among them are Solomon, who engaged in international trade, and Lydia, the seller of purple. But perhaps the best example of a successful entrepreneur is the woman described in Proverbs 31.

Proverbs 31 describes the qualities of an excellent wife who can be trusted to manage a household well, and many of these qualities are the same as those needed to be a successful entrepreneur. She recognizes a need and works willingly and diligently to fulfill it (13). She demonstrates a strong work ethic and a determination to complete her tasks. She is industrious, rising early in the morning (15) and staying up late at night (18). She engages in diverse activities, demonstrating a variety of skills from agriculture to sewing. In her decision to purchase a field, she evidences financial vision and wisdom. First, she scouts out the field to determine if it is worth the asking price and capable of sustaining the crops she plans to grow. Next, she reveals she has prepared long-range plans. She has considered which crops to plant in order to generate a profit, which she plans to use to plant a vineyard, and she intends to trade the vineyard's product for additional profit (16). She is discerning; she has the ability to recognize quality workmanship (18). She produces quality work and is dependable and punctual in delivering it to those who sell her goods (24).

This woman uses all her abilities to provide for her family. She creates and sells fine clothing (24). She uses her tailoring skills not only to make money but also to provide clothing for her family. She shows prudence in planning ahead for the coming winter and knits diligently to have proper clothing before the chill arrives (21). In all she does, this wise woman demonstrates the qualities that make entrepreneurs successful, and the industriousness of her labor is personally rewarded through a stable income and a contented family.

Consider what this chapter teaches about entrepreneurs and profits. Entrepreneurs organize, direct, and plan production processes. To do all that well requires prudence, time management, vision, and people skills. The Proverbs 31 woman clearly portrays these traits. Her compassion, generosity, and kindness are human relations skills that every entrepreneur should emulate (20, 26). To make a profit, entrepreneurs must recognize a need, develop a product to meet that need, and be able to produce and deliver it to consumers at a cost below what the consumers will be willing to pay. Here again, doing these activities well takes initiative, industry, awareness, and determination—qualities that the Proverbs 31 woman possesses. Though entrepreneurs may not acknowledge that they purposefully incorporate biblical principles in their lives, they are successful because they do. They have initiative and are skillful, prudent, industrious, determined, and decisive; and these ideas are manifested in the verses of Proverbs 31.

Whether you are male or female and whether God is calling you to be an entrepreneur or not, you should be developing now the skills and character qualities that Proverbs 31 describes. You will need these traits to be successful regardless of your calling. Begin by evaluating yourself. Ask yourself these questions:
- Do I show initiative, or are others forced to prod me to keep working and to motivate me to finish my tasks?
- Am I industrious and focused, or do I allow myself to be easily distracted?
- Am I regularly evaluating my performance and thinking of better ways to accomplish what I do?
- Am I determined that I will finish what I begin?

You know that whatever you do, you are to "do all to the glory of God" (1 Cor. 10:31) and that everything you do should be done "heartily, as to the Lord" (Col. 3:23). You also know that there is certainly nothing praiseworthy about half-heartedness, mediocrity, or slothfulness (Prov. 24:30–34). God and others deserve nothing less from you than the best you are capable of doing. By God's grace, seek to incorporate these Proverbs 31 traits in your life.

to business firms by purchasing bonds. The bond entitles its buyer to receive not only his original principal (the price paid for the bond) but also periodic interest payments.

- **Profit** is the difference between the revenues received from the sale of a product and the cost of the land, labor, and capital that went into its production. It is important that you recognize that profits are not just another expense. They are the rewards entrepreneurs receive for successful risk-taking. Entrepreneurial risks are great. To realize a profit, the entrepreneur must identify an unmet need, create a product to meet that need, produce it at a cost lower than the price buyers will be willing to pay, and be able to deliver it to his customers. Therefore, if an entrepreneur wishes to increase profits, he usually cannot simply raise the price of his product. He must instead lower its production costs.

The circular flow model is a simple representation of how an economic system operates. Looking again at Figure 2-7, you can clearly see the reason for the name *circular flow*. Households provide business firms the factors of production (land, labor, financial capital, and entrepreneurship) that the firms use to produce goods and services (GDP). In exchange, the households receive the factor costs (rent, wages, interest, and profit), which they use to purchase the businesses' goods and services (consumption expenditures).

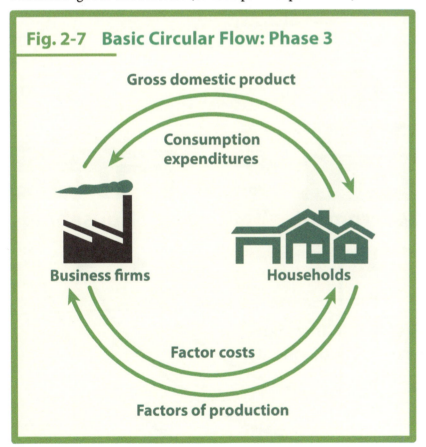

Fig. 2-7 Basic Circular Flow: Phase 3

THE GOVERNMENT AS AN ECONOMIC ENTITY

In its present form the circular flow model is too simple and unrealistic. To add a greater degree of reality, economists include another participant with whom you have contact every day of your life—the government. Figure 2-8 illustrates the circular flow model after adding the government. The term *government* refers to all levels of civil government, including federal, state, and local authorities.

To continue operating, the government, like households and business firms, incurs necessary expenses. It purchases goods and services ranging from the mundane, such as mops and buckets, to the

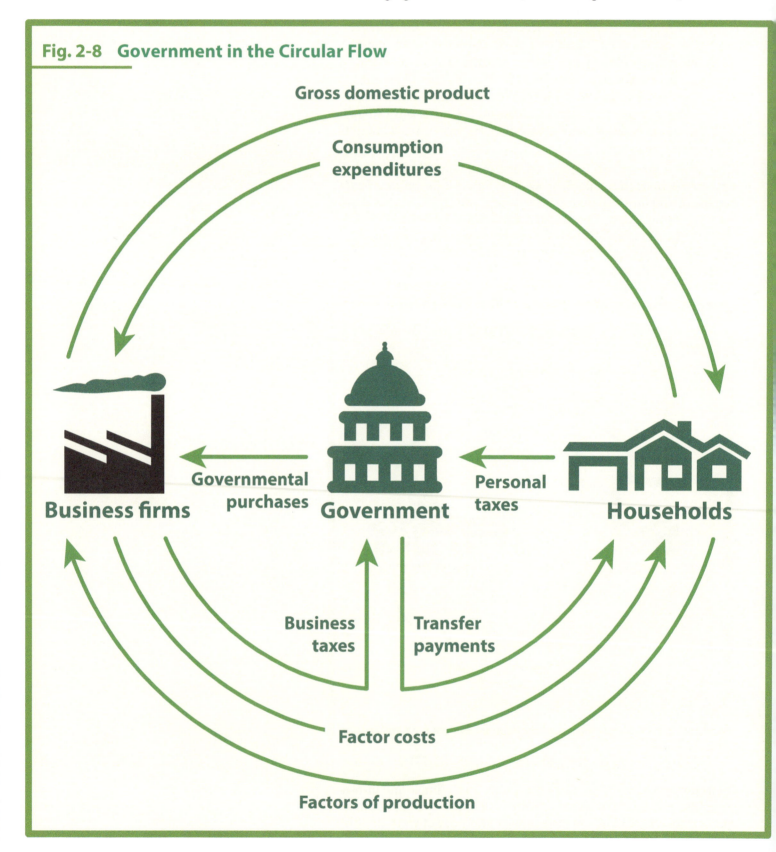

Fig. 2-8 Government in the Circular Flow

extraordinary, such as nuclear weapons and satellites. In addition to purchasing goods and services, the government provides transfer payments to households. **Transfer payments** are payments of money or goods to persons for which the government expects no specific economic repayment. Examples of transfer payments include paying social security benefits to the retired, welfare benefits to the poor, and unemployment compensation to those out of work.

To pay for its spending, the government imposes taxes. On households, it levies taxes on sales, income, and property. From business firms, it obtains funds through corporate income tax as well as social security, unemployment, and a number of other business taxes. Sometimes governmental spending exceeds the amount received in taxes. When this occurs, the government is operating under a **budget deficit**. If the government receives more in taxes than it is paying out, it is operating under a **budget surplus**.

THE FINANCIAL MARKET

The fourth player in the circular flow model is the **financial market**, which is the collection of a nation's financial institutions that receive deposits of excess funds from households and lend those funds to business firms. A principal function of the financial market is to circulate money from households to business firms effectively and efficiently. The financial market includes commercial banks, savings and loan associations, credit unions, insurance companies, finance companies, and stock brokerage firms. Looking at Figure 2-9, you will notice that households both save and dissave.

Economists consider households to be saving whenever they put money into a financial institution (for example, when they deposit money in a savings account or make a payment on a loan). On the other hand, economists apply the term **dissaving** any time households withdraw money from an account or borrow it.

A well-developed financial market is essential to the economic growth of a nation. Having a growing number of profitable business firms that have access to financial capital is a characteristic of a successful economy. As a population grows and tastes change, business firms must have access to available funds to adapt and grow. By taking the savings of households and channeling them to businesses, a well-developed financial market is able to meet this need efficiently.

Ideally, all savings in the financial market should be available to business firms, but the government often diverts some of the funds to itself to finance its budget deficit. As you read earlier, a budget deficit results when the government pays out more money than it receives in taxes. Suppose that you go to the grocery store and write a check for $120; but after you leave the store, you find that you have only $50 in your account. You must find $70 to deposit to your account before your check returns to the bank. Likewise, when the government operates under a budget deficit, it must either increase

> In a nation's economy, households, business firms, and financial institutions are referred to as the *private sector*, and government is referred to as the *public sector*.

taxes, an option that many consider politically unwise, or borrow an amount equal to the difference between its income from taxes and its expenditures.

To borrow money from the financial market, the government does not go to a bank, as you would, and fill out loan applications. Instead it sells bonds with very attractive interest rates to financial institutions. The federal government, for example, sells US savings bonds, Treasury bills, and Treasury notes.

On the surface there appears to be little difference in the effect on the overall economy whether business firms or the government is doing the borrowing; however, there is one subtle difference. Governmental

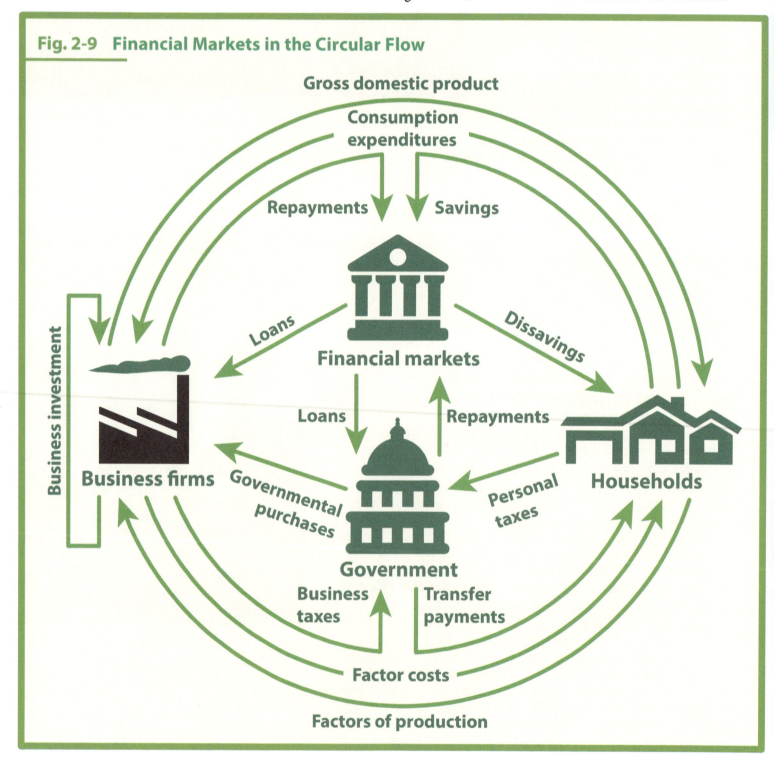

Fig. 2-9 Financial Markets in the Circular Flow

borrowing leads to a problem called **crowding out**. Money is finite like all other resources; therefore, every dollar borrowed by the government means one less dollar is available for business firms to use in purchasing the real capital they need to produce the goods that consumers want and need. In this way business firms are "crowded out" of the financial market by the government's budget deficits. Because the financial market is the heart of the economy, the money it provides to business firms is vital. If the government diverts too much money for too long, business firms will die, their plants will lie idle, and widespread unemployment will result.

The large model of the human eye your science teacher may have used provided a visual aid to help you understand his explanation concerning the function of that organ. Similarly, if you wanted to see how adjusting the flaps on an airplane alters the air flow over its wings, a model (perhaps in the form of a computer simulation) would be a great asset. Models are not perfect in their representations of other things, but because they allow us to see and study what we would otherwise not likely be able to examine, they greatly

LUDWIG VON MISES (1881–1973)
Advocate of Free Markets

Born in the Austro-Hungarian Empire, Ludwig von Mises (fon MEE-zess) studied and taught at the University of Vienna. After World War I, when Nazism was on the rise in Austria, he moved to Geneva. Then in 1940, when the repression of World War II was overspreading Europe, Mises fled to America, where he gained citizenship and spent the rest of his life teaching and writing.

Although Mises is not one of the most well-known economists of the twentieth century, his contributions to the science have had great influence. He is among those whose work served to establish the Austrian school as a leader in the field of economics. It was the founder of the Austrian school, Carl Menger, whose *Principles of Economics* turned Mises from a governmental interventionist to a free-market thinker. The writings of Mises, in turn, influenced another generation of economists at the Austrian school and led them to support capitalism.

Mises also became a vigorous opponent of socialism. He demonstrated in his 1922 book, entitled *Socialism*, that central planning under socialism or communism could not result in greater prosperity than that under a free market. His most significant work was the monumental *Human Action*, published in 1949. It was a comprehensive treatment of economic theory from the Austrian perspective and has been described as the most "profound, complete [and] persuasive exposition and defense of the free market."[1]

Mises wrote during a period in which mainstream economics had embraced the government-based solutions proposed in the works of John Maynard Keynes. As a result of the prevailing economic philosophy (and the fact that Mises wrote in German and had to have his works translated into English), his ideas were largely ignored. He also could not obtain a full-time position at an American university. In spite of these difficulties, Mises and his work still inspired a generation of economists to embrace and promote free-market economics.

1. Henry Regnery, "The Book in the Market Place," in *Toward Liberty: Essays in Honor of Ludwig von Mises on the Occasion of his 90th Birthday, September 29, 1971*, ed. F. A. von Hayek et al., vol. 2 (Menlo Park, CA: Institute for Humane Studies, 1971).

aid our learning. Tabular models, line graphs, production possibilities curves, and the circular flow model should all make it easier for you to grasp the economic concepts in this chapter. Perhaps you still are not entirely clear on some of those ideas, but you are likely to be closer to a working knowledge than you would have been without the help of the models. Models play a vital role in teaching economics, and you will encounter other models as you continue through this book. As you come to each one, take a moment to reflect on what you learned in this chapter, especially giving thought to what you may be modeling in your life by the choices you make each day.

SECTION REVIEW 2B

1. What does the circular flow model attempt to explain?
2. What are the four factors of production?
3. What four payments do business firms make in exchange for the factors of production?
4. What are the four major participants in the circular flow model, and what is the primary role of each in the circular flow?

CHAPTER REVIEW

CONTENT QUESTIONS

1. Why do economists use economic models? Give an example of an economic model from this chapter.
2. Name the two common types of models used in economics.
3. On a production possibilities curve, what do points on, inside, and outside the curve represent?
4. What is the difference between financial capital and real capital?
5. What is the most important factor of production? Why?
6. How is the Proverbs 31 woman an example of an entrepreneur? Use three examples from the box on page 30 in your answer.
7. Draw the basic circular flow (in which the only participants are households and business firms), labeling each of the four arrows or flows.
8. What economic functions does the government perform as illustrated by the circular flow model?
9. Why is the financial market necessary for the effective functioning of a developed society?
10. Explain what an economist means when he refers to the government as "crowding out."
11. With what economic principle do we most often associate Ludwig von Mises? Ludwig von Mises was influenced by what economist?

APPLICATION QUESTIONS

1. Suppose that a recent survey of high-school students revealed the following table of information equating hours of study per weeknight with grade point averages. Draw a line graph using the information given below. What relationship between hours of study and GPA does the slope of the curve indicate? Approximately how many hours of study would be necessary for a student to receive a GPA of 2.5? Mark this point on the curve.

Hours of study	GPA
2.25	4.0 (A)
1.25	3.0 (B)
0.75	2.0 (C)
0.25	1.0 (D)

2. Select one product currently on the market and list as many of the natural resources, types of labor, entrepreneurship, and capital that go into its production as you can.
3. If all financial institutions suddenly vanished and all deposits in those institutions were equally suddenly back in the pockets of the depositors, what would be some of the probable repercussions on the economy?

TERMS

tabular model	24
schedule	24
line graph	24
production possibilities curve (PPC)	24
circular flow model	27
consumption expenditures	27
factors of production	28
land	28
labor	29
capital	29
entrepreneurship	29
factor costs	29
rent	29
wages	29
interest	30
profit	31
transfer payments	33
budget deficit	33
budget surplus	33
financial market	33
dissaving	33
crowding out	35

PERSONAL FINANCE
PRINCIPLES OF PURCHASING

Proverbs describes the virtuous woman as a wise consumer who thinks about what she is about to purchase. "She considereth a field, and buyeth it: with the fruit of her hands she planteth a vineyard. . . . She perceiveth that her merchandise is good: her candle goeth not out by night" (Prov. 31:16, 18). Likewise, Christians should be wise stewards of whatever money the Lord entrusts to their care. Therefore, when a believer enters the marketplace, it is important that he keep in mind principles of wise purchasing.

Principle #1—Purpose to honor God with your purchases. Before purchasing an item, consider your motive for buying it and ask yourself how you will use it to honor God. "Whether therefore ye eat, or drink, or whatsoever ye do, do all to the glory of God" (1 Cor. 10:31).

Principle #2—Shop with knowledge. Before you go shopping, especially for major purchases, check the product's features and reliability with consumer product publications. Does the manufacturer guarantee the product and provide good service after the sale? In addition to checking published reports, investigate the dealer or store from which you are buying. Consult your local Better Business Bureau to see if the firm has a history of dissatisfied customers.

Principle #3—Shop with a plan. Before you shop, plan out exactly what you need to buy and what questions to ask. For example, when you shop for groceries, shop with a list of items you need for the coming week and

stick to your list. Of course, it takes time to "do your homework" before you shop; but if you shop without a plan, you will have a greater tendency to make impulse purchases. If you do not have a plan, you will be unsure of what questions you should ask salespeople. Most of these questions will likely arise from the research you do as part of shopping with knowledge.

BETTER BUSINESS BUREAU

Organized in 1916, the National Better Business Bureau has offices in all major US cities and counties. Businesses support this organization because it benefits an honest business's own reputation and discourages unscrupulous competitors. Not only does it provide customers with information about products and the business practices of local businesses before a purchase, but it also helps consumers get restitution for legitimate complaints against goods and services after they have bought them.

SMART SHOPPER TIP #1

A good policy to follow is never to purchase a major item without waiting twenty-four hours to pray, seek advice, and think the purchase over carefully.

Principle #4—Carry only necessary amounts of money. Romans 13:14 exhorts Christians not to make provision for the flesh or, in other words, not to make it easy to give in to fleshly desires. For many shoppers, a momentary desire coupled with having an abundance of ready cash or debit or credit cards very easily equals an unwise purchase.

FRAUD AND DECEPTION

A prudent man foreseeth the evil, and hideth himself: but the simple pass on, and are punished.
Proverbs 22:3

*CATCH?
Did you say CATCH?!*

There exists an old Latin maxim, **caveat emptor**, which means "let the buyer beware!" This saying acknowledges that it is the buyer's responsibility to ensure that he is not being deceived. While governmental regulations today protect consumers to a greater degree than they did a century ago, fraudulent business practices have not yet ceased, and the buyer must still beware.

It would be great if consumers could always trust salespeople and advertisements to be totally honest about their products. Unfortunately, the depravity of man is clearly evident in many such cases. One common advertising deception is the **bait-and-switch**. Using this tactic, a company advertises a product, such as a refrigerator or carpeting, makes it seem fine, and offers it at a very low price. That is the bait to draw customers into the store; however, when they arrive, they find that the product they came to buy is somehow undesirable or unobtainable.

*OooOOohh!
Sir, you wound me!
You cut me, Sir!
Ooohh!
All I want to do is show you the beauties of Duncewood Estates!*

...and give you, YES, GIVE you this fabulous TV—absolutely FREE—and you ask, "What's the catch?"

The refrigerator may be poorly built or not offer features that customers would assume it had, or the carpet may be of an obviously inferior quality. Often, the advertised product is "sold out." (There may have been only a few available for sale.) Then comes the switch as a salesperson tells the customer that what he really needs is a better model of refrigerator or a higher-quality carpet—items with significantly higher price tags.

Other forms of deceptive advertising include bogus contests and giveaways. The sales pitch tells the customer that he has won some prize or can have something absolutely free. Whether it be a new television or wonderful vacation package, there is likely to be a catch. Usually the "winner" must buy something else at a high price to receive his prize.

Fraud occurs when someone is deliberately dishonest to make a sale. He may give false information about a competing product or claim that his product can do something that it cannot do. He may trick a customer into signing a contract or charge for extra parts or services that he does not include. In a land scam, he may sell a "beautiful lot in a plush resort area" that turns out to be a small piece of unusable swampland. In a sly telemarketing scheme, he may sell get-rich-quick investments to people gullible enough to give their credit card number or send a check for the impossible deal. The fraud then disappears with the money.

Ingenious swindlers and unethical businesspersons are constantly finding ways to dupe unwary consumers, and today's Internet shopping has opened new windows for frauds and scams, such as "phishing" and "pharming." These schemes attempt to acquire sensitive, personal financial information, such as passwords and social security, credit card, and bank account numbers. Phishing uses the lure of a seemingly legitimate e-mail that asks for a response, and pharming utilizes computer codes to redirect Internet users to bogus websites.

You'll just need this $250 cord to run your free TV.

While advertising deception and fraud are illegal, innocent people who succumb to them are often too embarrassed to make the wrong known. Even if they do press charges, the inconveniences and expense of the ordeal can be frustrating and discouraging. Therefore, it is always best to remember *caveat emptor*!

Principle #5—Look carefully at the price tag and receipt. Do not be fooled by "sales." In some cases, merchants mark an item with a much higher price only to mark it down to a price that is still higher than you should pay. Also, pay attention to **unit pricing**. Unit pricing is the price per the product's unit of measurement. For example, when deciding between bags of potato chips of equal quality, do not look at the price tag on the bags as the sole determining factor; look at the price per ounce. One brand may sell a slightly smaller bag to display a smaller price while actually charging a higher price per ounce. If the store does not display unit prices, use the calculator on your phone to determine unit prices for yourself. After you shop, compare the price you paid with the actual price of the item. Even though stores generally use electronic scanners to scan UPCs, there is a chance that they programmed the prices incorrectly or that they did not enter a sale price to override the original higher price.

Principle #6—Consider the total cost. Remember, the cost of an item goes beyond its price tag to include all the costs associated with it throughout its life. For example, suppose you find a "terrific buy" on a popular sports car. Instead of paying its normal price of $30,000, you can purchase it for only $12,000. That looks like a great deal, but do not stop there. Check for other costs. Is the dealer charging a preparation fee? How about taxes and registration fees? Consider insurance; the cost of insuring a sports car may be prohibitively expensive. Have a reliable mechanic check its engine, transmission, and other parts that would be very expensive to repair or replace. If the price seems too low, check the car's history to find out if it was in a wreck or flood and has been restored to "almost" as good as new.

Principle #7—Ask for advice. When making a substantial purchase such as a house, automobile, or major appliance, it would be wise to have an expert provide counsel. For example, have a reputable mechanic look over a used car before making a commitment to purchase it. It may cost a few dollars, but it will be a few dollars well spent. He may be able to spot hidden costly problems that you would not have noticed until after a contract was signed. "Where no counsel is, the people fall: but in the multitude of counsellors there is safety" (Prov. 11:14).

SMART SHOPPER TIP #3

Always offer to pay someone who is looking over the item to give you advice, even if he is a friend. You do not want to earn a reputation as a freeloader.

Principle #8—Do not be fooled. Some salespeople prey upon the vanity or ignorance of shoppers by using deceitful advertising or fraudulent sales methods. Be aware of the techniques they might employ. Their sales tactics vary according to their targets: they approach newlyweds, new parents, and elderly folks according to their needs and interests.

Using these principles consistently should spare you from frequent frustrations of asking yourself why you bought something you should not have. Because the Christian recognizes that whatever money he has is from God, he knows he will one day give an account as to what he did with that money. Yes, there may be a way for you to return a faulty item or at least obtain some financial remuneration for the defective product you purchased. However, you would have fared better had you not made the purchase in the first place.

SMART SHOPPER TIP #2

Another good way to weigh the cost of an item is to think of its cost in terms not of dollars but of the number of hours you must work to earn the necessary money. For example, if you were earning $27.00 per hour, a $22,000 home theater system would cost you 814 hours, or 20.35 weeks of work.

REVIEW QUESTIONS

1. What are the eight principles of wise purchasing?
2. Why do businesses support the Better Business Bureau?

TERMS

caveat emptor	39
bait-and-switch	39
unit pricing	40

PERSONAL FINANCE

CONSUMERISM

Americans should be aware of the rights that their government affords them as consumers. The regulatory agencies designed to protect those rights may prove helpful in the event of unfair business practices.

CONSUMER RIGHTS

Because of a noticeable increase in fraudulent business practices during the first half of the twentieth century and the courts' *caveat emptor* attitude, American consumers rose up and demanded that their government protect them. The era of **consumerism**, the drive for the enforcement of consumer rights, began in 1962 when President John Kennedy sent a message urging Congress to guarantee four fundamental consumer rights:

1. The right to safety

   American consumers should have the right to be confident that the product they purchase will not be dangerous to their lives or health.

2. The right to be informed

   Americans should have the right to expect that businesses will provide enough information to assist consumers in making informed choices.

3. The right to choose

   American consumers should not be held at the mercy of monopolies. When competition thrives, consumers find a greater number of product choices at lower prices; therefore, the government should guarantee free competition.

4. The right to be heard

   When the government is making policy decisions, consumers should have the right to express their concerns.

Since 1962, other presidents have added to President Kennedy's list:

5. The right to an environment free of pollution

   American consumers have a right to clean air and water, uncontaminated by industrial pollutants.

6. The right to education on consumer issues

   American consumers have a right to be educated by the government about consumer issues.

7. The right to fight back

   If a consumer suffers as a result of buying a defective product or service, he should have the right to **redress**; that is, he should have the right to be heard in court and to receive reasonable compensation.

To enforce these consumer rights, the government created a number of federal agencies and empowered them to enact laws and to punish offenders.

In keeping with the first of President Kennedy's consumer rights, Congress authorized the Food and Drug Administration (FDA), created in 1906, to test all new drugs before they could be admitted to the marketplace. Additionally, Congress gave the FDA the power to require that drugs be not only safe but also "effective."

The Federal Trade Commission (FTC), created in 1914, maintains the second of President Kennedy's consumer rights, the right to be informed. It is the FTC that monitors advertising, labeling, and deceptive practices and reviews applications for complaints. If the FTC discovers a deceptive practice, it may take one of these corrective actions: 1) issue a **cease and desist order** that prohibits a firm from continuing a deceptive practice or 2) require **counteradvertising**, which is advertising that a firm must produce at its own expense to correct any false claims that its earlier advertising promoted.

In response to a growing number of unsafe consumer products that did not fall under the administration of the FDA, Congress passed the Consumer Product Safety Act (1972), which created the Consumer Product Safety Commission (CPSC). The CPSC has broad powers to detect and regulate potentially hazardous consumer

products. It has the power to devise safety standards for consumer products and may forbid sales of products it deems unsafe. For example, the CPSC has forced some toy manufacturers to recall products possessing parts that might be easily swallowed by small children.

In addition to these three, other governmental agencies exist to ensure consumer rights: the Department of Health and Human Services, the Environmental Protection Agency, and a number of state agencies. Several private watchdog organizations, including the Consumers Union and the Better Business Bureau, also exist to aid consumers.

CONSUMER RESPONSIBILITIES

Today many groups make much of the responsibilities of business firms to consumers, but what, if any, are the responsibilities consumers have toward business firms? While not codified into laws, there are common courtesies that all Christian consumers should extend.

1. Courteous treatment
   Many times the consumer demanding courteous service is himself rude in his dealings with business personnel. If we expect sympathetic and courteous treatment as customers, we should give sympathetic and courteous treatment to businesses. Remember, when placing an order or delivering a complaint, you may be dealing with a business firm; but a living, breathing person is across the desk or at the end of the telephone line. "And as ye would that men should do to you, do ye also to them likewise" (Luke 6:31).

2. Prompt and fair returns
   When customers purchase products, they expect them to perform as advertised. If a product is unsatisfactory, the customer should return it immediately for an exchange or a refund. Although some customers soon realize that a product is slightly defective, they use it for days, weeks, or even months before returning it and still expect a full refund. Had the item been returned immediately, it might have been repaired and resold. However, because of the delay, the damage may be irreparable, and the firm may suffer a financial loss. Also, if after purchasing a product a customer realizes that he really cannot afford it or that he does not like the style, he should return it without using it. "Recompense to no man evil for evil. Provide things honest in the sight of all men" (Rom. 12:17).

3. Prompt payment
   While many consumers would be irate at having to wait two months to receive their orders from a business, some seemingly have no problem withholding payment to a business for several months or longer. They may reason that they are denying money to a "big company" that really does not need it that badly or that they are simply paying

THE CONSUMER'S ADVOCATE

Ralph Nader, America's first and most vocal consumer advocate, published a book in 1965 called *Unsafe at Any Speed*. It condemned the automobile industry (and especially General Motors in its production of the Chevrolet Corvair) for allegedly sacrificing safety in its attempt to achieve a popular style. Nader carried on his attack by testifying before a Senate subcommittee. When it was later learned that General Motors had been harassing Nader for pursuing the issue, passage of the Traffic and Motor Vehicle Safety Act of 1966 was assured. Seat belts appeared in all new cars, and Nader won his reputation as a consumer advocate.

Nader did not limit his political action to matters of automobile safety, however. He built a network of organizations under the banner of Public Citizen Inc. to investigate corporate abuse of consumers and to lobby the government for regulative action. This work resulted in many federal laws involving everything from air and water pollution to meat and poultry inspection.

By the mid-1970s Nader's popularity began to wane as he pled for governmental regulation of America's private businesses and even the nationalization of industry. Most people rejected such socialistic ideas and abandoned Nader as he became more controversial.

late because their order was late. However, as regards the former reasoning, if a business experiences problems with its cash flow, the consumer will ultimately feel adverse effects. As the bills the company owes become past due, its suppliers will withhold shipments of raw materials, delaying production and shipment. If a customer cannot pay his obligation immediately, the least he should do is contact the firm, explain the situation, and work out a payment plan. As for the latter reasoning, it rises from vengeance, which belongs to God (Rom. 12:19). "The wicked borroweth, and payeth not again: but the righteous sheweth mercy, and giveth" (Ps. 37:21).

4. Consideration of other consumers' needs
An example of how a consumer practice can selfishly harm fellow consumers can be found in the airline industry. A common practice of airlines that has frustrated many passengers is that of overbooking flights—making more reservations than the airplane has seats. The reason this practice came into being, however, was that airlines noted a high probability that a percentage of booked passengers would not show up. Studies commissioned by the airline industry found that the reason for the predictable number of "no-shows" was that some passengers booked reservations under several names to ensure that they would receive a seat. They apparently had little regard for the effect of their actions on the airlines and the travel plans of other passengers. Such conduct has resulted in the inconvenience of many air travelers. These and other inconveniences could often be avoided if consumers would simply consider the effect of their actions on other customers. "Be kindly affectioned one to another with brotherly love; in honour preferring one another" (Rom. 12:10).

Perhaps you have heard the saying that with every privilege comes responsibility. As an American consumer you have many privileges. You have the right to have safe products, truthful product information, and governmental agencies to protect you from fraudulent business practices. You also have the right to seek redress when wronged. However, with those rights or privileges come responsibilities: being courteous, prompt, fair, and considerate. For Christians, fulfilling those responsibilities is an important part of glorifying their Savior and loving their neighbors.

REVIEW QUESTIONS

1. Describe the four basic consumer rights as outlined by President Kennedy in 1962.
2. Name the three federal agencies that have the responsibility to enforce consumer rights. Name a key function of each agency in relation to this responsibility.
3. Name four common courtesies consumers should practice when dealing with business firms.

TERMS

consumerism	41
redress	41
cease and desist order	41
counteradvertising	41

CHAPTER THREE
VALUE AND DEMAND

3A VALUE — 44

3B DEMAND — 50

3A VALUE

Danny loved auctions, and this one was no exception. As he elbowed his way to the front of the crowd, he heard the auctioneer call out, "All right, ladies and gentlemen, let's begin the bidding on this fine lamp at five dollars," and the auctioneer pointed to what, by some stretch of the imagination, might be called a lamp. Danny thought it was one of the ugliest things he had ever seen, but his amusement turned to shock and disbelief as twelve people began clamoring to purchase it. Several minutes later, after the hectic bidding had died down, the gavel fell: "Sold to the gentleman in the pinstriped suit for three hundred forty-seven dollars!" Danny's mind was reeling. Who on earth would be willing to pay any price for that thing? What a waste of money! As the victor happily paid the clerk and strode out the door clutching his prize, Danny muttered to himself, "It just doesn't make sense!"

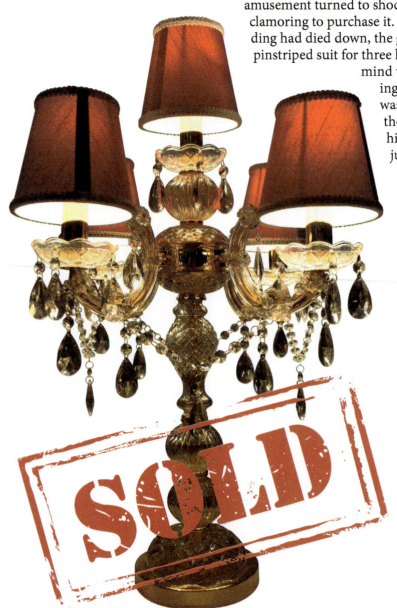

Actually the buyer's actions make perfect sense. Danny is just forgetting Carl Menger's rule of value: value (that is, economic value—the value of a good or service in dollars) is in the mind of the buyer, not in the thing being purchased. Danny is also forgetting that in a free market in which there is ample protection from fraud and force, people will almost always make choices designed to suit their own needs and wants. Perhaps the buyer of the lamp was interested in it for personal, sentimental reasons. It was just like a lamp his grandparents had owned and linked him with a special time in his past. Perhaps he knew something about that lamp that no one else there knew, such as it had a notable former owner or contained some hidden treasure. Or perhaps the man simply collected curious lamps, and this was just the one he needed to complete his collection.

Being unfamiliar with their circumstances and frame of mind, you, like Danny, may believe others are acting foolishly when, in fact, they are acting quite rationally. People dislike Menger's principle of subjective value because it is unsettling to think that their way of valuing goods and services is not the only way. In fact, the theory of subjective value lends itself to the possibility that a good actually may possess billions of different values, as many values as there are people on earth.

DIMINISHING MARGINAL UTILITY

While Menger's principle states that values are not constant from one person to another, a second principle holds that values are not constant even for a single person. An item that you hold dear right now, you may hold in lower esteem five minutes from now. For example, let us assume that you really enjoy eating So Good brand candy bars and that you are so hungry right now that you would place a value of $2.00 on the first So Good bar you could get. This is not to say that the price of a bar is $2.00, merely that you value one enough that you would be willing to pay $2.00 for it. Would you always be willing to pay that price? Would you pay $2.00 for a second bar, a fifth bar, a fiftieth? Probably not. How, then, is it possible for your value system to change dramatically in just a matter of moments? How could you at one moment be willing to pay $2.00 for a candy bar and a few minutes (and several bars) later be unwilling to buy one at any price?

William Stanley Jevons, an English economist, tackled and solved this riddle in 1871. In his book *The Theory of Political Economy*, Jevons developed the **principle of diminishing marginal utility**, which states that people tend to receive less and less (diminishing) additional (marginal) satisfaction (utility) from any good or service as they obtain more and more of it during a specific period of time.

To illustrate, let us return to the candy shop. If we attach to your brain the utility meter referred to in Chapter 1, we find that after eating your first So Good bar your satisfaction level jumps to six utils. After eating a second bar, which you enjoyed but not quite as intensely as the first, the meter jumps four additional utils to a total of ten. Your third bar results in a rise of three additional utils

to a total of thirteen. Notice how your total satisfaction is rising, but each increase tends to be less than the previous increase. You are experiencing diminishing marginal utility. Eventually you will reach a point at which additional candy bars will provide no added satisfaction. In fact, past this point, eating more bars will cause dissatisfaction.

Figure 3-1 is an example of a **marginal utility schedule**, a tabular model based upon the observation of your eating the hypothetical candy bars. Figure 3-2 is a **marginal utility curve**, a graphic representation of the marginal utility schedule.

You can easily see the principle of diminishing marginal utility applied in the accumulation of food items, but it is no less evident in the accumulation of other goods and services. For instance, a backpack is a useful item for you to be able to keep and carry your school essentials in, and it might be helpful to have a second backpack for going to the gym or playing sports. However, if you had two backpacks, how much additional utility would you gain from a third one? One kitchen table is a necessity in most houses, but who would want two or three? Services are equally subject to this principle. Having your car washed once a week might keep it looking good, but would you need it washed every day? Such frequent washes would often be unnecessary and a waste of time.

Fig. 3-1 Marginal Utility Schedule

Candy bar number	Total satisfaction after this candy bar	Minus	Total satisfaction before this candy bar	Equals	Satisfaction this candy bar provided (marginal utility)
1	6 utils	−	0 utils	=	6 utils
2	10	−	6	=	4
3	13	−	10	=	3
4	15	−	13	=	2
5	16	−	15	=	1
6	16	−	16	=	0
7	15.5	−	16	=	−0.5
8	14	−	15.5	=	−1.5
9	12	−	14	=	−2
10	2	−	12	=	−10

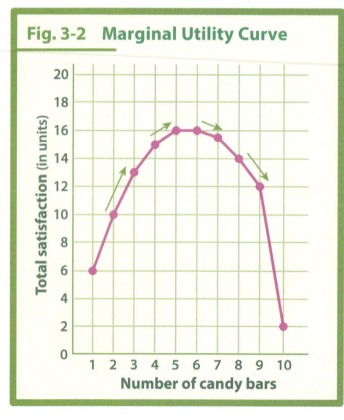

Fig. 3-2 Marginal Utility Curve

THE FUNCTION OF PRICES

In nearly every transaction, you compare your value of the good or service you are considering purchasing with the price tag on that item. If the value that product has for you is greater than or equal to the asking price, you will likely purchase it. If, however, the price of that item is higher than what it is worth to you, the merchant probably will not make the sale. You understand the concept of value, but what about the other part of the transaction? What is this thing called price? Prices are much more than numbers on little stickers

WILLIAM STANLEY JEVONS (1835–82)

Developer of the Law of Diminishing Marginal Utility

William Stanley Jevons was the ninth child in a relatively well-to-do family in Liverpool, England. However, his mother died when he was just ten years old, and his father's prosperous business collapsed shortly thereafter. Because of the resulting financial difficulties and because of his being a Nonconformist (one who practiced Protestantism outside the Anglican Church), Jevons did not have the opportunity to attend the best schools of his day. He entered college in London to study chemistry, mathematics, and logic but left after two years due to financial hardship. He took a job in Australia and remained there five years. After the death of his father, he returned to London to complete his bachelor's degree at the University College in 1860 and his master of arts in 1862.

Jevons had wide research interests. His earliest writings focused on applying mathematical principles to economic questions, but since these writings gained little attention, he turned to questions of logic. However, a number of years later, when a fellow researcher sent him a copy of a research paper in economics, his attention turned back to economics. His renewed interest motivated him to revisit his writings. Jevons's works addressed such topics as how individuals form subjective ideas as regards the utility they derive from goods and activities and how business activity tends to occur in cycles. His best-known work, *The Theory of Political Economy*, was the one in which he described an idea that earned him recognition as an economist: the law of diminishing marginal utility.

Jevons's presentation of the principle of diminishing marginal utility began with the idea that the value of a good was subjective (Carl Menger, see Ch. 1); that is, different people could value the same good very differently and derive different amounts of utility from it. Classical economists had taught that since the quantity of labor needed to produce a good determined its value, that good should have the same value for everyone. Jevons's work disputed that thinking and presented an alternative view. He demonstrated that individuals make decisions at the margin, or in terms of small increments, and that the quantity of any good or activity that an individual chooses to obtain is that amount at which the marginal benefit just offsets the marginal cost. Economists often illustrate Jevons's law of diminishing marginal utility with the familiar experience of eating pizza. As a person consumes each additional slice, he discovers it yields less satisfaction than the prior one until, ultimately, eating an additional piece yields less satisfaction than the slice of pizza would cost. This is true even if the person were to eat at a buffet where there was no additional cost for additional slices of pizza. In that case, the person would continue to consume pizza as long as he obtained any additional satisfaction from doing so.

Jevons and his contemporary Carl Menger put in motion a movement that became known as the "marginalist revolution." Their works helped to form what economists today call modern orthodox economic theory.

SCRIPTURE AND THE PRINCIPLE OF DIMINISHING MARGINAL UTILITY

So far in this chapter we have been talking about applying diminishing marginal utility only to the economic value of physical items. But many non-physical items have a value that is not economic. Things like God, His Word, truth, and relationships all have value even though no one can really put a price on them. Even though they aren't physical like So Good candy bars and the kitchen table, we can still apply the principle of diminishing marginal utility. We see examples in the Bible. In Malachi 1:13, God rebukes the priests for no longer recognizing the value of the sacrifices but viewing the process as "a weariness." In Revelation 2:4, Christ pointed out to the churches that they had "left [their] first love." They no longer had the same passion for things of God that they once had. The things of God had not changed in their value, but the churches' desire for those things had diminished.

We also see this principle around us in everyday life. For example, as people grow more familiar with others, they sometimes begin to esteem them less. Divorce comes too frequently when spouses forget to continue their submission to, acceptance of, and mutual respect for each other. Those who live in glamorous or luxurious places often do not enjoy their advantages. After growing up in Christian homes and being surrounded by Scripture, godly examples, and spiritual blessings, some children reject their blessings and come to despise the Bible, their parents, and their church.

On the other hand, the Word of God also points out that while diminishing marginal utility may be inherent in man's fallen nature, it is not an unchangeable situation. A person can be totally satisfied with a close personal relationship with God made possible through trust in the saving work of His Son, Jesus Christ. In John 6:35, Jesus talked about how He satisfies people's desire for something more: "I am the bread of life: he that cometh to me shall never hunger; and he that believeth on me shall never thirst." Only God can fully satisfy, and He says to His people, "Open thy mouth wide, and I will fill it" (Ps. 81:10). He invites all to come to Him for the satisfaction that can be found only in Him: "Ho, every one that thirsteth, come ye to the waters, and he that hath no money; come ye, buy, and eat; yea, come, buy wine and milk without money and without price. Wherefore do ye spend money for that which is not bread? and your labour for that which satisfieth not? hearken diligently unto me, and eat ye that which is good, and let your soul delight itself in fatness" (Isa. 55:1–2).

affixed to merchandise. Prices serve to transmit information, provide incentives, and redistribute income.

Suppose that for some unknown reason millions of people begin increasing the value they place on So Good candy bars. Thousands of stores will experience greater demand and, therefore, place larger orders with their wholesalers. Wholesalers, realizing that they have nowhere near the number of candy bars needed to satisfy the stores' demand, place larger orders with the candy manufacturers. The makers of the candy bars, now overwhelmed with orders from stores all over the country, will need to purchase greater amounts of ingredients from suppliers. To persuade producers to sell them more cocoa, milk, cream, and sugar, the candy makers must offer them higher prices. Seeing a potential for huge profits, cocoa producers will increase their production; dairy farmers will purchase more milk cows and will hire more farm hands. Sugar refineries will increase output, possibly necessitating adding an additional shift and hiring more workers. On and on this process continues until virtually all over the world business firms receive the information the price mechanism is sending them, telling what they ought to produce.

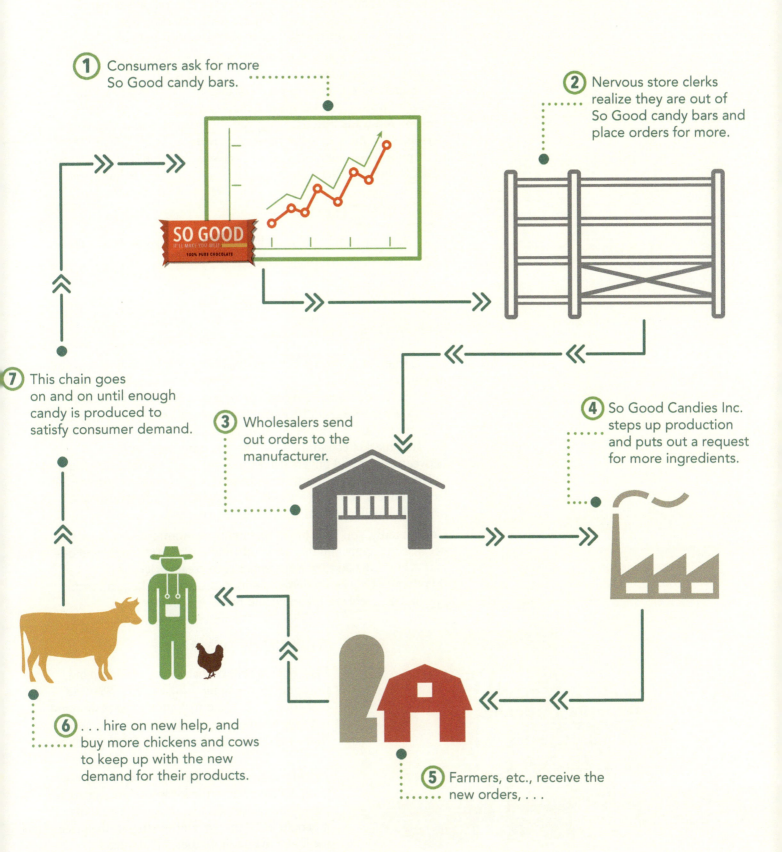

The price mechanism also provides incentives. The increased demand for So Good bars increases the prices that producers offer farmers for their goods. These higher prices act as incentives for the farmers to divert their production efforts to those goods with rising prices. Financial institutions, eager to make loans to candy makers and candy shops, will offer higher rates of interest on savings. These higher rates serve as an incentive for people to save, thus creating a large pool of money for the financial institutions to lend.

Prices also serve a third function of redistributing income. The farmers, chemists, and other producers who redirect their factors of production to help satisfy buyers' demands experience an increase in income. On the other hand, producers who ignore the information transmitted by the price mechanism and who are not persuaded to produce what the economy desires experience a loss of income. The potential increased income they could have seen is redistributed to others; consequently, they may declare bankruptcy.

SECTION REVIEW 3A

1. Who identified the principle of diminishing marginal utility?
2. What does that principle state?
3. What are the three functions of prices?

3B DEMAND

You learned in Section 3A that prices transmit information, provide incentives, and redistribute income, but you may wonder, "Where do prices come from?" After all, price tags on store items do not mysteriously appear in the night. Do producers charge whatever price they want? Does the government declare what prices will be? In a free-market economy, an unspoken, unwritten "agreement" between sellers and buyers determines prices. If a price is too high, sellers will have to lower their price or risk going out of business for lack of buyers. If buyers are willing to pay only a ridiculously low price, they will go unsatisfied, because firms will refuse to produce.

Undoubtedly, you have heard that many economic actions occur because of supply and demand, but what exactly are supply and demand, and how do they work together to create prices? The rest of this chapter focuses on demand—its definition and its relationship to price. You will study supply and prices in Chapter 4.

THE LAW OF DEMAND

Most people believe that consumers' demand for a good is the same thing as their "wanting" that good. The economist, though, sees **demand** not only as a willingness of consumers to purchase a product but also as their act of purchasing it.

The **law of demand** states that everything else being held constant, the lower the price charged for a good or service, the greater the quantity of it people will demand, and the higher the price, the lower the quantity they will demand.

The law of demand is nothing but common sense. If the price of a So Good bar at Candy City is $1.00, then only those people who value a bar greater than or equal to $1.00 will demand one. Figure 3-3a shows the subjective values of seven people for a So Good bar. At a price of $1.00 per bar, Candy City will sell only three bars to these seven people.

Now suppose that a discount from the manufacturer enables Candy City to lower its price to 90¢. Figure 3-3b illustrates that the price has dropped to a level where it is now attractive to two more buyers.

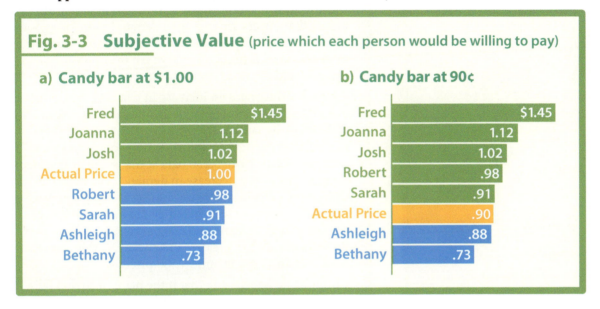

Fig. 3-3 Subjective Value (price which each person would be willing to pay)

a) Candy bar at $1.00

Fred	$1.45
Joanna	1.12
Josh	1.02
Actual Price	1.00
Robert	.98
Sarah	.91
Ashleigh	.88
Bethany	.73

b) Candy bar at 90¢

Fred	$1.45
Joanna	1.12
Josh	1.02
Robert	.98
Sarah	.91
Actual Price	.90
Ashleigh	.88
Bethany	.73

Fig. 3-4 Demand Schedule

Price charged per candy bar	Quantity demanded
$1.90	2,000 bars
1.55	2,250
1.00	3,500
.80	5,500
.75	6,750

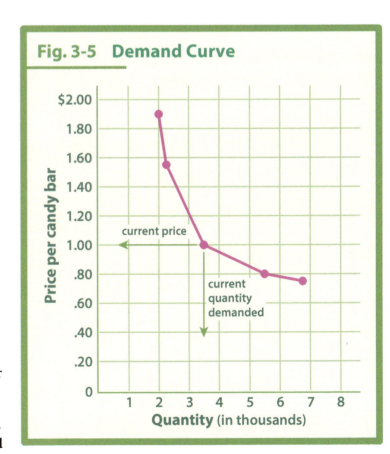

Fig. 3-5 Demand Curve

Economists, wishing to observe the effects of price changes on a product's demand, construct a **demand schedule**, a table listing various quantities demanded at various prices. Figure 3-4 is a demand schedule for Candy City's So Good bars.

To visualize the law of demand better, economists take the information from the demand schedule and put it into a line graph. The result is called a **demand curve**. Notice how the demand schedule contains a limited number of observations. However, putting it into a line graph form, such as in Figure 3-5, expands the information into an infinite number of points. Thus the observer has a better idea of the demand for the product at any given price.

Whenever a change in price causes a change in the number of items demanded, a **change in quantity demanded** has occurred. Suppose that Candy City has been selling

So Good bars for $1.00, but because of increases in the prices of ingredients, it must charge $1.90. Looking at Figure 3-6, we find that at a price of $1.90 per bar, the quantity demanded will be only 2,000 bars, a change of 1,500 bars.

CHANGE IN DEMAND

When a demand curve shifts, economists say that the product is experiencing a **change in demand**. A rightward shift, which represents an **increase in demand**, means that buyers are willing to demand more of a good or service at every price along the curve. A leftward shift, or **decrease in demand**, would mean the opposite; demand would decrease at every price.

Figure 3-7 illustrates an increase in demand. At a price of $1.00 per bar on the first demand curve (D_1), the quantity buyers demand is 3,500 bars. A rightward shift of the demand curve to D_2 indicates that consumers now demand a quantity of 5,250 bars at that same $1.00 price. Figure 3-8 shows a decrease in demand. The leftward shift of the demand curve means that at any given price buyers will demand less than they did before. Whereas they originally demanded 3,500 bars at $1.00, now, after the leftward shift of the demand curve (D_2), they demand only 2,750 bars at the same $1.00 price.

Common sense tells you that if the price of a good falls, people tend to buy more of it and vice versa, but what could cause people to buy more or less of a good or service when its price stays the same? Economists have

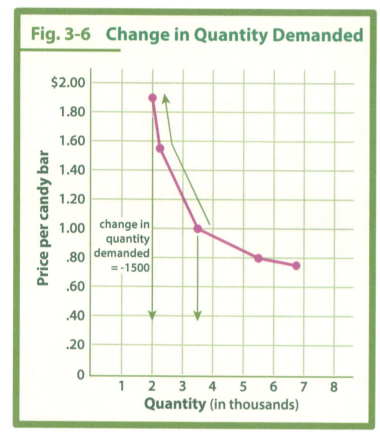

Fig. 3-6 Change in Quantity Demanded

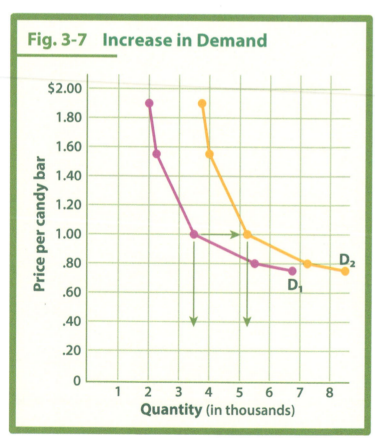

Fig. 3-7 Increase in Demand

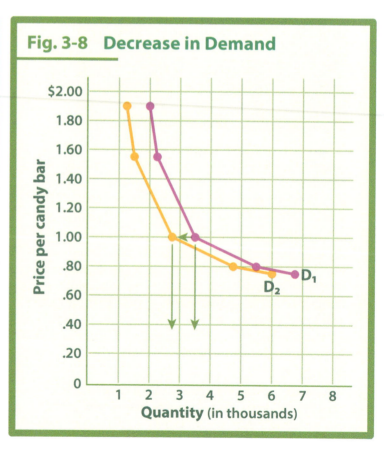

Fig. 3-8 Decrease in Demand

discovered that even though the price of a product does not change, there are four conditions that may cause a change in the demand for that product:
1. A change in people's incomes
2. A change in the price of related goods
3. A change in people's tastes and preferences
4. A change in people's expectations

Change in Income

One of the most important causes of a shift of the demand curve is a change in people's incomes. When people receive paychecks, they must divide their limited incomes among those goods and services they want most. For example, some families budget a given amount for eating in a nice restaurant once per month. When their incomes rise, they will probably allot more for this activity even though the price of dinners at the restaurant has not changed. Likewise with our candy bars, as buyers receive greater incomes, they will want to buy more. Parents will buy more for their children, boyfriends will buy more for their girlfriends, and some people will buy more for themselves. Whereas the previous income level supported a demand of 3,500 bars at $1.00 each, now the higher incomes enable purchasers to buy 5,250 bars at the same price.

Goods that experience an increase in demand because of an increase in consumers' incomes are **normal goods**. While most goods are normal goods, some goods actually experience a decline in popularity as buyers' incomes increase. Items such as recapped tires, travel on city buses, used cars, secondhand clothing, and powdered milk see a decline in sales as consumers' incomes increase. Economists label such items as **inferior goods**. Not only do inferior goods experience a decrease in demand as people's incomes increase, but the opposite is also true. As consumers' incomes decrease, businesses will sell more powdered milk, used cars, and recapped tires. No single good or service can definitively be called a normal good or an inferior good since an inferior good to one person may be a normal

For some individuals, travel on a city bus would be considered an inferior good.

good to another. A wealthy person may consider a used car to be an inferior good, while a less wealthy person may consider it to be a normal good.

Change in the Price of Related Goods

A second reason that demand may increase or decrease for a product without its price changing is that it may replace or be replaced with a similar good. Goods that households may use in place of others are called **substitute goods**. Examples of substitute goods include chicken and beef, hot dogs and hamburgers, and frozen yogurt and ice cream. As the price of one of the goods rises, consumers tend to buy more of the substitute. For example, as the price of beef rises, consumers will decrease their purchases of beef. Needing to make up for the decrease, consumers will purchase more chicken, even though its price has not changed. This increase in demand for a substitute good corresponds to a rightward shift of that substitute good's demand curve (see Fig. 3-9).

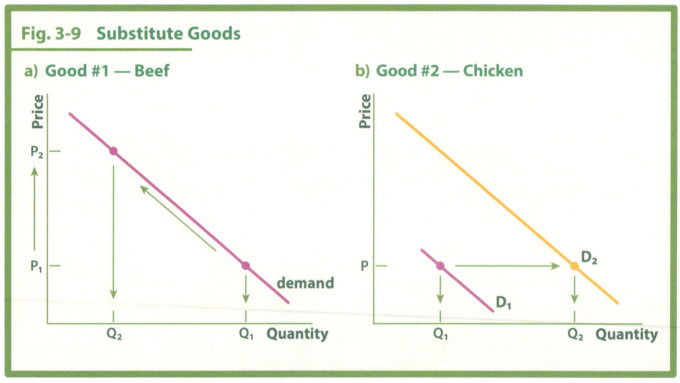

An increase in the price of beef (P_1 to P_2) causes a decrease in the quantity of beef demanded (Q_1 to Q_2), which eventually leads to an increase in demand for chicken, a substitute for beef.

There are also **complementary goods**, goods that are usually purchased or used together. Examples of complementary goods include cameras and memory cards, gasoline and automobiles, french fries and ketchup, and peanut butter and jelly. When the price of one of the complementary goods rises, demand for the other good decreases even though its price has not changed. For example, looking at Figure 3-10a, let us assume that the price of peanut butter rises from $1.80 to $4.50 per jar. Naturally, since the price has gone up, the quantity that consumers demand will decrease, in this case from three jars to one. Since many customers purchase peanut butter for peanut butter and jelly sandwiches, they will also cut their demand for jelly from three jars to one even though the price of jelly has not changed (see Fig. 3-10b).

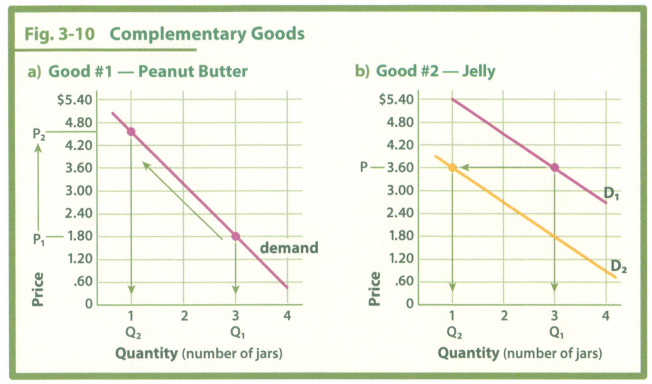

An increase in the price of peanut butter causes a decrease in its quantity demanded, which eventually leads to a decrease in demand for jelly, a complementary good.

Change in Tastes and Preferences

A third reason that people change their demand for goods and services is a change in their tastes and preferences. As a product gains popularity and people demand more at any given price, its demand curve experiences a rightward shift. As the product loses popularity, its demand curve begins to shift to the left. Most people associate this type of shift in demand with fad items. Fad items are those goods and services that appear quickly on the scene, receive heavy advertisement, and sell in great quantities over a short period of time. As quickly as it caught the market's fancy, the product loses favor and sales plummet. Examples of fad items in the past have included certain styles of haircuts, pet rocks, and mood rings.

Virtually all items, however, suffer the same fate as fad items, only over a longer period of time. Consider the horse and buggy, the typewriter, and VHS tapes. As time passed, each of these items gradually became less popular, and their demand curves shifted continually leftward until there was virtually no demand.

Change in Expectations

The final reason for a shift in the demand curve is a change in people's expectations of future prices. Suppose you have just received word from a reliable source that the price of So Good bars, currently $1.00 per bar, will be going up to $1.60 per bar because of a worldwide drop in cocoa bean harvests. In all likelihood, if you have the money, you will make a trip to the supermarket to purchase more bars than usual to beat the expected price increase.

Since the price has not yet changed but you have demanded more, your So Good bar demand curve has just made a rightward shift. The opposite also holds true; as people believe prices are going to decline, they postpone purchases so that they may buy at a lower

Peanut butter and jelly are an example of complementary goods.

price later. Assume you hear from your reliable source that there will be record-breaking harvests of cocoa beans resulting in a significant decline in chocolate prices, which will drop the price of So Good bars from $1.00 to 50¢ per bar. It is highly probable that your demand curve will shift to the left. That is, you will postpone purchasing any bars today in the hope of purchasing more tomorrow at the lower price.

Menger's principle of subjective value and Jevons's law of diminishing marginal utility work together to teach you important truths about what you value and how your value of something may change. The law of demand and the causes for shifts in the demand curve also highlight for you that economic principles arise from observations and study of human behaviors. As you review each of these concepts, you should notice that economic value is connected to what individuals will pay for certain items and that what they will pay often reveals the strength of their preferences for those items. Because your value of something comes from within, it is not surprising that saved and unsaved persons often differ greatly on the economic value they place on certain goods. The next time you go shopping, take time to consider the prices of goods. What does the price of a good and your opinion of that price tell you about that good's economic value to you? You can learn much about your likes and dislikes from prices. Would you be willing to purchase the good at full price, at 25% off, at half price, or would you walk away? Your answer reveals what the good is worth to you—its economic value.

SECTION REVIEW 3B

1. What is the economic definition of the word *demand*?
2. State the law of demand.
3. What four conditions may change the demand for a product?

CHAPTER REVIEW

CONTENT QUESTIONS

1. Give an example to explain the principle of diminishing marginal utility.
2. According to Jevons, when an individual makes a decision at the margin, how does he determine the amount to obtain?
3. Explain how prices act to transmit information.
4. Explain how the law of demand works in light of Figure 3-3.
5. What is the name of the graph that illustrates the demand for certain products?
6. Looking at Figure 3-5, what will be the approximate quantity demanded at a price of 90¢? $1.10? $1.70?
7. List five goods that you consider normal goods and five that you consider inferior goods. Be prepared to defend your answers.
8. Why is it that when the price of an original good rises we tend to purchase more substitute goods and fewer complementary goods?

APPLICATION QUESTIONS

1. If the market price for a candy bar should be $1.00 but the government, in its desire to decrease candy consumption, requires stores to charge $5.00 per bar, what disruptions may occur in the economy? (Hint: Review the list of the three functions of prices.)
2. How do business firms use advertising to shift an individual household's demand curves? Is it morally right for them to do so? Why or why not?
3. Is a demand curve positively or negatively sloped? Explain using the law of demand.

TERMS

Term	Page
principle of diminishing marginal utility	45
marginal utility schedule	46
marginal utility curve	46
demand	50
law of demand	50
demand schedule	51
demand curve	51
change in quantity demanded	51
change in demand	52
increase in demand	52
decrease in demand	52
normal goods	53
inferior goods	53
substitute goods	54
complementary goods	54

PERSONAL FINANCE
INSURING YOUR HOME, AUTO, AND LIFE

Owning your own house or car means assuming many financial responsibilities, such as taxes, utility bills, and maintenance expenses. Because of the ever-present danger of accidents, theft, or damage to these expensive possessions, insurance may be a wise purchase. Life insurance may also be a prudent choice, especially after marrying and beginning a family. Such responsibilities should motivate couples to ensure that there are adequate funds to meet the family's needs should one or both of them no longer be able to do so. However, insurance policies vary in coverage and in price, and not all insurance companies and agents have the same reputation for dealing promptly and fairly with claims. Consequently, consumers should shop carefully to purchase the insurance that best suits their needs.

 HOMEOWNER'S INSURANCE

Homeowner's insurance usually includes both liability coverage and a comprehensive policy. **Liability insurance** pays for property damage and bodily injury incurred by any visitor on the insured person's property (such as a delivery man tripping on the steps and breaking his leg). **Comprehensive insurance** protects the homeowner from heavy loss due to misfortunes that generally include fire, theft, windstorms, hail, and lightning damage. When buying such a policy, consumers should make sure that it covers the damages and losses that are most likely to occur where they live. Homeowners in certain areas of the country may want to add to their basic comprehensive plan special coverage for disasters such as earthquakes or floods. The amount of money at which to insure a home should be at least 80 percent of the replacement cost of the house, and preferably 100 percent. Periodic adjustments should reflect the home's increased value because of inflation.

A beneficial feature of a homeowner's comprehensive policy is that when there is damage or loss because of a covered misfortune, the insurance covers not only the house and other buildings on the property but also the policyholder's personal property, such as furniture, clothing, and appliances. This coverage extends to losses away from the property as well (e.g., a suitcase's being stolen out of the homeowner's car).

For those who do not own their own home but who want to insure their personal property, renter's insurance provides a similar coverage. Because a landlord's insurance does not cover a renter's personal property losses, renter's insurance is often advantageous.

AUTOMOBILE INSURANCE

There are several kinds of automobile insurance coverage; three of the most common are liability, collision, and comprehensive. Most states require car owners to carry liability insurance to cover the costs of bodily injury and property damage that they may cause to others. On a liability policy the limits of coverage will usually appear something like this: 200/600/80. In this example the insurance company would pay up to $200,000 for each person injured in a mishap up to a total of $600,000 for all personal injuries, and it would pay up to $80,000 for damage to property. In determining how much coverage he should buy in each of these categories, the consumer should consider the average court costs and settlements for accidents in his area of the country.

Collision insurance will pay to repair or replace the policyholder's car. If there is a mortgage on the vehicle, the creditor generally requires this coverage, and it is practical if the car has significant value. If, however, the car is more than a few years old and of no classic value, collision insurance is usually not cost-effective and therefore is unnecessary.

Comprehensive automobile insurance covers damage and loss to the vehicle by means other than traffic accidents. It generally includes protection against theft, vandalism, hail damage, glass breakage, and other misfortunes. Comprehensive auto insurance, along with collision insurance and homeowner's comprehensive insurance, usually stipulates a deductible. A **deductible** is the amount the policyholder must pay before the insurance policy will cover the remainder. If, for example, a typical comprehensive automobile insurance policy included a $200 deductible, then when the policyholder filed a $750 claim for hail damage, the insurance company would deduct $200 from that claim and pay the policyholder $550. In this way insurance companies avoid paying for many minor mishaps altogether, such as nicks in the car paint or the theft of a battery. Generally speaking, the higher the deductible a person is willing to pay, the less his insurance policy will cost.

Another kind of automobile coverage is medical payments insurance. It pays for the medical expenses of the policyholder and his family in the event of an accident. Because many health insurance policies already cover these expenses, this coverage may be unnecessary.

Uninsured motorist insurance pays for damages incurred in an accident that is the fault of another driver who does not have liability insurance. Many states require car owners to carry this insurance.

No-fault insurance is another form of coverage that a few states require. This insurance pays the policyholder for damage and injury in any accident, regardless of who was at fault. The intent of this insurance is to limit costly litigation in accident cases and provide speedy payment of claims.

The cost of automobile insurance varies widely not only with the type of coverage but also with the kind of car, the driver to be insured, and the conditions where the driver lives. Insurance companies keep many statistics to determine the probability of accidents involving various kinds of cars and drivers. As a result, high-performance sports cars are usually much more expensive to insure than compact economy cars. Because they tend to have far more accidents, single male drivers ages sixteen to twenty-five are more expensive to insure than are women and married or older men. Drivers can often reduce their costs if their insurance company allows discounts for installing antitheft devices on the car, having a good driving record, taking a driver's training course, or maintaining good grades in school.

LIFE INSURANCE

Because they associate life insurance with death, many people do not like to discuss it. Also, policy details are often complicated. Individuals must consider their present annual salary, present debts, family needs, possible medical expenses, and funeral and burial costs. Though he may find it difficult to determine the right type and amount of a policy, the Christian steward recognizes that procuring life insurance fulfills the obligation of caring for his family in the event of his death. Second Corinthians 12:14 teaches that it is not the children who "lay up for the parents, but the parents for the children."

The death of a family's income earner can bring financial hardship if the basic provisions of financial planning have been neglected.

Estimating the Amount of Life Insurance Needed

"Who needs life insurance?" is a question financial planners frequently hear. When a person insures his home or car, he does so to have the money to rebuild or replace his present one should something destroy it. Similarly, the main purpose for life insurance is to replace a family's lost income; it is not to console a grieving widow or to provide a "bonus" when someone dies. Therefore, it is important to carry life insurance on all income earners in the family if their income is necessary to the family's well-being. An unmarried person with no dependents may carry a small policy to defray burial costs, whereas a married man whose family depends not only on his income but on that of his spouse and perhaps the oldest child may need a larger policy on himself and policies on his wife and child.

Consumers also frequently ask, "How much insurance should I buy?" Out of a fear of not having enough life insurance, many families have become "insurance poor" by purchasing much more than they need. Others, however, find out too late that they secured an insufficient amount. To determine what is an adequate life insurance policy, a person needs to calculate his needs in two areas—death-related expenses and family-maintenance needs.

One reason for purchasing life insurance is to pay for death-related expenses. Obviously, the first of these expenses is funeral and burial costs. The average expenses for burial are in excess of $6,000. Estate taxes constitute the second of the death-related expenses. Currently people can transfer an unlimited amount of money to their spouses after death, but if the estate is over $2,000,000, then the spouse will have to pay taxes due. (The amount that is not subject to tax changes from year to year as Congress adjusts tax laws.) A third cost that often arises is medical costs not covered by insurance preceding the person's death. To avoid saddling survivors with unnecessary installment payments, a person should make provision for the fourth death-related expense, which is the payment of all outstanding consumer loans. A final death-related expense to consider is court costs. Costs for probate court services amount to between 3 percent and 7 percent of the value of the estate.

The second and most important purpose of life insurance is to provide financial maintenance for the surviving dependents. The method of calculating this need is somewhat involved. First, a person must calculate the expenses that his family will incur each month. The second step is to subtract all other sources of income. For example, a person might have interest from investments that provide a steady monthly income. It is likely that the Social Security Administration will also provide monthly benefits to surviving dependents. The amount of those benefits varies with the income of the decedent and the number of his dependents. Once the person has

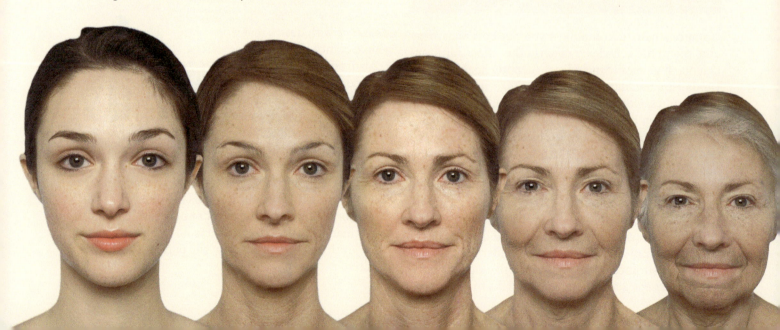

determined what income his family will need each month and what of that amount will be offset by social security benefits and investment income, he then looks at how to provide the remaining amount. He calculates what that amount translates into per year and determines how many years his insurance would need to maintain that rate. That number will likely be influenced by the number of years before his youngest child is of age to be financially independent. The person should also plan to adjust the annual amount to account for inflation. If the cost of living were to rise at a realistic annual rate of 5 percent, the person would need to increase the amount of his policy accordingly. The total inflation-adjusted amount needed to support his family would be the amount of a policy he needs to purchase.

Types of Life Insurance

Life insurance comes in two basic forms: term and whole life. A hybrid form called universal life has also entered the market, and it has some characteristics of both.

Term insurance is life insurance that provides only death protection. Consumers purchase term insurance for a specified period of time, and if they die during the life of the policy, the proceeds go to the **beneficiary** named on the policy. Term insurance is basically a simple contract that obligates the insurance company to provide a fixed death benefit in exchange for a monthly payment called a **premium**. When the term of the coverage expires, the customer ceases to be insured. However, some insurance companies provide term insurance policyholders the option to renew their policies for fixed periods of time without requiring a new medical examination to determine their eligibility. Term insurance provides more death protection per dollar of payment than any other type of life insurance; however, it has no savings component. Many insurance agents discourage potential customers from purchasing term insurance because it is less expensive than other types of insurance and therefore provides a lower commission for the agent.

Whole life insurance is the second type of life insurance. Unlike term insurance, it provides a savings component along with the death benefit. The premiums a purchaser pays on a whole life policy remain level over his lifetime. For a young person the premiums on a whole life policy are significantly higher than the premiums paid on a term policy with comparable death benefits; however, as a person grows older, the premiums on term insurance grow and eventually exceed the premiums paid on the whole life policy. The managers of insurance companies apply a portion of the whole life premiums to the policy's death benefit and invest the difference, providing the savings component. The savings value of a whole life policy is its **cash value**. The cash value of a whole life policy gradually increases during the early years of the policy and later increases until it equals the face value of the policy. At that point the insurance company considers the policy to be paid off. Holders of whole life policies may borrow from their life insurance company using the cash value as collateral for the loan.

During the late 1970s a rebellion of sorts occurred against the high cost of whole life insurance with policyholders choosing to purchase the less profitable term insurance. As a result, in 1981, insurance companies began offering **universal life insurance**. Universal life is a hybrid form of life insurance that provides policyholders with a term insurance type of death benefit but includes a flexible savings plan. The premium on universal life (called the "contribution") is not the high, inflexible premium of whole life policies. A portion of the contribution goes toward the payment for a term policy and for management charges, and a portion goes toward the buildup of cash value. The policy managers take the difference between the term insurance portion and the total contribution and deposit it into an interest-bearing account. Unlike whole life policyholders, universal life policyholders receive periodic statements that inform them of the cost of their term insurance and the interest earned on their investment account.

HEALTH CARE AND DISABILITY INSURANCE

Many of us, in the midst of a crisis, have heard the saying, "Well, at least you have your health." Many consider this expression trite until they experience the financial hardships of a prolonged medical problem. Writing a will and purchasing life insurance are necessary ingredients in the short-term portion of a total financial plan; however, they are useful only when the person dies. People should give even more serious consideration to medical emergencies, which can quickly sap a family's lifetime savings and investments. The most important types of health insurance plans include disability income, major medical, and hospitalization insurance.

Types of Health Care and Disability Insurance

Many people study the various life insurance policies, but it seems few consider what is perhaps the most important form of insurance—disability insurance. **Disability income insurance** provides the family with weekly or monthly payments that replace the income of someone who is unable to work as a result of an illness or injury. As with life insurance, it is prudent for a family to carry disability income insurance on all family members who provide necessary income. To provide an incentive for workers to continue working on the job rather than feigning illnesses or injuries, providers of disability income insurance usually replace only 60–70 percent of the insured's paycheck.

Insurance companies usually avoid paying large amounts of money on small claims made by persons suffering from illnesses or injuries that last a short time. They do so by requiring a waiting period, which may be as short as seven days or as long as one year, depending on the choice of the insured. Those buying disability income insurance can significantly lower their premium payments by selecting a policy with a long waiting period.

Another factor that affects the premium is the length of time during which the insurance company pays disability benefits. Individuals may select terms as short as one year or as many years as it takes for them to reach age sixty-five. If someone selects a policy with a long waiting period and a short payout period, he needs to have a liquid cash reserve to meet the expenses not covered by the disability insurance.

Major medical insurance provides benefits for virtually all types of medical expenses resulting from accidents or illnesses. It is called major medical insurance because the amounts of the benefits may range from several thousand dollars to millions. To prevent policyholders from filing minor claims, major medical insurance companies require the policyholder to pay a deductible. For example, many policies begin paying medical payments only after the insured person has paid $1,000 worth of medical bills in the same year. Some policies require the deductible for each illness or injury. In such a case the man who suffered a $700 injury in January and an $800 injury in July would receive no insurance benefits because neither of the injuries exceeded the $1,000 deductible amount per injury.

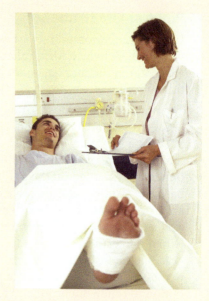

Major medical insurance pays for nearly all of the insured's medical expenses. Disability income insurance provides a percentage of his income while he is recuperating. **Hospitalization insurance** pays for the costs associated with staying in a hospital. Typically, plans cover a portion of the per-day hospital room-and-board charges, use of operating rooms, x-ray services, laboratory tests, and medication received while in the hospital. Usually, hospitalization insurance covers only a limited number of days' worth of hospital charges.

Sources and Costs of Health Insurance

The basic philosophy of all insurance companies is that of spreading the risk. That is, the insurance company collects relatively small premiums from each member of a large group of people and pays for the expenses of the few who die, contract diseases, or sustain injuries. Most health insurance, therefore, is **group health insurance**, and most group health insurance plans are part of an employee's nonsalary fringe benefits. Employer-sponsored health insurance is a double blessing for employees. First, it provides the insurance benefits the employees definitely need, and second, it is an untaxed fringe benefit. If employees were to receive the equivalent of the premiums in cash, they would receive only a fraction of the amount since the government would take a share in taxes. Then, the cost of buying their own policies would be much higher since they would be buying the insurance as individuals. The business firm, however, pays lower rates for the insurance because it insures a large number of employees. For those people with chronic health problems, employer-sponsored group health insurance can be perhaps the greatest benefit the employer provides, even greater than the paycheck.

Truly there is a lot to consider when looking at insurance, and as a high-school student, you may be glad that for now such decisions are not yours. However, it will not be long until you will be facing the need to purchase automobile, homeowner's or renter's, and possibly even life insurance. Before making such purchases, remember what you have learned in this class. Seek out godly counselors and pray over your decisions. You may think that there are too many papers and too much fine print in these various policies and that you cannot possibly know enough to make a wise choice. However, you should now know enough to ask good questions. Listen well to the answers, compare and evaluate the policies, and never forget that God promises to give wisdom to any Christian who asks Him for it (James 1:5).

REVIEW
QUESTIONS

1. What is the difference between liability and comprehensive insurance?
2. What is a beneficial feature of comprehensive homeowner's insurance that extends beyond the house and buildings?
3. Who are the most expensive drivers to insure?
4. What is the purpose of life insurance, and on whom should it be carried?
5. In disability insurance, why do insurance companies usually compensate only 60–70 percent of a person's income?

TERMS

liability insurance	58
comprehensive insurance	58
collision insurance	59
deductible	59
term insurance	61
beneficiary	61
premium	61
whole life insurance	61
cash value	61
universal life insurance	61
disability income insurance	62
major medical insurance	62
hospitalization insurance	62
group health insurance	62

CHAPTER FOUR
SUPPLY AND PRICES

4A SUPPLY — 65

4B DETERMINING PRICES — 71

In 2004 in the span of less than two months' time, four severe hurricanes made landfall in Florida. Ranging in intensity from category 2 to 4, hurricanes Charley, Frances, Ivan, and Jeanne caused catastrophic damage throughout much of the state. The fury of these storms severely damaged homes, cut off electric power for days or weeks, and left debris that hindered the movement of equipment and personnel needed for repairs and reconstruction. As a result of the widespread destruction, the demand for equipment and building materials—such as chain saws, gasoline-powered electric generators, and especially plywood—skyrocketed. Also, without electricity for air conditioning or refrigeration, there arose an enormous demand for ice to cool drinks on hot days and to preserve food. Keeping workers cool and fed so that they could rebuild required abundant resources.

However, because of the great demand for certain products, the prices of those products rose significantly immediately following each storm. Plywood sold at prices that were double the pre-storm amounts. For displaced residents, motels offered rooms at double the advertised rates. People began to complain of unfair pricing,

saying that just when they were in their greatest need, suppliers would raise the prices of essential goods and make it difficult to obtain them. The legislature passed laws against these practices, and thousands of Floridians called a special hotline to report instances of alleged price gouging.

Unfortunately, the laws that guaranteed consumers pre-hurricane prices also hindered the rebuilding process. As you will see in this chapter, high prices are the means whereby the market indicates to suppliers that it needs more supplies. High prices also provide the incentive for those producers to make additional goods and services available. When the state government enforced a limit on the prices that sellers could charge for their products, it eliminated an incentive for individuals and businesses to bring to the market greater quantities of necessary goods, such as plywood, generators, and ice.

One might respond that under emergency circumstances, it is the role of the government to provide these necessary goods to consumers. While the government certainly has a role to play in such situations, there is ample evidence that it cannot provide goods to consumers as quickly and efficiently as the free market. Moreover, when the government provides goods to consumers, it ultimately must increase taxes on all citizens to pay for those goods. In the end, therefore, consumers always pay, either directly or indirectly, for what the government supplies.

High demand for certain products during hurricane season causes the prices of those products to rise.

In this chapter you will see how supply helps to determine price in a free market and why the free market is more efficient at encouraging the correct supply of necessary goods, even during an emergency. The price of a good is not like an elevator that the government can raise and lower at whim. The market price of anything does not come from a law but from a compromise, an agreement between a buyer and a seller. In the previous chapter, you looked at this compromise from the demand side, or the buyer's point of view. Now you will examine the seller's perspective, or the supply side. Later, you will see how buyers and sellers agree, thereby reaching a market price. You will also learn how and why that market price can change and how a Christian should respond to price changes.

4A SUPPLY

Supply is the amount of goods and services business firms are willing and able to provide at different prices. For economists, business firms include all sellers of goods and services, not just major corporations.

THE LAW OF SUPPLY

As you recall from Chapter 3, the law of demand states that as the price of a good or service falls, other things being held constant, people will demand more of it and vice versa. The **law of supply**, on the other hand, holds that the higher the price buyers are willing to pay, other things being held constant, the greater the quantity of a

Whether their product is sheets of steel or bottles of sports drinks, suppliers will generally produce a greater quantity as the price rises.

Fig. 4-1 Supply Schedule

Price offered per candy bar	Quantity supplied
$1.90	5,000 bars
1.55	4,750
1.00	3,500
.80	1,000
.75	250

product a firm will produce and that the lower the price consumers are willing to pay, the smaller the quantity the supplier will produce.

To explain, let us return to the candy illustration from the previous chapter. This time, however, we will assume that you are not a customer but the owner of Candy City and that it costs you 70¢ to produce each So Good candy bar. Common sense says that if customers are willing to pay only 67¢ per bar, you would be unwilling to produce any because you would lose 3¢ on every bar sold. However, if the price that buyers are willing to pay rises above 70¢, you would be willing to start production, and the higher the price rises above 70¢, the more candy bars you would be willing to produce. Figure 4-1 presents a table with hypothetical data on the quantity of So Good candy bars you would produce at various prices. As a business owner you would recognize such a table as a **supply schedule**.

The information contained in a supply schedule could be more useful to you if it were plotted on a graph called a **supply curve**. Supply curves are positively sloped, meaning that as the price consumers

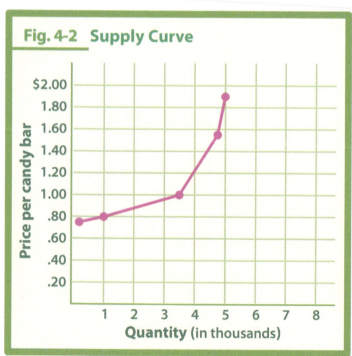

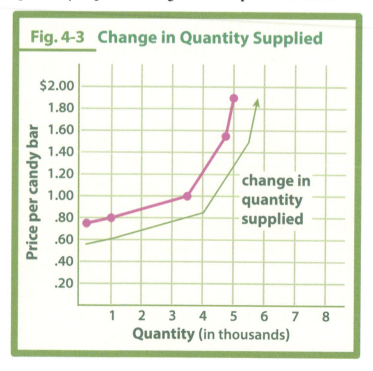

will pay rises, suppliers become willing to provide greater quantities and that as the price consumers will pay falls, suppliers tend to produce fewer quantities. Whenever a change in the price consumers are willing to pay causes a change in the number of goods produced and sold, a **change in quantity supplied** has occurred, as seen in Figure 4-3.

CHANGES IN SUPPLY

Just as a demand curve may shift to the left or right, a supply curve may shift to reflect **changes in supply**. A leftward shift indicates a **decrease in supply**, a situation in which suppliers produce less of their product at any given price. An **increase in supply**, shown in a rightward shift of the supply curve, demonstrates the willingness of business firms to produce more of their product at any given price. Figures 4-4 and 4-5 illustrate these two situations. Figure 4-4 illustrates a decrease in supply. Candy City shifts from being willing to supply 3,500 candy bars at $1.00 ($S_1$) to being willing to supply 1,750 candy bars at the same price (S_2). In contrast, Figure 4-5 demonstrates a rightward shift of the supply curve. Candy City moves from providing 3,500 bars at $1.00 ($S_1$) to supplying 4,250 at the same price (S_2).

It is understandable why business firms would be willing to provide more or less of a good as customers become willing to pay more or less, but what could cause a business to supply more or less of a product when its price has not changed? Economists have pinpointed three factors that lead to this phenomenon:

1. Changes in technology
2. Changes in production costs
3. Changes in the price of related goods

Changes in Technology

Technological advances are improvements in the tools used to produce goods and services. Recent technological advances include the

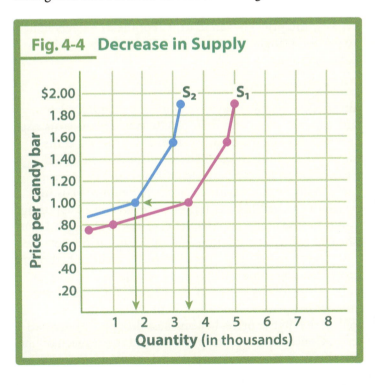

Fig. 4-4 Decrease in Supply

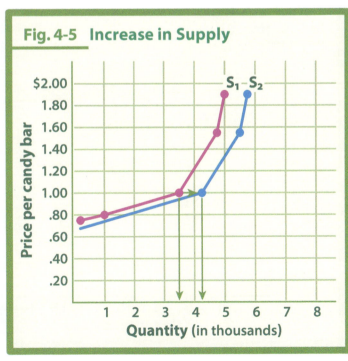

Fig. 4-5 Increase in Supply

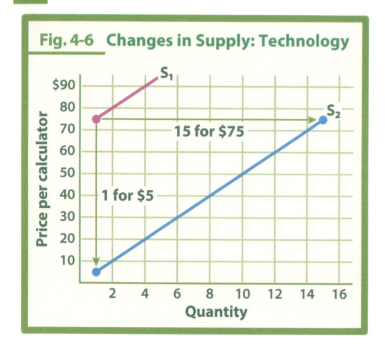

Changes in technology resulted in changes in the form and functions of calculators.

use of computerization and automated production machinery. As manufacturers improve the tools of production, businesses are able to offer more of the product at the same price (or the same amount at a lower price).

Consider the case of the electronic calculator. In the early 1970s a "pocket" electronic calculator (which was in fact very large) had the ability to perform only limited mathematical functions, and it cost around $75. As time passed and the tools of production improved, the components were miniaturized and the quality increased dramatically. As the tools used in producing calculators improved, businesses were able to manufacture them less expensively. The same amount of money that the producers once spent to manufacture a few early calculators now allowed them to make many more of the modernized versions. Supplies increased rapidly, and prices began to drop. For the $75 a person had to pay for a single calculator in 1973, he could now buy fifteen or more.

Changes in Production Costs

Business firms must pay for the natural resources, labor, and capital that go into their products. If a firm's costs rise, it must decrease the quantity of what it provides at the same price. For example, Beth, a business-minded ten-year-old, decided to open a lemonade stand in her front yard. With a hundred-ounce bottle of lemonade costing $1, Beth charged 10¢ per ten-ounce glass (we are ignoring profit for the moment). Her venture was so successful that she had to buy another hundred-ounce bottle the next day, but to her surprise and disappointment, its price had risen to $2. Making some quick mental calculations, she determined that for the same ten-ounce glass she would have to raise her price to 20¢. After Beth changed her sign to reflect the higher price, her business dropped off dramatically. Concluding that the price was out of the reach of her

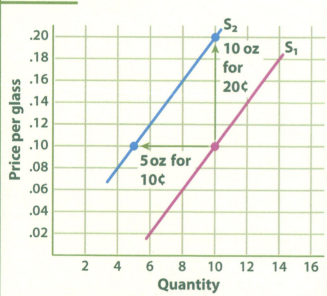

TELEPHONE TECHNOLOGY—CHANGES IN THE MARKET

From the wooden wall box with a mouthpiece and a dangling receiver to the tiny wireless cell phone—the telephone is a classic example of changing technological innovation. Improvements such as caller ID, voice-activated dialing, speaker phone, conference calling, digital imaging that allows a visual with the voice, and wireless headsets allowing hands-free operation have revolutionized the communications industry. Add to these, picture, Web, and computer-interface capabilities, and today's phones have far surpassed anything Mr. Bell could have envisioned.

What are the economic implications of these technological innovations and improvements? How have they affected the demand for phones? How have they changed the supply of phones? If they have, in fact, changed the demand and supply curves, what was the consequent effect on price?

Communications companies use the latest technology to increase demand for certain phones. How many advertisements have you seen in the last month for new phones? These ads are meant to increase consumer demand for a phone by convincing you that the new device can do much more than your current phone or can do the same things faster and with better quality.

In many cases you have to sign an agreement for a certain amount of time to get the phone you want at the lowest possible price. However, during that period, new, more technologically advanced phones will likely appear, spark your interest, engender a desire, and tempt you to buy. You will have to pay more, though, for these latest gadgets because you are still bound to the agreement from your previous purchase.

As the newest batch of phones hits the market and slowly begins replacing earlier models, think of what happens to the demand for and the price of those earlier phones. As the demand and supply curves shift leftward, demand, production, and price all decline.

Cell phones are a good example of supply and demand at work, and as you've learned, demand is an indication of what people value. People value the convenience of the anytime, anyplace communication that cell phones provide. Businesspeople find it convenient to be in touch with their clients even when they are away from their offices, travelers want the assurance that they will not have to find a pay phone if their vehicles break down or they become lost, and friends find it cheaper to stay in touch through various calling plans.

New technology, however, sometimes leads people to see only what they gain with the latest devices without noticing what they may be losing. Businesspeople may buy cell phones to increase their productivity only to find that the continual interruptions that come from ever-present phones actually decrease their productivity. Travelers who take cell phones as safety precautions may be distracted by calls while they are driving, which may even lead to accidents. The friends who buy phones to improve communication with each other may find that they actually have less face-to-face time and thus less meaningful communication.

In each technological advance a Christian needs to discern the potential gains and losses. You can use your cell phone to be a good Samaritan calling for help, to send important news quickly to several parties, or to respond to a need in a timely manner. However, you can get so caught up in texting that you miss important information, events, or conversations. You may forget that "in the multitude of words there wanteth not sin" (Prov. 10:19). The Christian must also consider how an ever-present phone may deprive him of time alone with his thoughts and with God.

This is not to say that advances in technology are bad or that Christians should shun them. However, you should be aware of how technological advances may reshape your values. Think about how you use technology and why you want the latest gadgetry. You need to see technology as yet another gift from God, another means whereby you can glorify Him, and another tool in your service for Him. Keep in mind that He is presently watching how you use it and will one day hold you accountable for that. Perhaps it will help you to think of technology and its offerings as one of the talents the Master has given you (Matt. 25:14–30). Ask yourself, "Am I currently using this talent in a way that maximizes its potential for my Lord's glory?"

ALFRED MARSHALL (1842–1924)
Architect of the Demand and Supply Model

Alfred Marshall came from a middle-class London family. His parents gave him a religious upbringing and encouraged him to prepare for the ministry at Cambridge University. However, after beginning his studies at Cambridge, Marshall evidenced a talent for mathematics and developed an interest in philosophy. As he pursued these fields of study, he abandoned any plans of filling a pulpit.

Marshall's interest in philosophy led him to travel throughout Europe and to read many of the classic works of philosophy. During this time the writings of Karl Marx, Charles Darwin, Friedrich Engels, and other communists and socialists were gaining in popularity. Marshall, however, did not agree with their conclusions and stated that the flaws of human nature would prevent communism from ever achieving the claims of its proponents. He viewed free enterprise with its rewards for diligence, industry, and creativity as being the best system. Dissatisfied with these philosophers' answers to life's problems and having seen much poverty in the cities of Europe, Marshall returned to England committed to the study of economics.

In 1868 Marshall became professor of political economy at Cambridge. He wrote many books and papers and worked to convert the study of economics from its undisciplined philosophical approach to a structured, mathematical, scientific, and practical profession. He published his best-known work, *Principles of Economics*, in 1890; and for the next several decades, it was one of the world's most influential works on economics. From the publication of this work until his death, Marshall was the leading authority on the study of individual markets and industries. He saw his *Principles of Economics* appear in eight editions and become the principal textbook for political economics throughout English-speaking higher education.

In *Principles of Economics*, Marshall developed a model that economists still use today to study markets: the model of demand and supply. His model demonstrated how changes in the underlying structure of demand or supply alter the consumers' desire to purchase goods or the suppliers' desire to offer them for sale at different prices. These changes ultimately influence the product prices in markets. His model addresses the impact of demand-related factors, such as the prices of related goods and consumer preferences, as well as supply-related determiners, particularly production costs. Marshall wrote of supply and demand, "Each may be compared to one blade of a pair of scissors. When one blade is held still . . . the cutting is effected by moving the other" (*Principles*, App. I). His model of demand and supply became the standard model, which appears in almost every introductory economics course.

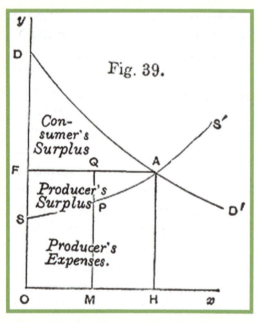

Marshall's early demand and supply curve

Marshall also developed and extended the study of markets to include an understanding of price elasticity, which describes the degree to which desired purchases or desired sales change as prices change under different circumstances. He expanded the study of the market economy to emphasize human behavior, marginal costs and benefits, and the major determiners of market price. Because of the extent and impact of his work, Marshall became one of the leading professors of economics in his day, and today economists still hold him in high esteem as one of the great leaders in the field.

young customers, she decided to offer a second alternative: a five-ounce glass for the old 10¢ price. This situation corresponds to a leftward shift of the supply curve (see Fig. 4-7). Had the price of lemonade at the store declined to 50¢ per bottle, Beth would have been able to offer a twenty-ounce glass for the 10¢ price and her supply curve would have shifted to the right.

Changes in the Prices of Related Goods

As the price people are willing to pay for a substitute rises, business firms naturally become willing to sell more of that good or service. To devote more resources to the higher-priced substitute, firms will decrease their supply of the original good even though its price has not changed.

Suppose that next door to Beth her best friend, Brenda, opened a much more popular iced-tea stand selling ten-ounce glasses for 10¢ and seeing a 3¢ profit on each. Receiving no profit on her lemonade and seeing her customers attracted to Brenda's stand, Beth decides to quit selling lemonade and to sell iced tea instead. The result: even though the price of Beth's lemonade did not change, her supply curve shifted to the left. Whereas she was once willing to produce ten glasses of lemonade at 10¢ each, she is now unwilling to produce any glasses at the same price (see Fig. 4-8).

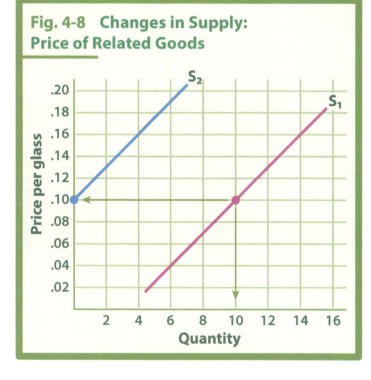

Fig. 4-8 Changes in Supply: Price of Related Goods

SECTION REVIEW 4A

1. State the law of supply.
2. Which way does a supply curve slope and why?
3. What three factors could lead to a change in supply?

4B DETERMINING PRICES

The beginning of this chapter states that the market price of every good or service represents an agreement, a meeting of the minds, between the buyer and the seller. How, though, can there be a meeting of the minds when the motives of the participants are exactly opposite? When prices are high, producers are willing to supply great quantities, but consumers are unwilling to buy. On the other hand, when prices are low, suppliers are willing to produce less than customers are willing to buy.

EQUILIBRIUM

The laws of demand and supply are in continual conflict except at one—and only one—critical point. At this point both parties agree that the price is fair, permitting goods to clear the market freely. Using the Candy City shop to illustrate, Figure 4-9 gives a graphic representation of the plans of both the buyers and sellers. The critical intersection point at which both parties agree is the **market equilibrium point**. It represents the price at which consumers are willing to take from the market the exact quantity of a product that suppliers are willing to put into the market. The price at which this

The market price represents an agreement between the buyer and the seller.

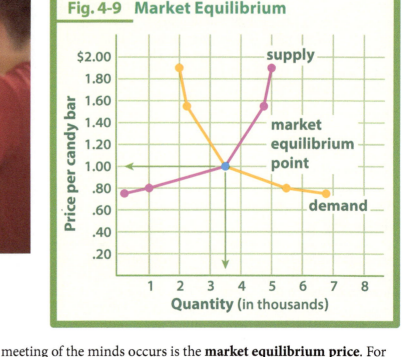

Fig. 4-9 Market Equilibrium

Talk is cheap because supply exceeds demand.

If a product is priced above the market equilibrium price, a surplus will result.

meeting of the minds occurs is the **market equilibrium price**. For Candy City and its customers, the market equilibrium price is $1.00.

This equilibrium price, which is determined by market forces, is fluid. The price and quantity at which buyers and sellers agree changes often and for a variety of reasons. Both the consumer and the producer need to recognize the importance of treating the other fairly, with respect and in the way each would himself want to be treated (Matt. 7:12). The biblical command to love your neighbor as yourself adds a moral element to the discussion of market equilibrium. On the one hand, the Christian buyer (consumer) wants to pay the best possible price for the largest quantity he can; on the other hand, he needs to recognize that the seller (producer) should be paid a reasonable price for a reasonable quantity at which he can make a reasonable profit. And the same scenario will be true for the Christian seller (producer) and his relationship with the buyer (consumer).

SURPLUS

At this point you may be asking yourself why Candy City would limit its price to $1.00 per bar. After all, we have been brought up to believe that businesses can charge any price they desire. Reality, however, is quite different. No one is totally exempt from the laws of supply and demand.

If a supplier raises the price of his product above the market equilibrium price, the law of supply will motivate him to increase the quantity of the product he puts into the market. At the same time, however, the law of demand will compel consumers to buy less of his product. The combined effect of the two opposite laws will result in a **surplus**, an excess of unsold products.

Looking at Figure 4-10, let us assume that Candy City's management becomes greedy and decides to raise the price of So Good bars to $1.55 each. Because of the higher price, the company stands to make a profit of 85¢ per bar sold as opposed to the 30¢ per bar it was making (assuming its production cost of 70¢ per bar remains unchanged). This rosy profit picture prompts Candy City's management to produce 4,750 candy bars (Fig. 4-10A), 1,250 more than it produced at the equilibrium price. Deciding that the price is too high, customers reduce the total demand by 1,250 bars (Fig. 4-10A). With the firm producing 1,250 candy bars more and buyers demanding 1,250 less, the combined result will be a surplus of 2,500 bars (Fig. 4-10B).

Because of the high costs associated with carrying large inventories, business firms find surpluses counterproductive. Carrying costs include such things as storage, security, insurance, spoilage, loss of income while the product is sitting idle, and interest costs on financing the unsold production. If a surplus continues for too long, carrying costs can drive a supplier out of business.

Obviously something must be done—the supplier must eliminate the surplus and decrease the carrying costs. The question is how. Three possible solutions exist: increase demand, decrease supply, or allow the price to fall to the market equilibrium point.

The first and best solution, from the standpoint of the supplier, is the one in which he may produce the greater quantity and charge the higher price at the same time. However, the only way for this to occur is for the demand curve to shift to the right. In the case of Candy City, the firm wants its customers' demand curve to shift rightward to a new market equilibrium point that would allow it to continue charging $1.55 per bar (see Fig. 4-11). The problem is how to accomplish this.

Some businesses try to shift the demand curve for their products by increasing consumers' tastes and preferences through advertising. Companies may also attempt to eliminate substitute goods by driving competitors out of business, buying rival firms, or persuading the government to forbid foreign competitors' products from entering the country. Occasionally similar businesses work together to persuade the government to purchase their surplus. When the government purchases surplus commodities to raise their prices, it is establishing a **price floor**, a barrier intended to prevent the prices of those items from falling below the market price.

If suppliers do not succeed at increasing the demand for their products but still insist on keeping the price artificially high, they have a second course of action: decrease supply. The object of decreasing supply is to shift the supply curve to the left where the new intersection point will be at the desired price. Figure 4-12 illustrates this alternative.

To decrease the supply of a good, a firm must cut production. As the product becomes scarcer, consumers become willing to pay a higher price. This solution is easy for the firm that has no competition, but it poses serious problems for those that share the market with other companies. Typically, as one business decreases its production, its competitors immediately increase their production to keep the product's price at the lower level. By

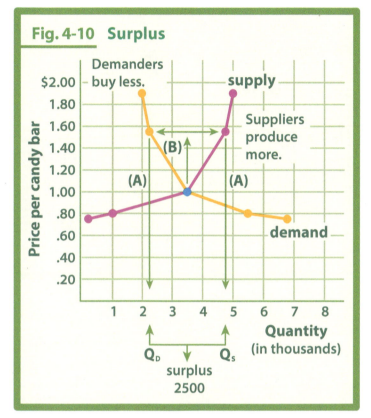

Fig. 4-10 Surplus

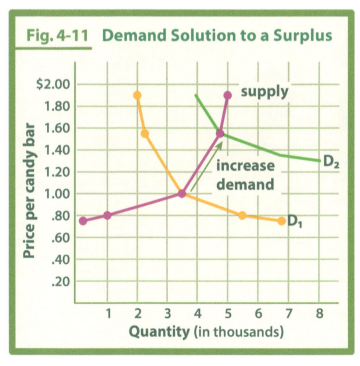

Fig. 4-11 Demand Solution to a Surplus

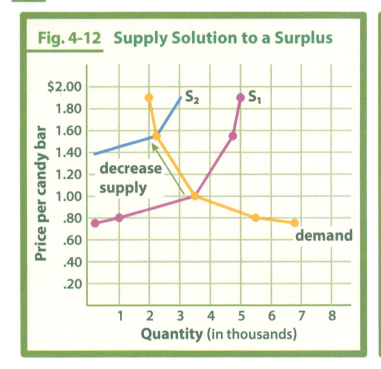

Fig. 4-12 Supply Solution to a Surplus

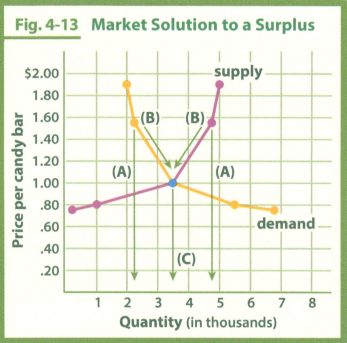

Fig. 4-13 Market Solution to a Surplus

cutting production in a competitive market, a firm risks driving itself out of business.

The simplest solution to the problem of surplus is to allow the market to work. A supplier, realizing that a surplus exists (see Fig. 4-13A), responds by slowly lowering his price (see Fig. 4-13B). As he lowers his price, he discovers that his surplus is shrinking, so he continues to lower his price until the quantity supplied exactly matches the quantity demanded (see Fig. 4-13C). At this point his excess inventory disappears, and the supplier has no reason to continue lowering his price.

SHORTAGE

Think back to some shortage you have heard about or experienced. Perhaps your experience went something like this: You heard that there was a terrific sale at a department store. There were discounts of 70–80 percent off the lowest ticketed price. By the time you got to the store, however, it was too late; everything worth buying was sold out. Why?

Whenever various factors hold the price of a good lower than its market equilibrium price, a **shortage** occurs. Suppose that for some reason the management of Candy City sets the price of So Good candy bars at 80¢ each, 20¢ below the market equilibrium price. At the lower price the quantity demanded by customers would rise to 5,500 bars (see Fig. 4-14A) while, due to a lack of producer incentives, the quantity Candy City would supply would fall to 1,000 bars (see Fig. 4-14A). The shortage, therefore, would be 4,500 bars (see Fig. 4-14B).

Virtually no supplier would deliberately sell his products at a price lower than the market price if profit is his goal. Many supermarkets advertise certain products at prices below the market equilibrium price, but they deliberately underprice these sale items to lure customers into the store to purchase other items that do provide a profit. What, therefore, could compel producers to act in a manner contrary to their own best interest? The government, usually with a

Businesses often place items on sale to reduce surplus merchandise, but if sale prices are below the market equilibrium level, shortages may result.

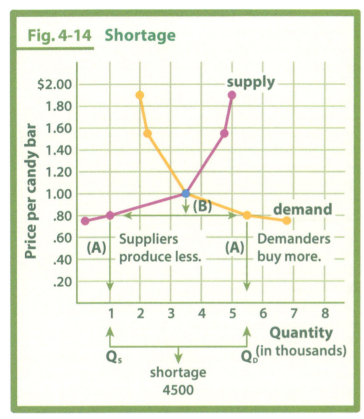

Fig. 4-14 Shortage

A shortage occurs when demand is greater than supply.

motive such as making certain products affordable to the poor, is often the compelling force that attempts to set aside the laws of supply and demand. It passes regulations dictating to firms in selected industries that certain prices may not rise, under penalty of law. Such mandates are called **price ceilings** because they prevent prices from rising to the market equilibrium price. Imposing a price ceiling will always cause shortages when the market price is higher. If the price ceiling holds the price below the market price too long, the affected businesses will eventually suffocate from a lack of profits and will die. Their goods or services will become unavailable to anyone at any price, including the targeted needy group.

The noblest of motives often fails to see the long-term effects of manipulating the market equilibrium price. For example, the desire to provide affordable housing has led some cities to pass rent-control laws that require landlords to charge rents that are lower than the

If unable to make a profit, a landlord may choose to leave the business and the building.

market price. The motivation behind these laws is to help low-income individuals obtain affordable housing; however, that has not been the result. As inflation drives up the cost of maintaining and running apartment complexes, the low rents become insufficient for the landlord to pay bills, make necessary repairs, and realize a profit. The landlord then faces the choice of either continuing to operate the apartment complex and paying for its losses each month out of his own pocket or evicting the residents, boarding up the windows and doors, and walking away, leaving the building to crumble. Unfortunately, but understandably, many landlords choose the latter, and now the poor people that the city was trying to help are as bad off as they were before, if not worse.

Just as there are three possible solutions to a surplus, there are three possible solutions to a shortage: decrease demand, increase supply, or allow the price to rise to the market equilibrium point.

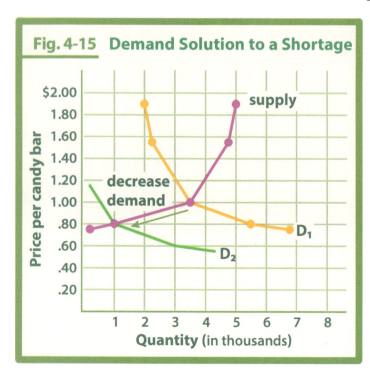

Fig. 4-15 Demand Solution to a Shortage

In the first solution, suppliers respond to a shortage by discouraging demand for their product, thus shifting the demand curve to the left (see Fig. 4-15). Business firms could accomplish this through advertising that discourages consumption. For example, during periods when demand exceeds their ability to produce, many electric power companies instruct customers in methods of conserving electricity. However, since most firms spend their marketing budget seeking to increase the demand for their products and they would probably have concerns that the decreased demand may become irreversible, not many companies opt for this solution.

A second solution to a shortage lies in the management of supply. Consumers tend to view a shortage as a problem of undersupply, with the solution being to boost production, an action corresponding to a rightward shift of the supply curve (see Fig. 4-16). Two ways of increasing supply are improving technology and boosting productivity.

Improvements in the production technology would certainly increase supply, but new tools and new production methods cannot be developed overnight. Technological advances occur gradually, certainly not fast enough to eliminate an immediate shortage. A more practical approach to increase supply would be for the firm to boost productivity, getting more production out of each machine and employee each hour. Companies hire efficiency experts and management consultants to analyze their production processes and determine if they could organize and operate their equipment differently to increase its output. To boost employee productivity, many businesses furnish training, award production incentives, and provide counseling and rehabilitative services for problems that decrease productivity, such as drug addiction and alcoholism.

The third, and in many cases the most sensible, solution to a shortage is to allow the price of the good to rise to the market equilibrium level. Many might argue that for the government to allow some prices to rise would be cruel to the poor. The problem with this line of reasoning is a belief that, at the lower price, supplies would exist in quantities large enough to satisfy everyone. In a sense, the government forgets the existence of the law of supply. Allowing the

SEVEN GOOD YEARS FOLLOWED BY SEVEN LEAN YEARS

A Biblical Example of Surplus and Shortage

Read Genesis 41:46–57 and 47:13–20.

1. How great was the food surplus during the seven good years?
2. What preparations took advantage of this surplus to prepare for the coming shortage?
3. How might the surplus have affected the price of grain during the seven plentiful years, and how might the government's stockpiling of the grain have changed the market price?
4. How bad was the shortage during the seven lean years?
5. What evidence indicates the rising price of grain during the famine?

price to rise to its market equilibrium point may be a better way of solving the plight of the poor for two important reasons. First, a realistic market price encourages conservation and discourages wastefulness. By establishing a price ceiling lower than the equilibrium price, the government sends out a signal that the supply of the commodity is so abundant that consumers may squander it. Second, a realistic market price acts as an incentive for entrepreneurs to enter the market either to produce more of the good at a lower cost or to invent less expensive substitutes that will fill the need.

The manager of Candy City first notices that there is a greater demand for the product than the company is currently producing (Fig. 4-17A); in this case the shortage is 4,500 bars. Responding to the excess demand, he gradually raises the price (Fig. 4-17B). As he does

THE AMERICAN REVOLUTION, PRICE CONTROLS, AND MISERY

Those who think that price ceilings are a modern phenomenon and long for the "good old days" of our forefathers who allowed the market to operate freely should consider the following.

During the winter of 1777–78, General George Washington faced many foes: the British, the mercenaries hired by the British, the traitors among his own ranks, and the bitter winter weather. The biggest enemy of all, however, the one that nearly wiped out his entire force without firing a shot, was the well-intentioned legislature of the Commonwealth of Pennsylvania. Realizing the high cost of outfitting and maintaining an army, this body sought some legislative way of helping the Continental forces.

The legislature passed laws setting the maximum prices that Pennsylvanians could charge the army for certain commodities; however, these prices were far below the market price. The result of creating price ceilings was as disastrous then as it is today. The prices of the same commodities imported from states not having similar controls rose to record heights. Pennsylvania farmers refused to sell their produce at controlled prices, which were lower than their production cost. Many farmers believed they had no alternative but to sell their goods to the British troops, who were willing to pay the market price in gold.

One positive result from this misguided attempt to help, however, is that our forefathers learned from their mistake. On June 4, 1778, the Continental Congress adopted the following resolution:

Whereas . . . it hath been found by experience that limitations upon the prices of commodities are not only ineffectual for the purpose proposed, but likewise productive of very evil consequences to the great detriment of the public service . . . resolved, that it be recommended to the several states to repeal or suspend all laws or resolutions within the said states respectively limiting, regulating or restraining the Price of any Article, Manufacture or Commodity.

Fig. 4-16 Supply Solution to a Shortage

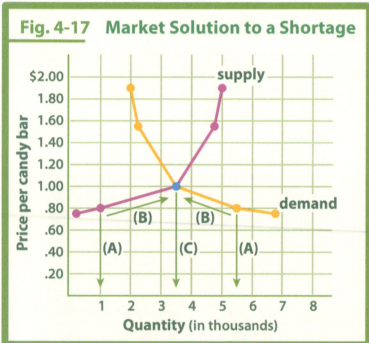

Fig. 4-17 Market Solution to a Shortage

so, he is pricing some consumers out of the market while creating an incentive for higher production. The manager keeps on raising the price until the quantity buyers demand is exactly equal to the quantity he supplies (Fig. 4-17C).

Whenever the price of a good changes from its market equilibrium price, regardless of the cause for the change, there will be negative results, either a surplus or a shortage. As a Christian who has now studied economics, particularly demand and supply, you know that waiting and allowing the market to solve these problems on its own is the best solution. In the interim, however, people may suffer financially as well as physically and emotionally. As a Christian you may not be able to help everyone, but you can have a part in helping to relieve those who are suffering and by so doing to give them an example of Christ.

What does it mean when a supply curve shifts to the right? to the left? How do technological advances, changes in production costs, and the price of related goods determine whether the curve shifts to the left or right? What does a price ceiling have to do with a shortage, and a price floor with a surplus? What causes surpluses and shortages, and what is the best solution for each? Prior to reading this chapter, answering these questions was probably beyond your ability. Now, however, you should be able to answer each one correctly. More importantly, though, you should be able to apply what you have learned in this chapter to better understand the economic events taking place around you every day and to understand them from a Christian worldview. How can the price of gasoline shift the supply curve for various types of automobiles? How might a bumper wheat crop prompt the agricultural lobby to push national and state legislatures to enact price floors? How have technological advances made it possible for a company's desire to make affordable laptops go from dream to reality? These events are just samples of economic changes that are shaping your world. Your ability to understand these events and their possible ramifications allows you to discuss them intelligently, to offer insights from a biblical perspective, and thereby to be a more effective servant of God.

SECTION REVIEW 4B

1. At what point do supply and demand intersect?
2. What occurs when the price of a product is higher than the price at which supply equals demand?
3. What is the simplest solution to a surplus?
4. What condition causes a shortage, and what are its possible solutions?
5. How can a Christian show Christ to others during a surplus or shortage?

CHAPTER REVIEW

CONTENT QUESTIONS

1. Who are suppliers?
2. What does a leftward shift in the supply curve indicate?
3. Do changes in technology cause an increase or a decrease in supply?
4. Alfred Marshall is best known for his model illustrating what economic law?
5. Why does a price above the market equilibrium price result in a surplus?
6. List the three possible methods of solving a surplus.

APPLICATION QUESTIONS

1. What would the supply curve look like for a product for which there is a finite supply (for example, stadium seats for a ball game)?
2. Use a graph to illustrate and explain the market equilibrium point.
3. Scalpers are people who purchase tickets for concerts and sporting events at low prices and attempt to sell them for significantly higher prices. Identify the advantages and disadvantages of scalping, using demand and supply curves as applicable to illustrate your points.
4. What would be the immediate effects if the government set a price ceiling that was below the market equilibrium price on a product? Illustrate with a graph.
5. Because market prices are fluid, name one of the biblical principles that should be used by both buyers and sellers in their relationship with each other.

TERMS

supply	65
law of supply	65
supply schedule	66
supply curve	66
change in quantity supplied	67
changes in supply	67
decrease in supply	67
increase in supply	67
market equilibrium point	71
market equilibrium price	72
surplus	72
price floor	73
shortage	74
price ceilings	75

PERSONAL FINANCE

THE CHRISTIAN AND DEBT

Perhaps no other topic in personal finance has proven as divisive among Christians as whether it is right for them to use consumer credit and enter into debt. The issue of debt has grouped Christians into those who totally oppose the idea of a Christian's willingly taking on debt and those who believe that Christians may use debt as a financial tool, provided they do so wisely and cautiously.

CHRISTIAN DEBT PHILOSOPHIES

Opponents of consumer borrowing declare that all debt is unscriptural and therefore wrong. They cite such verses as the following:

> *"For the Lord thy God blesseth thee, as he promised thee: and thou shalt lend unto many nations, but thou shalt not borrow; and thou shalt reign over many nations, but they shall not reign over thee" (Deut. 15:6).*
>
> *"Owe no man any thing, but to love one another: for he that loveth another hath fulfilled the law" (Rom. 13:8).*

Those taking this position state that since God told His people not to borrow or owe anyone anything, His position on debt is clear. Hence, they believe that the position His people take should be equally clear: do not enter into debt, period. Supporters of this philosophy believe these statements allow no exceptions. They maintain that rather than complaining that the position is unrealistic and impractical in today's society, Christians should reexamine their personal financial practices and make whatever lifestyle changes needed to align themselves with the principle these verses present.

A second group, however, maintains that debt is neither immoral nor unscriptural. They liken debt to fire—something very useful but also very dangerous. Members of this group offer several arguments to support their position. First, they point out that debt is a fact of life for everyone, even for the most conscientious debt-avoiding Christian. Whenever a person receives anything for which he has not yet paid, such as electricity, gas, or water, he is in fact a debtor until he pays his monthly statement. They then ask what the difference is between paying a utility bill and paying a credit card bill as long as both are paid on time without incurring any interest charges. Second, this group argues that God does not absolutely forbid debt and claims as evidence the Scripture's treatment of lending. They contend that if borrowing were a sin, then certainly lending would be considered equally sinful since it would be contributing to another's sin. To argue otherwise, this group believes, would be like condemning the person who consumes alcohol while approving of the one who sells it to him. Indeed, if lending is sinful, then even the most conscientious debt-avoider would be sinning by depositing money, for bank deposits are, in fact, loans to institutions, which in turn lend to individuals and businesses. What, therefore, does the Bible say about lending? Instead of condemning the practice, Scripture places restrictions upon it and even, at times, encourages it:

> *"And if thy brother be waxen poor, and fallen in decay with thee; then thou shalt relieve him: yea, though he be a stranger, or a sojourner; that he may live with thee. Take thou no usury [loan interest] of him, or increase: but fear thy God; that thy brother may live with thee" (Lev. 25:35–36).*
>
> *"Give to him that asketh thee, and from him that would borrow of thee turn not thou away" (Matt. 5:42).*
>
> *"Wherefore then gavest not thou my money into the bank, that at my coming I might have required mine own with usury?" (Luke 19:23).*

BIBLICAL CAUTIONS

Those who allow borrowing do not, however, believe that it is something Christians should practice without restraint. On the contrary, while they believe it may be useful in some situations, they insist that the Christian should be ever mindful of certain dangers and biblical cautions.

Scripture Associates Debt with Bondage

No matter what a person's reasons for borrowing money may be, the fact remains that the borrower becomes dependent upon the lender. A debt contract binds the borrower to repay a given sum of money. Hence, the Christian **debtor** is "bound" to his creditor, or in the words of Solomon, he becomes a "servant to the lender" (Prov. 22:7). Though debtors' prisons have gone the way of the horse and buggy and modern debt contracts severely limit the hold a **creditor** (or lender) has over a borrower, the lender still has some power over the debtor. By requiring the borrower to make periodic payments, the lender has a claim to a portion of the borrower's income. In some cases, if the borrower should **default** on his loan (fail to pay on time), the lender may obtain permission to **garnish** the borrower's wages. The borrower's employer would then take the payment the borrower owes on his debt out of his wages prior to his receiving his paycheck. Such an act requires a court order, and the specific limitations on the practice vary according to state law. Additionally, in some cases the lender also has a claim to the use of the item the debtor purchased with the borrowed money.

Debt May Prevent a Christian's Mobility

Closely associated with the idea that debt is a form of bondage is the fact that debt may limit a Christian's mobility. His debts may obligate him to keep his present job, thereby obligating him to stay in his current geographical location. For example, suppose a Christian businessman believes God has called him and his family to leave their present situation and serve the

PROBLEMS ASSOCIATED WITH CREDIT

Financial pressures are a leading cause of divorce, heart attack, suicide, and crime. Life has enough problems without adding those caused by debt brought on through credit.

First, credit exacts an emotional toll. Sudden, substantial, and unexpected bills—medical problems, broken appliances, a leaking roof—can be traumatic and can sap paychecks. The person who has borrowed has taken away money that he could have used to meet these expenses; consequently, the unexpected bills create a crisis in the home. The head of the household finds that the monthly bills are impervious to changing circumstances. The added burden of credit drains his energy, making him less effective at work and more susceptible to illness, anger, depression, and sin.

Second, credit actually lessens a consumer's buying power. A person who relies on credit frequently pays high interest rates. A young married couple with good credit might be able to buy quality furniture, an expensive entertainment system, and many other amenities now, but they may still be making payments when these things begin to break down and wear out. Over the same period another couple who makes do with less can earn interest on their savings and pay cash for even better things later. For example, suppose a credit-hungry couple buys a $900 stereo for $20 a month. By the time they finally pay it off—nearly four years and much wear later—a couple in the same circumstances who decided to save before buying could have saved enough to buy a new, more advanced stereo and have money left over. If these two couples consistently follow their opposing philosophies, one is likely to have old, worn-out possessions later in life, while the other is likely to enjoy newer possessions and money to spare for vacations, hobbies, and retirement.

Third, there is the temptation to abuse credit. Advertisements beg consumers to "buy now and pay later." A person with good credit finds his mailbox stuffed with "pre-approved" credit cards and loans. Those without self-discipline often use these to buy what they want rather than what they can afford.

In its worst form, abuse of credit leaves the consumer overextended. When credit payments (excluding mortgage debt) demand more than 20 percent of his take-home pay, the consumer begins to experience the stress of overextended credit. Signs of being overextended include late payment of bills, minimum payments on credit cards, loans for basics (such as food and gas), and new, higher loans to pay off old loans. Every unexpected expense becomes a crisis. Credit companies no longer extend new credit, and in its extreme form, overextended credit leads to bankruptcy.

Credit-happy Americans have been turning more and more to bankruptcy court to "solve" the problems created by their buying binges. Widespread debt causes excessive financial strain, as is evidenced by the over one million Americans that declared bankruptcy annually in the late 1990s and early 2000s. Changes in the bankruptcy law in 2006 made it more difficult for individuals to declare bankruptcy. As a result personal declarations of bankruptcy dropped dramatically but immediately began rising again.

Lord on a mission field; however, the family is bound by debt contracts on possessions and credit cards. Consequently, it may be years before they are able to obey the call. However, if they were debt free, they would be able to move much more quickly. It is therefore imperative that believers allow the Holy Spirit to guide them when contemplating purchases that could place them under potentially binding debts. As God exhorts in His Word, Christians are to avoid such possible hindering obligations: "No man that warreth entangleth himself with the affairs of this life; that he may please him who hath chosen him to be a soldier" (2 Tim. 2:4).

Debt Presumes upon an Uncertain Future

It is wise to make periodic deposits to a savings account and to allow the funds to accumulate interest over a period of time so that they can be used later to make a purchase. Debtors, however, choose to "save in reverse." That is, they first borrow money from the bank and "deposit" it later with the interest that they owe to the bank. The problem with this arrangement is that the borrower presumes his future conditions will enable him to repay the loan and the interest. Whenever a lender examines an applicant's ability to repay, he takes into account such factors as the likelihood that the borrower will continue to live in the area, that he will remain employed during the period of the loan, that his income will either remain constant or increase, that his health will remain good, and that his other expenses will not increase beyond his income. While such assumptions may be commonplace with the unsaved, the child of God must not fail to take into account that the Lord may have different plans for his residence, employment, income, health, and expenses. Consider the following verses:

> "Boast not thyself of to morrow; for thou knowest not what a day may bring forth" (Prov. 27:1).
>
> "Go to now, ye that say, To day or to morrow we will go into such a city, and continue there a year, and buy and sell, and get gain: Whereas ye know not what shall be on the morrow. For what is your life? It is even a vapour, that appeareth for a little time, and then vanisheth away" (James 4:13–14).

Many churches have gone into debt to finance building projects because they assumed that membership and offerings would continue to increase. Later, to their chagrin, they found that their assumptions were faulty. Their ability to repay the debt disappeared, and their testimony and effectiveness for Christ in their communities suffered irreparable harm.

Debt May Keep a Person from Seeing the Lord's Provision or Protection

Several cases in Scripture record the Lord's using someone's poverty as an opportunity to show His power. Several times He worked a miracle, and other times He provided through others, believers and unbelievers, by prompting them to give to that person's need. By using credit to meet a financial need, a Christian may either miss the blessing of seeing the Lord work on his behalf or deprive another saint of the blessing he would receive from assisting a brother in need. The Christian walks by faith, and his faith needs to be anchored in biblical truths, such as 2 Chronicles 16:9, "For the eyes of the Lord run to and fro throughout the whole earth, to shew himself strong in the behalf of them whose heart is perfect toward him," and Philippians 4:19, "But my God shall supply all your need according to his riches in glory by Christ Jesus."

The Lord may also use a lack of finances to prevent His children from purchasing something or involving themselves in an activity that is contrary to His will. Through the unwise use of credit, believers may circumvent the barriers that the Lord placed before them to protect them from making unwise purchases. By using debt financing, people today are able to purchase material possessions that were unaffordable to their counterparts in the past. As a result of this expansion of purchasing power, many Christians have fallen for one of the oldest of Satan's deceptions: that one can serve oneself and Jesus Christ at the same time. "Ye ask, and receive not, because ye ask amiss, that ye may consume it upon your lusts" (James 4:3).

Debt May Prevent a Person from Giving to the Lord and Others

God's Word commands Christians to give (2 Cor. 9:7) and exhorts them to be charitable toward others (Gal. 6:10, 1 Tim. 6:18). However, when a Christian enters into debt, he may encounter temptation to withhold monies he would otherwise have donated. As the pressure from his debts begins to weigh upon him, he may be tempted to use money set aside for his regular church giving and pledged offerings as a source of payment. He may attempt to justify his "robbing from Peter to pay Paul" by convincing himself that once the debt is paid off, he will redouble his giving. However, unless by the grace of God he changes his spending patterns, the paying down of one debt will more than likely be soon followed by the taking on of another one.

The issue of debt and the Christian is indeed a sensitive one. There are good people on both sides of the debate. Which side you take should result from your careful study of the Scriptures combined with seeking the counsel of godly elders. Regardless of which side you come to believe is right, you should be understanding of those who take the opposing view. Should you choose to allow yourself to use credit and to enter into debt, proceed with biblical discernment. You would be wise to heed well the cautions given here, recognizing there is good reason that they are labeled cautions.

Courtesy of Roger Harvell, Greenville News *(SC)*

REVIEW QUESTIONS

1. What are the five biblical cautions regarding debt?
2. How is debt associated with bondage?
3. How does debt presume upon the future?

TERMS

debtor	80
creditor	80
default	81
garnish	81

UNIT TWO

UNIT TWO

ECONOMICS OF THE NATIONS

Chapter 5
WHAT IS THE ECONOMIC PROBLEM? — 86

Personal Finance: The Consumer and Debt — 102

Chapter 6
ECONOMIC SYSTEMS — 106

Personal Finance: Types of Consumer Credit — 122

CHAPTER FIVE
WHAT IS THE ECONOMIC PROBLEM?

5A NATIONAL ECONOMIC GOALS — 86

5B THREE ECONOMIC QUESTIONS — 88

It is early Monday morning; another week begins. As the first amber beams of sunlight streak across midwestern fields, farmers start the huge machines that work the nation's heartland. Meanwhile, hundreds of miles to the east, Wall Street financiers begin flooding into the stock exchanges; and banks, shops, and businesses of all kinds prepare to open. Across the eastern half of the nation, thousands of assembly line workers break the silence of factories with the echoing of their footsteps and the starting of their equipment, while out West a few alarm clocks are going off, early morning newspapers are hitting driveways, and the first of the predawn delivery trucks are rolling out of parking lots.

This new day begins like thousands of days before it, and once again a remarkable occurrence passes unnoticed. Individuals rouse and set in motion the massive machinery of a nation's entire economic system. They will produce, trade, negotiate, buy, and sell; and these millions of women and men, though oblivious of each other, will work separately yet collectively to solve their society's economic problem.

5A NATIONAL ECONOMIC GOALS

Simply stated, the economic problem of a society is how best to accomplish its economic goals. Most societies have identified four primary goals:

- A low level of unemployment
- A stable price level
- A healthy rate of economic growth
- A fair distribution of income

GOAL #1: A LOW LEVEL OF UNEMPLOYMENT

Unemployment exists when someone who wishes to work cannot find a job. It is in the best interest of a society in general, and its members in particular, that every person who is able and willing to work be able to find employment. In addition to being a waste of the resource of human labor, high unemployment also often coincides with increased levels of poverty, crime, and despair.

Work is of God. Genesis 2:2 tells us that Creation was God's work: "And on the seventh day God ended his work which he had made; and he rested on the seventh day from all his work which he had made." God did not intend for man to be idle. When He placed Adam in the Garden of Eden, He made him caretaker of it. Adam was "to dress it and to keep it" (Gen. 2:15). In fact, refusal to work is sinful. In 2 Thessalonians 3:10 the Scriptures declare "that if any would not work, neither should he eat." Honest work is noble and commanded in Scripture. The Bible teaches that "in all labour there is profit" (Prov. 14:23) and that "an idle soul shall suffer hunger" (Prov. 19:15).

GOAL #2: A STABLE PRICE LEVEL

Numerous examples from history demonstrate that fluctuations between periods of inflation (when prices are rising) and deflation (when prices are falling) cause economic disruptions because the unpredictability of these ups and downs makes people unsure of their economic future. Whether prices are rapidly rising or falling, producers and consumers are unable to make accurate economic forecasts. They find it difficult to predict their production costs or monthly expenditures; consequently, both groups are hesitant to increase their buying and selling. A "wait and see" attitude begins to prevail. The undesirable result, then, of this instability in prices is that the nation's overall economic activity slows significantly.

In an atmosphere of instability we know that in God we can find stability. He is always the same yesterday, today, and forever (Heb. 13:8). We need by our example to demonstrate God's stability to others and by so doing draw them to Him and help them to see that the ups and downs of the economy are in God's control.

GOAL #3: A HEALTHY RATE OF ECONOMIC GROWTH

The term **economic growth** refers to an increase in the quantity of goods and services a nation can produce. Nations experience two types of economic growth: extensive and intensive growth. In a period of **extensive growth**, business firms are able to increase their production of goods and services because they have more land, labor, or financial capital available to them. From your study of US history, you may recall that America has experienced several periods of extensive growth, particularly through the 1800s. As the nation pushed westward, opened new lands, discovered new resources, developed new industries, and welcomed waves of immigrants, it experienced phenomenal increases in production. The nation tapped tremendous supplies of labor and natural resources and was able to produce more goods and services. However, as its untapped resources diminished, the country's extensive growth slowed significantly.

America now turned more to the second type of national economic growth, intensive growth. During times of **intensive growth**, a nation's business firms increase their production of goods and services by using their existing factors of production with greater efficiency. Invention and innovation promote intensive growth by developing the ways and means that encourage and permit companies to

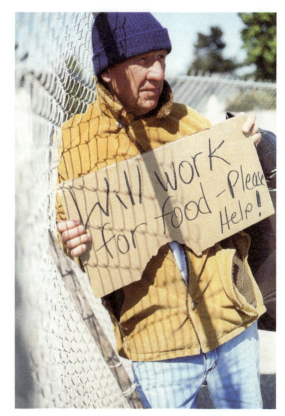

Because of the problems associated with a high unemployment rate, most governments list low unemployment as one of their most important economic goals.

produce more goods and services with the same quantity of resources. While a country can, to some degree, replenish some of its resources, there are others that, once depleted, cannot be replaced. Intensive growth, then, is essential for economic growth because a nation must develop alternative resources for production as well as newer, more efficient means of utilizing its present diminishing resources.

Christians recognize the value of economic growth. Scripture certainly does not praise stagnation and poverty, for it contains numerous verses extolling the virtues of hard work, diligence, foresight, prudence, and the maximizing of God-given talents that contribute to economic growth.

GOAL #4: A FAIR DISTRIBUTION OF INCOME

The final goal of most nations is a fair distribution of income, but with this goal come many problems and controversies. Economists and policymakers must answer such questions as, who defines fairness? how do they define it? and what role does that definition play in the distribution of a nation's income? For example, a society might question if fairness should be a guaranteed equality of income or simply an equal opportunity for success in an economy. If that society opts for the former, then who guarantees the equality and how? If it chooses the latter, then what constitutes an equal opportunity and who defines success?

In practical terms, policymakers must decide if the government should provide a safety net of economic benefits for the less fortunate or let the market determine each person's income.

As you may guess, there are more questions and possible answers as regards this topic than could possibly be adequately discussed in this brief section. Later in this chapter you will return to this discussion and consider it from a biblical perspective.

Almost daily you can find one or more of these economic goals in the headlines.

SECTION REVIEW 5A

1. What is a society's economic problem?
2. List the four economic goals of most societies and in your own words explain the economic importance of each.
3. List two biblical passages that can be used to evaluate any or all of these four economic goals.

5B THREE ECONOMIC QUESTIONS

In every society the economic system in place determines how that nation will achieve its economic goals. Whether its economic system imposes commands from some central authority or allows the free market to work, the nation's economic decision makers must answer three critical questions.

1. The output question: What will the nation produce?
2. The input question: How will the nation produce its goods?
3. The distribution question: Who will receive what the nation produces?

THE OUTPUT QUESTION: WHAT WILL THE NATION PRODUCE?

Every society must answer the output question, which is, what goods and services will it produce? Since resources are scarce and wants are limitless, every nation faces the predicament that it cannot produce everything that it wants; therefore, choices concerning what it will and will not produce are unavoidable.

The fundamental question concerns what types of goods the nation will produce. Rather than asking which particular goods to produce (such as microwaves, televisions, or shoes), economists are more interested in what mix of consumer goods and capital goods the economy generates. **Consumer goods** are those that individuals purchase for personal use, such as books, clothing, coffee, and school supplies. **Capital goods** are goods that firms use to produce consumer goods. Another name for capital goods is *real capital*. Examples of capital goods include printing presses, farm equipment, welding tools, and factory machinery.

Since a nation cannot produce everything its people desire, it must address the **consumer goods/capital goods tradeoff**. If a nation were to produce only consumer goods, it would create no new factories, tools, or replacement parts. Soon, factories and equipment would begin to deteriorate, fall into disrepair, and eventually stop operating, leaving households without a source of consumer goods. On the other hand, if a society determined to produce only capital goods, that choice would also cause the economy to collapse. By producing just the tools of production, the nation would abandon the production of food, shelter, clothing, medical supplies, and other consumer goods. Of course, no reasonable society would adopt either of these extremes. The best approach is a balance between the two. However, determining what that ideal combination is and how to achieve it often proves to be extremely challenging.

A nation's economy needs both consumer goods and capital goods and needs them in the proper balance.

CHOOSING BETWEEN CONSUMER AND CAPITAL GOODS

The choice between the production of consumer goods and capital goods can be illustrated with a production possibilities curve (PPC). By putting the production quantity of consumer goods on the horizontal axis and the production quantity of capital goods on the vertical axis, you should be able to easily recognize the tradeoff that is inherent in this decision. If the economy is producing at points A or B in the figure shown, points at which the production combinations of consumer and capital goods lie on the PPC, then the nation cannot increase its production of one type of good without reducing its production of the other type. Increasing production of one good, be it consumer or capital, entails an opportunity cost in terms of the other good.

The choice, however, is not just between the quantities of consumer and capital goods the economy is currently producing. It is more importantly a tradeoff regarding the present and future quantities of these goods. Choosing a greater quantity of consumer goods today permits not only a smaller quantity of capital goods today but also a smaller quantity of consumer goods later. The reason is that the capital goods the economy produces today are the tools it will need to produce consumer goods in the future. In contrast, if a country chooses to produce fewer consumer goods and more capital goods today, it will be able to produce and enjoy more consumer goods in the future.

For example, at point A in the diagram, the economy is producing more consumer goods than capital goods ($C_A > K_A$). Therefore, in that year there are more goods and services to consume, and the amount of capital goods manufactured will cause the PPC to move outward a small amount. On the other hand, at point B the economy is producing fewer consumer goods and services, but the increased manufacturing of capital goods will cause the PPC to move outward by a greater amount. In this example, the country choosing to operate at point B has chosen to reduce its current consumption to increase its future quantity of consumer goods.

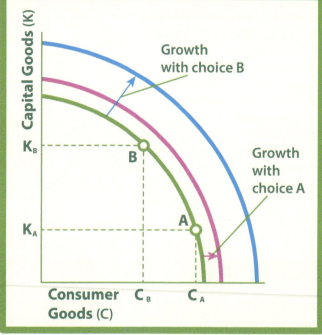

All economists recognize that the choice between producing consumer goods and capital goods is essentially a question of spending versus saving. When people spend money, they buy consumer goods. In a sense, when people save, they "buy" capital goods, because the money they put into financial institutions is then lent to businesses to purchase real capital.

Once a country sets its policy regarding the production of consumer and capital goods, it must make specific decisions about which capital goods and which consumer goods it will manufacture. Again, different economic systems answer these questions differently.

The Command Economy

In a command economy a powerful individual or a committee answers the three economic questions. The policymakers decide not only the proportion of consumer goods to capital goods that the nation will produce but also the specific items it will manufacture. They often justify their actions by saying that such decisions are too important to be left to the whims of the market. Those who favor a command economy point out that it may be necessary to override the self-interest of the individual and to subjugate the general welfare of the population in order to reach the society's goals.

Critics of the command economy ask two questions that prove difficult for its proponents to answer. First, if the market leads individuals to make wrong choices about spending and saving and if those choices produce undesirable results, would a central committee's making similar wrong choices not equally cause similar negative consequences? Second, if a government encourages too much consumer spending, would it not risk having the nation's factories and equipment falling into disrepair as spending on real capital declines?

The Market Economy

In a market economy, private individuals make the decisions that answer the three economic questions, and they do so with such an ease that it causes observers to marvel. Yet the real reason behind this ease is simple. A market economy, more so than its command counterpart, frequently gives the economic principles revealed in God's Word an opportunity to work. Some of these principles would be the following: the principle of work, Genesis 3:19; the principle of sowing and reaping, Galatians 6:7; the principle of counting the cost, Luke 14:28; and the principle of foreseeing the evil, Proverbs 22:3. When governments remove themselves from the market process, it tends to proceed effectively rather than to produce disarray.

Instead of waiting for committee decisions, as under a command economy, the free market automatically adjusts to the need for more or fewer capital goods by providing market-based incentives for businesses and consumers to change their spending practices. The regulating mechanism of market prices is the key to the market's ability to match consumption with production and personal saving with corporate borrowing. A central component of these market prices is the market interest rate.

Like a thermostatic valve that regulates the flow of cooling water to an automobile's engine, the market interest rate regulates the flow of money from households to business firms via the financial markets. As an illustration, consider the market for peanut butter. When, for whatever reason, consumers decide that they want more peanut butter, the market demand for peanut butter and its price will rise. Producers will recognize that because consumers are now willing to pay more for peanut butter, there is an increased profit opportunity in making it. To take advantage of this opportunity, manufacturers will produce more peanut butter, and in doing so, they will make an increased profit for themselves as well as provide the peanut butter that consumers want to buy. The market's rising price provided the incentive for manufacturers to increase production.

The peanut butter illustration can also apply to the decision about producing capital goods rather than consumer goods. When consumers want more peanut butter to the extent that producers must increase their use of capital goods to meet the demand, then the producers will demand more capital goods. The market interest rate

---

PLANNED ECONOMIES

Command economies are sometimes called *planned economies* because extensive planning is necessary to control the many economic activities of a nation. Communist states and countries ruled by dictators are examples of command (or planned) economies.

THE "GUNS AND BUTTER" ILLUSTRATION

In many early economics textbooks, students commonly found a representation of the capital goods/consumer goods tradeoff known as the "guns and butter" illustration. Textbooks usually portrayed this illustration as a PPC (with guns on one axis and butter on the other) and used it to demonstrate the necessity of production choices in an economy at the macroeconomic level. The guns represented the military or defense expenditures that a country deemed necessary, and the butter represented agricultural or consumer goods. The idea was to show that if a country was using all its resources, the only way it could produce more military resources was to produce fewer consumer goods and vice versa. However, political changes and economists' desire to expand the explanation of this tradeoff beyond just military spending versus domestic spending have lessened the use of this illustration.

will then mediate the tension between increased consumer demand and increased business demand for capital.

If interest rates are low, consumers have less incentive to save and will choose rather to spend a larger portion of their income on consumer goods. On the other hand, the financial market's lower interest rates provide an incentive for business firms to increase their borrowing in order to purchase more capital goods. To raise additional funds, banks offer consumers a higher interest rate on savings. As consumers save more, they spend less on consumer goods, further reducing the pressure on old equipment. The market interest rate will continue to rise until it has brought the consumers' desire to purchase down to where it matches the manufacturers' capacity to produce.

If, on the other hand, business firms have too much invested in capital goods, falling interest rates will bring the market back into equilibrium. Since businesses have too much equipment, they will decrease their borrowing from banks, and since banks no longer need as much money to lend to businesses, they will decrease the interest rate they pay on savings accounts. As consumers save less, they will spend more, prompting businesses to use their previously idle equipment.

During the first decade of the twenty-first century, the people of North Korea had a difficult time meeting their basic needs of food, clothing, and shelter. This hardship illustrates how a command economy's overspending on capital goods (military hardware) produces unsatisfactory results in consumer goods (agricultural products).

When nations allow the market to work, consumers wishing to buy goods will find them available, people desiring to save will see encouragements to do so, and business firms needing capital will be able to borrow enough to meet their needs. The society will balance the optimum proportions of consumer goods and capital goods, and it will have answered the output question in a way that has satisfied both consumers and producers.

THE INPUT QUESTION: HOW WILL THE NATION PRODUCE ITS GOODS?

The input question concerns how a nation chooses to produce its goods. A unique combination of the factors of production creates every economic good or service. However, in many cases it may be possible with two of the factors, labor and capital, to substitute one for the other. The input question asks therefore, Should a business firm use a greater amount of human labor or of capital goods (equipment) in its production process? If the firm takes a **labor intensive** approach, it relies more on human labor than it does on real capital, but if it follows a **capital intensive** policy, it uses more automated equipment than human labor.

Businesses that choose to be labor intensive enjoy certain advantages over their capital intensive counterparts. Human labor is trainable and versatile; that is, firms can teach workers to perform various

Handcrafted pottery is an example of a labor intensive product.

tasks. In contrast, equipment has limits to its applications. Labor intensive business firms also remain more flexible to meet changes in demand. As demand increases, a manufacturer can increase its workforce by the exact number of personnel it needs to meet the demand. Conversely, if demand decreases, the manufacturer may lay off a specific number of workers. To meet even a slight increase in demand, the capital intensive firm may have to purchase expensive equipment, and that investment will continue even if demand decreases and the equipment goes unused. By using a greater number of human laborers, labor intensive firms also benefit their society by contributing to a lower unemployment rate, which has the effect of reducing crime and poverty.

Business firms that are capital intensive, however, do possess several advantages of their own. First, in addition to not having to meet large payrolls, capital intensive business firms pay smaller hidden costs associated with employing workers. Examples of these costs include unemployment compensation, sick pay, vacation and holiday pay, medical and dental insurance, social security contributions, and profit sharing. Capital intensive firms also do not have to maintain large employee infirmaries, cafeterias, or lounges. Second, the capital intensive firm is unlikely to experience as significant a threat of union agitation or labor unrest as would a labor intensive firm. Third, by relying more on capital equipment than human labor, the company assures itself of a nearly constant rate of productivity. The productivity of human workers tends to rise and fall with changes in the weather, the day of the week, family problems, or the number of hours worked in a day.

A capital intensive assembly line reduces the need for human labor.

A labor intensive economy may increase the number of people working, but the nation may not necessarily be more prosperous as a result.

Of course, no firm could be totally capital intensive; and, as most operations require some tools, only those businesses in the simplest of industries could be totally labor intensive. Therefore, some combination of labor and capital is necessary for each business firm, but what combination is best?

The Command Economy

The command economy's solution to the input question depends upon who is commanding and what he hopes to achieve. In most cases command economies desire their business firms to be primarily labor intensive to produce a nearly fully employed workforce.

While labor intensive firms might bring about a lower unemployment rate, it is not necessarily true that a nation with a low unemployment rate is economically prosperous. In fact, one may legitimately question the validity of official statistics on unemployment in command economies because they may simply assign individuals to jobs to claim to have an extremely low unemployment rate. The problem in these countries is not that their citizens are unemployed but that they may not be employed efficiently. Assigning a worker to a job may guarantee that he is employed, but it does not mean that he is productive. He may not be qualified for what he is doing.

The Market Economy

In a free market each firm addresses the question of the proper mix of labor and capital by taking into consideration its unique needs. Whereas command authorities look to the immediate effects on unemployment, the incentives associated with production costs drive the market economy. Under the free market, business firms generally choose the mixture of labor and capital that will lower their costs, thereby allowing them to sell their products at lower prices, satisfy more customers, capture a larger share of the market, and reap a greater profit. For each industry this mix of labor and capital depends on the nature of the good or service it produces.

THE DISTRIBUTION QUESTION: WHO WILL RECEIVE WHAT THE NATION PRODUCES?

Of the three economic questions, none is as hotly debated as the distribution question: Who should receive the goods and services that the nation produces? In seeking to answer this question, politicians, economists, and other policymakers examine such questions as, should the rich receive more than the poor? are the highly educated entitled to a greater portion than the uneducated? should a person's age determine his share? and what is the fairest method of distributing a nation's limited goods and services? Since consumers need and use money to purchase the goods and services a nation produces, economists recognize that the distribution question relates directly to another question, who will receive the nation's money? The answers to these questions will be based on an individual's worldview. As a Christian your worldview must be based on the Bible. A biblical worldview will help to determine the answers to these questions and will help you as you are deciding whom to vote for in elections.

The Command Economy

It is undeniable that there is a significant disparity between the incomes of the richest and poorest Americans. Persons favoring the command solution are often those who seek to close this gap out of a commitment to egalitarian fairness. The policy of **egalitarian fairness** maintains that each person in a nation has a right to a part of that nation's wealth simply because he is part of the human race.

KARL MARX (1818-83)
Father of Communism

Karl Heinrich Marx was born in Trier in the German Rhineland. His father intended that he become a lawyer, but soon after Marx began his university training, he turned from studying law to exploring the philosophical and political developments of his day. He became associated with a group of radical students and teachers who openly criticized the government. They deplored the poor living conditions of the masses in nineteenth-century Europe and detested the wealthy landowners and businessmen who enjoyed their wealth while the lower classes struggled to eke out a living. When Marx began writing articles expounding these ideas, he quickly became an outcast in Germany. He went to Paris to continue his work, but again his radical ideas brought censure. He spent the last half of his life in exile in Britain. Because his work brought no steady income, he and his family lived in poverty, surviving by the charity of Marx's friend, Friedrich Engels.

Marx tirelessly studied the philosophical and economic ideas of his day and then meticulously formulated the details of his own beliefs. His bitter atheistic outlook on life centered on the ongoing conflicts of society. Marx agreed with the then-popular Hegelian thought that society continuously developed two antagonistic groups of people who would clash. The conflict would become a revolution that would bring these groups together into a new society. That society would eventually split into two new groups destined to clash. Seeing around him the upper classes (or bourgeoisie) and the lower classes (or proletariat), Marx believed that these groups would come into conflict because of their differences in wealth and living conditions. But he set forth his own opinion that man could change this pattern of history by using the conflict of the bourgeoisie and the proletariat to usher in an enlightened society. Marx's new harmonious society would strive for the betterment of all people by taking "from each according to his ability" and giving "to each according to his need." All greed would then be overcome in this setting in which society owned all things in common. Marx called this utopia communism.

Marx tried to encourage the fulfillment of his dreams by inciting the proletariat to rebel against the bourgeoisie capitalists, or owners of capital—the means of production. He despised capitalists, believing they gained their profits not by their own physical labor but by that of the oppressed proletarian workers. In 1848 Marx collaborated with Engels to write *The Communist Manifesto*, an appeal to the working classes to revolt against the capitalists. Europe was in political upheaval at that time, but even so, it rejected and suppressed Marx's radical ideas. Marx continued his study and his writings, especially the voluminous exposition of his ideas in a work called *Das Kapital*.

Marx was a revolutionary with some obviously unscriptural beliefs and erroneous predictions, but his ideas of perfecting society by human effort still appeal to men who seek human solutions for spiritual problems. His ideology also lends support to those who would increase their personal power by taking control of a nation's economic activities.

Some egalitarians argue in favor of **economic leveling**, or equally distributing the nation's pool of wealth to all its citizens regardless of what any individual has contributed to the pool. Less extreme egalitarians argue that principles of fairness, justice, and morality obligate a society to maintain an economic safety net that protects the poor from the devastating effects of economic hardships. This idea of safety-net egalitarianism is the basis of many of today's social programs including social security, unemployment compensation, Medicare, Medicaid, food stamps, and housing assistance.

Those who support the command solution frequently view taxes as the means to redistribute the nation's wealth. They seek to increase the taxes on those whose annual incomes are above the national average. Then, their goal is to transfer that money, primarily through social programs, to those whose incomes are below that average.

Every society faces the challenge of wealth distribution.

The Market Economy

Proponents of the market solution maintain that a nation should distribute its wealth solely to those who successfully satisfy the needs of others. They argue that those who cannot or will not work to create the products or services for which others pay are not entitled to some amount of the profit from those products or services. They should not receive a portion of the nation's wealth simply because they exist in that nation.

The market economy holds to the concept of libertarian fairness. Whereas egalitarian fairness maintains that every person deserves a share of the nation's wealth, **libertarian fairness** argues that the only economic right to which a nation should entitle its citizens is the right to own and use property free of governmental interference. Whether a person can or does accumulate any wealth is solely his personal responsibility. For the person who is unable to earn a living because of a lack of education, a libertarian would argue that it is that person's responsibility to secure the training he needs to gain a marketable skill. For one who is unable to work because of physical limitations, the answer would be that it is his responsibility either to discover a skill that is compatible with his disability or to secure private charity. Because libertarian fairness espouses these practices, some of its opponents have dubbed this policy "**economic Darwinism**," making a comparison to certain principles of species' survival that arose from Charles Darwin's theory of evolution. Libertarians believe that to transfer income from the productive members of society to the less productive members is to penalize the industrious while rewarding the indolent.

The Biblical Perspective

Basically, the distribution question addresses the topic of how a society should help its poor. This is not an issue that the Bible ignores. From the Law to the Prophets and from the teachings of Jesus to the Epistles, the Scriptures reveal how God's people are to treat the poor and cry out against the sin of exploiting them.

Unfortunately, throughout church history, believers have tended to gravitate toward extreme opposing views of economic fairness, citing a verse or two to defend their favored economic system. Christian libertarians use Christ's words, "ye have the poor always with you" (Matt. 26:11), to teach that economic leveling is impossible. Christian egalitarians counter with reference to Christ's admonition to the rich young ruler, "If thou wilt be perfect, go and sell that thou hast, and give to the poor" (Matt. 19:21). Egalitarian believers use such verses as Leviticus 19:9–10 and 23:22 to show that a biblical precedent exists for the government's helping the poor. They then use this precedent to advocate using tax revenues to create a safety net. Their libertarian brethren, however, go to the book of Ruth and

As long as there are those in need, Christians will always have opportunities to demonstrate a biblical love for their neighbors.

point out that though the law required leaving the gleanings of the harvest, the government did not harvest those gleanings and distribute them to the poor. The poor had to gather for themselves what others had left for them.

Rather than using phrases or isolated verses from the Bible to support personal economic preferences, Christians should use the whole of Scripture as the standard by which to evaluate all economic issues. For example, the Bible illustrates several causes for a person's poverty. Sometimes there are natural disasters, such as droughts or insect invasions, that can devastate harvests and leave whole societies impoverished. Slothfulness, lack of skills, and mismanagement of assets also create groups of poor people. Warfare often ravages crops and creates poverty in agrarian civilizations. Finally, corrupt governments and greedy, self-serving employers exploit certain classes of people and plunge them into poverty.

These different causes of poverty demand different responses. Underlying them all, however, are the biblical principles that Christians are to love their neighbors as themselves, that they are to do good to all men, and that their good works are to glorify their Father in heaven. The Christian who bases his treatment of the poor on these truths will do what is right in each situation.

Believers are to care first for the economic needs of their families: "But if any provide not for his own, and specially for those of his own house, he hath denied the faith, and is worse than an infidel" (1 Tim. 5:8). God also instructs His people to care for fellow Christians (Gal. 6:10) and those outside their families, to share the blessings they receive from His hand. "And when ye reap the harvest of your land, thou shalt not make clean riddance of the corners of thy field when thou reapest, neither shalt thou gather any gleaning of thy harvest: thou shalt leave them unto the poor, and to the stranger: I am the Lord your God" (Lev. 23:22). Though American Christians no longer live in an agrarian society, they can and should still follow the basic principle of loving their neighbors and look for ways to demonstrate that love to the poor. For those whose poverty results from factors beyond their control—natural disasters, war, disease, or governmental corruption—the Christian should show compassion in deed and not just in word.

The approach to those whose poverty results from slothfulness, however, differs. From the beginning God gave man work to do. He placed Adam in the garden "to dress it and to keep it" (Gen. 2:15). He provided all that man would need for food (Gen. 1:29); however, Adam had to gather that food through his own labor. The Scriptures also teach that economic leveling, or providing equal economic benefits regardless of a person's productivity, is wrong. God's Word states "that if any would not work, neither should he eat" (2 Thess. 3:10). Since work is the biblically given way to generate personal income (Prov. 10:4; 12:27; 22:29; etc.), a society needs to employ a variety of strategies to motivate its lazy members to become productive. Simply giving money to those who refuse to work is to perpetuate their indolence, and that does not show love to them. Real love seeks to help a person overcome his problem rather than participate in what simply indulges that problem.

The loving practice for those needing skills or training in financial management is to provide the training and education they need to enable them to obtain work or manage their own finances. Several states have taken advantage of volunteers or those willing to help for minimal pay to create and implement such job training and education programs. These programs provide enough money for a person to survive while also giving him job training and teaching him money-management skills. Helping the needy to find jobs and requiring that they actively look for employment are also valuable parts of such programs. Because of the emphasis on working for the benefits, these programs have been nicknamed workfare.

Christians should look for ways to help those suffering in poverty. Sometimes that help takes the form of donating money or material items. Other times it may be volunteering time in a training or educational program or helping to connect those looking for work with potential employers. Finally, it may be a matter of working in and with the government—federal, state, and local—to see that laws exist and are enforced to prevent the exploitation of the poor and to establish biblically sound, helpful programs.

Four goals and three questions were the focus of this chapter. Can you list all seven and identify how the questions relate to the goals? Most economies want low unemployment, stable prices, economic growth, and fair income distribution; and economic policymakers want to help their nation achieve its goals through what it produces, how it produces it, and for whom. However, as you now know from your study of this chapter, knowing what a society wants and achieving it are two separate things. Much depends upon who is making the decisions and upon what bases he makes them. As is often the case, the questions themselves may seem simple, but the answers and their applications can be very complex. As a Christian, it is your responsibility to examine each goal, each question, and each answer through the lens of God's Word and then to choose what is right accordingly.

SECTION REVIEW 5B

1. What are the three critical questions that every society must answer as it seeks to meet its economic goals?
2. How is the consumer goods/capital goods tradeoff a matter of spending versus saving?
3. What is the difference between a labor intensive business and a capital intensive business?
4. What should be the standard that Christians use to answer the distribution question?

CHAPTER REVIEW

CONTENT QUESTIONS

1. How is unemployment a problem for society?
2. What is the difference between extensive growth and intensive growth of an economy?
3. How does the market economy solve the consumer goods/capital goods production dilemma? How does the command system attempt to solve it?
4. What are the advantages and disadvantages of labor intensive and capital intensive business firms?
5. According to Karl Marx, how would his new society bring about the betterment of all people? What would his society then overcome, and how? What did he call his new utopia?
6. How does the market system decide who should receive what the nation produces? How does the command system address the problem?
7. Identify the three biblical principles that provide a basis for a Christian's treatment of the poor.
8. What way does the Bible give for a person to generate his own personal income? Use Scripture to support this position.

APPLICATION QUESTIONS

1. When looking at the economic goals of a nation, what verses from Scripture would you use to support those economic goals? (You may use verses discussed in the text or choose your own.)
2. Read an article from an online source or watch a television news report. List the circumstances in which the three economic questions were involved. Did the writer or broadcaster take the egalitarian or the libertarian point of view? Explain how you determined his or her point of view.
3. Choose five business firms in your community and answer these questions: Do they produce consumer goods or capital goods? Are they labor intensive or capital intensive? Explain your answers.
4. Using the information from the boxes on the consumer goods/capital goods PPC (p. 90) and the guns and butter illustration (p. 92), explain the political cartoon on page 93. You may use a PPC to illustrate your answer.

TERMS

economic growth	87
extensive growth	87
intensive growth	87
consumer goods	89
capital goods	89
consumer goods/capital goods tradeoff	89
labor intensive	93
capital intensive	93
egalitarian fairness	96
economic leveling	97
libertarian fairness	97
economic Darwinism	98

PERSONAL FINANCE

THE CONSUMER AND DEBT

While Christians may debate the appropriateness of debt, most people seemingly take a rather careless attitude toward it. For many Americans, going into debt has simply become a way of life. Consider, for example, that in the first quarter of 2015, American consumers accumulated over $3,363.4 billion in outstanding consumer debt while saving only about $574.1 billion.

Whatever an individual's belief about the propriety of debt, one thing is certain: to have a complete understanding of economics, a person must understand consumer credit. This article examines the reasons Americans choose to use debt. There are basically two reasons people borrow money. They use the borrowed capital either for current consumption or for purchasing investments.

CONSUMPTION BORROWING

Many consumers buy items using **consumption borrowing**, meaning they use debt to purchase goods that they will consume almost immediately. Examples of consumption borrowing include using a credit card to pay for a dinner at a restaurant, using company financing to buy a living room set from a furniture store, or borrowing money from a bank on a home equity loan to take a long summer vacation. The problem with consumption borrowing is that the consumer obligates his future income to pay for goods that provide him pleasure today.

Many people become trapped in a web of consumption borrowing. They fail to restrict their spending to amounts that they can pay completely with presently available funds. Had they limited their credit card balances to what they could pay in full, they would have avoided interest payments. However, by spending beyond their means, they find themselves paying off not only the original purchases but also substantial amounts of interest. As they continue to spend for immediate gratification, they begin to multiply their debts. Soon they must borrow increasing additional amounts against their income further and further into the future. Before they realize what has happened, they are hopelessly in debt. Scripture maintains that those who live only for the moment are not wise and warns, "He that loveth pleasure shall be a poor man: he that loveth wine and oil shall not be rich" (Prov. 21:17).

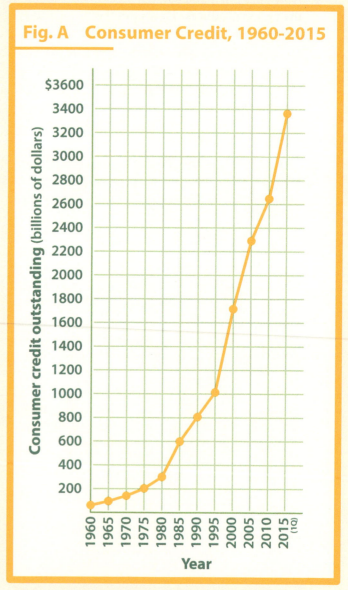

Fig. A Consumer Credit, 1960-2015

Covers most short- and intermediate-term credit extended to individuals. Credit secured by real estate is excluded.
Source: Board of Governors of the Federal Reserve System

Much of today's consumption borrowing results from either covetousness or a lack of financial planning. Covetousness is a person's strong desire to possess something he lacks but is convinced he should have. The covetous person sees the item he desires and believes he must have, and he buys it. However, lacking the money to pay for it, he willingly obligates his future income by using credit. The more he repeats this process, the further into debt he sinks. Scripture continually admonishes the believer to beware of covetousness (Luke 12:15) and to be content with what he has (Heb. 13:5). Rather than obligating tomorrow's income to pay for today's purchases, Scripture maintains that the child of God should trust the Lord to meet his current needs (Luke 12:28).

Others with debt problems may not be covetous, but their borrowing evidences poor financial planning. For example, a person may save the money necessary to purchase an automobile but fail to take into account all the expenses incidental to car ownership—property taxes, insurance, and maintenance. Once that person initiates the automobile purchase, he finds himself taking on debt to pay for what he failed to anticipate and add into the total cost of buying a car.

ROBERT MORRIS (1734–1806)

Financier of the American Revolution

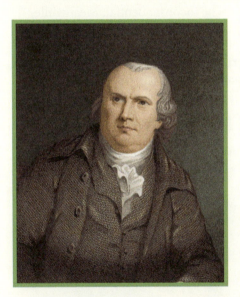

After emigrating from England in 1747, Robert Morris learned the responsibilities of business in a mercantile firm in Philadelphia. His industry and integrity propelled him into a very successful partnership in the import-export business. When the American colonies began their struggle for independence, Morris represented Pennsylvania in the Continental Congress; and he was one of only two men who signed all three of the nation's early and notable documents: the Declaration of Independence, the Articles of Confederation, and the Constitution.

During the Revolution, Morris devoted his efforts to financing the costly maintenance of the Continental Army. For a while he served as chairman of the Secret Committee of Trade, organizing the importation of vital military supplies. Then from 1781 to 1784, with the nation's financial problems intensifying, the Continental Congress called upon him to serve as superintendent of finance. In that office, Morris displayed remarkable skill and self-sacrifice as he steered the almost-penniless government through a continuous financial crisis. In this effort Morris used his own reputation and credit to secure precious funds and patience from increasingly skeptical creditors. Morris thus earned the widespread appreciation and admiration that later sent him to the Constitutional Convention and to the Senate for one term.

After the war Morris's success in renewed business interests added to his fortunes, and he determined to increase his wealth further by land speculation. Morris and two partners bought millions of acres of western lands and thousands of lots in the rising capital, Washington, D.C., incurring heavy debts in the process. When economic decline in Europe and other problems frustrated the finance and sale of these lands, Morris began to face his own financial crisis. Soon he was beset by angry creditors seeking promised payments. "I am latterly become so fully convinced that much wealth does not increase happiness that I cannot help regretting that so much of my time has been spent in the pursuit of it," he lamented, "and I would this moment give up a great deal of what I possess if by such a cession I could at once close the scene of business and become master at will of my time." And on another occasion he vowed, "If I can once get square, I will never contract another debt."

Morris saw the grand mansion he was building in Philadelphia stand unfinished because of his distress, and eventually his unpaid debts of $3 million brought full legal consequences. The frustrated financier spent three years, 1798–1801, in the Prune Street debtors' prison in Philadelphia. Though George Washington and other men of prominence visited him in prison and continued to offer their friendship, they could not extricate him from the financial pit into which he had fallen. Morris spent the last five years of his life humbly living on the support of his family and friends. The renowned financier of the Revolution died a pauper.

TRUTH IN LENDING ACT

Because borrowers were often unaware of the interest rates, finance charges, and other conditions of their loans, Congress passed the Consumer Credit Protection Act. More commonly known as the Truth in Lending Act, this legislation took effect in 1969 and has since been amended several times.

The law requires that creditors disclose the annual percentage rate of the interest they charge, the dollar amount of all finance charges, and all other conditions of the loan. The act also requires regulations for the advertising of credit terms by lending institutions, and it provides some legal guidelines for companies that issue credit cards. The Federal Trade Commission holds the most responsibility for enforcing these and other provisions of the Truth in Lending Act.

While much of the borrowing for current consumption is difficult to justify from Scripture, many Christians believe some circumstances exist in which this borrowing may be not only an acceptable practice but actually good stewardship. The first exception arises when the price of a good is rising faster than the cost of debt used to purchase it. If, for example, the price of an automobile were rising at a rate of 30 percent per year and the interest rate on debt were 20 percent, it would actually be less costly to purchase the car today with borrowed money. As an illustration, let us assume that you were planning to purchase a certain automobile at the end of the year. The present price of that car is $15,000, but with costs rising at 30 percent, you would pay $19,500 at the end of the year. However, if you purchased the car today with borrowed funds at an interest rate of 20 percent and repaid the $15,000 loan at the

Fig. B Car Buying: Present Credit v. Future Cash

	Purchased today with borrowed money	Purchased at the end of the year
Price of car	$15,000	$19,500
Cost of loan (20%)	$3,000	$0
Total cost of car	$18,000	$19,500

end of the year with a single payment, you would pay a total of only $18,000. Of course, in reality this would be an unusual circumstance.

Many believe that interest-free loans constitute a second possible exception to the warnings against consumption borrowing. For example, let us assume that you have been saving to buy a new piano. You have accumulated $2,000 in a savings account yielding 4 percent interest per year. Instead of withdrawing the cash to make the purchase, you use the store's "90 days same as cash" terms. That is, you are allowed to owe the store the $2,000 for three months, and provided you pay the full price at the end of the period, you incur no interest charges. At the end of the ninety days, you withdraw the cash and pay the bill in full. Now, during the three months between purchasing the piano and withdrawing the money, you earned over $19 in interest on your deposit. You would have lost that interest had you chosen to forgo using debt. In this example, many would commend you for good stewardship. You have not only the piano but also an additional $19. Note, however, this example worked only because you already had the money necessary for the piano.

Certainly circumstances exist in which consumption borrowing is less costly than paying cash for purchases, but such exceptions to the rule are few and the savings can sometimes be inconsequential. Meanwhile, the temptation to borrow can become overwhelming. Christians are well advised to proceed cautiously into consumption borrowing, prayerfully considering biblically justifiable reasons for their purchases.

INVESTMENT BORROWING

While consumption borrowing is often the impulsive use of tomorrow's income to obtain today's enjoyments,

An interest-free loan may actually allow a consumer to save money on a major purchase.

investment borrowing is the calculated use of debt to purchase goods that will increase in value, produce income in the future, or reduce expenses.

One type of investment borrowing uses debt to purchase **appreciating assets**, or goods that increase in value over time. Examples of appreciating assets include real estate, art, antiques, and diamonds. Obviously, if the price of an object rises faster than the cost of the money the consumer borrowed to make the purchase, the borrower will experience a profit. The problem, however, is determining which items are truly appreciating assets. Many believe that real estate is always an appreciating asset, but that may not be true. At various times many areas in the United States have experienced severe drops in the real estate market. The Christian needs to be very careful when purchasing what he believes to be appreciating assets; those items just might not appreciate. Seeking advice from those with knowledge and experience in dealing with those assets is a good, biblical course to follow (Prov. 11:14; 15:22; 24:6).

The second type of investment borrowing uses borrowed money to purchase goods that will increase a person's income. For example, some laborers borrow money to purchase the tools that they will need to earn income. Without those tools, they could not compete in their labor market. This situation is similar to business firms' borrowing money to purchase tools of production. An extension of this idea is a person's using credit to purchase an automobile to transport himself to his job. Some would also see the using of debt to finance a college education as an example of this type of investment borrowing. Their reasoning is that the loan pays for training that prepares the graduate for employment in a career that pays higher than one he would likely have without the education.

A third category of investment borrowing uses borrowed funds to reduce expenses. When a business firm purchases insulation to install in the ceiling of a factory, it is not purchasing an asset that will appreciate in value, and the insulation certainly will not generate additional sales. Management justifies its use of credit by pointing out that the insulation reduces its energy costs. The insulation could reduce the firm's electric bill by $2,000 per year, while the annual cost of the loan's interest is only $1,500. Likewise, many homeowners use debt to purchase cost-reducing goods for their homes. For example, depending on the rates in a homeowner's region, it may be financially advantageous to borrow the money necessary to switch from gas to electric power or vice versa.

Consumer credit can have profitable uses. Whether for consumption or investment borrowing, there are circumstances in which your using it demonstrates good stewardship. However, as with other financial practices, consumer credit can also be easily misused with disastrous consequences. Giving in to covetousness either for immediate gratification or for a desire to get rich has been the ruin of many. Before you avail yourself of consumer credit, remember that Christ said to "beware of coveteousness" (Luke 12:15) and that "the love of money is the root of all evil" (1 Tim. 6:10). Ask yourself why you are taking on the debt, and let biblical admonitions guide your decision.

REVIEW QUESTIONS

1. What are the two reasons for borrowing money?
2. Identify two situations in which consumption borrowing could be acceptable.
3. Some would see the using of debt to finance a college education as an example of which type of investment borrowing?
4. Develop your own biblical view of debt. Discuss three or more Scripture passages to support your view. (Passages may be ones that were discussed in the chapter.) Be prepared to explain your view to the class.

TERMS

consumption borrowing	102
investment borrowing	105
appreciating assets	105

CHAPTER SIX
ECONOMIC SYSTEMS

6A EARLY ECONOMIC SYSTEMS — 106

6B MODERN ECONOMIC SYSTEMS — 110

6A EARLY ECONOMIC SYSTEMS

Throughout history, men have sought to control entire civilizations, not only militarily and politically but economically as well. These leaders have wished to answer the three key economic questions (see Sec. 5B) according to their own desires and so have sought to control the economic choices of their own people and those they have conquered. However, in the latter part of the eighteenth century, new economic philosophies began to reshape the thinking and actions of those in power, and what many had viewed as a constant in history began to change.

MERCANTILISM

From around the year 1500 until 1776, most of the national leaders of Western Europe subscribed to an economic philosophy known as **mercantilism**. Mercantilism promoted the acquisition of precious metals, not as the means to an end but as the end itself. The European monarchs who accepted this philosophy pursued, then, one dominant economic goal—to increase their holdings of gold and silver. To be the wealthiest one on the continent, a nation had to possess the greatest amount of gold and silver. Mercantilism misled these rulers into thinking that stockpiling money was the same as accumulating wealth. In their efforts to amass fortunes, they committed themselves and their people to a five-point program:

1. Exploration: Discover and seize new sources of gold and silver by sending explorers abroad to plunder less-developed civilizations and by supporting privateers to steal from neighboring nations.

2. Trade: Increase exportation of goods and services while decreasing importation of foreign goods. Mercantilists recognized that when a nation sold more goods to other nations than it purchased from them, it had more gold coming in than flowing out; thus, it enjoyed a **favorable balance of trade**.

3. Domestic manufacturing: Increase domestic manufacturing (manufacturing within the country) to produce more goods to sell abroad. Mercantilists considered the manufacture of goods for the nation's own people to be of secondary importance because selling goods to its own citizens did not increase the nation's stockpile of gold and silver.

4. Colonization: Encourage the colonization of new territories to acquire new supplies of the factors of production. The motherland would use the new raw materials to produce goods that competing nations could not. To ensure maximum profit, the

mother country usually forbade the colonies from selling their raw materials to competing nations even when they offered higher prices. This policy usually increased tensions between the colonists and their monarchs.

5. Alliances/treaties/conquest: Arrange all foreign relationships in a way that minimizes competition, or conquer European neighbors to obtain their factors of production.

LAISSEZ-FAIRE LIBERALISM

Understandably, mercantilism fostered political discontent and economic distress within the home countries and in their colonies. By the mid-1700s a growing number of political philosophers began to argue in favor of abolishing monarchies and replacing them with representative governments; however, those who favored economic freedom had no prominent champion around whom they could rally. Then in 1776 a relatively obscure economist with the unassuming name of Adam Smith became the focus of attention. Smith published a treatise against mercantilism that was so logical in its presentation, so explicit in its condemnations, and so specific in its remedies that the world took notice; and the economic landscape of Europe changed forever.

Vessels such as these brought more than just people and goods from the Old World to the New; they also brought ideas, such as the mercantilist system.

In his lengthy book (with its rather lengthy title), *An Inquiry into the Nature and Causes of the Wealth of Nations*, Adam Smith argued that it is not the accumulation of gold and silver that makes a nation wealthy but that it is rather the economic prosperity of its people. Mercantilism, he maintained, was illogical. If taken to its ultimate conclusion, the "wealthiest" nation would be the one that had laid its own land waste to produce food that foreigners would consume. The people of such a nation would be cold, hungry, and angry as a result of their leader's selling to others the goods that they needed. Its persistent quest to obtain ever larger stockpiles of precious metals would often cause the mercantilist nation to take aggressive actions against neighboring countries. Consequently, while the mercantilist nation saw itself as prospering, it was actually creating a growing resentment and an increasing number of enemies. Though it may have been amassing a significant hoard of gold and silver, its policies did not result in its being a truly wealthy nation but rather a truly miserable one.

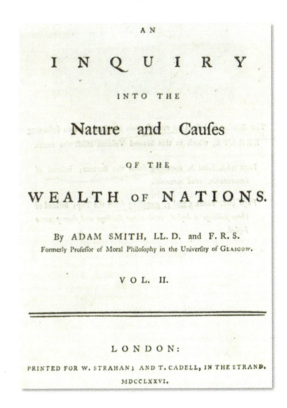

The root problem, according to Smith, was the misconception that money is wealth. From a purely economic standpoint, money is not wealth; it only enables a person to purchase wealth. Items that provide some measure of utility, such as food, clothing, transportation, homes, and other goods and services, constitute wealth. Money provides no utility of itself. You cannot live in it, eat it, wear it, or drive it. Money is only a means to an end, not the end itself. It is only a tool that individuals use to acquire economic wealth. To assume that the hoarding of money equates with being wealthy is like saying that the most successful carpenter is the one who accumulates the most hammers and screwdrivers.

After destroying the "money is wealth" myth, Adam Smith then presented what he saw as the true path to national enrichment: **laissez faire**. Loosely translated from the French, *laissez faire* means to "let alone." Smith argued that monarchs who wished their countries to prosper should leave their subjects alone and allow them to seek their own profit. People must be free to specialize in those jobs for which they are best suited and to exchange their products with others. Because of Smith's philosophy of limited government and

ADAM SMITH (1723-90)
Father of Laissez-Faire Economics

Adam Smith was born on June 5, 1723, in the small town of Kirkcaldy, Scotland, just a few weeks after his father died. A rather humorous (although at the time distressful) incident occurred when Adam was three years old. While his mother was visiting her brother, Hercules Smith, in his Strathenry home, Adam was left to play in the front yard. While playing, he was kidnapped by a band of gypsies. During the chase that ensued, Adam was dropped in a forest to hasten the gypsies' escape. "He would have made, I fear," said one biographer, "a poor gypsy."

Adam proved to be a bright student and entered the University of Glasgow at the age of fourteen. While studying there, he came under the influence of Francis Hutcheson, a professor of moral philosophy who, while a moral and upright man, instilled in Adam the philosophy that human reason is to be held in the highest esteem, even above the Word of God.

After three years at the University of Glasgow, Smith received a scholarship to attend England's prestigious Oxford University. The scholarship was set up to help train Scotsmen for the ministry of Jesus Christ. He accepted the scholarship but pursued a course of study leading to a degree not in religion, as was expected, but in political philosophy.

Because he knew that he would never become a minister of the gospel, Smith left Oxford in 1746, one year before graduation. He returned to Kirkcaldy intending to become a tutor, but parents were reluctant to hire him since he tended to be of "absent manner and bad address" (in other words, forgetful and sloppy). He did find employment as a traveling lecturer in 1748, and later, in 1751, his old school, the University of Glasgow, gave him a position teaching logic. In 1752 he was made chairman of the department of Moral Philosophy. He remained in this position until 1764 when he resigned to become the personal tutor of the young Duke of Buccleugh. While touring Europe with his young pupil, Smith met many of the influential European philosophers of the day, but eventually he became bored and began work on *The Wealth of Nations*, a classic work that earned him the nickname of "the economist's Shakespeare."

personal responsibility, he became known as the Father of Laissez-Faire Economics.

Critics of Adam Smith's new approach argued that his laissez-faire liberalism would create a nation of selfish, greedy, and antisocial people. In *The Wealth of Nations*, Smith countered that when governments leave people to practice their own self-interest, while enforcing laws to prevent theft and fraud, the people will actively seek out the needs of others to satisfy them in a profitable way—an outcome he believed to be far more satisfactory than the outcomes of mercantilism.

> But man has almost constant occasion for the help of his brethren, and it is in vain for him to expect it from their benevolence only. He will be more likely to prevail if he can interest their self-love in his favour, and show them that it is for their own advantage to do for him what he requires of them. . . . It is not from the benevolence of the butcher, the brewer, or the baker, that we expect our dinner, but from their regard to their own interest.

As a result of seeking their own profit, Smith argued, people will eventually make the nation wealthier since a nation is merely a collection of individuals.

> As every individual, therefore, endeavours as much as he can both to employ his capital in the support of domestic industry, and so to direct that industry that its produce may be of the greatest value; every individual necessarily labours to render the annual revenue of the society as great as he can. He generally, indeed, neither intends to promote the public interest, nor knows how much he is promoting it. By preferring the support of domestic to that of foreign industry, he intends only his own security; and by directing that industry in such a manner as its produce may be of the greatest value, he intends only his own

laissez faire (less ay FAIR)

ORIGIN OF LAISSEZ FAIRE

In France during the 1600s, Louis XIV ruled with a heavy hand in economic matters. The results of his economic decisions were disappointing, however, so his finance minister is said to have asked a leading French businessman what should be done to improve the economic situation. The reply, as it is told, was *"Laissez-nous faire,"* which can be translated as "Leave us alone."

In the eighteenth century, *liberalism* meant "liberty."

HELPING YOU SEE THE INVISIBLE HAND

A marvelous advantage of the market economy of capitalism is that the goods and services that people want are almost always available. The market self-adjusts to meet consumer demands. No one has to set up a master plan for providing just the right fruits, vegetables, meats, and other items in each community. Whether a person goes to the store on Monday evening to buy carrots or Saturday morning to buy bread, he will almost always find those goods because it is to the grocer's benefit to keep frequently desired items in stock. It is also in the best interest of grocery suppliers to keep providing the grocer with the things he wishes to stock. Furthermore, it is to the benefit of bakers, farmers, ranchers, factory owners, and other producers to keep grocery wholesalers supplied with those goods. Thus, all participants work independently for their own profit, but in doing so, they work together to ensure that consumers have desirable products readily available. This is Adam Smith's "invisible hand" at work.

gain, and he is in this, as in many other cases, led by an invisible hand to promote an end which was no part of his intention. Nor is it always the worse for the society that it was no part of it. By pursuing his own interest he frequently promotes that of the society more effectually than when he really intends to promote it.

Smith believed that society is better served by allowing the pursuit of self-interest because people rarely work as hard for others as they do for themselves: "I have never known much good done by those who affected to trade for the public good."

SECTION REVIEW 6A

1. What economic system prevailed in Europe from the 1500s to the 1700s?
2. What was the major economic goal of European countries from the 1500s to the 1700s?
3. According to Adam Smith, how might a mercantilist nation create bad feelings among its own people and with its neighbors?
4. According to Adam Smith, why would a laissez-faire economic policy work?

6B MODERN ECONOMIC SYSTEMS

In Adam Smith's day the great debate in economics pitted his laissez-faire liberalism against government-regulated mercantilism. The debate still continues between those who favor economic freedom and those who believe that the state should control economic events, but today the two sides of the argument are **capitalism** and **socialism**. To determine whether a nation follows a more capitalistic or socialistic philosophy, you need to know how that nation answers two fundamental questions:

1. Who owns the nation's factors of production?
2. Who answers the three economic questions?

If a central authority, a committee, or the people in common own the factors of production and make nearly all significant economic decisions, then the economic system is predominantly socialistic. If, on the other hand, private individuals own the factors of production and make almost all significant economic decisions, the economic system is strongly capitalistic.

Since all countries fall somewhere between complete (or radical) capitalism and extreme socialism (or pure communism), it is wise to think of capitalism and socialism as general categories containing many systems, which are variations on the themes of ownership and decision making. Figure 6-1 illustrates an economic spectrum with communism at one end and radical capitalism at the other. Between these two extremes, you see centralized socialism, social democracy, state capitalism, and classic liberal capitalism. These systems merge into one another as you move from one end of the spectrum with its emphasis on government ownership and government decision making to the other end of the spectrum with its emphasis on individual ownership and individual decision making.

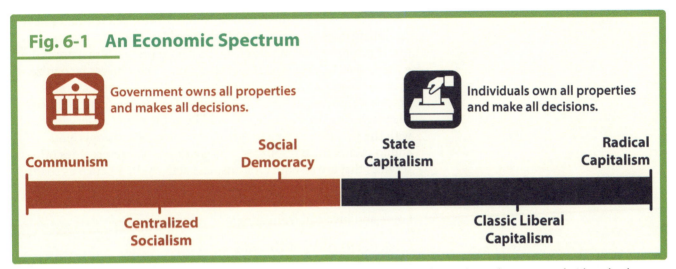

Rather than being capitalistic or socialistic, nations are relatively capitalistic or relatively socialistic when compared with each other.

FORMS OF CAPITALISM

The capitalist end of the economic spectrum can be broken down into three different forms of capitalism. You could classify these forms using different criteria and different names, and should you choose to pursue this study, you would likely find outside sources that offer more varieties or types of capitalism than are presented in this text. However, for your present study, this text presents three distinct forms: radical, classic liberal, and state capitalism.

Radical Capitalism

Radical capitalism is capitalism in its most extreme form and exists only as an economic theory. No country's economic system falls under radical capitalism. Were such a country to exist, you could identify it by the following characteristics: 1) private citizens would own all the factors of production, 2) private citizens would make all decisions regarding what and how to produce and who would receive what is produced, 3) there would be no government, and 4) the economic market would be free to operate without any outside regulations or interferences. While at first glance this theory may be attractive, a closer examination reveals that radical capitalism is unscriptural and impractical.

Radical capitalism is unscriptural because it denies the legitimacy of government. It places all decision making in the hands of private individuals, thus making government unnecessary. Each individual essentially becomes his own government, just as in Judges 21:25, "In those days there was no king in Israel: every man did that which was right in his own eyes." There is no need or desire for any higher power in this system, yet the Word of God teaches that God ordained human governments and specified their primary responsibility.

> Let every soul be subject unto the higher powers. For there is no power but of God: the powers that be are ordained of God. . . . For he is the minister of God to thee for good. But if thou do that which is evil, be afraid; for he beareth not the sword in vain: for he is the minister of God, a revenger to execute wrath upon him that doeth evil. (Rom. 13:1, 4)

Apart from its being unscriptural, another principal reason radical capitalism does not exist outside the world of economic theory is that it is impractical. As much as most entrepreneurs may want the government to leave businesses alone, they nonetheless recognize that free markets need government. The government maintains property laws and provides the means of enforcing them. Without such laws, smaller businesses would be at the mercy of larger ones with the financial means to infringe on patents and copyrights and to monopolize resources. The government also provides other services that are essential for business activity. Items such as roads, bridges, and national defense, if left to private individuals, would lack uniformity and consistency and would likely invite chaos at home and invasion from abroad.

Classic Liberal Capitalism

Classic liberal capitalism is the form of capitalism that arose from the writings of Adam Smith. It accepts the existence of government but allows it only minimal ownership of resources and decision-making power to perform its responsibilities.

Adam Smith's outline of the proper governmental functions in *The Wealth of Nations* became the outline for government under classic liberal capitalism. He declared that for citizens to enjoy economic and political liberty, they must strictly limit their government to the performance of three major duties. First, the government is to protect its citizens from foreign aggression. Today, this would also include the responsibility to protect citizens from terrorist acts. The government accomplishes this task by maintaining a national defense system: "The first duty of the sovereign, that of protecting the society from the violence and invasion of other independent societies, can be performed only by means of a military force."

Second, the government is to protect the rights of its citizens from infringements by others. Smith recognized that human nature is depraved and that left unrestrained, a free market would destroy itself. For example, a citizen might bargain with another to work for a certain wage, but without the threat of punishment, the employer could refuse to pay the employee. To protect citizens from one another, Adam Smith argued that the government should provide a legislature to enact just laws, a police force to restrain lawbreakers, and courts of law to judge and punish those who commit crimes.

> The second duty of the sovereign [is] that of protecting, as far as possible, every member of the society from the injustice or oppression of every other member of it. . . . Men may live together in society with some tolerable degree of security, though there is no civil magistrate to protect them from the injustice of those passions. But avarice and ambition in the rich, in the poor the hatred of labour and the love of present ease and enjoyment, are the passions which prompt to invade property, passions much more steady in their operation, and much more universal in their influence.

Third, the government is to provide **public goods**. Public goods are goods and services that benefit all or nearly all of a nation's people and that private firms or individuals would not choose to produce because they could not do so profitably. Highways, power plants, public schools, military operations, national parks, and a monetary system are examples of public goods. These types of goods could be produced privately, but the owners could not prevent those who refused to pay from utilizing the good. In short, public goods are necessary goods and services that if not provided by the government would not be available, would be available but not affordable, or would be available but not consistently reliable.

The third and last duty of the sovereign or commonwealth is that of erecting and maintaining those public institutions and those public works, which, though they may be in the highest degree advantageous to a great society, are, however, of such a nature that the profit could never repay the expence to any individual.... Works and institutions of this kind are chiefly those for facilitating the commerce of the society, and those for promoting the instruction of the people.

State Capitalism

Many modern economies operate under a variation of capitalism called **state capitalism**. Under this system private citizens own the vast majority of natural resources, financial capital, and labor, but the government freely intervenes in the decision-making process to carry out its economic and social goals.

To see this variation of capitalism at work you need look no further than the day-to-day interventions of the US government in the American economy. For example, Americans are free to own houses and factories, but the government creates policies to regulate which construction firms may build those houses and factories, how they may build them, and where they may locate them. Individuals may own businesses, but the government intervenes with decisions regarding the minimum wage that the owner must pay the workers, the jobs that certain workers may or may not perform, and the maximum number of hours that employers may require of their workers.

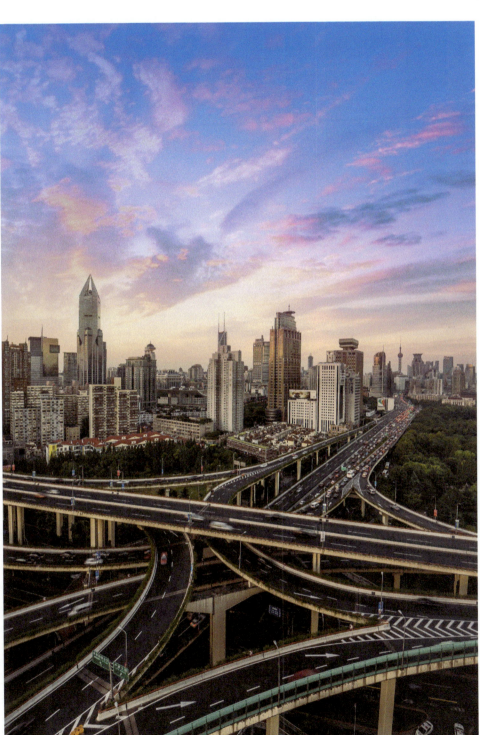

Public goods and services, such as highway construction and maintenance, are provided by the government in a classic liberal economy.

A nation under extreme state capitalism is known as a **welfare state**. In a welfare state, taxes are very high (generally averaging over 50 percent), and funds are redistributed in such a way that the government claims to care for its citizens from "the cradle to the grave." Several European nations could be classified as welfare states, with Sweden being perhaps the best example.

FORMS OF SOCIALISM

At this point you may be asking, "Just where does capitalism end and socialism begin?" While *capitalism* and *socialism* are relative terms, there does appear to be a clear dividing line between the two. As nations move further to the left on the economic spectrum, the government tends to take upon itself more ownership of resources and decision making. At the point, however, when the government actually steps in and takes possession of the majority of the principal businesses, that nation has crossed the line into socialism.

Social Democracy

Social democracy is a transitional economic system bridging the gap between capitalism and socialism. Its predominant characteristic is the state's taking possession of those industries that are the cornerstones of the economy.

These vital industries include transportation (auto manufacturers, airlines, shipping firms, and trucking companies), communications (telephone, television, and Internet), energy (nuclear power and petroleum—drilling, refining, and distribution companies), financial markets (banks, finance companies, and insurance companies), and health care (hospitals, clinics, and pharmaceutical businesses). This government tolerates individual ownership of smaller, nonessential businesses but highly regulates them. When a nation's government assumes ownership of companies on such a large scale, it is engaging in **nationalization**. Having experimented with nationalization for the sake of providing employment and low-cost goods and services and having found that it was too expensive to maintain unprofitable companies, many Western European governments decided to sell their nationalized businesses back to private stockholders, an action referred to as **privatization**.

Some economic systems nationalize the energy industry because of its importance to a nation's economy.

Centralized Socialism

Centralized socialism maintains that the national government should be both the central owner and the decision maker in all economic affairs of the state. It is this brand of socialism that Karl Marx envisioned for the world.

In his **Communist Manifesto**, Marx argued that any arrangement of the tools of production short of total state ownership would be counterproductive. Beginning with the statement "The history of all hitherto existing society is the history of class struggle," Marx announced that historically it has been the nature of mankind to oppress one another, most notably the rich oppressing the poor. Karl Marx believed that being an employee in a capitalistic system was nothing more than being a slave. The wealthy business owner would pay his employees poverty wages, which they would meekly have to accept. After all, the business owner possessed the tools necessary to create goods. Without the tools, the employees would have no work. Marx held that all the money received from the sale of goods rightfully belonged to the employees who created those goods. Instead, the capitalists were diverting the employees' money to themselves in the form of profits. Marx maintained that eventually employees in capitalist economies would realize that they were slaves, rise up in rebellion against their masters, and take possession of the tools of production. Then the fruits of their labors would be theirs indeed, not profits for indolent capitalist factory owners. Having taken possession of the tools of production, the workers would then turn them over to the state, which would ensure that every worker would receive a fair wage. The government would also be responsible for seeing that no business would ever again use any worker merely as a tool to make profits for another person.

Since the state owns all factories and equipment, centralized socialism treats the nation's economy like one big company, and the nation's leaders act like a board of directors. Opponents of centralized socialism have criticized it as being extremely inefficient. First, by taking over the tools of production and outlawing profits, it destroys the incentive for entrepreneurs to take the risks necessary to develop new products and services. Thus, a centralized socialistic society is doomed to live either with outdated products or the fruits of stolen technology. Second, by leveling wages it eliminates the incentive of individual workers to produce more and better goods and services.

Some economic systems privatize certain sectors of the economy to allow them to function more efficiently and economically than when they are owned and operated by the government.

THE DIESELIZATION FIASCO

In the early 1960s the Soviet Union decided to standardize all Soviet-owned trucks and tractors to diesel rather than gasoline engines. Their reasons were that diesel fuel was safer, more efficient, and less expensive than gasoline and that even American companies were making such a switch. However, the plan did not work. Why?

The Soviet planners made several mistakes. First, rather than calculating the cost of the equipment using the market rate on borrowed money, they used a rate dictated by the state. That rate was too low and caused them to underestimate seriously the total cost of new diesel equipment. Second, they failed to acknowledge that Soviet diesel fuel was inferior to the rest of the world's fuel and was unsuitable for use. Consequently, they mistakenly regarded their diesel fuel as significantly cheaper at their controlled price. The market price of higher-quality, non-Soviet diesel fuel was not much less than gasoline. To avoid paying that higher market price, the Soviet planners began to use their own inferior fuel. The high sulfur content of this fuel quickly damaged or destroyed almost all the engines in the state-owned equipment.

While several problems contributed to the Soviet "dieselization" fiasco, the fundamental error was that the Soviet planners did not realize that there can never be an "official price" contrary to the market price. The market price of anything—money, equipment, or diesel fuel—comes not from a governmental edict but from a compromise agreement between buyers and sellers.

Thus, the society must tolerate mediocre workmanship producing faulty merchandise. Finally, by controlling prices in such a way that they are unrealistically low, societies under centralized socialism must live either with shortages or an ever-growing black market.

Centralized socialism is not common among modern industrial countries. During the early 1900s a number of poor but determined leaders sought to establish such a system in Mexico. These leaders promised their poor countrymen that they would soon reap the profits of their work. As each new leader conquered the former dictator, the poor laborers never saw their hopes fulfilled. Greed was rampant, and profits went to the newest dictator. Though the dictators often took land from the rich and parceled it out to the poor, poverty remained.

Communism

Economically speaking, **communism** is socialism in its most extreme form. Like radical capitalism, pure communism exists only in economic theory, developed primarily from the writings of Karl Marx. According to Marx, centralized socialism is merely a stepping stone to a better society. When schoolchildren in the former Soviet Union were asked in catechism fashion, "What is socialism?" they replied, "Socialism is the long, hard struggle between capitalism and communism." Marx wrote that centralized socialism is a transition period: a "time out" in which the government wrests ownership and control of the factors of production from the capitalists, purges the state of the greedy, and teaches the new generation the glories of sharing. Marx promised that after eradicating capitalism and properly preparing its people, the government would happily disband and turn the management of the factors of production over to everyone in common. This was to be much like taking the training wheels off a bicycle after a child has outgrown them. After eliminating socialism the communist nation would then automatically govern itself. Everyone in the society would selflessly concern himself with the welfare of all the other members. Each person would voluntarily contribute as much as he possibly could and would demand of society only that which he absolutely needed.

The former Soviet Union established a centralized socialist economy but never achieved true economic communism.

None of the modern examples of communism have succeeded in establishing this utopian system, and none ever will because sinful men cannot establish anything perfect. In the former Soviet Union and in Cuba, North Korea, and China, communist systems have resulted in widespread poverty, shortages of necessary goods and services, and political and religious oppression. The few who lead these systems are very wealthy, but the masses do not benefit. Communism has the fundamental flaw of assuming that man is basically good and that if placed in the proper circumstances, he will naturally seek the good of his fellow man. Such a belief is directly contrary to the biblical truths that man is basically sinful and that, as such, he is basically selfish. Even if placed in an ideal environment, sinful man will seek first his own good, not that of others.

CAPITALISM/SOCIALISM CONTRAST

After examining libertarian and egalitarian fairness, the ideas of Adam Smith and Karl Marx, and the differences between capitalism and socialism, you may wonder which economic system is really the better one. Socialists point to their low unemployment rate and their classless society in which no businesses exploit the working class as arguments for the superiority of their system. Capitalists, however, make the case for their system by pointing to their higher standard of living.

Entire books have been written on this question, and the scope of this text certainly does not permit such an in-depth analysis. As you read in Chapter 5 regarding the distribution question, there may be Christians on both sides of this comparison who feel strongly about the correctness of their position. Rather than supporting capitalism or socialism simply because you associate one with being "conservative" and the other with being "liberal," you should be able to analyze these two systems in the light of God's Word and base your conclusions on biblical truth. While the Bible does not provide an economic blueprint, it does provide principles that allow Christians to evaluate any economic system. God also expects believers to be wise and promises to provide the wisdom they need to make right choices. As you look at capitalism and socialism, you should recognize that all systems created by humans, whether they are political, social, or economic, have flaws because man himself is sinful.

Capitalism finds support in Scripture in two important principles. First, it fits the principle of personal, private ownership of property.

STANDARD OF LIVING

When economists speak of the standard of living in a country, they are generally referring to a measure of the quality of life in that country. They focus particularly on the material aspects of life, which include the average level of real income (not the dollar amount a person earns but what that person's income can buy), the availability of goods and services, access to education, and the availability of health care. Of course, all these aspects relate directly to the economic activity in a country. A greater amount of economic activity coupled with a widespread opportunity for participation in that activity generally results in a higher standard of living. Capitalists are quick to state that their system produces this greater amount of activity and opportunity for participation in it.

Acts 5 illustrates this position in the story of Ananias and Sapphira, who sold a possession, donated a portion of the proceeds, and lied by saying that they had contributed all the money. Peter rebuked them, saying, "Whiles it remained, was it not thine own? and after it was sold, was it not in thine own power?" (v. 4). The two were punished, not for refusing to give away their property, but for lying to God about what they did with the proceeds. Also, some of the first laws God gave to the Israelites in the Old Testament dealt with the sanctity of property: "Thou shalt not steal" (Exod. 20:15), "Thou shalt not covet . . . any thing that is thy neighbour's" (Exod. 20:17), and "Thou shalt not remove thy neighbour's landmark, which they of old time have set in thine inheritance, which thou shalt inherit in the land that the Lord thy God giveth thee to possess it" (Deut. 19:14). Socialists argue that one of the primary evils in the world is the capitalist principle of property ownership. The Bible, however, does not support this argument.

Second, Scripture also supports the principle of individual accountability for decisions with its accompanying truths of individual rewards and punishments based on those decisions. The parable of the talents (Matt. 25:14–30) illustrates this principle. The master of the estate gave certain amounts of money to his three servants prior to his departure. One received five talents, another received two, and the third received one. The first two servants invested their talents wisely, doubling their master's money, but the third did nothing with his portion. Upon the master's return the responsible servants were honored while the careless servant was punished. Christ also taught that to whom much is given, much is required and that there will be some whose punishment will be more severe than that of others (Luke 12:47–48). Capitalistic systems promote individual accountability by advocating that private firms or businesspersons make their own economic decisions.

Capitalism supports the private ownership of property.

Socialistic systems emphasize the government's power to make economic decisions, and by doing so they tend to rob people of their personal accountability. Under socialism the group becomes more important than the individual. Unlike the biblical principle of rewarding the diligent and penalizing the irresponsible, socialist systems tend to reward laziness as a by-product of their egalitarian goal of leveling incomes. Though the Bible says nothing specifically about socialism, we can be critical of any aspect of it that encourages what the Bible discourages.

Americans living in the post–Cold War era tend to support capitalism since capitalism seems to work better than socialism, but capitalist societies have weaknesses as well. In some eras, business barons in capitalist societies have exploited their workers, paying them pitifully low wages while reaping substantial profits themselves. The Scriptures address this problem and clearly instruct Christian business owners to treat their employees with respect, pay them a decent wage, and pay them on time:

"Masters, give unto your servants that which is just and equal; knowing that ye also have a Master in heaven" (Col. 4:1).

"Woe unto him that buildeth his house by unrighteousness, and his chambers by wrong; that useth his neighbour's service without wages, and giveth him not for his work" (Jer. 22:13).

"Thou shalt not defraud thy neighbour, neither rob him: the wages of him that is hired shall not abide with thee all night until the morning" (Lev. 19:13).

Another danger of capitalism lies in its very success. Economic success is not a bad thing. God promised Israel material blessings if the nation would keep its covenant with Him (Deut. 8:6–10). However, God also warned the Israelites to beware lest prosperity cause them to forget Him (Deut. 8:11–20). The same danger applies to a successful capitalist society in which economic growth and the consumption of goods become the driving motivations of its citizenry. Scripture warns that the love of money is the source of all kinds of evil (1 Tim. 6:10), and Jesus warned against laying treasures up on earth because a person's wealth can very easily become his god. As He said, "Ye cannot serve God and mammon" (Matt. 6:24). The story of the rich young ruler illustrates Jesus' statement. Proverbs 30:8 expresses well what our attitude toward wealth should be: "Give me

CHOOSING AN ECONOMIC SYSTEM AT PLYMOUTH PLANTATION

William Bradford's history of the Plymouth Plantation records a shift from a socialist communal economy to a capitalist economic structure that promoted individual accountability and reward. He concluded that the latter was better than the communal system. He said their experience

> may well evince the vanitie of that conceite of Platos and other ancients, applauded by some of later times;—that the taking away of propertie, and bringing in comunitie into a comone wealth, would make them happy and florishing; as if they were wiser then God. For this comunitie (so farr as it was) was found to breed much confusion and discontent, and retard much imployment that would have been to their benefite and comforte. For the yong-men that were most able and fitte for labour and service did repine that they should spend their time and strength to worke for other mens wives and children, with out any recompence. The strong, or man of parts, had no more in devission of victails and cloaths, then he that was weake and not able to doe a quarter the other could; this was thought injustice. . . . Let none objecte this is men's corruption, and nothing to the course it selfe. I answer, seeing all men have this corruption in them, God in his wisdome saw another course fiter for them.

(*Bradford's History "Of Plimoth Plantation"* [Boston: Wright & Potter, 1898], 163–64.)

neither poverty nor riches; feed me with food convenient for me." Those whom God blesses with wealth should pray for the wisdom to use it wisely.

Based on what you have studied, you should recognize that Scripture does not advocate socialism and that it criticizes some of the results of capitalism. Scripture does, however, clearly teach 1) the right to private ownership and 2) accountability for financial decisions (the prudent should be allowed to grow their wealth; the foolish should face the results of their foolishness). As you study, you must remember to let Scripture dictate your philosophy regarding your personal finances and the measure of your involvement in your government and its economic system.

From mercantilism to communism, you've now had a brief overview of several economic systems. As you survey the current state of world economies, you may notice that several capitalist nations seem to be moving progressively leftward along the spectrum of economic systems. They are adopting more and more socialistic ideas. Their governments are growing in size and influence, and their economic policies are intruding more into their nations' businesses. Socialist nations, meanwhile, also seem to be moving. Many of them seem to be drifting rightward on the scale. They are incorporating an increasing number of capitalistic principles to nurture their economies and to keep their citizenry contented. If these systems continue their present movements, the result will likely be a blending of these opposing systems, a meeting in the middle, so to speak, that could create a somewhat unified worldwide economic system. Such a system would be an essential part of a unified world government. You should seek to keep informed of current events and to use what you have learned and are learning to help you understand them. Above all, ask God to give you wisdom and discernment to evaluate them according to the truths presented in His Word.

SECTION REVIEW 6B

1. The answers to what two questions can determine whether a nation is capitalistic or socialistic?
2. Name and briefly describe each of the three forms of capitalism discussed in this chapter of the textbook.
3. Name and briefly describe each of the three forms of socialism discussed in this chapter of the textbook.
4. Name two economic principles of capitalism that are supported by Scripture, and give a Bible reference for each.

CHAPTER REVIEW

CONTENT QUESTIONS

1. Identify the five points of mercantilism.
2. What is the full title of Adam Smith's landmark economic treatise?
3. What two parts of Adam Smith's philosophy earned for him the title of the Father of Laissez-Faire Economics?
4. What is liberalism according to the classical definition?
5. Why is radical capitalism unscriptural?
6. Which economic system is closest to Adam Smith's writings?
7. What did Adam Smith declare to be the three functions of government?
8. What kind of economy does the United States have?
9. Social democracy is marked by the government's nationalizing which vital industries?
10. To an economist, what is meant by the phrases *standard of living* and *real income*?
11. In what two areas do supporters of socialism say their economic system is successful?
12. In what area do supporters of capitalism say their economic system is successful?
13. Identify two potential weaknesses of capitalism. Give biblical support for your answer.
14. Complete the following chart of economic systems.

Economic system	Who owns the factors of production?	Who answers the three key economic questions?

TERMS

mercantilism	106
favorable balance of trade	106
laissez faire	108
capitalism	110
socialism	110
radical capitalism	111
classic liberal capitalism	112
public goods	112
state capitalism	113
welfare state	113
social democracy	114
nationalization	114
privatization	114
centralized socialism	114
Communist Manifesto	114
communism	116

APPLICATION QUESTIONS

1. Why is money not wealth?
2. Along the economic spectrum provided earlier in the chapter, where would you place the economy of the United States? Give examples to support your answer.
3. You are the leader of your own country and have the power to establish its economic system. From the six systems explained in this text, choose one you would like to implement. Defend your selection economically and biblically.

PERSONAL FINANCE

TYPES OF CONSUMER CREDIT

While people may list many reasons for borrowing money, you know from the article "The Consumer and Debt" (p. 102) that there are only two basic purposes for consumer borrowing: consumption and investment. On the lender's side of the consumer credit equation, there are also only two types of credit. Depending primarily on what the consumer wishes to purchase, lending firms may grant either installment or open-end credit.

INSTALLMENT CREDIT

When a borrower signs a contract in which he agrees to pay for a purchase by making scheduled payments, he is using **installment credit**. Lending institutions refer to some installment loans as **single-payment loans**, meaning, as the name implies, that the borrower pays off the loan in one installment. Most installment credit, however, involves paying a specified amount of money each month for a given **term**, or number of months. Figure A is an example of the payments a creditor would require for a $10,000 installment loan for various terms and at differing interest rates. By using this table you can determine close approximations of the payments that even larger loans would require. For example, to determine the payment required for a $100,000 loan at 12 percent interest for one year, you would multiply $888.49 (the payment required for a $10,000 loan with those characteristics) by ten, since the amount of the loan is ten times $10,000. The monthly payment would then be approximately $8,885.

While not readily apparent, each payment of an installment loan pays down the two parts of the loan—the principal and the interest. The **principal** is the original amount the consumer borrows, and the **interest** is the additional charge the creditor requires to cover the cost of making the loan and to provide a profit. Figure B illustrates how lending institutions divide the borrower's payments. It presents a schedule for a $10,000 loan at 8 percent interest that the borrower will pay off in twelve monthly installments. It is an **amortization schedule**, a table that breaks down each payment into its principal and interest components. Note that since the principal amount is greatest at the beginning of the loan's term, the interest portion of the payment is at its highest

> The word *amortization* is of French origin, and it literally means "to take to the death." Hence, an amortization schedule provides the plan by which a borrower pays down the loan until he has terminated the debt.

Fig. A	Monthly Installment Payment (Principal and Interest) Required to Repay $10,000									
Number of monthly payments	Annual percentage rate									
	5%	6%	7%	8%	10%	12%	14%	16%	18%	20%
12	$856.07	$860.66	$865.27	$869.88	$879.16	$888.49	$897.87	$907.31	$916.80	$926.35
24	438.71	443.21	447.73	452.27	461.45	470.73	480.13	489.63	499.24	508.96
36	299.71	304.22	308.77	313.36	322.67	332.14	341.78	351.57	361.52	371.64
48	230.29	234.85	239.46	244.13	253.63	263.34	273.26	283.40	293.75	304.30
60	188.71	193.33	198.01	202.76	212.47	222.44	232.68	243.18	253.93	264.94
72	161.05	165.76	170.49	175.33	185.26	195.50	206.06	216.92	228.08	239.53

Each payment rounded to the nearest cent

Fig. B Amortization Schedule for $10,000 Loan at 8% for 12 Months

Payment number	Payment amount	Principal	Interest	Principal balance after this payment
1	$869.88	$803.22	$66.67	$9,196.78
2	869.88	808.57	61.31	8,388.21
3	869.88	813.96	55.92	7,574.25
4	869.88	819.39	50.49	6,754.86
5	869.88	824.85	45.03	5,930.01
6	869.88	830.35	39.53	5,099.66
7	869.88	835.89	34.00	4,263.77
8	869.88	841.46	28.43	3,422.31
9	869.88	847.07	22.82	2,575.24
10	869.88	852.72	17.17	1,722.52
11	869.88	858.40	11.48	864.12
12	869.88	864.12	5.76	0.00
Total	10,438.61	10,000.00	438.61	

for the first payment and declines as the borrower pays down more of the principal.

If you add the principal and interest payments, you will find that the total amount repaid is $10,438.61, which is about the same as multiplying $869.88 times twelve.

Amortization schedules can be truly revealing, especially to a person who borrows money for a long period of time. If someone borrows $80,000 for twenty-five years at 10 percent interest to purchase a house, his monthly payments will be $726.96. However, from that $726.96 of his first month's payment, only $60.29 will apply toward reducing the principal balance. The remaining $666.67 will go toward paying the interest. The $80,000 that the home buyer originally borrowed will actually cost him $218,088 ($726.96 × 300 payments). In most cases, however, a borrower can reduce his total interest

CONSUMER LOAN CLAUSES

To protect themselves, lenders often include several clauses in the fine print of loan contracts. Some of the following may be standard, but they can cause anxiety and prove troublesome for a borrower who does not understand their ramifications before he signs on a dotted line.

Acceleration clause: This provision makes the entire debt due immediately if the borrower is late on one payment; consequently, it increases the likelihood of repossession.

Add-on clause: When a borrower makes two separate credit purchases at different times from the same business and has not completely paid for the first purchase before making the second, an add-on clause consolidates both loans into one. If the borrower then defaults, he loses both purchases to repossession, even if he had finished paying for the first one.

Balloon clause: This clause allows the borrower to make only interest or other small payments on a loan until the last payment. Then the creditor requires full payment of the remaining principal or some other large sum.

Prepayment penalty: Many loan contracts stipulate that the borrower must pay most of the interest on a loan if he pays it off early. The amount owed is based on what lending firms commonly call the *rule of 78s*. According to this rule, the borrower pays 12/78 of the year's interest for the first month, 11/78 for the second month, 10/78 for the third, and so forth, for what would be a twelve-month total of 78/78 of the year's interest. Thus, if a borrower were paying 10 percent interest on a $10,000 loan, which he paid off after six months, instead of owing only half ($500) of the annual interest of $1,000, he would owe 57/78 of $1,000, or $731.

Repossession: If a borrower defaults on his loan payments, the creditor can physically seize the security for the loan according to the contract's stipulations and the state's legal procedures. Some laws and agreements may make repossession relatively simple for the creditor.

Garnishment: A creditor may make provision in a contract to withhold a portion of the borrower's wages until the debt is completely paid, but this garnishment of wages is limited to approximately one-fourth of the borrower's take-home pay.

cost by paying a little more per month than the loan agreement stipulates. All money in excess of the regular payment applies toward the principal balance, thus reducing the total interest the borrower must pay.

An installment loan may be either secured or unsecured. A **secured loan** is one that is backed by **collateral**, valuable goods that the creditor may take and resell in the event that the borrower does not repay the loan. In contrast, an **unsecured loan** is one that has no collateral behind it. Unsecured loans tend to carry more risk for creditors than do secured loans; therefore, on these loans lenders often charge higher interest rates and have higher standards a borrower must meet to qualify.

OPEN-END CREDIT

The second type of credit is known as **open-end credit**. Also known as revolving credit, an open-end account is one from which a debtor may continually draw money.

CREDIT CARD FRAUD

If current trends continue, Americans will lose approximately $1 billion every year from credit card fraud. Commonsense precautions by alert cardholders could stop most of these schemes.

First, when dealing with cashiers make sure that 1) the receipt shows the exact amount you purchased, 2) the cashier made no extra receipts, 3) the card does not leave your sight (no honest cashier needs to go to a back room with your credit card), and 4) you get the card back immediately.

Second, do not for any reason give anyone your social security or credit card number over the phone or in an e-mail. Dishonest people use several ploys to defraud others, including the following:
- They congratulate you for winning an incredible prize that you can claim simply by providing "proper identification."
- They make you a "fabulous one-time offer you can't refuse," an unbeatably low price on a desirable product that can be yours but only with a credit card purchase.
- They purport to be conducting credit card surveys.
- They claim to be bank representatives trying to clear up confusion about an account with a number similar to yours.

Any information you give may enable a thief to use your numbers to make purchases directly or to apply for credit cards in your name (true-name fraud). Victims of identity theft tell horror stories about how credit frauds or identity thieves almost wrecked their lives.

Third, be careful what you put in your trash. Shred unused and expired credit cards, old bills, and receipts.

Fourth, carry only the credit cards you will need for the purchases you intend to make. People often carry every credit card they possess at all times; then if they lose their wallets or have them stolen, their headaches are multiplied.

As a further precaution, keep a list of your cards and numbers to call if a card is lost or stolen. Also, compare the items on your monthly statement with your sales receipts. Report any discrepancies immediately.

A final warning comes from a television news account about homeowners placing their budgets on their personal computers. The problem this story disclosed was that a person cannot erase all the data from the hard drive permanently. Consequently, discarded hard drives often still hold identification numbers, account balances, and other personal information that determined and skilled computer hackers can access and use or sell.

"The prudent man looketh well to his going" (Prov. 14:15).

These accounts are not truly open-ended because each one usually has a predetermined **credit limit**, or maximum amount the person may borrow. To determine credit limits, lending institutions usually examine such things as the borrower's employer, income, length of residence, and past credit experience. Examples of revolving accounts include bank credit cards, such as MasterCard and Visa, department store credit cards, and some oil company credit cards. Since the principal amount may vary from month to month, the monthly payment may likewise vary. When his monthly statement arrives, the open-end credit borrower has the option to pay the entire balance, the minimum payment due, or any amount in between. Nearly all revolving accounts are unsecured.

Perhaps your only experience with installment credit has been a parent-financed loan that you repaid as a single-payment loan with no interest. You may, however, have a credit card and some personal experience with open-end credit. If so, you should also be aware of the high interest rates many credit cards charge to customers who make minimum payments as opposed to paying the balance in full.

This article reminds you again that interest is a downside of buying on credit. You pay not only for the item but for the interest to the lender as well.

When used carefully, installment and open-end credit can be helpful and prudent choices. You can possibly save money and avoid having to carry large sums of cash. However, each can also be a means of making provision for the flesh (Rom. 13:14) and lead to unrestrained borrowing. Then, debt piles upon debt and interest upon interest until it becomes nearly impossible for the consumer to extricate himself from his debt. As regards consumer credit, Christians must indeed "walk circumspectly, not as fools, but as wise" (Eph. 5:15).

REVIEW QUESTIONS

1. What are the two types of credit?
2. Why is more interest paid out of the first payment of an installment loan than out of the last payment?
3. What is the difference between a secured loan and an unsecured loan?
4. Which type of credit involves a credit limit?
5. What type of credit is extended through a credit card?

TERMS

installment credit	122
single-payment loans	122
term	122
principal	122
interest	122
amortization schedule	122
secured loan	124
collateral	124
unsecured loan	124
open-end credit	124
credit limit	125

UNIT THREE

UNIT THREE

ECONOMICS OF THE BUSINESS FIRM

Chapter 7
Forms of Business Ownership — 128

Personal Finance: Sources of Consumer Credit — 142

Chapter 8
The Stock Market — 146

Personal Finance: Creditworthiness — 160

Chapter 9
Market Structure and Competition — 164

Personal Finance: Cash Management — 180

CHAPTER SEVEN
FORMS OF BUSINESS OWNERSHIP

7A   SOLE PROPRIETORSHIPS — 129

7B   PARTNERSHIPS — 132

7C   CORPORATIONS — 135

Take a moment to observe the various objects around you. Almost all the goods you see are the result of successful entrepreneurship. Entrepreneurship, as you recall from Chapter 2, is the ability to coordinate the factors of production and the willingness to take risks to produce a good or service for a profit.

You could liken an entrepreneur to an orchestra conductor who first recognizes a potential audience and determines what it wishes to hear. Then he organizes a team of talented musicians, motivates them, prepares them to perform, and leads them in performances to meet his goals of attracting audiences, generating applause, and meriting funding. The entrepreneur, too, sees a potential market and determines what it is willing to purchase. He hires managers and workers, encourages their efforts, and leads them; he does all this with the intent that his efforts will produce profits. Yet, in many cases the entrepreneur comes out the loser. Studies indicate that 25–30 percent of all new businesses fail within two years, and around 50 percent fail within five years.

Once an entrepreneur has decided to start a new business, he has several other important decisions to make. One of the most significant is to determine which form of business ownership he will use. Nearly all businesses in the United States today fall into three categories: sole proprietorships, partnerships, and corporations. Each form of ownership has distinct advantages and disadvantages, depending on such factors as the size of the firm, the abilities of the owner, and the firm's tax situation.

7A SOLE PROPRIETORSHIPS

As its name suggests, a **sole proprietorship** is a business firm that has one owner. Examples of sole proprietorships include various cleaning services, part-time sales businesses run out of the home, and lawn-care services. While sole proprietorships always have only one owner, many operate with a number of managers or employees. Sole proprietorships are the most popular form of business in America today, accounting for approximately 75 percent of all the nation's business firms.

ADVANTAGES OF SOLE PROPRIETORSHIPS

The sole proprietorship offers owners several freedoms. These freedoms account for its tremendous popularity as a form of business ownership.

Freedom to Enter and Exit the Market Easily

In most cases a person can start a sole proprietorship simply by registering his new company's name with the clerk of court of the county in which he resides. There are, however, instances when the proprietors must obtain various licenses. Examples of such businesses include medical and dental practices, daycare centers, and food-handling enterprises. Usually, though, starting a sole proprietorship is as easy as locating and renting a building, putting out an "open for business" sign, and selling a product or service.

Getting out of business is just as easy; the proprietor sells any remaining goods, collects the debts due him, pays his bills, and quits.

Freedom from Outside Control

While the government holds sole proprietors accountable for any laws that apply to all businesses, it imposes no special "sole proprietorship laws." As far as the government is concerned, the business and the proprietor are one and the same.

In addition to having no special accountability to the government, the sole proprietor reports to no one concerning his business decisions. He has no partners with whom to negotiate and no stockholders to please. The proprietor may apply for bank loans, offer new products or services, discontinue old product lines, expand or contract the business, change prices, or take all the money out of the cash register for a vacation to the Bahamas without having to seek approval or permission from anyone.

The owners of sole proprietorships enjoy the freedoms that this form of business ownership allows.

Freedom to Retain Information

One of the greatest fears of a businessperson is having his strategies, financial information, and production methods discovered by his competitors. Except for a possible audit by the Internal Revenue

Service, the sole proprietor may keep his business information as secret as he wishes. As regards what he chooses to do with his business, he need not consult with a board of directors, nor must he keep stockholders informed.

Freedom from Paying Excessive Taxes

All income of a sole proprietorship is subject to taxation at the personal income tax rate. While this may not sound like an advantage to you, it is of great benefit to the proprietor. Taxes on corporations tend to be significantly higher than those on personal income.

Freedom from Being an Employee

Sole proprietors possess the unique advantage of self-employment. The age-old ideal of rugged individualism, independence, and personal responsibility is most attainable under this form of business ownership. The sole proprietor is free to come and go without having to punch a time clock. The fruits of his labor, be they successes or failures, belong to him alone.

DISADVANTAGES OF SOLE PROPRIETORSHIPS

Because of the attractive advantages of becoming one's own boss, many people jump into a sole proprietorship without thinking about the limitations and problems that come with this decision.

Unlimited Personal Financial Liability

If a proprietor is unable to pay the obligations of his business firm out of the income it generates, he will have to make up the difference out of his own personal funds. For example, if a person sues a sole proprietor for several million dollars and wins the lawsuit, the proprietor will have to do all that is necessary to pay the debt, including selling all the business assets, using his personal savings, and selling his personal possessions. Before rushing into a sole proprietorship, the Christian needs to pay careful attention to the words of Luke 14:28–29 and the biblical principle of counting the

The person who owns his own business is required to wear many "hats" during a business day.

cost: "For which of you, intending to build a tower, sitteth not down first, and counteth the cost, whether he have sufficient to finish it? Lest haply, after he hath laid the foundation, and is not able to finish it, all that behold it begin to mock him." The child of God has more at stake in a business failure than the loss of dollars and cents. He is accountable for damages done to his personal Christian testimony and to the cause of Christ.

Limited Management and Employee Skills

In most sole proprietorships the owner performs all the duties needed to keep the business going. He often acts as the staff manager, salesman, bookkeeper, secretary, manufacturer, service technician, and janitor. With so many roles to fill, he is unlikely to excel at all of them. This lack of expertise poses a problem for the proprietor, especially when he finds himself competing with firms that fill entire departments with skilled personnel devoted to these various tasks.

Most proprietors would like to hire the same skilled talent available to their competition, but rarely can they match the high salaries, benefits, and prestige that the larger firms can offer. Employees of sole proprietors, therefore, tend to be friends or relatives of the owner or people with limited education, experience, or abilities.

Limited Life

By their very nature, sole proprietorships tend to be unstable. The continuation of the enterprise depends on many things that could change the business in an instant. Notable among these factors are the business savvy, health, and life of the proprietor. If he were to make an unwise business decision, it could prove financially disastrous for his firm. If he should become seriously ill or physically disabled, the productivity of his business would likely slow to the point of being unable to make payments and having to cease operation. If he were to die, the business would die with him, possibly leaving many legal entanglements for his survivors to resolve.

Limited Availability of Money

As long as the firm remains a sole proprietorship, the owner cannot sell a portion of his business interest to others to raise money for expanding or continuing operations. Therefore, the only option the proprietor has, apart from tapping into his limited personal savings, is to incur debt. When applying for a bank loan, many proprietors find limitations on this source too. Before deciding whether to grant the loan, the **creditor**, or lender, must determine the probability of the proprietorship's staying in business long enough to repay the amount. Given the unlimited financial liability, the limited business life, and the potentially limited management skills of sole proprietorships, most creditors are reluctant to lend money unless the proprietor is willing to use the deed to his home or other valuable property as collateral. In addition, if a financial institution does grant the loan, it may charge a high rate of interest to compensate for the high risk it is taking. In still other cases, if it considers the risk too high, the lender may refuse to make the loan under any conditions.

SECTION REVIEW 7A

1. What are the advantages of a sole proprietorship?
2. What are the disadvantages of a sole proprietorship?

7B PARTNERSHIPS

A **partnership**, also known as a **general partnership**, is a business enterprise with two or more persons as the owners. While a majority of all partnerships originate with only two individuals, some have over one hundred partners. The partnership is the least popular form of American business ownership. It accounts for approximately 10 percent of the total annual revenue and less than 10 percent of all businesses.

The laws of most states generally do not require that business partners have a written contract. However, attorneys recommend drawing up a partnership agreement that specifically answers the following questions:

1. Who are the partners?
2. What is each partner responsible to do?
3. How are profits to be divided?
4. How may a partner withdraw from the partnership?
5. How can the partnership be dissolved?

ADVANTAGES OF PARTNERSHIPS

Partnerships have several advantages that overcome many of the problems encountered by sole proprietorships.

Greater Management Skills

The logic behind engaging in a partnership is simple: partnerships combine the complementary talents of two or more people. One partner may be proficient at financial management, while the other may have skills in marketing or manufacturing. Two surgeons may form a partnership to replace each other during vacations, to share the cost of an office building and staff, or to share medical knowledge. By combining the strengths of two or more people, a business partnership has a much greater probability of success.

Greater Retention of Competent Employees

One great disadvantage of the sole proprietorship is its inability to attract or keep qualified and experienced personnel. Partnerships, on the other hand, have the ability to promote exceptionally well-qualified employees to the status of partner. Promotion acts as a great incentive for employees to work harder and to remain with the business. Many law and accounting firms use this incentive to their advantage.

Greater Sources of Financing

When it comes to raising necessary capital, partnerships have a definite advantage over sole proprietorships. A personal savings account is frequently the limit of financing available to a sole proprietor; however, the partnership, with its greater number of owners, has a greater quantity of money available to it. Also, because partnerships are more likely to have specialized management teams and qualified, competent employees, creditors are often more willing to lend money to these firms.

A partnership form of business can offer a number of advantages over a sole proprietorship.

Ease of Formation and Freedom to Manage

Like the proprietorship, the partnership is relatively easy to form and operate. Though the firm is subject to several laws unique to partnerships, it is relatively free to carry out its business activities with minimal governmental interference.

DISADVANTAGES OF PARTNERSHIPS

Knowing that this form of business ownership represents less than 10 percent of all American business firms, you may wonder why it is so unpopular. While it has several advantages, the number of significant disadvantages makes the partnership form of ownership unacceptable to most businesspersons.

Unlimited Personal Financial Liability

Perhaps the greatest drawback to partnerships is that each partner faces unlimited personal financial liability. Just as a sole proprietor must pay all company debts from his own personal wealth if need be, each general partner is responsible to pay all obligations of the firm. The history of partnerships contains numerous sad stories of businesspersons who abandoned unprofitable businesses and left their partners saddled with company debts to pay out of their own pockets. Not only is each partner liable for all of the firm's financial obligations, but each one has the ability to accept such obligations without the other partner's knowledge. Thus one partner could purchase thousands of dollars' worth of personal items under the firm's name, leave town, and obligate the other partner to pay the bills.

Uncertain Life

Of all the forms of business ownership, partnerships historically have the shortest lives. Many factors contribute to the dissolution of partnerships, including death, voluntary withdrawal of a partner, bankruptcy, or the failure of a partner to carry out his responsibilities as listed in the partnership agreement.

Conflicts Between Partners

Many partnerships begin their existence with smiles, handshakes, and bright hopes but often end relatively quickly with conflicts, bitterness, anger, and occasionally violence. There are many reasons for partners' having changes in attitude, but almost all of them stem from one basic problem—man's sin nature. Because we are all basically proud and selfish, it is very difficult for any business endeavor to have two or more masters and prosper for any length of time, and general partnerships are such endeavors.

In a general partnership each partner has an equal voice in business decisions. When significant differences of opinion present themselves, as in decisions involving company policies, finances, personnel, or business practices, each partner is likely to believe that his viewpoint is the correct one. Consequently, each is also likely to believe that his decisions

would best set policy, balance the ledgers, increase sales, and so on. Unless the partners are in complete agreement, one will have to yield to the other. If the partners are able to compromise, neither will see his decisions solely guide the firm. Unless the partners are able to overcome their innate selfishness and yield certain points of control to each other, over time the continuing tensions may prove too difficult for them to resolve.

LIMITED PARTNERSHIPS

To overcome some of the difficulties of the general partnership, the limited partnership was developed. In a **limited partnership** there is at least one general partner, who has unlimited personal financial liability, and at least one **limited partner**. The limited partner invests money in the partnership and has the right to inspect the books and to share in the profits of the firm, but he has no management responsibilities and makes no business decisions for the partnership. He is a limited partner because the amount of his investment limits the amount of his personal financial liability. In other words, the most money he could lose is the amount he has invested in the partnership.

SCRIPTURE AND PARTNERSHIPS

What does the Bible have to say about partnerships? Scripture does not provide specific rules for business partnerships, but it does give general warnings that anyone considering a partnership would be wise to heed.

First, there is the warning against unequal yoking. While the admonition of 2 Corinthians 6:14, "Be ye not unequally yoked together with unbelievers," aims primarily at the purity of the church, it can also apply to partnerships. Farmers in biblical times understood what a yoke was, the purpose it served, and the problems of yoking unequal animals. Differences in temperaments, strength, speed, and so on would hinder the work. Likewise, there are problems with connecting as equals those who are unequal in their spiritual lives. A Christian and his unbelieving partner have differing worldviews. Consequently, their goals for the business and the standards on which they base their values will also likely differ. While a Christian should derive his goals and values from Scripture, his unbelieving partner may form his goals and values simply from what works best for him. These differences in goals and values may create strain on the partners' relationship and on the business. The Christian partner could be pressured to conform to practices or policies that would require him to compromise his biblical convictions (e.g., cheating on taxes, using inappropriate advertising, employing unethical accounting practices). If a partnership with an unsaved person requires a Christian to participate in something unscriptural, it would be wrong for the Christian to remain in that partnership.

A second scriptural warning concerns **surety**, which is the act of becoming security for or pledging to undertake another's debt. Clear biblical admonitions regarding surety indicate that a general partnership, in which each partner becomes surety for debts that the other may incur, can be problematic even for two saved persons. Consider the following references:

"He that is surety for a stranger shall smart for it: and he that hateth suretiship is sure" (Prov. 11:15).

"A man void of understanding striketh hands, and becometh surety in the presence of his friend" (Prov. 17:18).

"Be not thou one of them that strike hands, or of them that are sureties for debts. If thou hast nothing to pay, why should he take away thy bed from under thee?" (Prov. 22:26–27).

While some argue that the Scriptures totally forbid becoming surety for another's debts, others maintain that the Bible allows for certain exceptions, such as a parent's cosigning on a loan for a son or daughter who is attempting to establish a good credit record. If you believe there are exceptions and choose to cosign for another, you should do so only after determining that, should it become necessary, you have the ability to pay the debt in full.

> The book of Proverbs provides abundant counsel on the wise use of money. This book is a treasure readily available for you.

> Occasionally a lender may promise to grant a loan to someone with inadequate credit if another more creditworthy person will also sign the note, promising to pay if the original borrower cannot. This practice is known as **cosigning**.

SECTION REVIEW 7B

1. What are the advantages of a partnership?
2. What are the disadvantages of a partnership?
3. What are the two forms of partnership?
4. What two biblical warnings related to partnerships are discussed in the text?

7C CORPORATIONS

Business owners create a corporation by incorporating their business, legally declaring that the business is its own organization, independent of and separate from the owners. A **corporation**, therefore, is a separate entity created and recognized by law. The government recognizes the right of the corporation to buy, sell, enter into contracts, own property, sue, and be sued, just like any legal person. The most famous definition of the term *corporation* appeared in 1803 from Supreme Court Chief Justice John Marshall. In the case of *Dartmouth College v. Woodward*, Justice Marshall stated this opinion:

> A corporation is an artificial being, invisible, intangible, and existing only in contemplation of law. Being the mere creature of law, it possesses only those properties that the charter of its creation confers upon it, either expressly or as incidental to its very existence. Among the most important are immortality, and, if the expression may be allowed, individuality; properties, by which a perpetual succession of many persons are considered as the same, and may act as a single individual.

TYPES OF CORPORATIONS

When you think of the corporate form of business ownership, what probably comes to mind are examples of the **private corporation**.

Recreational Equipment, Inc. is an example of a private corporation.

Private citizens are the owners of private corporations. Examples of private corporations include ExxonMobil, Disney, Coca-Cola, and General Electric. While most private corporations have many owners (sometimes hundreds of thousands), some have relatively few.

A second type of corporation is the **public corporation**. The general public owns and the government manages such businesses. Among public corporations are the Tennessee Valley Authority (TVA), some state-run liquor stores, and Amtrak. In the case of Amtrak, the federal government actually owns all the preferred stock of the public corporation, and the President of the United States appoints the board of directors.

OWNERSHIP OF CORPORATIONS

A person becomes an owner of part of a corporation by buying shares of its **stock**. The buyer receives a confirmation of his purchase from a stockbroker or transfer agent. This confirmation indicates the number of shares that the new stockholder owns and gives evidence that he is now a partial owner of the corporation.

The number of shares the stockholder owns divided by the total number of outstanding shares determines that person's degree of ownership. For example, if a business has one million shares outstanding and you own five hundred thousand of them, then you own one-half of the firm. You will learn more about stock and stock markets in the next chapter.

Amtrak is an example of a public corporation.

ADVANTAGES OF CORPORATIONS

Incorporation has several advantages that motivate business owners to choose this form of business ownership.

Limited Personal Financial Liability of Stockholders

After studying proprietorships and partnerships and learning that their owners face the disadvantage of unlimited personal financial liability, you can understand that the limited financial liability of corporate ownership is its primary advantage. Stockholders risk only what they invest in the corporation. The firm's creditors cannot touch the personal property of the shareholders. For example, if you owned $1,000 worth of stock in a corporation that owed $1 million when it went out of business, you would stand to lose your entire investment of $1,000, but your personal wealth would otherwise not be in jeopardy. Those seeking to collect the million-dollar debt could not seize your bank accounts, auction your home, or lay claim to your personal possessions.

Experienced Management and Specialized Employees

A board of directors, elected by the stockholders, runs a corporation. The board represents the interests of the stockholders and usually consists of people with experience in running other corporations. The board appoints a chief executive officer (CEO), who usually serves as president of the corporation. The CEO in turn appoints qualified persons to fill the top, middle, and lower management positions, and these managers then hire and oversee the development of the other employees.

An advantage of a corporation is that it may attract an experienced management team with the specialized abilities needed to help the business succeed.

Because of the expertise, specialization, and training of the management and employees within a corporation, the corporate form of ownership tends to be more profitable than either the proprietorship or the partnership.

> J. C. Penney used the golden rule as the foundation for his business practices. What biblical principle in Mark 12:33 supports this idea?

JAMES CASH PENNEY (1875–1971)
American Merchant

Born on a farm near Hamilton, Missouri, James Cash (J. C.) Penney was the son of a poor farmer who preached on Sundays at a Primitive Baptist church. Although the family remained in debt and barely kept food on the table, his parents made certain that their children obtained a proper education and that they learned scriptural principles as well. One of those principles that James learned at an early age was the golden rule. When he was only eight, his father informed him that he would have to buy his own clothes. James decided that to earn money for this new responsibility he would use the small sum he had saved to buy a pig, which he could fatten and sell for profit. He gathered table scraps from the neighbors to feed his animal and then sold it and bought more pigs. However, one day his father ordered him to sell the pigs immediately. James protested that they were not fat enough yet and would not bring a good price. Nevertheless, his father was firm because, as he explained, the smell of the pigs was beginning to bother the neighbors. The right thing to do was to follow the golden rule: "All things whatsoever ye would that men should do to you, do ye even so to them" (Matt. 7:12). Young Penney sold the pigs.

Penney's principled upbringing became a major asset during his career. Having decided that farming was not the life for him, he pursued becoming a merchant. His hard work at the new trade earned him a good job as a store clerk in his hometown. Poor health prompted him to move to the West, where he lost his savings trying to run a butcher shop. Dejected but not defeated, he returned to the merchant trade and found work again as a clerk. Once again his hard work and determination to succeed won him the admiration of his employers. The partners eventually offered Penney a management position and a one-third interest in a new store. Penney opened that store in Kemmerer, Wyoming, in 1902; and his fairness and eagerness to serve his customers brought him a loyal clientele. In 1907 Penney was able to buy out his partners' interest in the Kemmerer store and two other stores. He quickly expanded this chain, which he called Golden Rule Stores. By 1913 he had forty-eight stores. When he opened a store in his old hometown of Hamilton in 1924, the number of stores totaled five hundred. As his wealth grew, Penney became a generous philanthropist, supporting many religious organizations and charitable causes. Although he lost his fortune in the stock market crash of 1929 and the following depression, he earned it back again in later years by continuing to follow what were called the Penney Principles:

1. To serve the public, as nearly as we can, to its complete satisfaction.
2. To offer the best possible dollar's worth of quality and value.
3. To strive constantly for a high level of intelligent and helpful service.
4. To charge a fair profit for what we offer—and not all the traffic will bear.
5. To apply this test to everything we do: "Does it square with what is right and just?"

Continuous Life

If a proprietor or partner dies, the original proprietorship or partnership ends. In a corporation, however, if a board member dies, the stockholders replace him. If a manager or key employee dies, the firm seeks and hires another to fill the position. If a stockholder dies, his heirs inherit his shares, or they go up for sale on the open market to other investors. You can see that in each of these scenarios, the corporation does not cease to exist.

Ease in Raising Financial Capital

Since a corporation may have an unlimited number of owners, it may sell more shares of stock to raise needed additional funds. Corporations usually borrow money at lower interest rates than proprietorships or partnerships because they have a better record of being able to repay their debts with less risk of default. Lending institutions see the higher caliber of management, limited financial liability, and unlimited life of corporations as making them less of a credit risk than other forms of business ownership.

DISADVANTAGES OF CORPORATIONS

Of course the corporate form of business ownership is not perfect. If it were, the other forms would not exist. There are several disadvantages of incorporating.

Higher Taxes

Perhaps the greatest disadvantage of incorporation is the high tax rate the government levies on corporate earnings. Corporations pay taxes on a higher graduated scale than the personal income tax rate. In addition, after the firm pays out profits to its stockholders, they must pay personal income taxes on the dividends. This double taxation of earnings would be similar to having payroll taxes removed from your earnings before you get your paycheck and then paying additional income taxes on your after-tax income.

Greater Governmental Regulation

Because the government sees itself as having "created" the corporation, it exercises the right to oversee corporate operations. Thousands of regulations apply to all forms of businesses. Examples of regulations that all businesses must observe include rules for hiring, paying, retiring, and firing employees and standards for the safety and health of the workers and the general population. In addition to following these requirements, corporations must also obey laws on such matters as merging with other companies, selling new stocks and bonds, and setting prices of certain products. Corporations spend a great deal of time and money interpreting and obeying governmental policies in addition to keeping records and reporting to various governmental agencies.

Lack of Secrecy

As a result of much required reporting, corporations find that keeping business information secret is more difficult for them than it is for proprietorships or partnerships. By law, corporations must keep the government and their stockholders aware of the firm's sales, profits, advertising expenditures, costs of research and development, and other data. This information is of great interest not only to the

---

S CORPORATIONS

While most sole proprietors can see the obvious benefits of incorporating, they are reluctant to do so since corporations pay taxes at a higher rate than sole proprietorships. To encourage incorporation, the US government has created a corporate status for small businesses that allows them to continue being taxed at the lower personal income tax rates. A small business that fits into this category is referred to as a **subchapter S corporation**, or, more commonly, an S corporation. A business may incorporate as an S corporation if it has fewer than thirty-five shareholders and abides by certain restrictions regarding types of stock. (Chapter 8 discusses shareholders and types of stock.) A business owner whose company meets these requirements and who desires his business to become an S corporation must file the appropriate paperwork with the federal government.

shareholders but to the firm's competitors as well. Some corporations have solved the secrecy problem by "going private," a situation in which the managers of the firm purchase all outstanding stock, allowing the corporation to keep sensitive information from reaching the public.

Impersonality

Many large corporations suffer because employees become depersonalized by the sheer size of the firm. Workers begin to feel that they are only a small part of the giant corporate machinery and then

LIMITED LIABILITY COMPANY (LLC)

Many people incorrectly refer to a **limited liability company (LLC)** as a limited liability *corporation*. Though similar to a corporation, an LLC is a different form of business organization that combines the benefits of a corporation with those of a partnership. As in a corporation, the owners of an LLC are not liable for the acts and debts of the LLC, and as in a partnership, the owners avoid the double taxation of company earnings. If the owners set it up properly, the LLC is not subject to corporate taxes. All company earnings become part of the income of the members who receive them, and they pay income taxes accordingly.

An LLC and a corporation also differ in how individuals create, own, and operate them. Whereas the law requires that there be three or more persons to establish a corporation, a single person can create an LLC. Also, an S corporation can have no more than thirty-five shareholders, who all must be US citizens or resident aliens; however, an LLC may have any number of shareholders, who can be citizens, resident aliens, nonresident foreigners, other LLCs, partnerships, or corporations. Unlike a corporation, an LLC does not have a board of directors who must meet regularly on a published schedule, nor must it hold regular meetings of shareholders. The financial reporting requirements are also less burdensome for an LLC than they are for a corporation.

Yet another difference between an LLC and a corporation concerns what governs each. Corporations have sets of bylaws that govern their formation and operation; however, a document called an *operating agreement* governs an LLC. This agreement sets the rules for the company; defines the rights and responsibilities of its members; specifies who provides the capital and how much; designates who receives profits, losses, gains, and credits; and determines how and under what circumstances the company will be dissolved.

There are, however, some disadvantages of an LLC. Many states still seek to tax the profits of the companies by levying a "franchise," "capital values," or "margin" tax on LLCs. Another problem is a lack of personal liability that may make it difficult to raise needed capital. It may be necessary for at least one owner to forfeit his limited liability benefit and to assume financial responsibility for the LLC before banks or other lending institutions and investors will commit their resources to the business. Of course, if the members have sufficient capital without having to borrow, an LLC may be the ideal way to organize the business. Finally, an improperly worded operating agreement can result in several serious difficulties and even severe legal complications. Those establishing an LLC must use great care in writing an operating agreement for several reasons; perhaps the most important one is that the IRS will use this document to determine whether it will tax the LLC as a corporation or a partnership. An LLC could lose most or all of its desired tax benefits from a carelessly or inappropriately worded agreement. Because of this, potential owners often employ competent and experienced legal assistance in crafting the operating agreement, though few states have laws requiring such expertise.

Rather than individual owners making the operating decisions, a board of directors runs a corporation.

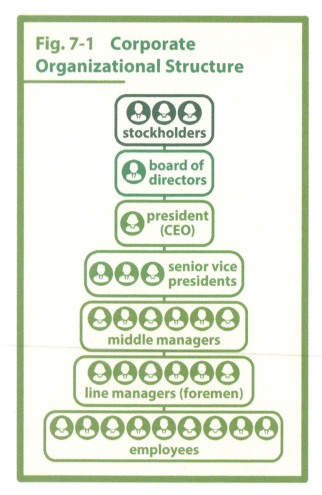

tend to minimize the overall importance of their work. To solve this problem, some large corporations seek to help employees feel appreciated and part of the corporate team by sponsoring a variety of opportunities from company picnics and softball teams to programs that give workers a voice in business operations.

Rigidity

The owners of proprietorships and partnerships can react quickly to market changes; corporations generally move at a much slower pace. For example, a proprietor may develop a new product one day and begin selling it the next. The proprietor's complete control of the business operations allows him to make speedy adjustments. In contrast, a corporation's new product ideas may take months or years to gain the approval of the various decision makers. Depending on their size and organizational structure, corporations often receive criticism for being unresponsive to the market when in reality their responses are just very slow.

Perhaps now, even as a high-school student, you believe that God may be calling you into the world of business. Perhaps you were among the many childhood owners of a lemonade stand. Looking back at that, what you probably considered a sole proprietorship you may see now as actually a limited partnership, with your mom or dad as the limited partner. Looking ahead, though, what do you see? Perhaps you see yourself and a friend starting a lawn care business, or maybe you have several friends who have discussed combining their various computer, artistic, sales, and leadership talents into an entrepreneurial venture. Of course, included in any such potential business plans should be plans for all members of the future firm to seek God's will as well as additional education and training. Having read this chapter, you should be aware of the advantages and disadvantages of proprietorships, partnerships, corporations, and even LLCs. Such knowledge should prove invaluable as you enter the marketplace; however, there is much to learn, and there should be much prayer before proceeding.

SECTION REVIEW 7C

1. How did John Marshall, Chief Justice of the Supreme Court, define a corporation?
2. Explain the difference between a private corporation and a public corporation.
3. How does one become a partial owner of a corporation?
4. What are the advantages of incorporation?
5. What are the disadvantages of incorporation?

CHAPTER REVIEW

CONTENT QUESTIONS

1. What are the three basic forms of business organization?
2. Which is the most popular form of business in the United States? What accounts for this type of business's popularity?
3. What disadvantage of a proprietorship does the partnership form of business ownership solve?
4. What are the key differences between a general partnership and a limited partnership?
5. What does it mean to be surety for someone?
6. What is the primary advantage of being incorporated?
7. Explain the biblical principle J. C. Penney applied in the foundation of his company. Cite the applicable reference.
8. An LLC combines the benefits of which two forms of business ownership?

APPLICATION QUESTIONS

1. If you were given $100,000 to start your own business, what kind of business would you undertake (a bicycle shop, a craft supply store, a bookstore, etc.)? Assuming that this business is a sole proprietorship, what will be some of the necessary tasks that you will have to complete to form your business and begin operation?
2. If you and three of your closest friends were going to start a business, which form of business ownership would you recommend to your friends and why? Give reasons from the text to support your answer.

TERMS

Term	Page
sole proprietorship	129
creditor	131
partnership	132
general partnership	132
limited partnership	134
limited partner	134
surety	134
cosigning	135
corporation	135
private corporation	135
public corporation	136
stock	136
subchapter S corporation	138
limited liability company (LLC)	139

PERSONAL FINANCE
SOURCES OF CONSUMER CREDIT

Most American consumers seem ready and willing to apply for and use credit to make their purchases, and it seems a host of financial institutions are willing to extend credit to them. However, three major sources grant the majority of credit in the United States: commercial banks, thrift institutions, and finance companies.

COMMERCIAL BANKS

The first source of credit that comes to almost everyone's mind is the commercial bank. Commercial banks offer a wide range of loan options to both consumers and business firms. They offer installment loans on secured and unsecured bases. Because it offers the best protection to the bank, one of the least expensive types of secured (backed with or by collateral) installment bank loans is the assignment of savings account. An **assignment of savings account** is a loan for which the borrower's savings account serves as collateral. The bank places a hold on the savings account that allows the borrower to withdraw funds only to the degree that he has reduced the loan principal. If the borrower defaults on the loan, the bank simply repays itself for the loan using the remaining funds it kept on hold. Since banks bear practically no risk on these loans, they charge an interest rate that is usually much lower than that charged for other types of installment loans. Most banks charge an interest rate just 2–3 percent above the rate they are paying on the deposit. Thus, the person earning 4 percent on a regular savings account would pay only around 6–7 percent for a savings assignment loan.

In addition to accepting savings accounts as backing for installment loans, commercial banks also accept other substantial forms of collateral, such as vehicles, real estate, stocks, and bonds. Banks also grant unsecured installment loans, but because unsecured loans increase their risk of loss, they usually limit this type of loan to their most creditworthy customers and often charge a high interest rate as well.

Open-end loans in the form of revolving charge accounts are another method of borrowing from a commercial bank. One of the most popular types of open-end bank loans originated to keep checking account holders from experiencing overdraft charges. As a result of either bad bookkeeping or carelessness, many checking account holders occasionally bounce checks (write checks for more than is in their accounts). When a depositor writes a check that overdraws his account, the bank generally charges a fee to cover its costs for returning the check through the national check clearing system. In addition, many merchants who receive overdrawn checks also levy a service charge on returned checks. As you can see, it could become very costly for a consumer who accidentally writes several overdrawn checks before he discovers his error.

To protect their customers as well as to provide additional interest income, many commercial banks offer an open-end line of credit that serves as **overdraft protection**. Customers paying for this service know that the bank will automatically deposit funds into their checking accounts, up to a predetermined credit limit, whenever the account balance falls below zero. While this service may be financially helpful, consumers need to inquire about the terms and conditions that their bank places on its overdraft protection loans. While some banks deposit only the exact amount needed to cover an overdraft, others deposit fixed increments, such as $100, and as a result, customers may have to pay more interest than necessary. Another item customers should

SOURCES OF CONSUMER CREDIT

question is the rate of interest. Overdraft protection interest rates are generally higher than those on simple loans.

Many commercial banks offer a second type of open-end bank credit—a bank-issued credit card. Bank customers can use these cards to purchase merchandise from numerous retailers, and many bank credit cards offer the added bonus of a **cash advance** feature that enables the cardholder to receive cash against his account. Customers can take advantage of this feature at either the bank counter or an ATM. Though the interest rate on merchandise purchases is often higher than that on cash advances, the customer needs to be aware of an important difference. On cash advances, the bank begins charging interest the day of the advance; whereas on merchandise purchases, the interest charges usually do not begin until approximately twenty-five days after the bank issues the credit card bill. Typically, interest rates on bank credit cards are higher than those on simple loans, and many bank cards also require an annual fee.

THRIFT INSTITUTIONS

Savings and loan associations (S & Ls), one type of thrift institution, appeared in the United States in the late 1800s to help those with modest incomes purchase homes. Home loans typically take one of two forms. A **first mortgage** is the loan that many use to purchase a home. Homebuyers use the property as collateral to secure the first mortgage loan. To obtain a **second mortgage**, homeowners use the **equity** they have in their house as collateral. To calculate a home's equity, the lending institution determines the difference between the amount the homeowner owes on his mortgage and the house's current market (resale) value. For example, a couple wants to purchase their first home. They find

DEBIT CARDS VERSUS CREDIT CARDS

The bank just gave you a Visa card. It has the same logo as other Visa cards, and you use it much the same way—to pay for goods at the store when you do not have your checkbook or sufficient cash. But this Visa card is not a credit card; it is a *debit card*. A key difference is that with a debit card, you are not using credit to make your purchases. When a cashier rings up a purchase on a debit card, the amount is subtracted directly from your checking account.

Like a credit card, a debit card affords its user around-the-clock access to funds. Its primary advantage, however, is that the cardholder can draw on the bank's services at an automatic teller twenty-four hours a day—cash withdrawals, deposits, and inquiries. Withdrawals can also be made at stores by requesting "cash back" on debit purchases. And unlike many credit cards, the debit card is usually free because when you use it, you are not borrowing from the bank.

Yet debit cards have some obvious—and not so obvious—disadvantages. Just as you can accumulate credit debt without realizing its amount, you can easily forget to record debit transactions and suddenly be overdrawn. Furthermore, if your card is lost or stolen, you are protected by the weaker Electronic Funds Transfer Act, not the consumer credit acts. You can be liable for up to $500 if you fail to inform the bank within two days, and your liability is unlimited if you fail to inform the bank within sixty days of your last bank statement.

a modest starter home for $90,000. Able to put $15,000 down, they take out a first mortgage for the remaining $75,000. Later, they want to build an addition on their house but lack the capital, so they explore the option of a second mortgage. The loan officer finds that their home is now worth $100,000 and that the principal balance on the original mortgage is $45,000. The difference between the value of the home and the amount the couple owes on their first mortgage is $55,000. This amount represents the equity they have in their home and the amount available for a second mortgage to pay for the addition.

Until the mid-1970s, S & Ls continued the tradition of only accepting savings deposits and extending first and second mortgage home loans, but after that time they began to aggressively market new services to increase their profitability. To encourage second mortgage lending, many S & Ls began to offer a version of overdraft protection. Though their plans acted much the same as a commercial bank's overdraft service, S & Ls offered their customers far greater credit limits by basing their lines of credit on the equity that borrowers had in their homes.

Credit unions, a second type of thrift institution, also provide a source of credit for potential borrowers. Instead of depositing money into an individual savings account, credit union members purchase shares of ownership in their credit union as they add money to their accounts. From this pool of funds, other members may borrow. When a member needs a loan, a volunteer committee of members reviews his application. When a credit union grants a loan, it can arrange for payments to be made in several ways, such as payroll deduction or direct account debit. Since they are nonprofit organizations and incur very low overhead expenses, credit unions can usually issue loans with a lower interest rate than loans granted by commercial banks or S & Ls.

FINANCE COMPANIES

Finance companies are private companies that extend loans to the general public. Two types exist: consumer finance companies and sales finance companies.

Consumer finance companies make personal and debt consolidation loans to the general public. People use a **personal loan** to pay for a vacation, to finance an education, or to cover personal temporary cash deficits. Many consumers use their credit cards, credit lines, and installment loans to amass a burden of debt that they cannot manage. To relieve some of the pressure caused by this abundance of debt, a borrower may seek a debt consolidation loan. A **debt consolidation loan** combines all outstanding debts into one loan that carries a single monthly payment that is lower than the combined payments of the individual debts. Financial advisors warn those considering a debt consolidation loan to examine carefully the costs involved. While the monthly payment may be lower, it is usually because the creditor stretches the loan over a longer period of time, a factor that may significantly increase the amount a person pays in interest.

Finance companies range in size from large, nationally known firms to local companies with limited lending capacity. State laws usually regulate the maximum amount that consumer finance companies may lend and the maximum interest rate they may charge. Typically they make relatively small loans. In addition to setting lending limits, state laws usually mandate that the interest rate the finance companies charge must decline as the size of a loan increases. For example, some states permit finance companies to charge a maximum interest rate of 48 percent on loans of $500 or less and a maximum of 24 percent on loans over $2,000.

While borrowers might complain that finance companies charge excessive interest rates, they should recognize that these firms make much smaller loans with considerably greater risk than those made by thrift institutions. Loans with a higher risk of default require consumer finance companies to spend more money to investigate applicants' creditworthiness and to collect the loans that have gone into default. In addition, the source of the funds that consumer finance companies lend is not low-interest savings and checking deposits; rather, it is capital borrowed from commercial banks and thrift institutions.

Unlike consumer finance companies, **sales finance companies** do not function to meet the personal or debt consolidation needs of the general public. They are usually subsidiary companies that larger business firms create to provide financing for consumers wishing to purchase their products. For example, the General Motors Acceptance Corporation (GMAC) provides loans to enable buyers to purchase General Motors products. The interest rate on loans from sales finance companies tends to be lower than those from consumer finance companies for two reasons. First, sales finance companies do not make the high-risk loans associated with consumer finance companies. Sales finance companies tend to screen loan applicants and choose only those with the best credit. Second, firms the size of GMAC and Ford Motor Credit do not have to borrow their funds from financial institutions. They can issue their own bonds to the general public at a much lower interest rate.

OTHER SOURCES OF CREDIT

Besides thrift institutions and finance companies, several other sources of credit exist. Individually, they play a relatively minor role in the extension of credit; combined, however, they are responsible for a great deal of the credit issued in the United States.

One such source is life insurance companies. If clients have life insurance policies with an optional investment feature, they may borrow from the insurance company using their accumulated cash values as collateral.

A second source is companies that make loans by mail or over the Internet. Other than the facts that they do not operate out of typical retail offices and they make loans of even higher risk, these firms are virtually indistinguishable from consumer finance companies.

A third source of funds is educational loan companies. Borrowers who wish to finance their college education borrow money from governmental and private educational loan services. Usually creditors grant these loans on the basis of the borrower's financial need and academic achievement.

Pawnbrokers are a fourth source of credit. **Pawnbrokers** provide loans that a customer usually must repay in a single payment within six months of the loan. The pawnbroker normally accepts as collateral some item of value, such as jewelry or electronics. Rather than signing a formal note, the borrower receives a pawn ticket and cash in exchange for the collateral. If the borrower fails to repay the loan by a specified date, the pawnbroker has the authority to sell the collateral. Credit

counselors strongly discourage this type of borrowing because the amounts pawnbrokers loan are usually significantly less than the property's value and interest rates on pawnbroker loans may sometimes be as high as 100 percent.

Finally, some people borrow from family or friends to avoid high interest rates and the impersonal commercial aspects of borrowing. In many situations loans from family members are thinly disguised gifts. Those who wish for family or friends to take personal loans seriously should make the loan as businesslike as possible and draw up an informal written repayment promise detailing the terms and conditions.

The consumer looking for credit has many options. That credit opportunities may be readily available does not mean, however, that you need to take advantage of them. Whether you are applying for credit from a bank, S & L, or finance company, always take the time to read carefully the terms and interest rates. Make sure that you understand the type of loan for which you are applying and its requirements. Knowing the nature and function of different lending entities should help you make an informed decision. Also, knowing that the way a Christian uses credit can support or damage his testimony should help guide your choice.

REVIEW QUESTIONS

1. What are the three sources of consumer credit in the United States?
2. Why do commercial banks consider an assignment of savings account virtually risk free?
3. How is a second mortgage connected to the concept of equity?
4. Name an advantage and a disadvantage of a debit card.
5. What kind of loans do sales finance companies provide?

TERMS

assignment of savings account	142
overdraft protection	142
cash advance	143
first mortgage	143
second mortgage	143
equity	143
consumer finance companies	144
personal loan	144
debt consolidation loan	144
sales finance companies	144
pawnbrokers	145

CHAPTER EIGHT

THE STOCK MARKET

8A STOCK — 146

8B STOCK MARKETS — 150

8C THE MARKET AND THE ECONOMY — 154

The owner of So Good Candy Bars needs to expand his business. Demand for his product is rising, and the increasing demand is increasing his sales. He needs to purchase a larger facility and more equipment to keep pace. Like nearly 75 percent of businesses, though, his is a proprietorship. As you read in the previous chapter, one difficulty many proprietors encounter is raising capital. The owner of SGCB has limited personal assets and is hesitant to incur debt at the interest rates he, as a sole proprietor, is likely to face. So, he weighs his options.

First, he considers finding a partner or partners. While their combined assets may prove sufficient for the expansion he desires, he also knows that partnerships, like proprietorships, face the risk of unlimited personal liability. Should SGCB experience financial failure, the owners would lose not only the amount of money they invested in the business but also their personal assets. To be able to raise the necessary funds and avoid this risk, the owner of SGCB opts for incorporation.

Once he has met all the requirements to transform his proprietorship into SGCB Inc., the owner is ready to raise the capital he needs by selling stock. He has made all necessary decisions regarding common and preferred shares and maintaining majority ownership. Financial advisors at his investment bank have guided his considerations of the various exchanges—whether to offer his stock on the NYSE or NASDAQ. Then, they set a date to launch his corporation's IPO.

You may have followed this story until that last paragraph. What is stock, and what are common and preferred shares? What is majority ownership, and what do all those letters mean? You will learn the answers to these questions and much more about stock and stock markets as you continue reading.

8A STOCK

If you own shares of **stock**, you own shares, or a portion, of a corporation. When the owners of a corporation choose to sell shares of stock, they realize that they are, in a sense, selling partial ownership of that corporation. Anyone purchasing one or more shares can now participate in the activities of an owner. Shareholders have the opportunity to cast votes on business decisions proposed by the corporation's board of directors. Voting takes place in periodic shareholder meetings, and items that may be voted on include hiring or firing managers, expanding the business into new markets, and choosing measures that will best promote the financial wellbeing of the firm.

Those who own large portions of the stock have an obviously greater part in the ownership responsibilities. If you, for example, were to own over 50 percent of the stock in a corporation, you would be its majority owner and would have control of that corporation.

Until a few years ago, stockholders received pieces of paper called stock certificates as evidence of their ownership of the company. Today, however, companies generally forgo printing stock certificates.

TYPES OF STOCK

As stated earlier, should you wish to become a partial owner of a corporation, you would purchase shares of stock in that firm. In some American corporations you can choose to purchase shares of either common or preferred stock.

Common stock is the most prevalent type of stock that companies offer and represents true ownership of the firm. That is, if you own ten thousand shares of common stock in a corporation that has one hundred thousand common shares outstanding (available for sale), you own 10 percent of that corporation. At the annual shareholders' meeting, common shareholders elect the firm's board of directors, the body that actually runs the corporation. After paying all of the business's expenses, the board of directors may decide to pay the common shareholders **dividends**, a distribution of a portion of the corporation's profits. As the company's profits increase, the dividends paid to the common shareholders may likewise increase. Of course, the board may also decide to retain the funds to purchase needed assets, such as equipment, raw materials, land, buildings, or other resources.

Stock certificates once verified ownership of stock. Today many have become little more than collector's items.

However, because they are the owners of the corporation, common shareholders are the last to be paid if the firm fails. If a corporation files for bankruptcy, it may be forced to sell all its assets. From the money raised by such a sale, the company must make several payments. First, it must pay any wages it owes its employees. Second, it must pay the government for any outstanding tax bills. Third, it must pay its creditors, banks, or other lending institutions. Lastly, from any leftover revenue, the business pays the common shareholders in proportion to their ownership of the corporation. That payment, however, is likely to be significantly less than the previous value of their stock.

Shareholders of **preferred stock** receive their dividends before the common shareholders, and should the corporation suffer financial failure, preferred shareholders receive their portion of any leftover

Traders watch prices on the electronic board.

revenue just ahead of the common shareholders. Hence, for many would-be stock purchasers, these shares are "preferred." However, do not let that word mislead you into thinking that preferred stock is significantly better than common stock. Comparing preferred to common stock is like comparing apples to oranges. They are fundamentally different; each has advantages and disadvantages. For many, preferred stock carries less risk of loss because preferred shareholders have claim to the company's assets before the common shareholders if business losses force the corporation to close. However, preferred stock does not equate to true ownership of the corporation; consequently, preferred stock shareholders usually do not have the right to vote on matters of importance to the business. To the corporation, preferred stock is perhaps more like debt than ownership. The dividends the firm pays to its preferred shareholders are fixed, like the interest on a loan. While these dividends may come on a more regular basis than those paid to the common shareholders, there is no guarantee the preferred shareholders will receive any dividends. If the company's expenses consume all its profits, it is not obligated to pay dividends to its preferred shareholders any more than it would be to its common shareholders.

SELLING STOCK

Business owners may seek to take advantage of the limited liability and legal status they gain by organizing their business as a corporation yet choose not to offer any of their corporation's stock for public sale. These owners decide to hold all their company's stock and thus retain complete control of the business and all its profits.

However, if the owners need to raise money for business purposes, they may have to sell shares of stock. To do this, they must register

STOCK TRADING 101

Individuals wishing to buy and sell shares of stock initiate stock trades. Suppose that you want to buy one hundred shares of Coastal Cola stock at a price of $20 per share. You contact a **stockbroker**, a person who generally works for a brokerage company and who specializes in buying and selling stocks on behalf of his clients. Stockbrokers work for a fee called a **commission**. Your broker calls one of his company's stock traders to pursue the trade you have requested. Stock traders, also called **floor traders**, are physically present on the trading floor to execute requested trades. Your trader then tries to locate another trader on the floor who is willing to sell one hundred shares of Coastal Cola stock for $20 per share. Once the traders find each other, they carry out the trade through the brokerage firms they represent. The market indicates the transaction on the "**tape**," which used to be paper tape from a stock ticker but is now an electronic message board.

Electronic trading has opened new doors for buying and selling stocks. More stock exchanges have begun adopting electronic trading systems that enable brokers and other individuals to initiate and finalize transactions without the face-to-face work of floor traders. Some exchanges have no trading floor at all and execute all trades electronically. Even the more well-established exchanges, like the NYSE, are increasing their use of electronic trading. As more firms offer e-trading services, the e-trading business continues to grow.

their business with a stock market, such as the New York Stock Exchange, and arrange for the sale of their company's stock through an investment bank. The investment bank then schedules the sale of a certain quantity of stock through the exchange in what is called an **initial public offering (IPO)**. When issuing an IPO, however, it is not uncommon for the owners to sell less than half the stock. This allows them to raise the necessary capital but still retain majority ownership of their corporation, thereby maintaining control because they always have a majority of the votes. Corporations use the capital they raise from selling stock for various business needs, such as expanding production by building a new plant or initiating additional research and development of the good or service that the business already provides.

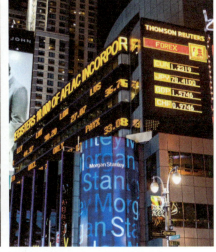

The Waldorf-Astoria Hotel displayed stock information for its patrons on boards in the lobby (1918). In the 1960s the mechanical ticker and tape were replaced by computers and electronic boards.

BUYING STOCK

Individuals purchase shares of stock primarily for one of two reasons: to make a profit or to receive dividend payments. Investors earn a profit by following the old rule "Buy low and sell high." That is, they want to buy stock at what they consider to be a low price for shares that they believe are going to increase in value and then to sell those shares later at a higher price, thus making a profit. To a certain extent, then, stock prices reflect the opinion of buyers as regards the financial future of a company.

Investors may purchase stocks they believe will steadily increase in value, thereby providing them with consistent income growth, or they may purchase stocks based on the quality of projected dividend payments. Either way, they are looking to expand their investment and earn a profit from their initial purchase. Since dividend payments depend largely on profits, those investing in stocks for this

Ticker tape was often cut up and recycled as confetti for big-event parades, which became known as "ticker-tape parades."

reason, like those seeking to make a profit, look for companies they anticipate having a reasonably high prospect of financial success.

SECTION REVIEW 8A

1. Owning shares of stock not only makes a person a partial owner of a corporation but also gives that person what other opportunity?
2. What is the most prevalent type of stock that most corporations offer?
3. Why do corporations sell stock?
4. What are the two principal reasons that individuals purchase shares of stock?

8B STOCK MARKETS

Stock markets have existed as long as corporations. Since shares of company stock are like other valuable assets that consumers may buy, sell, or trade, markets where such transactions could occur developed rapidly.

EARLY MARKET DEVELOPMENT

The street that has become synonymous with American finance

Originally, merchants traded stocks at locations called **stock exchanges**, or bourses. They first appeared in Great Britain and North Holland (now part of the Netherlands) sometime prior to 1700. It is not surprising that these exchanges began in Great Britain because the corporate form of business initially developed there, undergoing gradual changes before becoming the now-familiar corporate model. Well-organized stock exchanges, however, did not develop until the corporate form of business became more widespread, generally between 1800 and 1850. Then similar exchanges quickly developed in other European countries, including France and Germany.

The Philadelphia Stock Exchange, founded in 1790, was the first stock exchange in the United States. The New York Stock Exchange, organized in 1792, eventually outgrew the Philadelphia exchange due to the development of New York City as America's financial center. Today there are several stock exchanges in the United States, including those in such cities as Los Angeles, Boston, Cincinnati, and Chicago.

The NYSE originated outdoors under a buttonwood tree.

The NYSE in the early days of the exchanges

THE STOCK MARKET

ORGANIZATION

Stock markets are like other markets with which you are familiar. Just as a supermarket brings together people who want to buy and sell groceries or household items, so a stock market is a location (literal or virtual) at which people come together (physically or electronically) to buy and sell shares of stock.

The stock market is also like other markets in that the prices of its products usually reflect what consumers are willing to pay for them. When potential buyers perceive the value of a stock to be increasing, they will likely increase their demand for that stock and thereby bid up its price. When they believe that a business will make a profit in the future, they will be willing to pay a higher price for that company's shares of stock. Conversely, when buyers believe a stock is losing value, they will decrease their demand and its price will drop. Their belief that profits will be low or that the company may even lose money will cause the price of the stock to fall. Traders will seek to sell the stock but will find investors willing to pay less for it.

> Remember the laws of demand and supply? Do you see their application in the discussion regarding the price of shares of stock?

EXAMPLES OF MARKETS

There are many stock markets. The most well-known are the **New York Stock Exchange (NYSE)** and the **NASDAQ** (National Association of Securities Dealers Automated Quotations). Though actual markets function in different ways, they all exist to bring together those seeking to sell and those wanting to buy stock.

Stock exchanges differ by reputation. The NYSE is the most well-known and reputable stock market in the world. The importance and prestige of the NYSE as compared to other exchanges result from its history, its location in the financial center of New York, and its listings, which include many of the most economically significant companies not only in the United States but also in the world. Because these characteristics are widely known and held to be true, companies enjoy a great status boost when their stock trades on the NYSE.

The NASDAQ has become a well-established stock exchange even though it is less than fifty years old. The NASDAQ market best illustrates one innovation in stock trading—"over-the-counter" trading. In over-the-counter trading, there is no physical location at which traders meet as there is with markets like the NYSE. The NASDAQ is the largest exchange that does not have a trading floor. Instead, the market posts stock price information to an electronic network, and dealers who are registered with the market perform the trades.

The front of the NYSE

The trading floor of the NYSE has modernized from days of the past.

This is an excellent illustration of how markets may function without a physical location.

Lesser known but still reputable American markets include the **American Stock Exchange (Amex)** and a number of stock exchanges that operate exclusively in certain regions of the country. There are also many well-established stock exchanges in other industrial countries. These include Japan's Tokyo Stock Exchange with its Nikkei index, the London Stock Exchange, and the Hong Kong Stock Exchange.

CHARLES DOW (1851–1902)
Creator of the Dow Jones Industrial Average

Charles Dow was born into a farming family in eastern Connecticut in 1851, but he soon determined to avoid farming as a career. At twenty-one, he left home and found work as a reporter at a Massachusetts newspaper. After five years he returned near home to work as a business reporter at the *Providence Journal*. He learned about the world of business and finance through meticulous research and reporting. Seeking a greater challenge, the twenty-nine-year-old Dow moved to New York in 1880 to work for a Wall Street news company that served the financial and banking community. At this company he joined forces with Charles Bergstresser and a former coworker, Edward Jones, and in 1882 the three formed their own Wall Street news service, Dow, Jones & Company.

In 1889, after seeing their news service enjoy a successful beginning, Dow and Jones began the *Wall Street Journal*. They quickly developed a reputation for honest reporting in an environment in which it was common for reporters to slant the news in exchange for bribes. They often printed the names of companies that refused to provide information about profits and losses and thus gained respect from the financial community.

During the boom of the 1890s, corporations grew in number and size. As a result, investors found it difficult to obtain reliable information about individual companies and their stock prices, as well as information about the overall changes in the stock market. In response to this need, Dow developed the first stock index, the Dow Jones Industrial Average, by adding the stock prices of twelve prominent companies and dividing the sum by twelve. The company published this index daily, and it quickly became a popular indicator of stock market activity. Dow also developed the first technical stock analysis, called the *Dow theory*, in which he related his stock index to overall business activity in a way that permitted economic forecasting.

Charles Dow's character and integrity earned respect in an often dishonest business world, and in that regard, he is a good model for those in today's business world.

Charles Dow's partner, Edward Jones

STOCK INDICES

In every stock market many different types of corporations trade their shares. As a result, it is often difficult to determine from the whole market what trends are occurring in specific industries. To help identify stock trends in specific industries, stock exchanges and other independent companies group together stocks of certain industrial categories and report the behavior of prices within these categories. A group of stocks that analysts use for this purpose is a **stock index**, and investment companies as well as the various stock exchanges commonly report the activity of these indices in the news media. These reports provide more concise information about particular markets than the information available from the total market transactions.

In 1896 Charles Dow, one of the founders of the *Wall Street Journal*, developed the most well-known index, the **Dow Jones Industrial Average (DJIA)**. It is an example of a stock index published by an investment company. The index consists of the prices of thirty stocks, most of which are traded on the NYSE, that economists consider to be the leaders of industrial production in the United States. It includes such well-known companies as IBM, General Electric, and AT&T. Economic analysts consider it to be the best representation of the health of American industry. Consequently, more media outlets report the DJIA than any other stock index.

The **Standard and Poor's 500 (S&P 500)**, like the DJIA, is a commonly reported investment index. It includes five hundred stocks and is intended to give an even broader perspective on business in the United States. The S&P 500 tracks not only corporations engaged in industrial production but also other types of businesses, such as those that provide services. Given that spending on services composes the majority of consumer spending in the United States, the S&P 500 is indeed an important stock index.

The various stock exchanges publish indices that serve as economic indicators of various industries. The NYSE indices include a composite index (covering the entirety of the over two thousand stocks it lists), a financial index, a utilities index, a transportation index, and an energy index. Various groups use these indices to gauge the health of specific types of industries. The NASDAQ also has a composite index. This index appears regularly in business reports and is one to which economic analysts often refer. The NASDAQ also publishes numerous industry-related indices. The Amex, too, publishes a composite index.

SECTION REVIEW 8B

1. In what two ways is a stock market like other markets?
2. What is the most well-known stock exchange in the world, and what accounts for its importance?
3. What is the largest US stock exchange that has no trading floor?
4. What is the most well-known stock index in the United States, and who developed it?

CHAPTER EIGHT

The bull and bear are symbols economists use to describe stock market movements. When the market is rising and investors are buying stock, economists refer to such increases as a bull market. The bear market is the opposite: the market is falling, and investors are selling off shares.

A **stock portfolio** is a collection of stocks from different individual corporations.

8C THE MARKET AND THE ECONOMY

Both the corporation and the investor hope to benefit from the sale of stock. The corporation looks for needed capital to improve and increase its productivity and profitability, and the investor seeks to increase his income. Both of these results occurring in significant industries and significant numbers indicate that the nation's economy is moving forward.

THE IMPORTANCE OF STOCK MARKETS

Stock markets provide a venue for the sale of stock, which is essential for a corporation to raise needed revenue. The corporate ownership structure developed so that businesses could undertake projects that an individual owner or partnership would not have the money to undertake. Though business owners relinquish some control of the business and its profit, they can, by selling stock, raise the financial capital necessary to purchase items that could significantly boost productivity and profits. For example, they can invest in highly advanced production technology that not only increases the efficiency and profitability of their operation but also permits the increased standard of living enjoyed in free economies.

The market also provides opportunities for individuals to invest. The *2014 Investment Company Fact Book* states that 53.2 million households, or 43.3 percent of all US households, own **mutual funds**, which are privately managed stock portfolios (see Fig. 8–1). Approximately half of the nation's households own stock through mutual funds, individual investments, or retirement packages. Stock ownership is no longer an exclusive privilege for the rich; it has become an important part of retirement planning for many Americans.

Fig. 8-1 43 Percent of U.S. Households Owned Mutual Funds in 2014

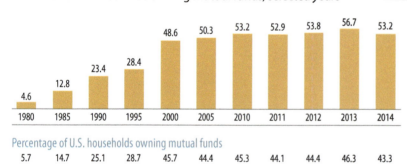

Millions of U.S. households owning mutual funds, selected years

Year	1980	1985	1990	1995	2000	2005	2010	2011	2012	2013	2014
Millions	4.6	12.8	23.4	28.4	48.6	50.3	53.2	52.9	53.8	56.7	53.2
Percentage of U.S. households owning mutual funds	5.7	14.7	25.1	28.7	45.7	44.4	45.3	44.1	44.4	46.3	43.3

Finally, the stock market indices provide information to corporate leaders, economic analysts, and governmental policymakers. The various market indices, such as the DJIA or the S&P 500, help investors to see trends and be better able to predict the risks and returns of various investment options. They give guidance to business owners as to whether it is a good time to expand production or to follow a more conservative fiscal strategy. For economic analysts and governmental policymakers, the various indices supply valuable data for determining the overall health of the nation's economy and what interventions, if any, may be necessary.

PAST PROBLEMS AND PRESENT SAFEGUARDS

The important role of stock exchanges in the financial history of the United States most vividly evidences itself in times of crisis. The most memorable example, by far, is the stock market crash of 1929, which many identify as the beginning of the Great Depression.

The 1920s was a decade of prosperity in the United States. Many people sought to transform their new-found wealth into an

THE STOCK MARKET AND THE CHRISTIAN

Is it consistent for a believer who refuses to engage in gambling to be involved in trading stocks? There is certainly no biblically definitive answer to that question. To make an informed decision consistent with the Scriptures, the believer ought to prayerfully examine what gambling is, how it differs from investing in the stock market, and what biblical principles apply to this question.

To gamble is to wager or bet some stake, usually money, on the uncertain outcome of a game or event in the hopes of gaining a higher stake, usually more money. Whether betting on horses, purchasing lottery tickets, playing cards, or rolling dice, the goal is to win, and winning almost always means money, sometimes significant amounts of it. There is the element of chance, the anticipation of possibly high returns, and the adrenaline rush if successful. For many, these elements make gambling addictive and leave players unable to stop in spite of financial losses and the harm those losses may create.

How then does gambling differ from investing in stocks? Is not the goal of investing to earn a profit, and is not the investor also uncertain of the outcome? There are, no doubt, those who enter the stock market as a gambler enters a casino. Their primary motivation is greed. They are not looking to invest as much as to "play the market" in the hope of getting rich quickly. This approach to stock trading is wrong, and those who practice it are guilty of gambling. The purchase of stock should be as an investment rather than as a game of chance played for a remote opportunity to make money. Stock trading and gambling can and should be greatly different.

One important distinction between gambling and stock trading is that to buy stock is to purchase partial ownership in a corporation and thereby have a personal interest in its successful operation. Stock ownership is comparable to the ownership of a proprietorship or a partnership. As a partial owner of a corporation, the shareholder has a say in the direction and operation of the company, although his say is small unless he owns a significant number of shares. If he believes the managers are running the business inappropriately, he can seek to have them dismissed or he can sell his share of the ownership.

Another distinction between stock ownership and gambling is that the stock market need not carry the risk of a gambling game. The person who buys and sells stocks with only the intent of "striking it rich" may indeed take unnecessary risks. That kind of investor will likely purchase stocks that offer possible high returns but at a high risk; consequently, he may well lose his entire investment. Wise investing in stocks, however, includes research into the background, products, and financial stability of a corporation, thus reducing the uncertainty of the outcome of the investment. If an investor plans to stay informed as regards the progress of his corporation and to hold his shares for a long period of time as the business grows, then he lessens his risk of financial loss and increases the likelihood of seeing a positive return on his investment. Careful purchasing of stocks can be a prudent means of increasing God-given resources.

There are several biblical principles that apply to this question. You should take the following as a start and do further study on your own.

Stewardship

Believers are to be good stewards of whatever financial resources God provides. Risking those resources in gambling ventures is to ignore biblical warnings regarding wealth obtained through vain means (Prov. 13:11). Gambling is not exercising wise stewardship over God-given resources. Those who operate gambling enterprises do so to make money for themselves, not their customers. Consequently, the odds on their games work against the players. There is just enough of a chance to win and a high enough prize to convince a player that he could be the next winner and that he will be rich if he is. The truth, however, is that there is not nearly as great a chance to win as there is to lose. Because this is true, gambling clearly violates the biblical principle of stewardship. It is unnecessarily risking what God has entrusted to a person. On the other hand, investing in stocks can be good stewardship, similar in principle to the parable of the talents in which the master told the wicked servant that he should have given the talent to the exchangers so that the master could have collected it with interest (Matt. 25:27).

Covetousness

The Bible warns against covetousness (Deut. 5:21 et al.) and identifies it as idolatry (Col. 3:5). While there may be a certain thrill to gambling, the primary motivation for most is money, and you have seen several times the warning against the love of money (1 Tim. 6:9).

Love for God

Rather than loving God with all his heart (Matt. 22:37), seeking first the kingdom of God and His righteousness (Matt. 6:33), and striving to please God and to glorify Him (1 Cor. 10:31), the gambler is primarily interested in enriching himself. His desire for monetary winnings puts him at odds with Christ's teaching on the inability to serve two masters (Matt. 6:24).

Love for Others

Addiction to gambling is real and creates numerous heartaches. The gambler who becomes obsessed with winning and convinced that the next game or card will bring him instant wealth often spends on himself what he should have spent on family or used to pay living expenses. He is not loving his neighbor as himself but is rather just loving himself (Matt. 22:39).

ever-increasing income in a quest to join the ranks of the truly rich. The stock market served as a primary means of achieving this goal. Along with the increase in individual wealth, the value of stocks exchanged on the stock market (as reflected by their prices) had grown significantly. Buying stocks when prices were low and selling them when prices rose enabled investors to make a good deal of money. Those who actively buy and sell stocks for the purpose of taking advantage of short-term price changes are engaging in a practice that market analysts call **speculation**. Speculation is risky and is closer to gambling than it is to investing.

Though the values of many stocks were rising in the 1920s and making the stock market more attractive to those seeking wealth, all was not as well as it seemed. Sometimes stock prices rise not because the true value of the company they represent is increasing but simply because investors expect the price to rise. In a sense, the investors' expectations create an increased demand for that company's stock, thereby raising its price. When stock prices rise in an industry or across the entire market simply because of expectations and they rise in excess of the corporations' true value, economists call it a **speculative bubble**. As long as the bubble continues to grow, investors can make money, sometimes significant amounts. Such was the case throughout much of the 1920s. However, when stock traders realize that the value of the stocks exceeds the real value of the corporations, they begin selling shares in large quantities. The quantity of the selloff causes prices to fall dramatically, and investors lose money. Then, the bubble bursts.

In the late 1800s there were those who recognized the problems of speculation. This Currier and Ives lithograph grouped speculation with other dubious forms of making money, some of which have since become illegal. By contrast, the other half of the lithograph highlights the value of hard work and industry (Prov. 13:11).

TULIPMANIA

One of the most interesting historical examples of a speculative bubble occurred in the early 1600s in Holland. Tulip bulbs are not native to Holland; traders introduced them in the late 1500s. Tulips proved very popular, and suppliers found that the flowers were susceptible to a nonfatal virus that caused the development of petals with contrasting colors. The widespread demand, the increased variety, and the limited supply caused the price of tulip bulbs to rise significantly through the 1620s and early 1630s. Based on this pattern of rising prices, Dutch citizens

of all economic levels sought to make money in speculation on tulip bulbs. They bought and sold the bulbs in tulip exchanges developed specifically for the purpose. Prices continued to rise until a single bulb of some varieties sold for today's equivalent of tens of thousands of dollars. The bubble eventually burst in 1637, when those who held and grew bulbs could no longer sell them and lost a great deal of their investment.

The 1920s' surge in stock prices was, in large part, a speculative bubble. As the economy began to slow in late 1928 and early 1929, speculation became more dangerous. Investors had less money to invest, the nation's productivity lessened, and then the speculative bubble burst. Mass stock selling occurred during a period of just over a week and culminated on Tuesday, October 29, 1929—one of the greatest one-day losses in the history of Wall Street stock trading. Shareholders, both large and small, lost most of their investments, and in some cases they lost everything.

Some market analysts have voiced concern that the events of 1929 and the Great Depression could happen again. It would be irresponsible to suggest that such a calamity is impossible today, but the federal government has implemented safeguards to make a recurrence less likely. For example, the government formed the **Securities and Exchange Commission (SEC)** in 1934 to ensure that corporations provide accurate and current information to the public about their financial situations and their business dealings. The purpose for this reporting is to prevent investors from making decisions in ignorance. Consequently, investors are now less likely to buy a corporation's stock believing that it is financially sound when in fact it is not.

Outside the NYSE on the day after the October 24, 1929, stock market crash

This chapter presented you with considerable information about corporate America. You have been introduced to types of stock, stock trading, stock indices, the SEC, and the history, types, and functions of stock markets. You have read how the stock market plays an important role in a modern market economy, allowing individuals to enjoy the benefits of business ownership without investing a life savings and permitting business owners to finance economically beneficial growth in technology and production. You have also seen that stock markets, exchanges, and private organizations generate a great deal of information about stock behavior and, correspondingly, the

THE SECURITIES AND EXCHANGE COMMISSION

Following the Great Depression and in response to concerns that investors expressed about the behavior of some corporations, the US Congress created the Securities and Exchange Commission. During the speculative bubble of the 1920s, some corporations had encouraged investors to purchase their stock by falsifying or concealing information about their financial stability. This inaccurate information led investors to buy what they may not have purchased had there been a truthful financial disclosure. Also, at times stock exchanges and stockbrokers who had financial interests in additional investments encouraged their clients to purchase stocks when such purchases may not have been in their clients' best interests.

The intent in establishing the SEC was twofold: 1) to require companies to fully disclose their financial status so that potential investors could make informed investment decisions and 2) to regulate the activities of stock exchanges and brokers in the best interest of the investor. To encourage full disclosure, Congress passed a law requiring corporations to make regular financial reports to the SEC, as well as to notify the commission about any significant changes in the structure or activity of the company that may affect its operation and profitability and, thus, affect investors' decisions. Commission personnel compile this information in a database that they make available to the public electronically. The SEC has also designed its website to educate the public about investment and corporate activity.

nation's economic condition. You are also now aware that businessmen, economists, and policymakers use this valuable information to make the decisions and determine the policies that direct the economy. You were also challenged to apply scriptural principles to market investment to find a biblical answer to whether the stock market is indeed a venue in which the Christian steward can wisely invest the resources his Master entrusts to him.

SECTION REVIEW 8C

1. List three reasons that stock markets are important to the economy.
2. According to the text, what are two distinctions between gambling and stock ownership?
3. List two circumstances contributing to the crash of 1929.
4. What is the danger of speculation?
5. When and why was the SEC founded?

CHAPTER REVIEW

CONTENT QUESTIONS

1. What is the evidence of ownership of a corporation?
2. How does a person control a corporation?
3. What is the primary reason for a corporation selling shares of its stock?
4. What do the owners of a corporation lose when they sell shares of its stock?
5. Identify each of the following as being associated with common (C) or preferred (P) shares of stock:
   a. shareholders receive dividends first
   b. owners have voting rights
   c. considered true ownership
   d. less risky
   e. if the corporation fails, these shareholders receive any leftover revenue ahead of other shareholders
6. When launching an IPO, how could the original owners maintain control of their corporation?
7. Explain how the phrase "buy low; sell high" applies to buying stock for profit.
8. In what two countries did stock exchanges originate?
9. Where and when did the first US stock exchange develop?
10. What stock index gives a broader perspective than the DJIA, and why is it important?

APPLICATION QUESTIONS

1. For each of the following, explain how the stock markets and the various stock indices are important:
   a. a corporation's board of directors
   b. an individual investor
   c. a governmental economic policymaker
2. Had the SEC existed in the 1920s, how might its regulatory policies have prevented the stock market crash of 1929?
3. A communications firm has recently acquired patents for new technology that will result in significant growth for the company. Consequently, you are considering purchasing shares of stock in this company. Should a friend ask you how you would explain the difference between your stock purchase and gambling, how would you answer? Support your answer using biblical and economic principles.

TERMS

Term	Page
stock	146
common stock	147
dividends	147
preferred stock	147
stockbroker	148
commission	148
floor traders	148
tape	148
initial public offering (IPO)	149
stock exchanges	150
New York Stock Exchange (NYSE)	151
NASDAQ	151
American Stock Exchange (Amex)	152
stock index	153
Dow Jones Industrial Average (DJIA)	153
Standard and Poor's 500 (S&P 500)	153
mutual funds	154
stock portfolio	154
speculation	156
speculative bubble	156
Securities and Exchange Commission (SEC)	157

PERSONAL FINANCE

CREDITWORTHINESS

The word *credit* comes from the Latin word *credere*, which means "to believe," and in the context of finances, it means to entrust something into another person's care. Before a credit institution entrusts its capital (the loan) into the care of the borrower, it seeks to ascertain the creditworthiness of that person. But how does a lender determine who is worthy of credit?

Most professional lenders require loan applicants first to complete a credit application. By carefully scrutinizing the loan application and other sources of information, the lender determines what is popularly known as the potential borrower's five Cs of credit: character, capacity, capital, collateral, and conditions.

CHARACTER

If a friend wanted to borrow $100 from you, one of the first questions that would likely go through your mind would be, "Will he pay me back?" Internally, you are assessing an aspect of your friend's character. Do you know him as a person of integrity and dependability? Likewise, the first area a potential creditor examines is the character of the applicant, or his honesty and reliability. While determining character may be a fairly easy task for a person considering a loan to a friend, it is very difficult for a lender who is not acquainted with the applicant. To determine an applicant's character, a lender examines his history of repaying loans by checking the records of a credit bureau.

In periodic reports to credit bureaus, major lenders detail the performance of those to whom they have lent money. **Credit bureaus** serve as central warehouses storing in-

formation about borrowers for seven years (they retain information about personal bankruptcy for ten years). They charge lenders for examining the files of particular applicants. A credit file includes the names of lenders, the amounts of loans previously granted, the term of the loans, any outstanding balances, and the borrower's performance in repaying the loans. These factors commonly comprise a person's **credit score**, an index of the person's overall creditworthiness. If an applicant lacks credit experience, as evidenced by insufficient information in his credit file, or if the information indicates that he cannot be trusted with a loan, the lender will likely decline to make a loan. If so, the lender must notify the applicant in writing.

CAPACITY

Capacity takes into consideration a loan applicant's ability to repay his debts. If a friend has exceptional character but has just lost his job, you might still be reluctant to lend him $100. Why? Because without a job or other source of income, your friend has no apparent means to repay you. Banks and other commercial creditors must likewise be assured that an applicant has the capacity to repay a loan; therefore, they require that potential borrowers disclose all sources of income. Examining where an applicant works, his present income, and how long he has worked for that employer contributes to the lender's assessment of a loan applicant's ability to pay off the loan he is requesting.

A lender determines an applicant's "credit health" during an application to ascertain whether he's a good risk, much as a physician determines a patient's health during an exam.

CAPITAL

When a banker or other lender mentions the word *capital*, he is speaking of the borrower's net worth. The **net worth** of a borrower is what he owns minus what he owes. In other words, the financial net worth of someone is what he would have left if he sold everything he owned and paid off all his debts. You might consider someone who has $4 million in houses and other assets to be a wealthy and prosperous individual; however, if he owes various creditors $3,990,000, a bank or other lending agency may consider him a poor loan risk. To determine an applicant's capital, lenders sometimes require a borrower to complete a personal financial statement that lists all his assets and all his liabilities.

COLLATERAL

If an applicant's character is good, his capacity to repay is sufficient, and his capital is adequate, a lender next

SYLVIA PORTER (1913-91)

Economic Reporter and Tutor for the Masses

After her widowed mother lost most of their family savings in the stock market crash of 1929, Sylvia Field Porter decided to change her major at Hunter College from English literature to economics. In the midst of the economic difficulties the nation was beginning to experience, she was curious to find out what did or did not make an economy work. That curiosity and a talent for explaining the technicalities of economics in a clear and simple manner soon led her into an impressive career in economic journalism.

After she graduated (magna cum laude) in 1932, Porter gained work experience at several brokerage firms while taking graduate courses at New York University. Her writing career took off in 1935 when she began to produce a regular financial column for the *New York Post*. She also contributed articles to many popular magazines and in 1939 wrote her first book, *How to Make Money in Government Bonds*. By the end of the decade she was called "the girl wonder of Wall Street."

At first the young writer used the name S. F. Porter to conceal that she was a woman in the male-dominated realm of economics. However, the merit of her work soon brought respect to the lady economist, and she changed the byline of her syndicated financial column to simply Sylvia Porter.

Many of Porter's major book titles reflect the practical nature of her writing. Among them are *How to Live Within Your Income* (1948) and *How to Get More for Your Money* (1961). Also, beginning in 1960, Porter annually published *Sylvia Porter's Income Tax Book*. She updated her 1975 bestseller, *Sylvia Porter's Money Book: How to Earn It, Spend It, Save It, Invest It, Borrow It, and Use It to Better Your Life*, with a new version "for the '80s" in 1979. It also became a bestseller. In 1984 she began publishing *Sylvia Porter's Personal Finance*, a magazine that offered financial information and advice. Her final book was *Sylvia Porter's Your Finances in the 1990s*.

Before succumbing to complications from emphysema in 1991, Sylvia Porter had done much to mainstream many economic principles. Through her writings she admirably attempted to eradicate economic ignorance with down-to-earth economic instruction and practical advice for the general public.

examines the collateral that the applicant plans to use to secure the loan. Lenders must determine if the collateral would be sufficient to repay the loan should the borrower be unable to do so.

Contrary to what some people believe, lenders such as banks are not in business to repossess collateral. Taking possession of collateral is an expensive, time-consuming, and often emotional experience. The sole aim of a bank's repossession of collateral is the protection of its depositors' funds. Banks and other lenders, therefore, are reluctant to make a loan solely on the basis of good collateral.

CONDITIONS

The final C of credit, conditions, refers to the current general economic conditions. If the economy is healthy and financial institutions have plenty of money available for lending, they will likely make many loans, even some marginal ones that they would probably otherwise have denied. If economic conditions are poor, however, lenders may screen their loan applicants more tightly and deny some loans, even to those who have been their very good customers.

A significant economic downturn can have a negative impact on the other Cs as well. If the downturn costs a person his job, he may find himself suddenly unable to make payments on his debts; and if he should default on those debts, his credit score will likely drop. If unemployment is rising and a loan applicant's future employment is uncertain, a lending firm may view him as having less capacity and thus as a higher risk. A poor economy can also see a decline in real estate or other markets, and such declines can decrease a loan applicant's capital as well as the value of his collateral, both making it more difficult for him to obtain loans.

The five Cs of credit—character, capacity, capital, collateral, and conditions—should help you remember

CREDIT SCORE

If a friend asked to borrow money from you, you would no doubt review your history together. If he's borrowed money before and repaid it, you would probably be more willing to lend than if he had failed to pay you (or other friends) back. What if a complete stranger asked you for a loan? What assurance would you have of ever seeing your money again? That is the situation banks and other lenders face when people apply for credit cards and loans. They have a limited amount of money available to lend, so they must decide who will be a good investment—those who will pay back their loans.

To provide lenders with objective information, credit bureaus collect data and calculate credit scores. Lenders use credit scores to determine who qualifies for credit, what interest rate the applicant must pay, and how much credit they will grant him. Major factors in calculating the score include the frequency of on-time payments (late payments over thirty days drop the score), the amount of current outstanding debt, a comparison of the amount of debt to the amount of available credit, and the length of the person's credit history. Since each bureau has varying information and uses different scoring methods, no person has just a single credit score. For example, the Fair Isaac Corporation created the FICO score, which the mortgage industry uses extensively, and the three

major credit reporting agencies—Equifax, Experian, and TransUnion—each have different credit scoring systems.

By law, US residents have the right to request a free credit report every twelve months and to challenge any inaccuracies. Occasionally, a person with the same name as someone else in the community may find that credit records of the other person have become part of his credit reports. If the other person has a poor credit record, the results could be damaging to the person with a commendable credit history. The best way to raise your credit score is to pay off all outstanding debts in a timely manner, have only a few credit card accounts open, and apply for new credit only when necessary.

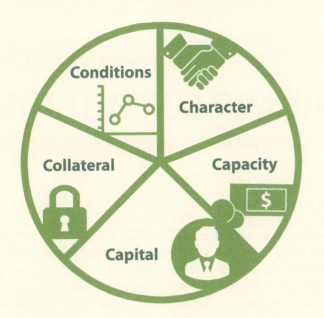

what lending institutions look at to determine a person's eligibility for a loan. They want to know a person's past performance with credit, his financial status, the present state of the economy, and the security that can be offered for the loan. Perhaps you have seen television commercials or printed advertisements for credit reports; now you know how they originate, what they contain, and why they are useful. You should also now realize that to lending firms, a person's character does matter. The Christian knows the importance of godly character, and since he realizes a poor credit score could be interpreted as a poor character score, he certainly seeks to keep his score high. Perhaps you do not presently have enough credit history to have a credit report score, but you could have one amongst your peers. If you want to know that score, just ask a friend for a loan.

REVIEW
QUESTIONS

1. What are the five *C*s of credit?
2. How do lenders investigate the character of a potential borrower?
3. When a lender speaks of a borrower's capacity, of what is he speaking?
4. What three things do lenders use credit scores to determine?
5. How often can US residents request a free credit report?

CHAPTER NINE
MARKET STRUCTURE AND COMPETITION

9A   MARKET DIFFERENCES — 165

9B   TYPES OF COMPETITION — 168

9C   ANTITRUST POLICY — 175

The owner of a business firm believed there was a great need for a certain product, and he developed that product and a way to produce it as a high-quality item. Anticipating that the demand for this product would necessitate expanding his business, the owner examined the advantages and disadvantages of the proprietorship, partnership, and corporate forms of business organization and chose the one best suited for his firm. However, in just six months he was bankrupt—a scenario all too common in American business.

What went wrong? It seems small American business firms are almost an endangered species. Nearly half of all new businesses close their doors within five years. Why is it so difficult for them to succeed? You can find the answer in one word: *competition*.

Choosing the right form of organization is not enough to ensure a business's success. Every business firm must also be able to meet its customers' needs in a way that is better than rival companies that produce a similar product. It must make a better or different product, have better customer service, or devise a better marketing strategy to persuade consumers to buy its product. In short, it must be able to compete successfully in the market.

But what does it mean for a business to compete in the market? After studying the previous chapter, when you read the word *market*, you may first think of the stock market and how firms compete there. Perhaps you still first associate the word with a supermarket or department store, and your thoughts went to competition between stores. Still another possibility is that you are one who looks at the business section of your local paper and connects *market* with a particular segment of the economy or *group of buyers*, such as the fast-food, new-car, or real-estate markets. In that case, you would think of competition within those groups. From an economist's point of view, however, the word **market** refers to the arrangements that people have developed for trading with one another, and competition is the struggle each firm experiences as it seeks to survive and then thrive within those arrangements.

This chapter examines three basic market questions. First, what are the fundamental differences that distinguish one market from another? Second, based upon these differences, what types of competition exist in the market? Third, how does the US government attempt to preserve market competition through federal laws?

9A MARKET DIFFERENCES

Each business has unique characteristics and differing ways of bringing its products and services to its customers. Almost all businesses, though, fit into groups that form specific markets, such as automobile, banking, publishing, electronics, construction, and so on. Economists and business analysts refer to each of these markets as an **industry**. An industry is a group of businesses that share common concerns: they sell a similar product, serve a certain group of customers, or produce their products in a similar way. Although there are a great many ways to distinguish each industry from every other one, economists have identified four key differences.

Businesses compete with each other with a fervor similar to that of children scrambling for the candy from a broken piñata. As long as there are profits to be made in a market, businesses will be drawn into the competition.

NUMBER OF FIRMS

The first and most obvious distinguishing difference is the number of firms that make up any one industry. In some industries, such as fast food, there are a large number of separate companies, while in others, such as jet airplane manufacturing, there are only a handful of competitors.

PRODUCT DIFFERENCES

Differences in the goods they sell also distinguish one industry from another. Many industries consist of firms that sell **differentiated products**, products that are visibly different from one firm to another. Other industries, however, produce **undifferentiated products**, products that are exactly alike regardless of which firm produced them. For example, dairy farmers produce an undifferentiated product—milk. The milk coming from one farm is virtually indistinguishable from that coming from a neighboring farm. Producers of undifferentiated products often go to great lengths with advertising and publicity methods to set their products apart from those of their competitors.

Firms in the automobile industry sell differentiated products. These two brands of automobiles may both provide transportation, but they are not alike.

CONTROL OF PRICE

A third difference that separates industries is the amount of control that firms have over setting the price of their products. In some industries, companies have considerable freedom to raise the prices of their products without significantly hurting their sales, yet firms in other industries do not have such control. If, for example, there is very little competition in a certain industry, consumers of that industry's product must either accept the price the few suppliers offer or go without the product. In contrast, other industries have so many competitors that if one firm raises its prices, most of its customers will simply go to other firms with lower prices.

ENTERING/EXITING THE INDUSTRY

The final difference among industries is the ease or difficulty with which firms can enter and leave the market. Remember the lemonade

ANDREW CARNEGIE (1835–1919)

Businessman and Philanthropist

In 1848 Andrew Carnegie and his family immigrated to America from Scotland. After the family located in the Pittsburgh area, thirteen-year-old Andrew set out to help provide for his poor family. Working first in a cotton factory and then in a bobbin factory, the lad eagerly accepted a new job in 1850 as a messenger boy for the telegraph office. Although it paid only $2.50 per week, the position became an important stepping stone for an amazing career.

While quickly learning about Pittsburgh and its prominent people, Carnegie proved that he was a dependable, hard worker worthy of greater responsibilities. He learned telegraphy on his own initiative and became a telegraph operator at age seventeen. Thomas Scott, a superintendent for the Pennsylvania Railroad, noticed Carnegie's skill and hired the young man as his personal clerk and telegraph operator. As Scott's able assistant, Carnegie climbed through the ranks of the railroad company. In 1859 he became superintendent of the Pittsburgh division and earned a yearly salary of $1,500—an impressive sum in those days, especially for a man not yet twenty-five.

Carnegie's earnings from his work with the railroad allowed him to begin investing in promising industries. He avoided stock speculation (a practice he regarded as gambling) and invested his money instead in businesses he knew and believed in. Although he acquired considerable stock in several companies, it was his investments in iron and steel that multiplied his wealth. First, he formed the Keystone Bridge Company, a successful partnership that replaced hazardous wooden bridges with iron ones that could span great rivers like the Mississippi and the Ohio. The need for high-quality iron for these bridges led Carnegie to build iron mills and expand his interests to all phases of iron production. His business acumen, his determination to manufacture quality products, and his practice of bringing talented men into these businesses as partners further increased his earnings. In 1865 Carnegie resigned from the railroad to oversee his other interests. Three years later he was making $50,000 per year and was considering retiring at the age of thirty-three.

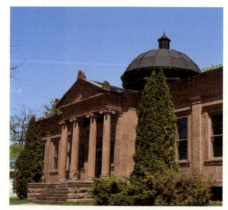

Carnegie Public Library, located in Escanaba, Michigan, was built in 1902.

However, he continued in his business activities and soon jumped into the emerging steel industry. Realizing that steel would be a major construction material in the future, Carnegie and his partners built their own steel mills in Pittsburgh, and later they bought the Homestead mills. In 1899 they consolidated these operations and their subsidiaries into the Carnegie Steel Company, and two years later, they sold them to J. P. Morgan. For his interests in this industry alone, Carnegie received more than $250 million.

In later years Carnegie became determined to dispose of his wealth by philanthropic endeavors. He wrote, "The man who dies . . . rich dies disgraced." In his essays "The Gospel of Wealth" and "The Best Fields for Philanthropy," Carnegie outlined how "surplus wealth should be considered as a sacred trust, to be administered during the lives of its owners, by them as trustees, for the best good of the community."[1] Accordingly, he donated vast sums (amounting to about $350 million) in America and abroad to build libraries, further education, aid the needy, and support other charitable concerns.

Despite his generosities and his admirable diligence and integrity, Carnegie was not a Christian. Like many today, he rejected organized religion and orthodox theology in favor of spiritual beliefs that relied more on his personal feelings than on Scripture. While Carnegie believed in a "Heavenly Father," he put more stock in humanist philosophy, evolutionary teaching, and his own intellectual enlightenment.

---

1. "The Best Fields for Philanthropy," *North American Review*, CCCXCII (July 1889): 684.

stand from the discussion on forms of ownership? If you were one of those who had such a first entrepreneurial experience, do you remember how easy it was for you to enter the market? You made a stand and a sign or two, chose your location, conducted minimal marketing, purchased the lemons, made the lemonade, and began sales. Now think of how difficult it would be were you to start a nuclear power plant. In addition to meeting thousands of regulations, you would need to locate and purchase a great deal of land, skilled labor, and technical machinery. These requirements, among others, would make it extremely difficult for you to enter that market.

Economists use the term **barrier to entry** to refer to any significant obstacle that prevents or hinders a new firm from entering an industry and competing on an equal basis with established firms. They do not, however, include in this definition the normal start-up difficulties of financing, attracting customers, hiring managers, and producing a product.

Barriers to entry may be either natural or artificial. **Natural barriers to entry** occur when firms already in the industry own all of a vital natural resource that a new firm would need to enter the market or when production costs favor high-volume production over production in small quantities. **Artificial barriers to entry** result from governmental regulations, such as licensing requirements or patents, which are exclusive rights to manufacture new inventions. In some cases the government makes it impossible to start up new businesses in certain industries.

ROLES IN PRICE CONTROL

Businesses that have the power to control the price of their products are known as price setters. It is important to note that even though a firm has the power to set the price of a good, it cannot control the demand for that good. The laws of demand and supply still hold. The firm may have the power to set a high price in the market, but customers still have the power to forgo purchasing the good. Businesses that do not have the power to control the price charged for the goods they sell are called price takers. These businesses are limited to charging the price that others in the market are charging.

SECTION REVIEW 9A

1. List the four key differences that distinguish one industry from another.
2. Based on the definitions given for differentiated and undifferentiated products, give an example of each. (They can be examples provided in the text or ones of your own.)
3. What is the difference between a natural barrier to entry and an artificial barrier to entry?

9B TYPES OF COMPETITION

Basing their analysis upon the four distinguishing market differences, economists have identified four major types of competition and have placed them on a continuum. As you move farther to the left on the continuum, you will notice the following: the number of firms in the industry declines, the differences in products increase, the firms are more able to control the market price, and it becomes more difficult to enter and exit the industry. Were you to move to the right on the continuum, you would notice that the opposite of each occurs.

PERFECT COMPETITION

Perfect competition exists when there are many producers selling an identical product, no single firm controls the price, and businesses find it relatively easy to enter and exit the market. One of the best examples of perfect competition is the production of crops, such as soybeans, corn, or wheat.

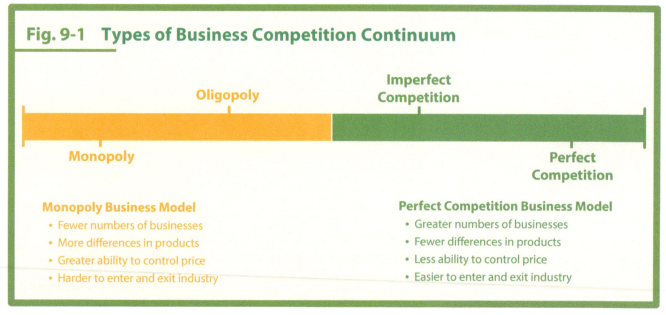

Fig. 9-1 Types of Business Competition Continuum

There is no example of a true monopoly or of truly perfect competition in the United States. As you can see on the above continuum, the four types of competition blend into one another. They are not bound by strict definition.

Number of Firms

In perfect competition there are a great many manufacturers, each of which has a very small share of the total market. For example, the number of soybean farmers in the United States is so large that even if one farmer owned a one-hundred-thousand-acre farm and produced over 3.5 million bushels of soybeans annually, he would still be producing less than one-fifth of 1 percent of the total US soybean production.

Product Differences

Another characteristic of perfect competition is that each firm in the industry sells an undifferentiated product. For example, consider soybeans again; the ones produced on one farm are indistinguishable from those grown on any other farm. Since there are no differences between the products, customers are indifferent as to whose they buy. Consequently, they tend to base their buying decision solely on the lowest price.

Control of Price

When perfect competition exists, there are so many businesses producing identical products that no individual firm can control the price. Imagine what would happen if Mr. MacDonald, a soybean farmer, decided to raise his price from the standard $10.50 to $12.50 per bushel. All of Mr. MacDonald's customers would likely abandon his product immediately and purchase soybeans from other producers. Likewise when many firms are producing similar products for price-conscious buyers, each tries to sell its product at a price lower than its competitors. Since this practice would eventually drive the price down to the minimum-profit level, profit-minded businesspeople generally shy away from participating in perfectly competitive industries.

Entering/Exiting the Industry

Under perfect competition, firms may enter and exit the market with relative ease. In our soybean farming example, the farmer may be faced with difficulties such as buying land and equipment and working the long, hard hours that farming requires; however, as long as the obligations of finance, technology, labor, and infrastructure are met, our farmer can get into and out of soybean farming

Soybeans are an example of an undifferentiated product.

WHAT'S IN A NAME?

Inventors apply for patents to protect their designs from being copied, and authors can gain copyrights to preserve their works from unauthorized duplication. Manufacturers also have an interest in protecting the names of their products, and they gain a measure of protection by registering a product's name as a trademark. Trademarks, which are names and symbols for a particular brand of product, have legal protection. No doubt you could easily list some familiar trademarked names, such as Mountain Dew, Oreo, and Ford. No one but the owners of those trademarks can legally put those names on products. The trademark may cover even pictorial designs, such as McDonald's golden arches. The owner of a trademark can prosecute anyone who uses that name or symbol without authorization.

A business has a vital interest in preventing impostors from using its product names and symbols. The owner of a trademark has undoubtedly spent an enormous sum of money on advertisements to build the reputation of a product. If another company were to market a product using the same name, it would be taking unfair advantage of the advertising already done by the original company without bearing any of the expense. Also, poor-quality products that are counterfeits of a name brand can severely damage the brand's reputation. Clothing is particularly susceptible to product name infringements. Violators may easily sew designer labels or identifying ornaments on their products to exploit trademarked names such as Levi's or Tommy Hilfiger. However, manufacturers other than those in the fashion industry must also beware because nearly every product, including counterfeit auto parts and bogus food products, has appeared on the market with phony logos.

Businesses must not only keep a watch on willful name infringements but also protect their names from becoming "generic" terms. If a trademark becomes too commonly used for a class of products, it can lose its protection under the law. Linoleum, aspirin, and shredded wheat are just a few of the familiar brand names that lost trademark protection. Some companies today (e.g., Coke, Kleenex, Xerox, and Scotch tape) are ready to legally prosecute every infraction to preserve their trademarks because so many people use these names as general terms.

with few entanglements. There is no true example of perfect competition in the United States. One or more of the four market differences will not be fully achieved. An example of this is the above illustration of the soybean farmer. In today's modern economic world, it can be extremely difficult for an individual to enter/exit the agriculture industry.

IMPERFECT COMPETITION

Imperfect competition is probably the most prevalent form of competition in America today. Within imperfect competition there are many producers of slightly differentiated goods, and each firm has some control over price and can enter or exit the market with relative ease.

JOAN ROBINSON (1903-83)
Teacher of Imperfect Competition

British economist Joan Robinson studied at Cambridge University and taught there for most of her life. Her work included such wide-ranging inquiries as a study of the economics of Karl Marx, the development and exposition of J. M. Keynes's General Theory, and a masterful critique of the generally accepted theory of the relationship between a country's accumulation of capital and its long-term economic growth.

Robinson is best known, however, for her development of the concept of imperfect competition. Economic models generally represent business firms as operating under perfect competition. Unfortunately, the characteristics of perfect competition are not very realistic for the vast majority of industries. In her book *Economics of Imperfect Competition* (1933), Robinson demonstrated that relaxing the assumptions of perfect competition affects the decisions of firms in terms of the prices at which they offer their products for sale and the quantity of the products they will produce. In particular, Robinson showed that firms under these new assumptions (the characteristics of imperfect competition) will reduce their production and increase the price of their product. Robinson's analysis, along with that of American economist Edward H. Chamberlin, provided the widely accepted concept of monopolistic or imperfect competition that schools of economics teach today.

Robinson is notable not only for her lasting contributions to economics but also for arguably being the only significant female economist born prior to 1940. Although her writings and work were comparable to those of Nobel Prize winners of her time, she was never considered for the prize. Some believe she never received the prize because of her gender, some claim it had more to do with her espousal of leftist political views, and others argue the reason was her diverse and sometimes unconventional economic teachings.

Number of Firms and Product Differences

Under imperfect competition there are a large number of firms, and they sell products that are differentiated in some way. The product itself may be differentiated, as with perfumes, which differ in scent from brand to brand; or the manufacturer may attempt to differentiate the product superficially by distinctive packaging, special warranties, and advertising crafted to establish a brand name.

Control of Price

Firms in an imperfectly competitive market do have the ability to affect the price of their products but only to a small degree. They have a relatively good idea of what their competitors are paying for natural resources, labor, and financial capital; how the overall economy will affect their own sales; and what customers desire to buy. To gain more information, some firms conduct extensive market research that surveys customers and analyzes competing products.

However, a firm's primary ability to control price relates directly to its ability to differentiate its product. Some firms are highly successful in setting their products apart from those of their competitors and in gaining customers' *brand loyalty*. Such loyalty allows the business to raise its prices and earn a greater profit. This phenomenon is readily apparent in the market for clothing with designer labels. While not always significantly different from their nameless counterparts, brand-name products have the ability to command a higher price.

Entering/Exiting the Industry

Economists use the phrase *relative ease* to describe the level of difficulty that firms experience when trying to enter or leave an industry under imperfect competition. The costs of entering and exiting the industry may be higher than under perfect competition, but there are certainly no insurmountable barriers.

OLIGOPOLY

As you move further to the left on the continuum of market organization, you encounter the **oligopoly**. The word *oligopoly* literally means "selling by a few." An oligopoly contains only a few firms, and their products can be either highly differentiated or undifferentiated. Each firm has a great deal of control over price and would find it relatively difficult to enter and exit the industry. The most important characteristic of an oligopoly is what economists call *mutual interdependence*. Because there are only a few large firms in this type of industry, the production decisions of one affect the profits of the others. Business strategy, therefore, is very important in an oligopoly.

Number of Firms

When should you consider an industry to be an oligopoly? Is it when two firms dominate the market? six? nine? The term *oligopoly* is used, in fact, quite broadly. Because for years three firms controlled most of the market, the US automobile industry was more obviously an oligopoly than it now appears to be due to the significant increase of foreign competitors. The petroleum-refining, breakfast-cereal, and airline industries are also oligopolies though

Distinctive packaging helps some manufacturers to differentiate their products from those of their competitors.

SYNERGY

Oligopolies are formed by many small sellers merging into larger companies. One important reason for mergers is synergy. **Synergy** occurs when the total is greater than the sum of the parts. The larger company will need only one quality-control department, personnel office, and so on—departments that each smaller firm had to maintain separately. Thus, the larger company is more economically efficient as it concentrates its resources to increase productivity. Synergy is the business equivalent of one plus one equaling three.

The manufacturers of breakfast cereals are an example of an oligopoly.

duopoly (doo OP uh lee)

each has differing numbers of firms. To make a distinction, economists identify a **tight oligopoly** as an industry in which the top four firms account for 75 percent of the market sales. A **loose oligopoly** is one in which the top four firms account for 50–75 percent of the industry's total sales. An oligopoly composed of exactly two business firms is a **duopoly**.

Product Differences

Some oligopolies manufacture products that are undifferentiated, while others produce differentiated goods. The petroleum industry produces an undifferentiated product. Other oligopolies, such as makers of automobiles, produce highly differentiated products.

Control of Price

In an effort to gain a larger share of the market and thereby gain greater control of prices, some firms aggressively try to determine their competitors' costs, production methods, prices, and any other factors that may give them an advantage. Yet, as in imperfect competition, the principal way for a firm in an oligopoly to control the price of its product is to differentiate its product successfully. Automobile makers who manufacture a distinctive car can command a higher price than they can on less differentiated models. Oligopolies that produce an undifferentiated product, however, do not have the option of improving their product to gain more customers. For example, a small number of big producers dominate the market for oranges. In a free market, competition among these producers would

CORPORATE SPYING

Keeping up with the competition is a major concern of modern oligopolies. Gaining or losing a small percentage of the market to a rival can mean millions of dollars in profits or losses. Therefore, corporations have stooped to some unorthodox means of observing the activities of their competitors to find ways to get a step ahead. While these practices are generally legal, you will notice that many of the following examples are less than ethical.

Some modern businesses have been known to use the following tactics to spy on their competition:

- Taking a tour of the competitor's factory
- Using aerial photographs of factories and warehouses to analyze activities
- Sifting through the competitor's garbage
- Keeping track of the competitor's help-wanted ads
- Paying workers inside the competitor's business for information
- Analyzing products made by the competitor
- Hiring employees away from the competitor to gain their information and skills
- Questioning the competitor's customers and former employees
- Studying labor contracts negotiated by the competitor
- Watching and counting goods being shipped to and from the competitor's buildings
- Obtaining information from consultants or suppliers who have worked for or done business with the competitor
- Conducting deceptive job interviews for the competitor's employees to gain information

Another means of corporate spying has come with improved cell phone technology. Employees of one firm can use their phones to take pictures of information on computer screens, assembly lines, or other facets of their company's operation and send those photos to cell phones or e-mail accounts of persons working for rival firms. Hence, some firms have banned personal cell phones from the workplace.

result in significantly lower prices for oranges. While consumers would benefit, producers would earn minimal profits.

Under some circumstances, these few orange producers might agree to cooperate rather than compete. If the producers were to agree to restrict production of oranges, the price would rise and profits would increase. This kind of agreement among a small number of producers to reduce their output and increase prices is called **collusion**. In the United States, collusion of this kind is illegal. The federal government seeks to protect consumers from the intended results of collusion—high prices and decreased quantities of certain products.

When producers form collusive agreements in countries in which they are legal or when the agreements span across national borders, the cooperating producers may choose to formalize their agreements by contracts or other official statements. This type of formalized collusion is called a **cartel**. The most well-known and successful cartel is OPEC, the Organization of the Petroleum Exporting Countries. Thirteen nations that produce and export crude oil form the OPEC cartel. Their cartel intends to prevent competition among oil producers, thereby maintaining oil prices at a high level.

Saudi members of OPEC converse during an OPEC summit in 2007.

Entering/Exiting the Industry

Firms seeking to enter an oligopoly face several barriers to entry that usually make it very difficult to break into the industry. Many oligopolies have few competitors simply because of the high up-front cost of entering the market. Consider the expenses you would face should you seek to start manufacturing a new line of automobiles. Other oligopolies have few competitors because there are laws that limit the number of firms that can exist in that industry. For example, the Federal Communications Commission (FCC) limits the number of licenses it grants to firms wanting to start radio or television stations.

In an oligopoly it is likewise difficult for a firm to exit the industry. Firms in oligopolies tend to use specialized and expensive production equipment for which there is a limited market. Again consider your automobile manufacturing endeavor. Should you need to exit the industry, to whom would you sell your equipment? The limited market could hinder your ability to sell the items at your cost, resulting in significant financial loss.

MONOPOLY

Have you ever played the board game Monopoly? If you have, you probably remember that success depends on obtaining a monopoly—owning all four railroads, all the utility companies, or all the best properties, especially Boardwalk and Park Place. With your monopoly of those properties, you could eventually place a hotel on each one and force your opponents into bankruptcy. The term *monopoly* reveals the number of firms in the industry, and by its nature, that one business is the price setter. It is also impossible for new firms to enter the industry and very difficult for the existing firm to exit.

Number of Firms

The word *monopoly* means "one seller." A **monopoly** is a form of market organization in which there is only one supplier in the industry. Several monopolies probably exist in your community. Your

ORIGIN OF THE MONOPOLY GAME

Though there is some controversy regarding the origin and development of the board game Monopoly, the most widely known and accepted account is that presented by the game's manufacturer, Parker Brothers.

In the midst of the Great Depression, a man named Charles Darrow developed a game that appealed to man's basic desire for wealth. He based the game on the idea of cornering a market and used locations from Atlantic City, New Jersey. He made and distributed his early versions by hand. His first offer to sell his game to Parker Brothers met with rejection, in part because of how long it took to complete a game. However, as the game grew in popularity, Parker Brothers accepted his second offer, and the game went on to become a highly successful product.

Public utility companies, such as those providing electricity, are given a legal monopoly to provide service in a particular area.

city's water/sewer, electricity, natural gas, cable television, and garbage disposal services are probably monopolies.

To gain a monopoly in the board game takes successful rolls of the die, good judgment, and shrewd trading; but how does one gain 100 percent of a market in the real world? One way is to own or control 100 percent of a resource that is essential to an industry. A firm in this circumstance enjoys a **natural monopoly**. When this occurs, there is a natural barrier blocking entry for any firm that would try to compete. Natural monopolies are hard to find since very few firms have total control of a single natural resource.

A second way is the **legal monopoly**, which exists because the government has allowed a firm an exclusive right to provide a good or service. For example, the government has granted the natural gas, water/sewer, and electric companies in your town monopolies because it has decided that to have more than one firm providing such services would be too inconvenient or expensive. You can understand this reasoning when you consider the possible havoc resulting from two or more companies digging up yards and roads to run gas, water, or sewer lines or setting up utility poles and running multiple power lines. The government also argues that if it allowed two electric companies to compete in the same area, the customers would end up having to pay higher individual bills to pay for the construction and operation of two power plants.

Product Differences

Since there is only one firm in the industry, there is only one product available with no substitutes. Other than the threat of losing the monopoly, the firm has little incentive to innovate and improve its products or services. For example, prior to the entrance of parcel-carrying competition from United Parcel Service (UPS) and Federal Express, the US Postal Service had no incentive to innovate. Indeed, complaints persist about the US Postal Service's lack of service in those areas in which it still enjoys monopolistic power.

Control of Price

Since there is no direct competition, the monopoly controls the price for the industry; that is, whatever price a monopoly sets for its product is the price that customers must pay if they want that product. Out of a fear that firms will "gouge" consumers, the government regulates the prices that many monopolistic companies can charge. To set that price, a governmental board determines the level of profit it will allow the firm and adds the firm's projected expenses to the profit to determine its allowable revenue. For example, an electric power company would determine its cost per kilowatt hour, and the governmental board would add the allowable profit, thereby setting the rate the power company may charge.

One firm's control over price does not necessarily render buyers totally at the mercy of the monopoly, for when dissatisfaction sets in, it creates an incentive for entrepreneurs to develop alternative products. If the price of electricity were to become prohibitively expensive, customers would switch to using natural gas or coal for their heating and cooking needs. If no close substitute for a product were available, entrepreneurs in search of profits would scramble to invent a substitute. For this reason, consumers in a free economy need not overly fear the power of a monopolistic firm.

BENEFITS OF COMPETITION

A monopoly is usually undesirable because of the lost benefits of competition. Competition stimulates efficiency because only the more efficient producers are able to compete successfully. It also encourages quality. Producers of inferior products find it difficult to retain customers and thus to compete. These benefits testify to the truth of biblical principles regarding diligence and industry. Competition serves as an impetus for producers to practice these principles.

Proverbs 10:4 and 13:4 illustrate how the person who puts hard work and skill into his labor rises above the ones who are careless. The result of the producer's putting his might into his work (Eccles. 9:10) is that his business prospers in the competitive market. His efficiency and quality also benefit the consumer with the best possible products at the best possible prices.

Entering/Exiting the Industry

By definition it is impossible for another firm to enter a monopolized industry. Some significant barrier to entry—whether natural, legal, or regulatory—blocks potential competitors from entering the market. Furthermore, monopolies have a vested interest in preserving their status and will spend a large amount of time and money to influence regulators and governmental officials to maintain the monopoly. If another firm were to succeed at entering the monopoly, it would become an oligopoly.

Also, it is very difficult for a monopolistic firm to leave the industry. Consider your electric company. Since it is the only provider of electricity, the government has made it virtually impossible for the firm to shut down. In certain cases in which strikes have threatened to shut down a service operated by a monopoly firm, the government has called upon the military to take over the operation temporarily.

SECTION REVIEW 9B

1. What type of business is one of the best examples of perfect competition?
2. What is the most prevalent form of competition in America today?
3. What is the most important characteristic of an oligopoly, and what does this term mean?
4. Why is it extremely difficult for a monopolistic firm to exit the industry?

9C ANTITRUST POLICY

Let us return to the game Monopoly. You may have participated in a game in which another player managed to get a monopoly on Boardwalk and Park Place. He then placed a hotel on each and waited. Eventually, one by one, the other participants landed on one of the expensive properties and declared bankruptcy, leaving the monopoly holder victorious.

Although most people enjoy playing the game, they draw the line at actually living it, especially when they are on the paying end of the transaction. Fear of a monopoly's power to charge exorbitant prices has prompted many laws prohibiting even the hint of the beginnings of an unlicensed monopoly. In the 1800s and early 1900s, Americans saw an era of tremendous growth. During this period the steel, oil, automobile, and banking industries became oligopolies. Realizing the direction many of these oligopolies were taking and fearing the results of monopolistic power, Congress took action.

THE SHERMAN ANTITRUST ACT OF 1890

Prior to 1890 one of big business's favorite ways of limiting competition without actually forming a monopoly was to form a trust. To create a **trust**, the head of the largest company in the industry would persuade the other firms to put their stock into a trust account. The manager of the trust would then look after the affairs of the larger group and would distribute the profits. To ensure that cutthroat

> In a nation's economy, households, business firms, and financial institutions are referred to as the private sector, and government is referred to as the public sector.

Political cartoon showing a Standard Oil tank as an octopus with many tentacles wrapped around the steel, copper, and shipping industries, as well as a state house, the U.S. Capitol, and one tentacle reaching for the White House.

competition would not occur and that profits would remain high, the trust manager would control the promotion, quantity, and prices of the products offered by each firm.

As a response to the tremendous control of the market by the trusts, Congress enacted the Sherman Antitrust Act in 1890. The act stated that "every contract, combination in the form of a trust or otherwise, or conspiracy, in restraint of trade" was illegal. The law also declared it illegal to "monopolize, or attempt to monopolize, or combine or conspire . . . to monopolize" business. Penalties for violation of the Sherman Act are fines and imprisonment.

THE CLAYTON ACT OF 1914

The Sherman Act led to the 1911 breakups of the Standard Oil Company and the American Tobacco Company. Some American legal analysts noted, however, that because of certain vague points in the Sherman Act, many businesses were still conducting themselves in ways that hindered competition without technically monopolizing the industry or combining firms.

The Clayton Act of 1914 closed most of the gaps found in the Sherman Act. It enumerated, clarified, and made illegal certain anti-competitive practices. Specifically, the act prohibited the following practices:

1. **Interlocking directorates:** Firms were skirting the Sherman Act by placing one or more directors on the boards of competing firms.
2. **Tying contracts:** A few big companies, to secure more business for themselves, would require that smaller companies

desiring to buy from them had to purchase their full line of products. For example, suppose that the owner of a small retail store wished to sell a certain manufacturer's line of shoes. That company would force the store owner by contract to carry its less desirable line of costume jewelry in order to carry its shoes. In fact, many large businesses would even refuse to sell any of their products to smaller firms if those firms carried any products of a competitor.

3. **Anticompetitive takeovers:** Corporations were taking over other firms by purchasing their common stock, limiting competition significantly.

MONOPOLY, ANYONE?

American Telephone and Telegraph (AT&T) used to be the largest privately owned company in the world. It was incorporated in 1885, shortly after Alexander Graham Bell first successfully spoke over wire. It was the parent company of the Bell System, a company that gained a monopoly under the protection of governmental regulation. With this monopoly, AT&T operated all long-distance telephone lines as well as most of the local telephone systems in the United States.

Another one of AT&T's subsidiaries was Western Electric, a company that manufactured telephones and telephone equipment. The government did not, however, give Western Electric approval for a monopoly. Nonetheless, AT&T required all twenty-three of its local or regional Bell System companies to use Western Electric equipment. These companies simply passed along to their customers the high prices Western Electric charged for telephone equipment, and AT&T profited. Customers had no alternative because they could not change to another telephone company.

The US government had long noticed the problems caused by AT&T's monopoly. Under the terms of an antitrust case in 1956, AT&T had to limit its operations to the telephone business. Still, the problems remained until the Justice Department's 1974 antitrust suit against AT&T under the provisions of the Sherman Antitrust Act. In the suit the government requested that Western Electric, Bell Labs (a research division), and all the local and regional telephone systems separate from AT&T, the parent company. When the case was finally settled in 1982, AT&T both lost and won. It lost the right to retain its local and regional telephone companies, and on January 1, 1984, they reorganized into seven independent regional firms. It won because it was allowed to keep Western Electric and Bell Labs and allowed to enter the new technologies of the computer industry.

In today's technology-dominated marketplace, many companies have such a large portion of their particular markets that they seem to be monopolies. Research and development are costly processes for companies, and new technologies are initially expensive for consumers. Few companies are willing to spend money to challenge an existing technology, and few consumers see the need to replace original purchases that are still functional. By default, then, the company that gets into a market first often dominates it. Examples of companies that are in or have been in this situation are Microsoft, Google, iTunes, Google Chrome, and Safari. The European Union has criticized several of these corporations for imposing dominance over competing firms. Some have argued that as it did with AT&T, the United States government should break up these firms into smaller companies. Others recommend simply waiting for rival companies to expand the market.

Companies that have a large amount of the market share of an industry are often viewed as a monopoly by some, as evidenced by the EU's concern over the dominance of Google.

4. **Price discrimination:** Firms were selling the same good to different buyers at different prices.

OTHER LEGISLATION

To promote competition further, Congress passed three additional landmark acts. The first of these was the Federal Trade Commission Act of 1914. This law provided for the establishment of an agency called the Federal Trade Commission (FTC). Its purpose is to enforce the Clayton Act. The FTC investigates alleged violations, holds hearings, and issues cease-and-desist orders if a suspected firm is found guilty of "unfair methods of competition" or "unfair acts or practices." Congress later amended the Federal Trade Commission Act to protect consumers as well as competitors.

Congress passed the second act in 1936, the Robinson-Patman Act. Small retailers were complaining that large chain stores were receiving price discounts as a result of quantity buying. The large stores were then able to sell their products at lower prices than the small retailers. The Robinson-Patman Act made it illegal for suppliers to hinder competition by selling "at unreasonably low prices."

Finally, in 1950 Congress closed another loophole by passing the Celler-Kefauver Act, often called the Antimerger Act. The Clayton Act of 1914 had prohibited firms from buying enough of a competitor's shares of stock to control the market and lessen competition, but it made no provision to prevent one firm from purchasing the assets of another firm. Many firms skirted the spirit of the Clayton Act by purchasing a competing firm's buildings, equipment, and inventory, enabling them to control the market all the same. The Celler-Kefauver Act made this kind of quasi merger illegal.

Seemingly every day, another business closes its doors, unable to compete any longer in the market. Were there too many other firms and too much competition to allow another newcomer to survive in that industry? Was the business unable to differentiate its product successfully and create its niche in the market? Was the business just not able to compete against rival firms who were better able to control prices? Having read this chapter, you should be able to answer such questions. When you read articles about local businesses, you should be able to make sense of references to imperfect competition, oligopolies, and monopolies. You could even look at some of the more prominent industries in your town and be able to classify them by industry and identify the number of firms, the differentiation of products, the control of price, and the ease of market entry and exit within that industry. You should also be able to explain the primary reasons for and the principal points of the Sherman, Clayton, and Robinson-Patman Acts. In addition to all this, a board game, perhaps one of your favorites, now takes on a whole new meaning for you. It may be time to play.

SECTION REVIEW 9C

1. What is the difference between a monopoly and a trust?
2. List the five congressional acts that were passed between 1890 and 1950 to preserve competition. Include the date of each.

CHAPTER REVIEW

CONTENT QUESTIONS

1. From an economist's point of view, what is a market?
2. What is an industry?
3. Complete the following chart.

	Number of firms	Product differences	Control of price	Entering/exiting the market
Perfect competition				
Imperfect competition				
Oligopoly				
Monopoly				

4. Why is collusion illegal in the United States?
5. What is the most well-known and successful cartel, and what does it control?
6. What legislation did Congress pass to make trusts illegal?
7. What four practices did the Clayton Act of 1914 end?
8. What governmental agency was created to enforce the Clayton Act, and what additional responsibility was that agency later given?

APPLICATION QUESTIONS

1. Why can a firm in a perfectly competitive market not slightly raise its price so that it might make a little more profit?
2. Why is it unlikely that a new firm would enter an oligopolistic market?
3. Select ten business firms in your town, and identify the form of competition under which each operates.

TERMS

market	164
industry	165
differentiated products	165
undifferentiated products	165
barrier to entry	167
natural barriers to entry	167
artificial barriers to entry	167
perfect competition	168
imperfect competition	170
oligopoly	171
synergy	171
tight oligopoly	172
loose oligopoly	172
duopoly	172
collusion	173
cartel	173
monopoly	173
natural monopoly	174
legal monopoly	174
trust	175
interlocking directorates	176
tying contracts	176
anticompetitive takeovers	177
price discrimination	178

PERSONAL FINANCE
CASH MANAGEMENT

Whether the topic is time, talents, or cash, the Christian who understands the stewardship principle knows that proper management is essential. He accepts that, as a steward, his primary responsibility is to "be found faithful" (1 Cor. 4:2). He recognizes that he has a responsibility to his Lord to "[redeem] the time" (Eph. 5:16), to seek to improve the talents given him, and to manage properly the earthly assets entrusted to him. Whether the Lord provides you with great wealth or just enough money to meet your basic needs, He demands that you use that amount wisely.

Successful personal financial stewardship entails correctly handling money on three levels. The first level is properly controlling cash in the short run. In contrast with the wise use of cash to make purchases, this level involves good management of the cash itself over a period of days and weeks. The second level is the prudent utilization of money in the intermediate run. As opposed to managing cash today or next week, the intermediate period is wise saving over a period of months. The final level of personal financial management focuses on the long-run investment of excess funds and considers saving for retirement. This article looks at only the first of these levels.

Cash management is a person's or business's system of handling the financial activities of accounting for cash inflows, storing short-term cash balances in ways that are most profitable, and making timely payments on financial obligations. (*Cash*, in the sense of cash management, refers not just to currency but to money in general; see p. 187.) Though some individuals, business firms, churches, and Christian schools might not be suffering financially as a result of poor cash management, they could be making better use of their limited assets and thereby improving their service to the Lord. By taking a more studied approach to the handling of their day-to-day financial transactions, they could accomplish more with their present capital and perhaps discover money for projects that had been tabled because of insufficient funds. For example, the principal of one Christian school noticed that thousands of dollars sat idle each month between the first of the month when parents made tuition payments and the middle and end of the month when the school distributed payroll checks to the faculty. He decided to open an interest-bearing account for the school into which he deposited all tuition payments. When payroll came due, he withdrew only the amount necessary to cover expenses and left the rest to draw interest. By the end of the year, the school had earned over $3,000 in interest. Because of this principal's wise cash management, the school could provide the faculty with a modest salary increase without raising the students' tuition.

PURPOSES FOR HOLDING CASH

A first step in examining how people might better manage their money is to determine why people hold cash balances. Generally, people hold cash for three reasons: to pay for routine transactions, to pay for unexpected emergencies, and to act as a store of value.

To Pay for Routine Transactions

Each day almost everyone engages in one or more routine cash transactions. Perhaps already today you have participated in such a transaction. You may have left your house with a specific amount of cash to pay for a breakfast item on the way to school, something for lunch, or some class expense. Most adults hold cash for the same reason, only on a larger scale. They have cash inflows from their paychecks, and in turn, they pay certain bills that arrive in their mailboxes regularly—house payments, utility bills, and home and auto insurance premiums. Since the amount of each of these transactions is fairly predictable, those receiving such bills usually plan to hold a certain portion of their income in cash to meet these expected obligations. Of course, with the increase of online payments, more people are holding this income in bank accounts from which their payments are electronically deducted rather than in physical currency.

To Pay for Unexpected Emergencies

The second reason people hold cash is to be prepared for rainy-day expenses. If households keep only enough cash to pay for their routine transactions, they can find themselves in serious financial trouble when they encounter unexpected problems. If emergencies arise for which they are unable to secure sufficient cash, they may have little choice but to draw from the funds they normally use to pay their monthly obligations. Then, when those regular bills come due, they may need to sell personal possessions or borrow to generate enough cash to stay current with their creditors.

The amount of money someone should hold to meet unexpected needs depends partially on his income. Economists have found that those with relatively high incomes tend to have "rainier" days than those with lower paychecks. For example, a student working part-time and making minimum wage may need to keep only a few dollars on reserve against some unforeseen emergency; however, a homeowner with three children and two cars would need to hold a greater amount of cash.

The amount a person needs to hold in reserve against a possible financial emergency also depends on the amount of other resources he has available. Consider, for example, the possibility of an incapacitating injury. A person with disability insurance may not need to hold as much money on reserve as someone without the insurance because his policy will continue to pay his salary while he is convalescing. Many financial consultants advise their clients to keep three to four months of income on reserve to meet unexpected emergencies.

To Act as a Store of Value

The final reason people hold cash is to store it for some predetermined future use. They may be saving for a major purchase, such as an automobile or major appliance, or they may be accumulating sufficient funds to invest in an income-producing or appreciating asset.

WAYS OF HOLDING CASH

Having answered the question of why people hold cash balances, we turn our attention to the ways in which they hold those balances. Basically, there are only two options. Either a person can hold the cash in the form of the money itself, generally paper currency or coins, or he can establish some type of transaction account.

Paper Bills and Coins

Obviously, the primary way someone can hold cash is to hold the money itself. Perhaps you have heard stories of wealthy eccentrics who, out of a distrust of banks, buried substantial sums of money in their yards or stashed it in the walls of their homes. Upon their deaths, neighbors or relatives ransacked their homes and property searching for the hidden treasure.

There are two specific dangers of holding money in the form of paper bills and coins. First, there is the danger of losing the money because of carelessness or theft. When it becomes commonly known that a person holds great amounts of currency, he becomes a target for thieves. The second danger is the threat of loss because of inflation. If a twenty-year-old had buried $10,000 in 1938 and as a ninety-seven-year-old had dug it up at the end of 2015, he would still have had $10,000 in cash; however, that cash would have lost a significant amount of its purchasing power. Since a dollar in 1938 could purchase over fifteen times more goods than a dollar in 2015, the person would have lost the purchasing power of a tremendous amount of money.

Transaction Accounts

Most people use cash for buying goods from vending machines or making other small purchases, but for larger purchases they prefer to use transaction accounts. A **transaction account** is an account at a financial institution against which a person may write a note instructing the institution to pay a specific sum of money to the person named on the note. Commercial banks offer the most popular transaction account, the **checking account**. The law permits only commercial banks to offer checking accounts, but it also forbids them from paying interest on those accounts. To circumvent these laws, commercial banks devised a second type of transaction account, a savings account called a **negotiable order of withdrawal (NOW) account**. Against his NOW account, the account holder can write withdrawal slips and transfer them to others. In appearance, a negotiable order of withdrawal is virtually indistinguishable from a check. The only difference is that a NOW account pays interest, whereas most checking accounts do not. Most banks require NOW account holders to maintain a minimum monthly balance of perhaps $1,000 for the account to be eligible to earn interest.

INSTANT CASH

Walk up to a bank at any time, day or night, punch a few buttons, and—presto!—cash at your fingertips. The electronic *automated teller machine (ATM)*, first implemented in 1969, has revolutionized banking to meet the demands of today's fast-paced society.

ATMs provide convenience. You can find them nearly anywhere people need ready cash—banks, shopping centers, malls, or airports. Customers can avoid long lines and perform routine business transactions, such as deposits, withdrawals, transfers between accounts, instant cash loans, and loan payments. To use the ATM, you simply insert your debit card into the machine, enter your *personal identification number (PIN)* on the keypad, and follow the instructions on the screen to complete your transaction.

Even if you go out of town or overseas, your debit card can help you obtain cash. Many of the over 420,000 ATMs in the United States belong to a network, and the numbers are growing daily. The Cirrus/MasterCard network has over 1 million ATMs in 210 countries, and the Plus/Visa System has more than 1.8 million ATMs in 200 countries. With this many ATMs, you can travel abroad and easily withdraw yen or pounds at the best rates without carrying traveler's checks, taking a loan, or paying commissions. For example, were you to enter a request for £20 at an ATM in London, a computer would convert the amount to dollars and call the main network office in Denver, which would then relay the request to your home bank. Provided that your account contained the money, the Denver office would approve your instant cash within fifteen seconds, and the bank would withdraw the money directly from your home bank account. Of course, the withdrawal from your account would be slightly more than the equivalent of the £20 you requested because most financial institutions charge a fee for the international exchange. This fee is usually a percentage of the withdrawal.

Along with the advantages of the ATM comes the disadvantage of an opportunity for new forms of crime. In one form, criminals obtain sets of access codes for the ATMs. In one instance the thieves had the help of a telecommunications consultant and planned to steal $14 million. Fortunately, they were caught. Another form of theft utilizes stolen cards and codes. One thief used a bank ATM's master security card, which can enter any account, and took $237,000. In a simpler form of crime, smalltime crooks simply hide near ATMs and rob customers who have just withdrawn cash.

Although thieves can break almost any code or barrier, the industry has taken extreme precautions. Bank computer programmers have developed random code systems that make it nearly impossible to eavesdrop on your computer line, even for someone who knows the system. The customer, however, should take some obvious precautions: 1) never give your card or PIN to anyone, 2) avoid out-of-the-way ATMs, 3) take a friend, and 4) beware of anyone loitering suspiciously around an ATM. The law says that you can suffer unlimited losses if you do not notify the bank within sixty days of an unauthorized withdrawal from your bank account.

Perhaps you chuckled to yourself as you began this article because internally you were joking about not having any cash to manage. Your amusement may have continued as you read about why and how people hold cash, and you wished that you had some to hold. Yet, the truth is that many who think that they have no cash to manage or hold are actually revealing their need for better personal financial management. If Christians were better stewards of the small amounts that God provides for them, they might find that He would entrust them with increasingly larger amounts (Matt. 25:21). Rather than wishing you had more money at your disposal, perhaps it would be better to examine critically how you are managing what you have now.

REVIEW QUESTIONS

1. What are the three areas that must be addressed for personal financial stewardship?
2. Why do people hold cash?
3. What are the two ways of holding cash?

TERMS

cash management	180
transaction account	182
checking account	182
negotiable order of withdrawal (NOW) account	182

UNIT FOUR

UNIT FOUR

ECONOMICS OF THE FINANCIAL MARKET

Chapter 10
MONEY AND THE FINANCIAL MARKET — 186

Personal Finance: Opening and Maintaining a Transaction Account —202

Chapter 11
CENTRAL BANKING — 208

Personal Finance: Ways to Save — 228

CHAPTER TEN
MONEY AND THE FINANCIAL MARKET

10A   MONEY — 187

10B   THE FINANCIAL MARKET — 195

Perhaps no other single item has been more beneficial to the economic development of mankind nor has been at the heart of more of mankind's problems than money. The consuming desire for it has been a cause of countless wars, murders, kidnappings, broken friendships, failed businesses, treasons, thefts, and wrecked marriages. The belief that they have too little of it motivates some people to steal or defraud to obtain more, while many of those who possess much of it find that it only inflames their desire to possess even more. Satan deceives people into believing that all they need to satisfy their unlimited wants is to acquire just a little more money. Scripture warns of the disastrous consequences of succumbing to this deception: "But they that will be rich fall into temptation and a snare, and into many foolish and hurtful lusts, which drown men in destruction and perdition. For the love of money is the root of all evil: which while some coveted after, they have erred from the faith, and pierced themselves through with many sorrows" (1 Tim. 6:9–10). Sadly, in spite of such a clear warning, some Christians, as well as many in the unregenerate world, still become obsessed with accumulating money.

Though money has been the principal cause of many problems, it has also been central to many benefits. The proper use of money allows man to provide for the needs of his family, to purchase clothing for the destitute, to obtain food for the hungry, to care for the sick, and to spread the gospel to the nations of the world. Christians who have a proper relationship with God recognize that money is a tool God provides for His people to use in His service.

10A MONEY

So far in this text we have taken money for granted. It first appeared in Chapter 2 in the circular flow model as the key ingredient that allows an economy to function. Yet what exactly is money? Some would say that money is paper bills and coins; others would include checking accounts and traveler's checks. While all these things may serve as money, the term has a much broader definition. **Money** is anything that a society commonly uses and generally accepts in payment for goods and services. Thus, anything can serve as money. This truth is evident in that different cultures in different ages have used such a variety of objects as fur, dried fish, seashells, tobacco, human hair, and shark's teeth as money.

Remember, though, for an item to serve as money, the members of a society must commonly use and generally accept it. To ensure that everyone in the American economy accepts your money, the US Congress has declared it **legal tender**. So, if you tender (or offer) it as payment for a debt, all creditors must accept it.

FUNCTIONS OF MONEY

In the minds of most people, money has but one function: to buy things. Although money functions primarily as a means of payment for goods and services, it also serves as a measure of value and a means of storing purchasing power.

Means of Payment

As a means of payment, money reduces the cost of doing business. What do we mean by "the cost of doing business"? To illustrate, let us suppose that you want to purchase a used car. How would you go about locating one at an acceptable price? Would you walk down a busy street asking each passerby if he has a car to sell, go door-to-door asking the same question, or stand at a busy intersection shouting and waving a sign bearing your request? You are probably thinking, "That's crazy! It would take way too much time and effort and would be too costly," and you are absolutely correct. Economists have found that rational people do everything possible to reduce the cost of doing business. To lower the cost of buying a car, you, as a rational person, would likely use the Internet, your local newspaper's classified ads, or visits to a used car lot. Likewise, a society uses money as a means of payment to reduce the cost and effort of doing business.

Money serves as an easy means of payment.

Consider the alternative to using money. Before using a standardized monetary system, primitive societies used **barter**, the exchange of one person's goods or services for another's. Barter is an expensive and time-consuming process. Once again we illustrate with another automobile example. Let us assume that a carpenter living in a barter economy needs to have his car repaired. He takes a day off from work, and after spending several hours searching, he locates a mechanic. There is, however, one problem: the mechanic does not need any carpentry work done. He wants some steaks. Now the carpenter goes in search of a butcher who will trade steaks for carpentry work so that he can trade the steaks for car repairs. Now imagine the butcher wants something else—the process

could go on and on. Because of the lack of a **double coincidence of wants** (both parties involved in the trade wanting what the other has to offer), barter for any economy is not only a frustrating way to do business but also an exceedingly inefficient practice. The two or three days that you spent lining up the multiple exchanges could have been used to produce carpentry work. By imagining many others engaged in similar multiperson exchanges, you can recognize how barter severely hinders the development of a nation's economy. Because the use of money as a common means of payment eliminates barter's multitude of time-consuming trades, it is far less costly to the economy.

Measure of Value

What would you do if you were driving down a highway and saw all the road signs displaying distances in kilometers? You would probably attempt to estimate those distances in miles because the mile is how you commonly measure distances. Economics is no different. Every society must have a common and consistent measure for economic value. Hence, whatever a nation uses for money becomes the yardstick by which its people express the value of goods and services. If a person tells you that an item sells for $10,000 or that a service costs $20 an hour, you have a pretty clear understanding of its value—far better than if the person expressed its cost in terms of a certain number of books, cows, beads, or seashells.

Values expressed in terms of money are easy to record and understand.

> Inflation is a general rise in prices.

Means of Storing Purchasing Power

Another problem with barter is that the recipient of bartered goods often cannot store them to prevent them from losing their original value. Food spoils, household items break, livestock dies, and clothes go out of style. Money better retains its face value. Rather than attempting to store your purchasing power by buying commodities and constantly reselling them before they spoil, you can hold your purchasing power considerably longer in the form of money. Though money does retain its face value over a period of time, it is subject to a type of economic spoilage. If the nation experiences inflation, it will likely reduce the purchasing value of a person's savings.

DESIRABLE CHARACTERISTICS OF MONEY

Whatever the form of money a nation chooses, there are certain characteristics that are most desirable for the money to have.

Convenience and Portability

That a barter system is inconvenient and that a monetary system is far better goes without saying, but not all standards (forms of money) are equally convenient and portable. The ancient Spartans used bulky slabs of iron, and many early American colonists used bales of tobacco, neither of which would be easy to carry or use. Today, however, most societies choose a standard, such as gold, silver, or paper, that is definitely easier to carry and far more convenient.

Divisibility

A nation's money should be divisible. That is, you should be able to divide the money relatively easily into smaller denominations. The Spanish dollar, the monetary unit from which we derived the US

MONEY ON YAP

Throughout human history, money, as the medium of exchange in a society, has taken such forms as blocks of salt, beaver pelts, and cattle. However, one of the most curious forms of money still exists on the Micronesian islands of Yap. The traditional Yapese currency consists of large stone wheels. The country has over six thousand of these wheels, and they range from two to twelve feet in diameter, although most are five feet across or smaller. Each limestone wheel has a hole in the center so that it may be carried by a log slipped through the opening. The larger stones may require as many as twenty men to transport them.

The islanders have used this stone money for over one thousand years. Tradition says that a warrior named Anagumang brought the first (and most valuable) stones from a distant island in outrigger canoes. Sailors and traders of the late nineteenth and early twentieth centuries brought additional stones, but because of the comparative ease with which they came to the islands, their value is less, regardless of their size.

Obviously, because the large stones are difficult to carry around as pocket change, the Yapese also use other money. For minor transactions they have used necklaces of stone beads as well as large seashells. Today the islanders also use US currency for many of their purchases. (Yap was a part of the US Trust Territories in the Pacific until it became a part of the independent Federated States of Micronesia.) However, the Yapese still commonly use the stone money in large transactions, such as buying land, purchasing canoes, and winning permission to marry. Also, when given as a token of apology or reconciliation, the money works well to settle arguments.

When not using their stone money, the Yapese typically prop the stones against their houses or park them in a "village bank." They rarely move such parked stones, and any change in ownership is declared publicly so that everyone knows who the new owner is. One positive feature of this stone money is that its owners have little fear of its being stolen. Thieves could not easily carry away the big rocks, and any that they could pilfer would be difficult to hide or use without being identified.

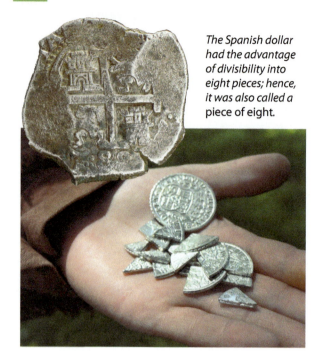

The Spanish dollar had the advantage of divisibility into eight pieces; hence, it was also called a piece of eight.

dollar, was actually physically divisible into eight pieces, or "bits." Since each bit was one-eighth of the whole, many Americans came to call our one-fourth dollar piece (the quarter) "two bits." Though our present-day currency may not be physically divisible, the amount it represents is easily divisible into smaller denominations that are more suitable for smaller transactions or for giving change.

Durability

Currency material must also be durable. Currently in the United States, a paper dollar has an average life of eighteen to twenty-two months. Coins, on the other hand, may last several decades. In its effort to cut costs, the US government has on several occasions introduced dollar coins, but, to date, such coins have proved unpopular.

The Eisenhower dollar, the Susan B. Anthony dollar, and the Sacagawea dollar, though durable, have not been well received by the public.

Stability

A monetary system should not only be convenient, portable, divisible, and durable but also keep a constant value over time. A society will not use a money standard very long if, for example, the amount it takes to purchase a car one day will buy only a loaf of bread the next. Such is the case with the money of nations that do not follow sound economic policies.

MORE THAN MONEY

Money is valuable. Regardless of what a society chooses to use as money—furs, shells, salt, beads, animal teeth, or even stones—its members use it because they have assigned it great value. Because money has such value, some people spend their whole lives trying to amass huge quantities of it. Others are willing to steal or even kill to obtain more. Whether they seek to acquire it legally or otherwise, people do so because they value money, often more intensely than they should. The Bible puts these desires in perspective by reminding us that God values other things far more highly. The Word of God reveals that God values each of these above gold, silver, or gemstones:

- wisdom (Job 28:12–19, Prov. 3:13–15; 16:16)
- the testimony, commands, judgments, and fear of the Lord (Pss. 19:7–10; 119:72, 127)
- the instruction and knowledge of wisdom (Prov. 8:10)
- understanding (Prov. 16:16)
- loving favor (Prov. 22:1)
- faith (1 Pet. 1:7)
- the blood of Christ (1 Pet. 1:18–19)

We are to seek the knowledge of God with the same zeal with which we would seek for silver and gold (Prov. 2:4). If we do so, the promise is that we will find it (Prov. 2:5), and what we will find is of infinitely greater value than any amount of gold. Though wisdom, understanding, faith, and knowing God may not be commodity items you can use as money, you should understand how their value supersedes any monetary form. "For what shall it profit a man, if he shall gain the whole world, and lose his own soul?" (Mark 8:36). Give your effort to pursuing what God values, and your reward will be greater than anything money could buy.

MONEY STANDARDS

There are only three kinds of money: commodity money, representative money, and fiat money. Since barter is an inefficient way of transacting business, primitive societies usually graduate to using a **commodity money** standard. A commodity money system is one in which some single commonly used good becomes the economy's medium of exchange. Anything can serve as a monetary commodity, including seashells, salt, and gold; but the use of an abundant commodity has a tendency to lead to inflated prices. For example, suppose you live in an island society that chooses to use seashells as money. When you go to a store to buy a shirt that costs ten shells, you discover that you have only five shells in your pocket. You thought you had more, and you have none at home. Now what do you do? Do you go to work to earn more shells or simply run down to the beach with a bucket? If the commodity a society uses as money is not rare, prices will tend to skyrocket. In our island example, the shirt could rise in price to hundreds of shells.

As societies progress, they turn to using rarer commodities that people cannot easily obtain or duplicate, such as gold or silver coins. Whenever a coin contains an amount

The real value of a one-ounce gold coin would depend on the current market value of gold, not necessarily the denomination stamped on the coin.

A PENNY FOR YOUR THOUGHTS

In today's society, the term *penny-pinching* has seemingly become anachronistic. Why bother to stoop down to pick up a penny off the sidewalk when it would take a pocket full of them just to buy a candy bar? Redeeming a jar or box full of pennies now hardly seems worth the time it takes to wrap them in rolls of fifty. (Remember the concepts of opportunity cost and opportunity benefit from Chapter 1? They apply here.) Many people also find it frustrating to make a purchase that totals just over a whole dollar and then have to fumble for those few pennies. The answer to the penny problems could be simple—abolish the penny.

Some economists seriously advocate taking the penny out of circulation. A penny costs about 2¢ to manufacture, and the minutes and seconds "wasted" in transactions involving pennies deprive businesses and individuals of valuable time. The anti-penny people generally advocate that the government and businesses adjust all taxes and prices to the nearest nickel. They argue that lower prices would almost certainly offset any inflation that this action might cause. For instance, a merchant selling an item for $19.99 would probably change the price to $19.95 instead of $20.00 because of its greater psychological appeal.

One major roadblock to abolishing the penny is its sentimental value. Americans are naturally reluctant to give up a coin that they have collected, carried, flipped, and thrown in wishing wells ever since they can remember.

The recent advent of coin-counter apparatus in many grocery stores and banks might also help to keep the penny alive. They make it easy for users to exchange their pennies (and other coins) without having to roll them. The owner of the small-change jar empties his container into the machine, which counts, sorts, and stores the coins. The owner then receives a receipt for his amount, which he redeems for dollar bills at the check-out counter. The machine keeps a

small percentage as a fee, but the owner is now free to spend his larger bills.

It remains to be seen whether pennies will become mere curiosities in coin shops and attic chests or whether they will continue to circulate despite those who consider them obsolete.

WORTHLESS WAMPUM

Counterfeiting, as well as inflation, can undermine the stability of a form of money and its function as a means of storing purchasing power. For instance, if a large quantity of undetected phony $20 bills enters circulation, people will soon be unwilling to accept $20 bills in financial transactions for fear of being stuck with a forgery.

An example of counterfeiting's devaluing a currency occurred in colonial America when wampum, small beads that the Native Americans wove into colorful strips, was the commonly accepted currency among the Iroquois and other tribes. The English and Dutch colonists also accepted the wampum as money until both the Indians and the colonists began to counterfeit this commodity. It seems that the Indians learned how to dye beads made from conch shells to make them look like the more highly valued dark beads made from the hearts of quahog clamshells. Colonists were often duped by the counterfeit wampum until they learned to spit on the shells to see if the color would come off.

One of the colonists found another way to increase his supply of wampum. William Pynchon acquired a large quantity of the wampum beads and then hired women and children from the Massachusetts Bay Colony to assemble them. Eventually, the business substituted glass beads for the shell originals, and the colonists strung so many wampum that the wampum economy collapsed. Wampum became worthless, and no one in the colonies could use it any longer as a form of money.

---

of gold or silver equal to its face value, it is a **full-bodied coin**. A coin that contains a quantity of metal less than its face value is a **token coin**. Thus, a one-ounce $20 gold piece would be full bodied if the price of gold were $20 per ounce, but it would be a token coin if gold were worth less than $20 per ounce. All the coins commonly used in the United States today are token coins.

Representative money is money that represents a commodity that some entity holds in store. In the fifteenth and sixteenth centuries, Western Europeans who sought convenience and feared being robbed began to deposit their gold coins with local goldsmiths. For a fee, these early bankers would accept the gold and issue receipts to the depositors. Whenever the depositor wanted to make a purchase, however, he would first have to go through the inconvenient and time-consuming process of redeeming his receipt for gold. Eventually, after merchants became familiar with certain goldsmiths, they began accepting the gold deposit receipts from their customers instead of actual gold; thus, paper money was born.

Until 1934 US paper currency was redeemable for gold or silver held in the national treasury; therefore, it was an example of representative money.

The third kind of money, **fiat money**, does not have gold or something of substantive value backing it. Fiat money came into use when governments took over the function of issuing money. Many governments confiscated their nation's gold and then passed legal tender laws that required businesses to continue to accept receipts that had no gold backing them. All money in the United States today is fiat money. The government uses its stockpiles of gold not for

> *Fiat money* means "money by governmental decree." *Fiat* (FEE at) is from the Latin, "let it be done."

The nation's money supply consists of more than coins and paper dollars. Checks and credit cards are also forms of money.

backing its money but for some international transactions. If gold is not backing our dollars, what, then, provides value to our money? Two things keep our current fiat money system functioning: the faith that others will accept the money we have accepted and the limited quantity of money that exists.

MEASURING THE MONEY SUPPLY

Exactly how much money exists in the United States? The answer to this question depends on how you measure it. Since money represents purchasing power, you cannot just count the paper dollars in your pockets. You must include every means of buying goods and services. The first measure of the money supply, which economists refer to as **M-1**, attempts to measure the money Americans have available for immediate spending and reflects the role that money has as a medium of exchange. M-1 includes paper and coin money held by the public, traveler's checks, and checking accounts. In the beginning of 2016, M-1 accounted for $3,090 billion. A broader measure of the money supply, which economists call **M-2**, represents money that consumers could immediately spend (M-1) plus all money that is available to spend after a short delay. In the beginning of 2016, M-2 amounted to $12,421 billion. In addition to M-1, M-2 comprises a variety of different types of savings accounts.

CREATION OF MONEY

If a nation is using gold coins as money, its money supply can grow only if its gold supply increases. If a nation is using paper money, however, it is possible to increase the money supply by merely increasing the quantity of paper bills in circulation.

The banking system has the ability to create money through the use of what is called **fractional reserve banking**, in which a banker lends out more paper money than he can back in gold. European goldsmiths discovered this phenomenon shortly after they began

Fig. 10-1 M-1: US Money Supply, 2016 (in billions of dollars)

currency and coin	$1,345
demand deposits	$1,229
other checkable deposits	$513
nonbank traveler's checks	$3
total M-1	$3,090

Note: Components may not add to totals due to rounding.
Source: Board of Governors of the Federal Reserve System

Fig. 10-2 M-2: US Money Supply, 2016 (in billions of dollars)

M-1 money supply	$3,090
savings deposits	$8,224
small-denomination time deposits	$405
retail money market funds	$702
total M-2	$12,421

Note: Components may not add to totals due to rounding.
Source: Board of Governors of the Federal Reserve System

CHECK IT OUT

Just about everyone knows what a check is—an authorization to pay a designated amount of money out of an established account. But what does a check look like? The obvious answer is that a check is a piece of paper that has special printing on it giving the name and number of the bank, the name and account number of the holder, and blanks to fill in amounts, reason, and signature. A person usually tears one of these papers from a checkbook. Although most checks would meet this description, not all checks have been so conventional.

Unless laws or regulations specify otherwise, any legitimate written authorization to pay money out of an account is an acceptable check. Thus, checks have been written on newspapers, boards, handkerchiefs, and countless other unusual materials. A man in the lumber business was known for writing his checks on wooden shingles, a sailor once wrote a check with a blowtorch on a metal plate from a battleship, and a Canadian bank cashed a check written on the shell of a hard-boiled egg. The Chase Manhattan Bank Museum of Moneys of the World has a remarkable check on display. It was made of solid steel and was so heavy that two men had to carry it. This check for several thousand dollars was cashed in Cleveland in 1932. The bank promptly canceled it by riddling it with a submachine gun.

A person can create a check on anything as long as it
- is in writing,
- is signed by the maker,
- is payable to the bearer or to the order of a specific person,
- orders the bank to pay a specified sum of money, and
- bears a date no older than six months.

Miss Myrtle Berheim, White House Secretary, holding a check for $70,000, which was written on the wood and metal wing flap of a Japanese airplane

WANTING MONEY MOST

Having wealth is not evil. God blessed Abraham (Gen. 24:35) and the Israelites in the Promised Land (Deut. 8:18) with great wealth. God also tells His people that riches can be a reward for diligence (Prov. 10:4), hard work (Prov. 13:11), and generosity (Prov. 11:24). God gives wealth and possessions as a gift to rejoice the heart of man (Eccles. 5:19). Wealth can also be used to advance the Lord's work. The Old Testament speaks about giving tithes (Lev. 27:30), and the New Testament speaks of Christians' giving to the Lord's work as they have the ability (2 Cor. 8:2–4).

Nevertheless, throughout the Scriptures, God repeatedly warns of the spiritual danger of pursuing riches. In the first commandment God tells us to have no other gods before Him, and seeking wealth with a greater intensity, earnestness, and relentlessness than we seek God is to make money a god before Him. We are to love God with all our hearts; yet, if our hearts are bent after the pursuit of wealth, then we cannot give God the love we owe Him. In Matthew 6:24 Christ makes it clear that we cannot serve two masters; we cannot serve God and riches. In Deuteronomy 6:10–11 Moses speaks of the Israelites' possessing houses and lands in Canaan that would make them instantly financially comfortable. Though this wealth would be a gift from God, verse 12 nonetheless follows with the warning, "Then beware lest thou forget the Lord." Deuteronomy 8:8–18 repeats this warning. Psalms 49:6–10 and 52:7 and Proverbs 11:28 warn against trusting in riches. God's people need to guard against thinking they have made themselves rich (pride) and placing their trust in their riches rather than in God (idolatry).

The introduction of this chapter features the warning from 1 Timothy 6:9 that those who pursue wealth "fall into temptation and a snare, and into many foolish and hurtful lusts, which drown men in destruction and perdition." You would do well to remember these verses and take to heart their warning.

letting customers deposit their gold in exchange for receipts. With people using their receipts as the medium of exchange, the goldsmiths found that their inventories of gold constantly increased. Realizing that the owners were not likely to redeem their receipts, the goldsmiths began to lend much of their customers' gold, keeping only small emergency reserves on hand. Borrowers, not wanting to carry bulky gold coins, began requesting paper receipts instead. To oblige them, the goldsmiths issued new receipts—backed by the same gold that was already backing up other receipts. Through this process, they actually created new money. The receipts served as money, but the quantity of gold backing the receipts did not change. As long as all the depositors did not return to the goldsmith at the same time to demand their gold, the goldsmith was safe. Today, this process works the same way, but instead of having one piece of gold backing two or more paper bills, no gold backs the US dollar. You will learn more about this process of increasing and decreasing the US money supply and creating money in Chapter 11.

SECTION REVIEW 10A

1. What term implies that a merchant must accept in the payment of debts whatever the government declares to be money?
2. What three functions does money serve?
3. What characteristics should an effective monetary system possess?
4. What are the three kinds of money that can circulate in an economy?
5. Name the two measures of the money supply discussed in your book and list what each includes.
6. What does the Bible say about the value of money? Include Scripture references to support your answer.

10B THE FINANCIAL MARKET

Economists speak of the "financial market." You realize, of course, that the financial market is an abstract institution; you cannot get into your car and drive there as you can to a supermarket. The **financial market** is the collection of organizations that assist households in channeling their money to businesses and the government (see Fig. 2-9 on p. 34). Although it includes thrift institutions, insurance companies, investment firms, and finance companies, the largest participant in the financial market is the commercial banking industry.

COMMERCIAL BANKS

Bank institutions accounted for $14.6 trillion of the financial market's total assets in 2011. Banks function primarily by accepting deposits from customers and making business, mortgage, and consumer loans.

History of Banking in the United States

From 1836 until the National Banking Act of 1864, the United States experienced a period of *free banking*. During that time there was no

---

RENAISSANCE BANKING

Modern banking practices began as a simple but essential service amid the growing markets of the Renaissance. Italian moneychangers in sixteenth-century Florence sat in the marketplace at benches called *bancos*. This word passed with the banking trade through Western Europe and into England as *banks*.

If a moneychanger, or goldsmith, were to lend out too much money and not keep enough in reserve to pay out withdrawals, the magistrates would take the goldsmith's bench (*banco*) and would break it in half (*rupturo*) to signify that the goldsmith was insolvent (had no money) and was out of business. He was "bankrupt."

national banking system, and individuals could start private banks simply by meeting certain minimal requirements to obtain a charter from the state. Consequently, hundreds of new banks sprung up representing states, towns, canal companies, and railroad lines. Each of these banks was free to issue its own bank notes, resulting in a multitude of different sizes, colors, and denominations of currency entering circulation. Because many of these unregulated banks were financially unsound (and because counterfeiting became prevalent), the worth of the bills was often in doubt. To end this confusion and to provide revenue for the government during the Civil War, Congress passed the National Banking Act, which established a system of national banks, extended the control of the Department of the Treasury, and issued a uniform currency. In addition, the government placed taxes on the currency issued by the private banks. This action forced the banks to discontinue issuing such notes. The pressure of the legislation actually broke many of the private banks, giving rise to the expressions "broken banks" and "broken bank notes." Those banks that survived often kept their state charters because of the less strenuous requirements, while new banks began either as state banks or under federal charters as national banks. Because the legislation left the nation with both state and federally chartered institutions, it resulted in the nation's *dual banking system*.

At one time in US banking history, each bank printed its own bank notes.

Dual Banking System and Regulation

The government formally defines a **commercial bank** as a financial institution that accepts deposits and makes commercial loans. Recognizing the importance of banking in the American financial system and desiring to ensure that depositors' funds are safe, the government heavily regulates the commercial banking industry. Indeed, from the day they create their businesses, bank owners feel the weight of governmental regulations. For a bank to open its doors, it first must receive an authorization to exist, or a **charter**. Both federal and state authorities issue charters. Federal authorization comes from the United States Treasury's Comptroller of the Currency, while each state's banking commission provides state charters. Of the nation's over thirteen thousand banks, only about one-fourth receive federal charters.

Once a commercial bank receives its charter, it is subject to one of four regulatory authorities. First is the Comptroller of the Currency, which supervises and regulates only those banks with national charters. Second is the Federal Reserve Bank, which regulates only those state banks that have chosen to join the Federal Reserve System (FRS). If a state bank does not choose to join the FRS but desires to be insured, it falls under regulation by the Federal Deposit Insurance Corporation (FDIC). Finally, those state banks that are neither members of the FRS nor insured by FDIC are under the supervision of their state's banking authority. Figure 10-3 shows the distribution of commercial banks in terms of their regulatory status.

Functions of Commercial Banks

Commercial banks fulfill three important roles in the US financial market: accepting deposits, extending loans, and providing miscellaneous services.

Accepting and guarding customers' deposits, a function that began with the early goldsmiths, continues today. Not only is a bank to ensure the physical safety of deposits by maintaining strong vaults

MONEY AND THE FINANCIAL MARKET 197

Fig. 10-3 Regulation of US Commercial Banks

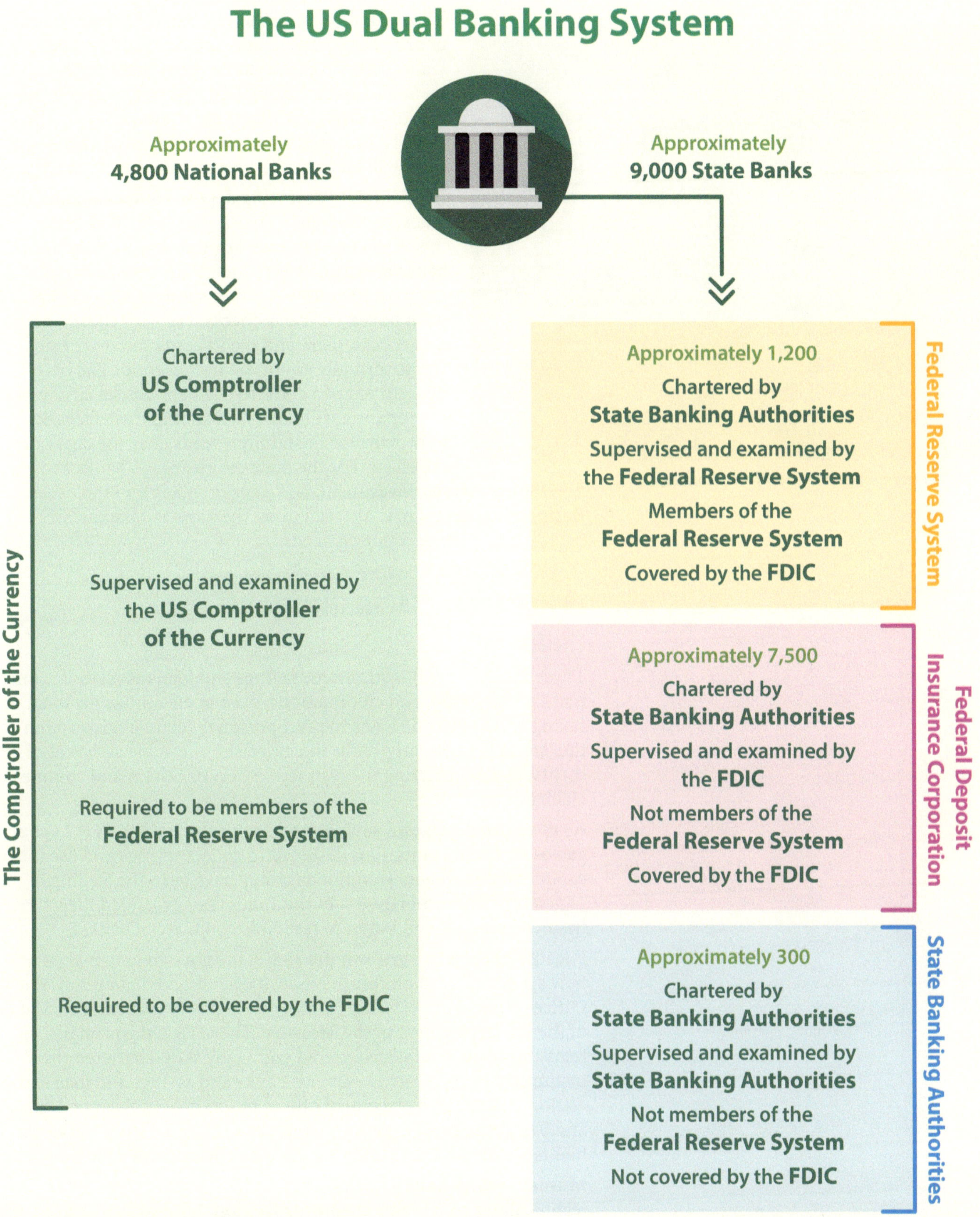

The US Dual Banking System

Approximately **4,800 National Banks**

Approximately **9,000 State Banks**

The Comptroller of the Currency

Chartered by **US Comptroller of the Currency**

Supervised and examined by the **US Comptroller of the Currency**

Required to be members of the **Federal Reserve System**

Required to be covered by the **FDIC**

Federal Reserve System

Approximately 1,200

Chartered by **State Banking Authorities**

Supervised and examined by the **Federal Reserve System**

Members of the **Federal Reserve System**

Covered by the **FDIC**

Federal Deposit Insurance Corporation

Approximately 7,500

Chartered by **State Banking Authorities**

Supervised and examined by the **FDIC**

Not members of the **Federal Reserve System**

Covered by the **FDIC**

State Banking Authorities

Approximately 300

Chartered by **State Banking Authorities**

Supervised and examined by **State Banking Authorities**

Not members of the **Federal Reserve System**

Not covered by the **FDIC**

and hiring guards, but it is also to ensure the safe use of the funds by making sound investment decisions. Functioning in this capacity, commercial banks have developed an array of creative deposit plans, including checking accounts, savings accounts, individual retirement accounts, and money market deposit accounts.

The second role commercial banks perform is that of providing loans. Banks extend many types of loans, including loans to business firms for equipment and inventory, real estate loans to people purchasing homes, and loans for automobiles. As the risk of a borrower's not repaying a loan increases, a bank will increase the interest rate that he must pay.

In addition to accepting deposits and extending loans, commercial banks typically provide other miscellaneous services. For this reason, commercial banks are often referred to as full-service banks. Most banks offer consumer services such as safe-deposit boxes, traveler's checks, cashier's checks, certified checks, debit and credit cards, and wire transfers to virtually anywhere in the world. The trust department of a commercial bank assists customers in preparing wills and establishing trust accounts to provide for the family's needs after the death of the client. For the business customer, banks assist in developing savings, investment, and pension plans for employees. Business customers may also call upon the bank to take care of their payroll and other accounting needs.

Banks accept deposits and provide a safe place to keep those deposits.

OTHER FINANCIAL INSTITUTIONS
Thrifts

Three kinds of thrift institutions, savings and loan associations, mutual savings banks, and credit unions, exist to encourage personal saving and to provide loans to meet personal needs. Legislation in the late 1970s and early 1980s increased the allowable activities of thrifts, thereby blurring the distinction between them and commercial banks.

As their name suggests, **savings and loan associations (S & Ls)** began as financial institutions designed to collect savings and use that capital to make loans. Traditionally, they have been the leading financiers of home mortgages. In the 1980s they expanded their other financial services and began to resemble commercial banks.

Because of the S & L crisis in the 1980s, the government created a new agency to head off future crises. It established that agency, the Office of Thrift Supervision (OTS), on August 9, 1989, as a bureau of the US Department of the Treasury. The OTS is the primary regulator of all federally chartered and many state-chartered thrift institutions, which include savings banks and savings and loan associations. The OTS has regional offices in Jersey City, Atlanta, Dallas, and San Francisco. Funds to operate the OTS come from the assessments and fees it levies on the institutions it regulates.

Mutual savings banks resemble savings and loans except for some technicalities concerning their organization. Like savings and loans, they offered only savings accounts and mortgage loans until the

1980s. These banks exist almost exclusively in the northeastern United States.

Credit unions originate with groups of people who have a common interest, such as company employees, teachers, or union members. These groups form cooperative institutions to pool the savings of their members and make consumer loans available to them. They can now make mortgage loans and offer checking accounts as well.

Savings and loan associations, mutual savings banks, and credit unions still exist today. However, because of the Depository Institutions Deregulation and Monetary Control Act of 1980 (see Chapter 11), there is little difference between the day-to-day operations and services of these financial institutions and those of commercial banks.

Contractual Savings Institutions

As their name implies, contractual savings institutions operate under a contract between the customer and the institution. The business receives regular payments or premiums from its customers, invests that money, and returns to the customers stipulated amounts of money under prescribed conditions. These institutions include insurance companies and pension funds.

MILTON FRIEDMAN (1912-2007)
Spokesman for the Monetarist Approach

One of the leading economists in the second half of the twentieth century was Milton Friedman, a long-time professor of economics at the University of Chicago. His views strongly supported laissez-faire capitalism and roundly denounced governmental interference in the marketplace.

As the chief spokesman for the monetarist approach, Friedman held that the stability of the economy depends on the supply of money in circulation. For example, Friedman stated, "Inflation is always and everywhere a monetary phenomenon."[1] That is, inflation over the long term is caused by changes in the supply of money in the economy. A larger money supply will cause inflation. On the other hand, if the money supply does not grow adequately, the economy will go into a recession. Therefore, Friedman advocated the establishment of a strict rule whereby the government would control the money supply, raising it slowly and steadily to facilitate economic growth. This, however, is the only intervention the government should make. Businesses should be free to make natural adjustments to the conditions of the market through the activities of private enterprise.

The philosophy of Friedman and his associates represented what many call the Chicago school of economics. Their ideas came to the forefront of American thought during the 1970s and 1980s. Friedman expounded his monetary approach along with the danger of governmental involvement in economics in several works:

Bright Promises, Dismal Performance
A Theory of the Consumption Function
The Optimum Quantity of Money and Other Essays
Monetary Statistics of the United States
Monetary Trends in the United States and the United Kingdom
A Monetary History of the United States, 1867–1960
Free to Choose
Capitalism and Freedom
Tyranny of the Status Quo

In 1976 Friedman's efforts were recognized when he was awarded the Nobel Prize for Economics.

---

1. Milton Friedman and Anna Jacobson Schwartz, *A Monetary History of the United States, 1867–1960* (Princeton: Princeton UP, 1963).

Fig. 10-4

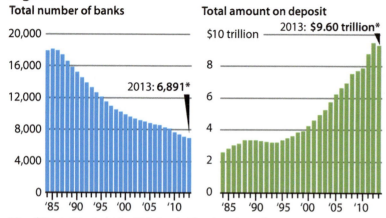

*As of Sept. 30, excludes U.S. banks' foreign deposits
Source: Federal Deposit Insurance Corp., The Wall Street Journal

Reprinted with permission of The Wall Street Journal, Copyright © 2013 Dow Jones & Company, Inc. All Rights Reserved Worldwide. License numbers 3677710807642 and 3677711141523.

Finance Companies

Finance companies make consumer loans for purposes such as home improvements and automobile purchases. They also lend money to small businesses. The interest rates charged by finance companies are usually higher than those of commercial banks and thrifts, largely because the finance companies take greater risks.

Investment Companies

Operating under the principle that it takes money to make money, mutual funds and other investment companies pool the financial resources of their shareholders. They use these combined assets to buy stocks, bonds, real estate, and other investments that they believe will return profits. The companies then divide these profits to their shareholders in proportion to each shareholder's investment.

Money—before reading this chapter you thought you knew what it was and what it did: it was the paper currency you carried in your wallet and used to "buy stuff." Now, however, you understand there is much more to money than just dollar bills and making purchases. You understand the differences between commodity, representative, and fiat money. No doubt you are glad that the United States has a monetary economy rather than one based on barter. You are probably also glad that your fiat money is portable, divisible, durable, and stable and that it provides you a reasonably good measure of the value of items while retaining its purchasing power. The terms *M-1* and *M-2* take your understanding of the money supply beyond your own personal finances, and you have been introduced to one way the banking system creates money (you already knew from your parents that it did not grow on trees). As regards your personal finances, you should also have a better understanding of the bank in which you may have a savings, a checking, and perhaps even some type of investment account. Whether your bank is state or federally chartered and what it means by describing itself as full-service are also concepts that this chapter should help you to appreciate better. Yet with all that you have learned from this chapter about money and banking, make sure you take with you the truth that ultimately whatever money you possess you have as a gift from God. Use it as you are to use all of God's gifts—wisely and well for His glory.

SECTION REVIEW 10B

1. What does it mean to say that the United States has a dual banking system?
2. What are the three functions of commercial banks?
3. Which type of thrift usually originates with a group of people who have something in common (usually employment)?
4. Give an example of a contractual savings institution.

CHAPTER REVIEW

CONTENT QUESTIONS

1. Up to this point in your life, with what function of money are you most familiar?
2. How does money act as a store of purchasing power?
3. Name an advantage and a disadvantage of the traditional money used on the Yap Islands.
4. Which characteristic of money do you consider most important and why?
5. Are today's US coins full-bodied or token coins? Explain your answer.
6. What is the name given to unbacked money when it is issued by governmental decree?
7. What two factors keep a fiat monetary system functioning?
8. What type of money does the United States currently use?
9. Why can commercial banks also be referred to as full-service banks? Give examples in your answer.
10. For what economic position was Milton Friedman a leading spokesman, and what did that position see as the principal cause for inflation?

APPLICATION QUESTIONS

1. What are some disadvantages to having a monetary system backed by some precious commodity, such as gold or silver?
2. Should the potential income of a particular degree program be the primary reason for your choosing that college major? Why or why not? Support your answer with biblical principles.

TERMS

money	187
legal tender	187
barter	187
double coincidence of wants	188
commodity money	191
full-bodied coin	192
token coin	192
representative money	192
fiat money	192
M-1	193
M-2	193
fractional reserve banking	193
financial market	195
commercial bank	196
charter	196
savings and loan associations (S & Ls)	198
mutual savings banks	198
credit unions	199

PERSONAL FINANCE

OPENING AND MAINTAINING A TRANSACTION ACCOUNT

In the article "Cash Management" (p. 180) you read that one of the most common ways people hold cash is in transaction accounts. You also learned what transaction accounts are and how consumers use them. This article continues the discussion of transaction accounts by examining how a person opens and maintains an account.

OPENING A TRANSACTION ACCOUNT

The requirements for opening a transaction account are very simple. A person must be of legal age and fill out a signature card. The signature card authorizes the institution to maintain an account and serves as a security device to permit the institution to verify the account holder's signature. If two or more persons share an account, it is a **joint account**.

When opening a joint account, applicants should consider the laws of survivorship. For example, if a husband and wife want an account that would ensure that upon the death of one the funds would become the property of the other, they should open a joint account with **right of survivorship**. If, on the other hand, two people want to open a joint account without right of survivorship, they should ask for a joint account as **tenants in common**. Without right of survivorship, the deceased tenant's share could simply become part of his estate rather than passing to the other tenant.

WRITING CHECKS

After a customer opens a new transaction account, the institution's customer service representative may provide the new account holder with a small packet of blank checks to use until his printed checks arrive. Writing checks is a very simple procedure; however, the account holder must pay attention to details, even such a simple one as the date on the check. The recipient may not be able to cash a check if it is postdated or if he has allowed it to become stale dated.

A **postdated** check bears a future date. Consumers sometimes postdate checks to pay bills or to buy items before sufficient funds are actually present in their transaction accounts. Because such checks often clear the bank undetected, this is not a good practice. For example, a couple wrote a postdated check to their landlord to pay the rent that was going to be due while they were on vacation. They had automatic deposits on their paychecks and knew the next deposit would not take place until the normal due date. So, they gave their landlord specific instructions not to deposit the check until the normal due date; however, he forgot and deposited the check a few days later. The postdated check slipped through the bank's operation center undetected, and that withdrawal caused several of the couple's other checks to bounce.

A **stale dated** check bears a date that is more than six months old. Many financial institutions have policies against cashing stale dated checks. An illustration of stale dated checks that could have been heartbreaking but fortunately turned out well is the story of a couple that devised a "unique" way of saving to purchase a new car. They lived off his paycheck and each week placed her paycheck in a bank safe deposit box. Three years and over 150 paychecks later, they were stunned to discover that the bank could cash only the most recent six months' worth of her stale dated paychecks. They were relieved, however, when her employer agreed to redeem the checks.

The second step in writing a check is to fill in the name of the **payee**, the person receiving the check. The name needs to be present and legible. A blank name line or an illegible name is an opportunity for a thief to fill in his name or to scribble a name that resembles the one on the check.

Writing the amount of the check is the third step. For safety's sake, printed checks provide two places for the amount. One line requires the amount written in words, and the other asks for the sum in numerals.

GUARANTEED CHECKS

While most people make payments in cash or by using a transaction account, there are times when buyers cannot use either of these means of payment. Occasionally the price of the purchase is so large that it would be impractical for the consumer to use cash. At the same time, if the price of the item is substantial and if the merchant is unfamiliar with the buyer, he may refuse to accept a personal check. In such cases customers may purchase checks that guarantee payment.

A **guaranteed check** is so called because it provides the merchant a 100 percent guarantee that when he cashes it he will receive the funds. Four types of guaranteed checks exist—certified checks, cashier's checks, money orders, and traveler's checks.

A **certified check** is a customer's personal check that a financial institution guarantees to pay upon presentation. To have a check certified, the buyer writes a personal check listing the payee and the amount. The bank then verifies that the customer's account contains sufficient funds to cover the check and places a hold on those funds to ensure that the money will be available for payment. The bank imprints the word *certified* on the check, and a bank officer signs the certification. This certification means the bank guarantees payment of the check. Banks do, however, generally charge a fee for certifying checks.

With a **cashier's check**, payment for the check comes out of an account the bank itself holds. Since the bank is selling a check that it guarantees to pay, it will accept only guaranteed funds in exchange. Banks sell cashier's checks only if purchasers present cash, a checking or savings withdrawal drawn on the bank itself, or a guaranteed check from another institution. After receiving the guaranteed funds, the bank affixes the name of the payee and imprints the amount of the check in such a way that it is nearly impossible for someone to alter the check. A bank officer then signs the check, which is numbered to enable the bank to record its details for future reference. Banks usually charge a fee for the purchase of a cashier's check.

A **money order** operates much the same as a cashier's check, but it generally serves people who do not have checking accounts to pay for small routine transactions, such as utility bills and car payments. A variety of sources, such as financial institutions, branches of the US Post Office, and convenience stores, sell money orders. The fees they charge depend upon the amount of the money order.

People going on vacations or business trips anticipate that local merchants will not likely accept their out-of-town personal checks, and they recognize that carrying a sizable amount of cash is not wise. So they may opt for **traveler's checks**, which they can purchase in varying denominations and which nearly every merchant accepts. Most major financial institutions and credit card companies will issue traveler's checks, and some banks and travel companies allow their customers to obtain the checks without charge as part of package accounts. Financial institutions that sell traveler's checks usually charge about 1 percent or more of the face amount of the checks. The bank, in turn, typically keeps 90 percent of the fee and remits 10 percent to the issuer of the traveler's checks. Thus, if you were to buy $1,000 worth of traveler's checks, you would pay a $10 fee of which the bank would keep $9 and send the remaining dollar to the company that issues the checks.

The buyer signs each of the traveler's checks in the presence of a bank officer, and later, when purchasing goods with a traveler's check, he countersigns the check next to his original signature. If the signatures match, the merchant accepts the check just as he would cash. Most traveler's check companies ensure merchants that they will redeem all their checks, even if evidence later proves they were stolen or counterfeited.

The use of traveler's checks is declining because of the spread of ATMs. ATMs that are part of international networks conveniently provide withdrawals in local currency, thus reducing the demand for traveler's checks.

CASHING CHECKS

Occasionally, people become angry when banks will not cash checks they present. However, it is not difficult to understand why the banker is reluctant to cash some checks. Imagine that you sold your car and received a check drawn on First National Bank for $4,000 from John Smith, a man completely unknown to you until he responded to your classified advertisement in the newspaper. You, however, do not have a checking account at any bank, but you go to the bank nearest your house, Second National Bank, and request that they give you $4,000 for the check. Most banks would refuse to cash your check for two reasons.

First, they do not know you. You could have stolen the check from the original recipient and are now trying to cash it fraudulently. You could have altered a legitimate $40 check to be $4,000. You could also perhaps have a computer and the capability of printing checks, and you are going from bank to bank collecting a harvest of $4,000 at each stop.

Second, the banker does not know the check writer. Because Mr. Smith's account is not at Second National Bank, that institution has no way of knowing if the real Mr. Smith is the one who wrote you the check, if there are sufficient funds in his account at First National Bank to cover the check, or even if such an account exists. True, Second National Bank could contact First National Bank and confirm that there are sufficient funds at present; however, depending on how many outstanding checks Mr. Smith may have, there may not be sufficient funds when Second National presents its check for payment. In the words of one banker, "The unknown check casher has everything to gain while the bank has everything to lose." Second National is in business to make a profit, and there is nothing profitable about cashing potentially fraudulent checks when the bank knows neither the person writing nor the person cashing the check.

So, how could you cash this $4,000 check? Very simply, you take the check to the bank on which it is drawn. If you can identify yourself and if the bank can confirm that an account holder wrote the check, then the bank must cash it. Verifying that the account holder wrote the check may involve checking the account holder's signature and, in the case of checks involving large amounts of money, calling the depositor to verify that he did indeed write the check. But what if First National Bank is on the other side of the city or the country? To cash an across-town or out-of-town check, you may take the check to any bank, and for a small fee, it will send the check to the bank on which it is drawn. The out-of-town bank will then send a cashier's check that you can cash at your bank with no risk of loss. You could also send the check via registered and insured mail to the out-of-town bank and request a cashier's check.

Now that the banking industry and its customers are increasingly utilizing computers, a person can verify a check and receive payment much faster than previously possible.

If the two amounts disagree, the bank accepts the amount in words as the legally correct figure.

Each time a person writes a check, he should immediately subtract its amount from his previous account balance to avoid overdrawing his account. To present a blameless testimony in the community and to avoid possible criminal charges, a Christian should purpose never to overdraw his transaction account. An overdrawn account means that a person presents to the bank a check for which sufficient funds for payment are not on deposit. Though most overdrawn checks result from careless record keeping, many are intentional attempts to defraud a merchant.

Should you make an error in completing a check, draw a line through the incorrect item, write the correction above it, and initial the change.

As the final step in completing a written check, the account holder signs the check. He should sign each check exactly how his signature appears on the account's signature card.

An account holder should safeguard his checks from being lost or stolen. If a checkbook is stolen, an account holder should contact the institution immediately to close the account. The depositor can then promptly open a new account from which the bank will make payments on legitimate checks written on the old account.

MAKING DEPOSITS TO A TRANSACTION ACCOUNT

Making deposits to a transaction account is a fairly simple process. The account holder enters the correct amount of currency on a deposit slip and lists individually each check he wants to deposit along with its routing number. This number helps the bank

THOMAS SOWELL (1930-)

Critic of Affirmative Action

Born in North Carolina and raised in the Harlem ghetto, Thomas Sowell was a high-school dropout, but he succeeded in rising above his circumstances and achieving what many, based on his beginnings, would have declared impossible. He joined the Marines, and after finishing his enlistment, he used the provisions of the GI Bill to attend Harvard, Columbia, and the University of Chicago. Sowell eventually earned a PhD in economics, and along the way, his economic philosophy made an about-face from espousing Marxist thought to adamantly supporting capitalism.

In 1971 Sowell began a prolific writing career that produced books not only on economics but also on education, law, and racial issues. His writings have won the admiration of many of his fellow economists and political philosophers. His most noted and most controversial work deals with race and economics. Sowell believes that governmental civil rights activities in recent decades have led to policies that are harmful to African Americans. He thinks that affirmative action and other governmental meddling to produce social progress have simply made some blacks dependent on the government and have discouraged personal improvement.

Sowell has taken much criticism from African American leaders who want increased governmental aid and protection for the interests of their communities. Nonetheless, Thomas Sowell can point to the hard work that took him from the ghetto to academic accomplishment without preferential treatment from governmental programs.

PERSONAL FINANCE

trace the deposit in the event a check is lost during processing.

A depositor must endorse a check to cash or deposit it. To **endorse** a check is to acknowledge receipt of the amount written on the front of the check. A person endorses a check by signing his name exactly as it appears on the front. After endorsing the check, the payee may receive cash from a bank, make a deposit to his account, or transfer the check to a person to whom he owes money.

STOPPING PAYMENT ON A CHECK

Occasionally, a check writer does not want his bank to cash a check he has written. This situation occurs most often when a customer finds that a product he purchased is defective or incomplete. To ensure nonpayment of a check, an individual can go to his bank in person or online and issue a **stop payment order**. If the payee has not yet cashed the check, the bank will guarantee that for the next six months it will not honor that check. Instead, it will return the check to the payee and notify him that the account holder stopped payment. After the six-month period, the check will be stale dated and nonnegotiable. Most banks charge a fee for issuing a stop payment order.

Stopping payment on a check can be a very serious matter. If a customer stops payment on a check, the merchant who sold the item might easily believe that the customer is a thief. He has refused to pay for goods now in his possession. To maintain a blameless testimony, a Christian needs to return all goods for which he has stopped payment and offer an explanation as to why he decided a stop payment order was necessary.

RECONCILING A TRANSACTION ACCOUNT

One of the biggest responsibilities in maintaining a transaction account is for the customer to reconcile his account balance with the statement from the bank. **Reconciling** is commonly called balancing the checkbook. Each month most banks send a statement to each checking account customer listing all deposits, all checks and debit card transactions for which the bank has made payment, and the customer's final account balance.

The end-of-the-month account balance on the bank's monthly statement may not agree with the balance in the customer's checkbook register for several reasons. First, there may be deposits that the account holder has already added to his balance but that the bank has not yet received or processed. Second, there may be checks that the account holder wrote and subtracted from his check register that have not yet cleared the bank. Third, the account holder may have added a deposit or subtracted a check in his register incorrectly. Fourth, if it is an interest-bearing account, the account holder may have forgotten to add the interest. Fifth, the bank may have made an error in adding the customer's deposits or subtracting his checks.

One mistake many checking account holders make is failing to record all the checks they write or all the uses of their debit cards. When they believe that they may be nearing the end of their funds, they need to call their bank or go to their bank's website. Most banks offer access to account information via the telephone or Internet. These services provide hassle-free ways of verifying account activity so that the account holder does not overdraw his account. However, account holders should not use such services as a substitute for balancing their accounts.

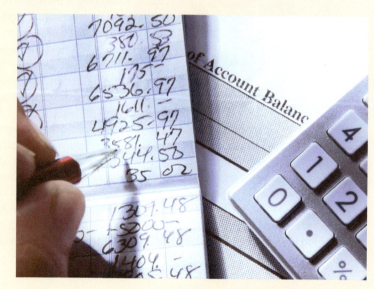

It is true that the growth of Internet banking and online bill paying is steadily reducing the use of checks. It is also true that because of these options, you will likely not be as dependent upon a checkbook as your parents and grandparents were. However, it is nonetheless good for you to know the terms and to understand the workings of transaction accounts. As part of a basic understanding of consumer finances, you should know the concepts of joint accounts, postdated and stale dated checks, stop payment orders, and reconciling a transaction account. Again, though you may not use them often, you should be familiar with the various types of guaranteed checks. Having a working knowledge of these financial tools may keep you from misusing one, and that could keep you from seriously harming your testimony. Remember, the Christian seeks to live blamelessly, to be above reproach, and to avoid all appearance of evil.

REVIEW QUESTIONS

1. What is a joint account with right of survivorship?
2. How long can a check be held before it can no longer be cashed?
3. What are the four types of guaranteed checks?
4. What must a depositor do before cashing or depositing a check?

TERMS

joint account	202
right of survivorship	202
tenants in common	202
postdated	202
stale dated	202
payee	202
guaranteed check	203
certified check	203
cashier's check	203
money order	203
traveler's checks	203
endorse	206
stop payment order	206
reconciling	206

CHAPTER ELEVEN
CENTRAL BANKING

11A ORGANIZATION OF THE FEDERAL RESERVE SYSTEM — 209

11B FUNCTIONS OF THE FEDERAL RESERVE SYSTEM — 214

11C MONEY AND THE ECONOMY — 222

You saw in Chapter 10 that money is an essential element for an economy to function smoothly. Without some stable form of money, our present sophisticated economic system would not be possible. If some type of money did not exist, people would be forced to return to barter. Because barter requires individuals to make numerous trades to obtain what they desire, they tend to generalize; that is, they stop specializing in what they do best and endeavor instead to meet as many of their own needs as possible. The effect of this "every man for himself" attitude proves detrimental to a societal economy.

Now that you understand how vital money is to the efficient operation of our economy, you may have come to an obvious and oft-asked question: Who creates our money? Chapter 10 briefly touches on this question when it describes the creation of money by the goldsmiths of Western Europe in the sixteenth and seventeenth centuries and the development of what economists now call fractional reserve banking. Today in the United States three organizations create money: the United States Treasury, financial institutions, and the Federal Reserve System.

The US Treasury creates money by minting and selling coins to the Federal Reserve Banks. For example, it minted approximately 13 billion coins in the year 2014. The Treasury is able to make a handsome profit in this exchange because its cost to mint coins is only a fraction of their face values, and it sells the minted coins at full face value to the Federal Reserve.

The second creator of money is the financial institutions that make up the US financial market. These institutions, which include commercial banks, savings and loan associations, and credit unions, create money by lending money. They lend their customers' deposits to other businesses and individuals, who in turn redeposit this money into other institutions that lend it yet again. Later in this chapter you will learn more about how this process creates money.

The vast majority of new money, however, begins its life at the Federal Reserve Bank, the central bank of the

United States. The term **central bank** refers to the government's use of this bank to control and accommodate the nation's finances through the bank's various functions.

11A ORGANIZATION OF THE FEDERAL RESERVE SYSTEM

The **Federal Reserve System**, or "the Fed" as most Americans know it, is a governmental institution responsible for overseeing the issue of currency, regulating banking activity, and providing banking services to the nation's commercial banks. The Fed also attempts to control prices, unemployment, and economic growth by controlling the nation's money supply.

Many nations of the world established central banks long before the United States did. England, for example, founded its central bank, the Bank of England, in 1694. France created the Bank of France in 1800, and Japan opened the Bank of Japan in 1882. The United States did not introduce its central bank until 1913.

The Federal Reserve Building in Washington, D.C.

INDIVIDUAL FEDERAL RESERVE DISTRICT BANKS

In 1913, the United States was a nation of regional distinctions. The East was the financial center, the South and the Midwest were the agricultural sectors, the North was the hub for manufacturing, and the West was still largely an undeveloped frontier. Realizing that each section of the nation had diverse financial needs and not wanting any region to be at the financial mercy of another, Congress divided the nation into twelve districts and gave each its own central bank. Each Federal Reserve district bank performs numerous economic tasks. For example, each district bank supplies the currency and coins to commercial banks that enable them to pay out checking and savings account withdrawals.

President Woodrow Wilson signed the Federal Reserve Act in 1913.

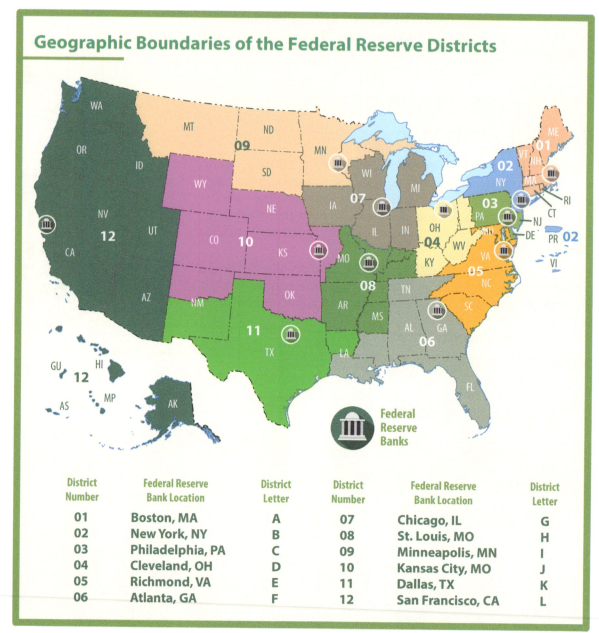

Geographic Boundaries of the Federal Reserve Districts

District Number	Federal Reserve Bank Location	District Letter	District Number	Federal Reserve Bank Location	District Letter
01	Boston, MA	A	07	Chicago, IL	G
02	New York, NY	B	08	St. Louis, MO	H
03	Philadelphia, PA	C	09	Minneapolis, MN	I
04	Cleveland, OH	D	10	Kansas City, MO	J
05	Richmond, VA	E	11	Dallas, TX	K
06	Atlanta, GA	F	12	San Francisco, CA	L

The Federal Reserve Bank of San Francisco, one of the twelve district banks

A board of directors supervises each district bank. Each board has nine members: three bankers, three businesspersons outside the banking industry, and three representatives of the general public. While each district's board of directors still governs the day-to-day affairs of its Federal Reserve district bank, these directors have little to do with controlling the nation's money supply. Since the mid-1930s, the Fed's Board of Governors and the Federal Open Market Committee have made virtually all decisions regarding the money supply.

BOARD OF GOVERNORS

The seven-member **Board of Governors** guides the Federal Reserve System. The board members acquire their seats through a selection and confirmation process. The president of the United States selects and Congress must confirm each member. To ensure a balanced board, no two members may be from the same Federal Reserve district. Congress legislated that one membership would become vacant every two years and that each member may serve a term of fourteen years without reappointment. Even though the maximum number of years a board member may serve is fourteen, the average term each serves is six years. Many board members choose to return to private business or retire before their terms expire.

The Board of Governors meets in Washington, D.C., where its members have access to governmental officials and many economists. One of the greatest responsibilities of the Board of Governors is to set the reserve requirement. The sixteenth-century Western European goldsmiths had the power to lend all their customers' gold; however, the Board of Governors dictates that American banks keep on hand the **reserve requirement**, a specified percentage of their deposits. Other functions of the Board include supervising and regulating commercial banks, supervising the twelve Federal

J. P. MORGAN (1837–1913)
Formidable Financier

John Pierpont Morgan was born into wealth. His grandfather was a farmer in Connecticut who acquired a small fortune through real estate, insurance, banking, and other business interests. His father, Junius Spencer Morgan, increased the family fortune through successful banking and investment interests in New York City and London. J. P. (often called Pierpont) Morgan used his inherited financial position and personal talents to rise to the top of the American business world by the end of the nineteenth century.

While a partner in the New York financial firm of Drexel, Morgan and Company, J. P. Morgan extended his business interests into financing and railroad reorganization for the United States government. His solid character led him to support men and business ventures of merit without undue regard to his own monetary reward, but the results of his judicious dealings were increased riches.

His financial firm was renamed J. P. Morgan and Company in 1895, and this "House of Morgan" took a leading role in the American economy. In 1895 Morgan used his resources and ideas to help President Cleveland avoid a national crisis because of a depleted gold reserve. In 1907 Morgan once again stepped in to aid the country as it faced a severe financial panic by risking his personal financial assets to restore business confidence. In the meantime, Morgan had put together the largest corporation of his time, US Steel Corporation, as well as taken control of other large business concerns. Because Morgan exerted influence over a large segment of the American economy, he faced opposition in his later years from a public suspicious of great wealth and increasingly concerned over monopolies and trusts.

Though Morgan had wielded influence over untold billions in his lifetime, at his death his estate was valued at a relatively meager $68.3 million (plus a valuable art collection that he intended to be put in a public museum). His will set aside a $3 million trust for each of his three daughters, a $500,000 bequest for his church in New York City, and various other provisions for charities, relatives, and employees. The remainder of his estate was left to his son, J. P. (Jack) Morgan Jr., who carried on as leader of the House of Morgan. Although Morgan had supervised his financial empire admirably, his death signaled the demise of such economic power. Fearing that future financiers would abuse their powers, the government began regulation in earnest, starting with the organization of the Federal Reserve System. In a sense, the Fed was intended to replace the economic wisdom and stability that J. P. Morgan had provided for the country in the decades prior to World War I.

Reserve district banks, and administering financial consumer protection laws, such as those that require equal credit opportunity and fair housing lending.

FEDERAL OPEN MARKET COMMITTEE

The **Federal Open Market Committee (FOMC)** affects the money supply by buying and selling governmental securities, such as Treasury bills, Treasury notes, and Treasury bonds. This function, as you will see later in this chapter, is the Fed's most important tool in changing the quantity of money in the money supply. The FOMC has twelve members, which include the seven-member Board of Governors and five of the Federal Reserve district bank presidents. The president of the Federal Reserve Bank of New York is always a member in order to act as account manager to monitor the purchases and sales of securities that occur in the financial market in New York City.

The FOMC meets to discuss the buying and selling of government securities.

CHAIR OF THE BOARD

Janet L. Yellen was appointed chair of the Board of Governors in 2014.

The chair of the Federal Reserve's Board of Governors is the most influential individual in the Federal Reserve System. The chair often advises the president or Congress on economic issues, and the actions of the Fed usually reflect this important leader's economic philosophy. The president designates one member of the board to act as chair for a four-year term that can be extended for multiple terms.

INDEPENDENCE OF THE FEDERAL RESERVE SYSTEM

Believing that the nation needed a central bank but fearing that such a bank might be used by self-serving politicians, Congress, in its original Federal Reserve Act, sought to keep the Federal Reserve System independent of outside influence. Legislation made the Fed free from outside control in three ways.

First, the Fed is politically independent. With one term on the Board of Governors expiring every two years, it is difficult for one president to control the Fed for a long period of time by "packing" the board with those whom he favors.

Second, the Fed is financially independent. It sets and operates under its own budget. Congress has learned by experience that the federal budget is a powerful force that it can use to reward cooperative agencies and to punish those that do not carry out the legislature's wishes. For example, if the Federal Reserve System were under the federal budget, the potential would exist for congressional representatives aggressively seeking reelection to threaten the Fed with extinction if it did not create and lend billions of dollars to

ALAN GREENSPAN (1926–)
Chair of the Fed

Alan Greenspan was born in New York City to Hungarian immigrants. He is best known as a former chair of the Federal Reserve Board of Governors, but his successful career as an economist came after an attempted career in music. After completing high school, Greenspan studied at the Juilliard School of Music for a while but dropped out to play music full-time. His musical career, however, was short-lived, and he soon returned to school to pursue studies in economics. He eventually received three degrees from New York University: a BA (1948), an MA (1950), and a PhD (1977).

His first employment as an economist came in 1948 at the National Industrial Conference Board, a private think tank oriented toward business and industry. He formed an economic consulting partnership called Townsend and Greenspan in 1954 and served as its president for twenty years. During that time he made short-term contributions to the government, including serving a four-year period as chair of President Gerald Ford's Council of Economic Advisers (1974–77). He has also served as director on the boards of many large corporations, including J. P. Morgan and Company, Mobil Corporation, and General Foods Inc.

In 1987 President Ronald Reagan nominated Greenspan for chair of the Federal Reserve Board of Governors. He was soon tested by the severe stock market crash of October 1987. On Black Monday, the market lost 20 percent of its value in one day. Many economic analysts have credited Greenspan's solid leadership with helping to stabilize the economy after that crisis. Over time, Greenspan earned a reputation as an inflation fighter. Since the reputation of the Fed Chair is as important as the policy tools used, many of Greenspan's public statements were able to avert potential inflation without significant policy changes.

Greenspan, who retired from the Federal Reserve Board of Governors in January 2006, was followed as chair by Ben Bernanke (2006–14) and then Janet Yellen (2014–). Greenspan's successful tenure as chair has been recognized in numerous ways, including many honorary degrees and the Presidential Medal of Freedom.

banks in their districts. To avoid this problem, the framers of the Federal Reserve Act provided that the Fed would not depend on Congress for its operating funds. Instead, the Fed provides for its own needs by charging fees for the services it provides to banks, by selling its stock to new member banks, and by collecting interest on the securities it holds and the loans it makes.

Finally, the Fed is operationally independent. Though Congress requires the chair of the Board of Governors to report to it periodically, no one may dictate what actions the Federal Reserve System must take. Also, the Fed's financial records are exempt from audit by any agent or agency. No one, including the president of the United States or members of Congress, may examine the Fed's books without its permission.

The Fed chair appears regularly before congressional committees.

This extensive independence does not mean, however, that the Federal Reserve may act irresponsibly in carrying out its duties. There are two specific checks in place to ensure the Fed's stability. First, Congress may remove members from the Fed's Board of Governors "for cause," a legal term that Congress may interpret as narrowly or as broadly as it wishes. Second, and most importantly, the Fed depends on Congress for its very existence. The leaders of the Fed are well aware that Congress created the Federal Reserve System by legislative action and that by an opposite piece of legislation Congress could abolish it.

SECTION REVIEW 11A

1. Who are the three creators of money in the United States?
2. Into how many districts did the Federal Reserve Act divide the nation, and why?
3. Who or what is responsible for guiding the Fed?
4. In what three ways is the Fed independent of outside control?

11B FUNCTIONS OF THE FEDERAL RESERVE SYSTEM

Congress passed the original Federal Reserve Act of 1913 as "an act to provide for the establishment of Federal reserve banks, to furnish an elastic currency, to afford means of rediscounting commercial paper, to establish a more effective supervision of banking in the United States, and for other purposes." In keeping with this act, the Federal Reserve System exists to perform six national economic services:

- To provide a uniform currency
- To regulate member banks
- To clear checks and debit card transactions
- To act as the nation's fiscal agent
- To serve as the banker's bank
- To create money

War bonds are an example of securities sold by the FOMC.

PROVIDING A UNIFORM AND ELASTIC CURRENCY

One of the first responsibilities Congress delegated to the Federal Reserve System was to provide an **elastic currency**. Congress desired that our country possess a money supply that could expand as our economy grew. However, before the Federal Reserve System could even think of establishing such a money system, it had to furnish a uniform currency that every person and business from coast to coast would recognize and accept. To this end the Fed initiated the series of Federal Reserve notes that are in use today. The Federal Reserve System, however, does not create these Federal Reserve notes. The Bureau of Engraving and Printing (BEP) under the US Treasury prints the notes, and the Federal Reserve places them into circulation through its twelve district banks.

REGULATING MEMBER BANKS

Originally, banks that were members of the Federal Reserve System enjoyed certain benefits, such as free check clearing and free currency and coin delivery, but these banks also faced burdensome requirements to maintain membership. For example, the percentage that the Fed required member banks to hold on reserve against deposits was much higher than what state banking authorities required of nonmember banks. As the regulations grew more oppressive, member banks withdrew from the Federal Reserve System and put themselves under the less demanding regulations of state banking authorities. The number of banks fleeing the Fed alarmed Congress. Therefore, it passed the Depository Institutions Deregulation and Monetary Control Act of 1980, which required all financial institutions to abide by the regulations set by the Federal Reserve, including the reserve requirement in the above example. This legislation gave the Fed greater influence in the financial sector of the US economy.

CLEARING CHECKS AND DEBIT CARD TRANSACTIONS

The twentieth century saw an explosion in the number of checks people were writing. In the 1990s, checks accounted for $95 of every $100 in business transactions. Now, however, consumers use credit cards, debit cards, and electronic funds transfers (EFTs) more prevalently than they use checks; therefore, billions of electronic transactions take place each year.

Each check, debit card transaction, or EFT requires clearing—that is, the receiving business or institution must send each transaction to the bank that holds the purchaser's account for payment. To handle the huge volume of transactions requiring clearance, the Federal Reserve System has developed a check and debit clearing system.

ACTING AS FISCAL AGENT

The Federal Reserve System also functions as the nation's **fiscal agent**, or the government's bank. Just as a commercial bank accepts customer deposits, makes loans to borrowers, and offers financial advice to those requesting it, the Federal Reserve's job as the government's fiscal agent is likewise threefold. First, it holds the US Treasury's checking account. The Internal Revenue Service (IRS),

The Fed supplies all states with a uniform currency.

CHECK PROCESSING

- The check as a payment method is being replaced over time by electronic forms of payment, such as credit cards, debit cards and online account transfers.
- Nearly all the checks the Federal Reserve Banks process for collection are now received as electronic check images.
- Regardless of whether checks are cleared as paper or electronic images, financial institutions have several alternative ways to receive payment for, or clear, checks deposited with them.
- In line with the electronification of check processing and the downward trend in the use of checks as a payment method, the Federal Reserve Banks have reduced the number of their check processing centers.

The check as a payment mechanism is being replaced by the increased use of electronic payments. The number of checks written in the United States has been falling since the mid-1990s. At the same time, the number of checks being processed electronically is increasing.

Instead of transporting and sorting paper checks as was done in the past, financial institutions such as banks and credit unions and some businesses process the checks that they receive electronically.

In line with this trend, the Federal Reserve Banks reduced the number of places at which paper checks are processed. Before their restructuring initiative that began in 2003, Federal Reserve Banks processed checks at forty-five locations. Since February 26, 2010, the Federal Reserve Banks have processed all paper checks at just one location.

One of the initial pushes for the electronification of checks occurred when companies were first allowed in 2002 to capture the information on the magnetic ink character recognition (MICR) line at the bottom of a consumer check, keep an image of the check and process the payment as an automated clearinghouse (ACH) transaction. Companies that receive a large number of paper checks, such as credit card processors, public utilities and phone and cable companies, took advantage of this change.

The shift from paper to an electronic format moved forward in October 2004 when the Check Clearing for the 21st Century Act became effective. This legislation—commonly called Check 21—facilitated electronic check collection by introducing a new negotiable instrument called a "substitute check." A substitute check is a special paper copy of the front and back of an original check that is the legal equivalent of the original. Previously, to collect checks electronically, all financial institutions in the collection process had to agree to do so. Otherwise, original paper checks had to be presented to the institution on which they were drawn. Under Check 21, institutions that wish to process checks electronically may do so provided that if, in the process of collecting a check they encounter an institution that insists on receiving paper items, they provide that institution with a substitute check created from the electronic image file.

Today, the Federal Reserve receives almost all the checks it processes for clearing as electronic check images. Regardless of whether checks are processed as paper or electronic items, financial institutions have several alternative ways to receive payment for, or clear, checks deposited with them.

In 2009, interbank checks, which are checks that are deposited at and drawn on different depository institutions, accounted for about 74 percent of the checks paid that year. The remaining 26 percent of checks were "on-us" checks, which are deposited at and drawn on the same depository institution.

To clear on-us checks, the institution makes the appropriate entries on its books, by debiting the payor's account and crediting the depositor's account. To collect the remaining interbank checks, a financial institution may:

- present the paper checks or transmit images of the checks directly to the paying bank,
- forward the paper checks or images of the checks to a correspondent for collection,
- exchange checks, in paper or electronic form, with a group of banks participating in a clearinghouse arrangement, or
- forward the paper checks or images of the checks to a Federal Reserve Bank for collection.

Generally, smaller deposit-taking financial institutions either deposit checks for clearing with a Federal Reserve Bank or with a correspondent. A correspondent may be a larger commercial bank, a bankers' bank or a corporate credit union. Larger institutions may deposit exclusively with a Federal Reserve Bank or use a combination of methods to clear checks. All depository institutions, either directly or in conjunction with a correspondent, may deposit checks with a Federal Reserve

Bank. Check deposits are received as either bundles of paper checks called "cash letters" or, more commonly, computer files of imaged checks called "image cash letters." The Federal Reserve Banks charge depositors a fee for check-clearing services.

When cash letters or image cash letters are deposited with Federal Reserve Banks, they credit the Federal Reserve account of the depositing institution or its correspondent. The Reserve Banks debit the Federal Reserve account of the paying institution or its correspondent when the checks drawn on the paying institution are presented to that institution for payment. A paying institution may choose to receive checks drawn on it in image files or in paper form. If the financial institution elects to receive check presentments in paper form, it will most likely receive substitute checks. The paying institution then charges the accounts of the customers who wrote the checks in accordance with its account agreement.

Regulation CC of the Board of Governors of the Federal Reserve System and certain state laws limit how long financial institutions may hold funds deposited by check before making the funds available for withdrawal by a depositor.

"FedPoint: Check Processing," Federal Reserve Bank of New York website. Used by permission.

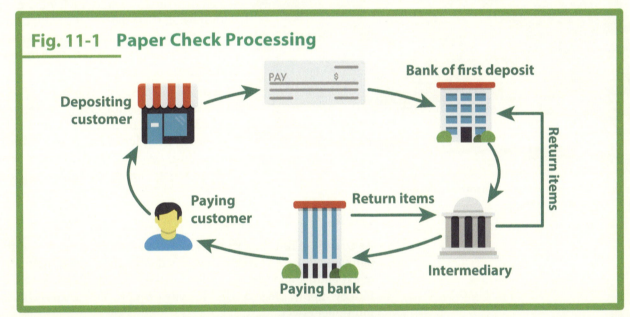

Fig. 11-1 Paper Check Processing

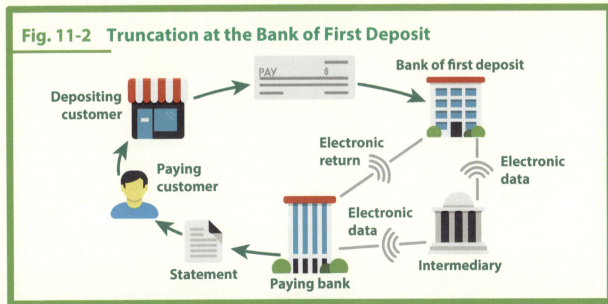

Fig. 11-2 Truncation at the Bank of First Deposit

Adapted from Joanna Stavins, "A Comparison of Social Costs and Benefits of Paper Check Presentment and ECP with truncation," New England Economic Review, July/August 1997

the government's tax collector, deposits all tax revenues into the government's checking account at the Fed, and out of this account the government pays its bills. Second, the Fed makes loans to the US Treasury by having the FOMC purchase governmental bonds. Third, through the chair of its Board of Governors, the Fed supplies a wealth of economic information and advice to both the president and Congress.

SERVING AS THE BANKER'S BANK

As mentioned in the previous chapter, paper currency and coin account for a relatively small portion of the total money supply, while checking accounts make up a significantly larger part. Problems arise, therefore, when a greater than expected number of people want to receive cash from their accounts. If a bank cannot meet their withdrawal requests, people panic, and a **run on the bank** may occur, in which depositors rush to the bank seeking to withdraw all their money. If a bank cannot supply the cash its customers are demanding during such a run, it may face insolvency and failure.

Part of the purpose for creating the Fed was to prevent such panics. Congress designed the Fed to be the banker's bank, and as such it serves as a **lender of last resort**. It creates and lends enough currency to banks to allow them to satisfy their panicking depositors.

The Fed takes action to prevent runs on banks, like this one in New York City in the early 1900s.

CREATING MONEY

As a result of fulfilling its roles as the nation's fiscal agent and the banker's bank, the Fed has developed several powerful methods of expanding and contracting the money supply. To increase the money supply, the Fed relies heavily on a process called the money multiplier effect.

The Money Multiplier Effect

The **money multiplier effect** is the expansion of the money supply as a result of commercial banks' lending their depositors' money to others. Let us look at an example of how it works. Suppose Mrs. Jones deposits $10,000 cash into her checking account at First National Bank. Assuming the Fed requires banks to hold reserves equaling 10 percent of their deposits, First National must keep at least $1,000 either in its vault or on deposit with its Federal Reserve district bank. The bank may now lend the remaining $9,000 in "excess reserves." Later that day Mr. Smith walks into First National Bank and requests a $9,000 auto loan. The bank grants the loan, and he takes the check to Honest John's Auto Sales and purchases a car. John deposits the $9,000 check into his checking account at Second National Bank. To meet its reserve requirement, Second National holds 10 percent (or $900) of the $9,000 as reserves and then lends out the excess $8,100 to another borrower, who in turn deposits the check to his account in Third National Bank. On and on the process continues. If all the participating banks lent out all the deposits in excess of their required reserves and if all the recipients of those loans redeposited the entire amounts, Mrs. Jones's original $10,000 would multiply into $100,000 worth of new deposits! The reason for this phenomenon is simple: if Mrs. Jones had personally lent Mr. Smith $9,000, she would have relinquished ownership of the money. However, when her bank lent the money, Mrs. Jones still retained ownership of the $10,000 in her account while Mr. Smith gained ownership of $9,000.

To determine how much the money supply may grow, you could add up all the new deposits as depicted in Figure 11-3, or you could use a simple formula:

$D \times \frac{1}{rr}$ = increase in money supply,

where D = initial deposit and
rr = reserve requirement.

For example, by how much could the money supply grow if a person deposits $10,000 and the Fed requires the bank to hold 10 percent on reserve?

$\$10,000 \times \frac{1}{.10} = \$100,000$

The factor $1/rr$ is the **money multiplier**, and it represents the number of times a deposit may be multiplied. In our example, the money multiplier is 1/.10, which is equal to 10 times the initial deposit.

In attempting to predict changes in the money supply, the money multiplier formula tends to be a poor tool. The participants in this process will never fully multiply the money supply for two reasons. First, financial institutions will not lend all their excess reserves. Historically, banks have tended to hold slightly more of their depositors' money on reserve than the Fed requires. Second, not all recipients of the loaned money will redeposit the entire amount. Whether

Fig. 11-3 The Money Multiplier Effect in Action

Bank	Amount deposited	−	Amount held on reserve	=	Amount loaned	Money supply
						$10,000.00
1st National	$10,000.00		$1,000.00		$9,000.00	$19,000.00
2nd National	9,000.00		900.00		8,100.00	27,100.00
3rd National	8,100.00		810.00		7,290.00	34,390.00
4th National	7,290.00		729.00		6,561.00	40,951.00
5th National	6,561.00		656.10		5,904.90	46,855.90
6th National	5,904.90		590.49		5,314.41	52,170.31
•	•		•		•	•
					Total increase =	$100,000.00

they desire the convenience of available cash or simply distrust banks, some people will choose to hold their money in the form of currency as opposed to depositing it into their checking accounts. Such decisions short-circuit the money multiplier, for money that is not redeposited cannot be re-lent. The combination of these two actions significantly reduces the money multiplier. For example, given that the average reserve requirement in the United States today is about 6 percent, the multiplier should be about 16 times (1/.06) the initial deposit. Yet, because people choose to hold currency and because banks do not lend all that they could, the real multiplier is approximately 2.9 times the initial deposit.

The Tools of Money Creation

To change the quantity of money in the nation's money supply, the Fed may either change the amount of money subject to the multiplier effect or change the multiplier. The Fed can do this in three ways: change the discount rate, change the reserve requirement, or buy and sell securities in the open market.

Changing the discount rate. The first way the Federal Reserve may increase or decrease the nation's money supply is through a process called **discounting**, which is lending money to banks. When a bank borrows money from the Fed, there is no need to print new money, to write or clear checks, or for any gold or silver to change hands. The Federal Reserve simply creates the money by informing the bank that it has credited the funds to the bank's reserve account. With the extra money, the bank may now make additional loans that cause the money supply to grow via the multiplier. Just as a bank attracts more borrowers by charging a lower interest rate, the Fed attracts banks to borrow more money by lowering the **discount rate**, the interest rate it charges on the loans it grants to banks. By raising the discount rate, the Fed could also discourage borrowing and cut the growth of the money supply.

Federal Reserve Bank of New York

Although the Fed can use changes in the discount rate as a powerful tool to change the money supply, it has rarely chosen to use the rate for that purpose. The Fed uses discounting primarily for its intended purpose, that of assisting banks that find themselves temporarily unable to meet large demands for withdrawals. The Fed also publicly advertises the availability of reserves to banks during times of economic uncertainty to discourage depositors from making runs on banks out of unnecessary panic. Immediately following the events of September 11, 2001, the Fed did just this to maintain the stability of the US financial system. As a result, there were no problems of financial panic associated with the 9/11 crisis.

Changing the reserve requirement. The second way the Federal Reserve may alter the money supply is by changing the reserve requirement. You saw earlier that if the reserve requirement is 10 percent, it could potentially multiply new deposits by a factor of ten (1/.10 = 10). If the Fed wanted to increase the money supply, it could simply lower the reserve requirement, which would have the effect of increasing the money multiplier. For example, if the reserve requirement were lowered to 5 percent, the money multiplier would rise to twenty (1/.05 = 20). Similarly, it could decrease the money supply by raising the reserve requirement. Because small changes in the reserve requirement can cause dramatic changes in the money supply, the Fed has been hesitant to use this method to adjust the money supply except in the direst economic circumstances.

Using open market operations. In contrast to its infrequent use of changes in the discount rate and the reserve requirement, the Fed continually uses its open market operations to control the quantity of money in circulation. An **open market operation** is an action whereby the Fed purchases or sells governmental securities in the open market to inject money into or withdraw money from the economy. If the Federal Reserve wishes to increase the nation's money supply, it simply purchases bonds in the open market, placing into the banking system new funds that flow into circulation. If, on the other hand, the Fed wishes to decrease the money supply, it sells bonds, thereby pulling money into itself and away from the general population.

Suppose that the Federal Open Market Committee meets and decides that the money supply needs to be $10 billion higher. Assuming a money multiplier of ten, the FOMC would direct the president of the New York Federal Reserve Bank to purchase $1 billion worth of governmental bonds. To pay for these bonds, the Fed would write checks totaling $1 billion to the securities dealers holding the bonds. Sellers of the bonds, in turn, would deposit the money into banks, and from the banks the money would enter the lending and borrowing cycle until the original $1 billion became $10 billion by the money multiplication process. At this point you may ask, "Where did the Fed get the $1 billion to buy the bonds in the first place?" Very simply, the Fed created the new money through a bookkeeping entry. Unlike ordinary customers of a bank, who must deposit money into their accounts prior to writing checks, the Fed may write checks on funds it creates by merely adjusting its books. After all, it controls the bank.

Fig. 11-4 The Fed's Monetary Policy Tools

Tool	Action	Effect on the money supply	Impact on the economy
discount rate	increase discount rate	reduces money supply	rising interest rates and a slowing of the economy
	decrease discount rate	increases money supply	falling interest rates and an acceleration of the economy
reserve requirement	increase reserve requirement	reduces money supply	rising interest rates and a slowing of the economy
	decrease reserve requirement	increases money supply	falling interest rates and an acceleration of the economy
open market operations	sell governmental securities	reduces money supply	rising interest rates and a slowing of the economy
	purchase governmental securities	increases money supply	falling interest rates and an acceleration of the economy

SECTION REVIEW 11B

1. List the six functions of the Federal Reserve System.
2. Explain the money multiplier effect.
3. To decrease the money supply, how would the Fed change the discount rate?
4. Which would decrease the money supply, an increased or decreased reserve requirement?
5. Which method of changing the money supply does the Fed use most often?

11C MONEY AND THE ECONOMY

Now we come to the ultimate question in this chapter's discussion: What difference does it make if the Fed increases or decreases the quantity of money in circulation? To answer that question correctly, you need to understand the economic effects of monetary policy changes and the effects of the money supply on prices and interest rates. Conversations about monetary policy and its effects can develop into lively discussions, with proponents on both sides of the issue holding strong opinions. Individuals, whether consumers, producers, economists, or politicians, form opinions based on how they perceive the ability of monetary policy to affect their jobs, their savings, and the prices they pay. Because Christians have an obligation to love their neighbors as themselves, it is important that they understand monetary policy and its ramifications and be able to apply Scriptures to their position.

MONETARY POLICY

Monetary policy is the increasing or decreasing of the money supply to influence the economy. The Fed governors examine economic data on a regular basis to determine whether there are any potential problems in the economy. If they perceive a potential problem, they use the tools at their disposal to adjust the money supply accordingly. For example, when the Fed has concerns about high inflation, it may enact a **tight monetary policy**, using one or more of the policy tools to reduce the money supply. If, on the other hand, the Fed has

The Fed's monetary policy decisions can affect unemployment.

concerns about a possible recession and rising unemployment, it may implement a **loose monetary policy**, which uses one or more of its policy tools to increase the money supply. You should note that there is always a tradeoff with any Fed policy. A tight monetary policy tends to curb inflation, but it increases the risk of slower economic growth and higher unemployment. On the other hand, a loose monetary policy encourages economic growth and helps to fend off a recession, but it makes inflation more likely.

THE SUPPLY OF MONEY AND PRICES

The first means whereby changes in the supply of money affect the economy is through prices. As the nation produces more goods and services, the supply of money must increase to the same extent so that the same quantity of dollars will purchase the same quantity of goods. If the supply of money grows more quickly than the growth in production of goods and services, it will require more dollars to buy any given good, thus creating a general rise in prices. Economists refer to this situation as inflation. If the supply of money grows more slowly than the growth in production of goods and services, prices will generally decline, and because there will not be enough dollars in circulation to purchase all the goods produced, a recession may ensue.

Prices will rise or fall depending on the amount of money available to purchase goods.

THE SUPPLY OF MONEY AND INTEREST RATES

The second means whereby changes in the supply of money affect the economy is through interest rates. The power to control interest rates gives the Fed tremendous control over the nation's economy. In a free-market economy the intersection of the demand and supply curves determines the price of any particular good. Likewise, the intersection of the demand and supply curves for money determines the price of money, or the interest rate. Figure 11-5 graphically depicts the demand for money. People and business firms will demand

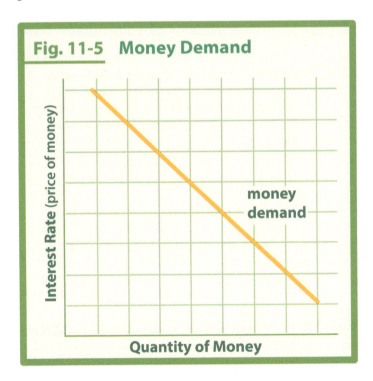

less (borrow less) money as interest rates rise. Why? Because as interest rates rise, it becomes less profitable for business firms to borrow money to purchase buildings and machines. The higher interest rates will reduce the firms' profits. Therefore, as interest rates rise, businesses will forgo expansion projects that would require them to borrow money. On the other hand, as interest rates fall, people and business firms will want to borrow more money.

The supply curve for money, as seen in Figure 11-6, is unusual in that it is a vertical line. Most supply curves slope upward from left to right, illustrating that as the price of a good rises, producers are willing to supply more. Money, however, comes from a supplier (the Fed) that is not interested in making a profit. The Fed simply chooses the supply of money that suits its policy purposes without regard to the prevailing interest rate; therefore, its money supply line is perfectly vertical.

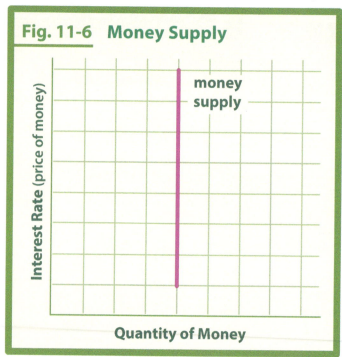

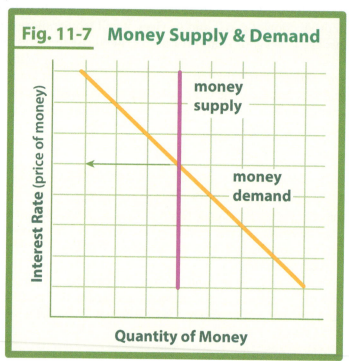

Figure 11-7 shows the combination of the two curves. The intersection point determines the interest rate (i). If the Federal Reserve should increase the supply of money, the vertical money supply curve would shift to the right, causing a decline in the interest rate (Fig. 11-8). Conversely, if the supply of money declines, the curve will shift to the left, leading to a rise in the interest rate (Fig. 11-9).

But how does the ability to control interest rates give the Fed the ability to influence the economy? You may recall that the interest rate is the mechanism that opens and closes the financial valve that controls the flow of money to business firms. If the Fed increases the supply of money, the interest rate on loans will fall, making it less costly and more profitable for businesses to borrow. The stock market will surge as people scramble to purchase stock in the now more profitable business firms. Consumers will also feel the effects of lower interest rates as houses and cars will be more affordable to finance. In short, as interest rates fall, businesses will expand, consumption expenditures will rise, and, more importantly, unemployment will fall.

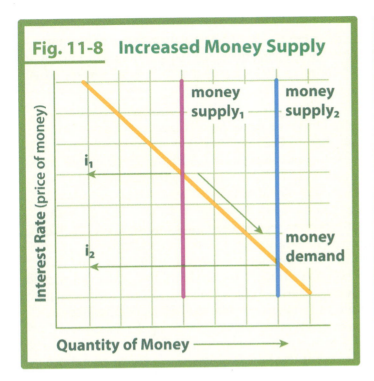

Fig. 11-8 Increased Money Supply

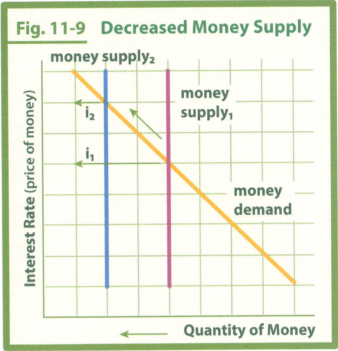

Fig. 11-9 Decreased Money Supply

THE FED POLICY TRADEOFF

An obvious question you may ask at this point is, Why does the Fed not continually print more money to stimulate the economy? The answer is that such activity would accelerate the economy too much. There is a point at which the economy would not be able to produce any more goods and services. At this point, equipment would be running twenty-four hours a day, people would be working at full capacity, and natural resources would be stretched to their limits. If the Fed were to continue to increase the money supply after the nation's economy had reached this point, demand would begin to exceed supply. The goods that could still be produced would rise in price and would be rationed out among buyers, who would become increasingly fewer and somewhat frantic. When this situation occurs, economists say the economy is "overheating."

To "cool down" an overheated economy, the Fed would decrease the growth rate of the money supply, causing interest rates to rise. As interest rates rose, businesses and consumers would be discouraged from borrowing additional funds. If the Fed should decrease the money supply too much, the economy might cool to the point that businesses would be left with idle machines and employees. To cut losses, businesses would begin laying off workers. In short, an artificial depression in the economy may closely follow an artificial expansion. This is one possible explanation for the Great Depression. After the Fed expanded the money

"IT SAYS, 'THESE DROPPING INTEREST RATES ARE A GIFT FROM YOUR FRIENDS AT AMERICA'S FEDERAL RESERVE.'"

CARLSON © 2001 Milwaukee Journal Sentinel. Reprint with permission of UNIVERSAL UCLICK. All rights reserved.

supply throughout the 1920s, perhaps causing the period of unprecedented economic prosperity, business activity began to heat up. The Fed reacted by reducing the money supply from $26.5 billion in 1929 to $19.5 billion in 1933—a reduction of over 25 percent, which may have cooled the economy into a chilling depression.

So, now you should be able to answer the question, What does it matter if the Fed increases or decreases the money supply? You know that whether the Fed pursues a tight or a loose monetary policy influences prices, interest rates, employment, the stock market, and the nation's overall economic growth. Having read this chapter, though, you should be able to do more than just answer this question. You should have a better understanding of a term you have perhaps often seen or heard in the news media but maybe never really paid much attention to—*the Fed*. Perhaps you did not know what the Fed was or did not think that whatever it did really had much effect on your life. Now you know differently. You should understand why Congress formed the Federal Reserve System, how it is organized, and what its purpose and principal functions are. When you read of the Fed's raising or lowering the discount rate or issuing new Treasury notes, you should understand not only what these actions are but also how they affect your family economically. You have learned much about open market operations, the power of the FOMC, the functioning of an elastic currency, the money multiplier effect, and how checks clear. As with other chapters you have read so far, this new knowledge should give you a greater understanding of and appreciation for economic events happening in your world and should also increase your desire to learn even more.

SECTION REVIEW 11C

1. What is the difference between a tight and a loose monetary policy?
2. The Fed's changing of the supply of money affects the economy in what two areas?
3. Why does the Fed not continually expand the money supply?

CHAPTER REVIEW

CONTENT QUESTIONS

1. Give the position or title of the most influential person at the Federal Reserve System.
2. Although the Fed is an independent organization, what are two specific checks on its power?
3. What is a run on a bank? Why is it a problem? How does the Fed attempt to prevent or control it?
4. For what two reasons will the money supply not ever be fully multiplied?
5. If the Fed were to decrease the discount rate, what kind of monetary policy would it be following?

APPLICATION QUESTIONS

1. In what way is the Federal Open Market Committee more powerful than any foreign army that could march against the United States?
2. If the reserve requirement is 8 percent and the money supply is $500 billion, what dollar amount of governmental securities will the Federal Reserve need to purchase if it wants to increase the money supply by 10 percent?
3. Imagine you have just heard a news reporter announce the following: "The Fed's Board of Governors announced today that it will begin pursuing a tight monetary policy for the next twelve months. The chair announced that, effective immediately, the discount rate and the reserve requirement would be increased and that the FOMC would begin selling governmental securities." Discuss the effect such a policy might have on prices, interest rates, employment, economic growth (the growth of the nation's production of actual goods and services), and the stock market.
4. How would you react to a tight monetary policy, and what effect would it have on both your short-term and long-term plans and goals?
5. How does Proverbs 22:3 apply to a discussion of monetary policy?

TERMS

Term	Page
central bank	209
Federal Reserve System	209
Board of Governors	210
reserve requirement	211
Federal Open Market Committee (FOMC)	212
elastic currency	215
fiscal agent	215
run on the bank	218
lender of last resort	218
money multiplier effect	218
money multiplier	219
discounting	220
discount rate	220
open market operation	221
monetary policy	222
tight monetary policy	222
loose monetary policy	223

PERSONAL FINANCE
WAYS TO SAVE

Whereas the first level of good financial stewardship is handling money in the short run (cash management; see p. 180), the second level is the proper handling of money in the intermediate run—short-term saving. "We can't afford to save." "We can barely keep our heads above water as it is." "It seems as if there is always too much month left over at the end of the money!" Such are common complaints of many individuals and families. They think that their expenses are so great that they cannot afford to save. The truth, however, is that with diligence and a little creativity they can often find some money to save.

There are actually two aspects to saving. The first aspect is reducing expenditures, that is, not spending any more money than is necessary. This is the idea of developing a budget and sticking to it. The second aspect is setting aside a specific amount of money before there is an opportunity to spend it. Clearly, the person who occasionally puts away a small amount is not the one who accumulates a sizable savings account, but rather it is the one who develops and maintains a disciplined and systematic savings schedule. Of course, the Christian's first financial responsibility is that of scriptural giving, but after that, his second goal should be saving a fixed portion of his income. Most financial planners advise clients to save 10 percent of their paychecks each month. There are a few options available that can help a person generate savings by setting aside a specified portion of his income.

AUTOMATIC PAYROLL DEDUCTION

Many employers provide a service whereby they automatically deposit a prearranged percentage of an employee's paycheck in a savings account. Having the funds deducted before he receives the paycheck often makes it a little easier for a worker to live on what is left as opposed to his having to make a deposit personally. If your employer deducted only $50 per month from your paycheck and deposited it at a 3.5 percent simple annual interest rate, you would have a savings of $621 dollars at the year's end. That amount would grow to over $3,300 in five years, over $7,400 in ten years, and over $17,800 in twenty years. Those who adopt a payroll deduction plan early in their working careers will not only accumulate sizable balances over a period of years but also begin a savings habit that could last a lifetime.

EMPLOYER SAVINGS PLANS

Closely related to payroll deduction is an employer-sponsored savings plan. To encourage savings, provide an added employee benefit, and on occasion encourage ownership of the company's stock, many business firms provide matching savings plans. The employer will contribute a predetermined amount of money toward a savings and investment plan for each dollar an employee contributes, up to a maximum amount. For example, were a company to contribute 50¢ for each dollar an employee contributed to the plan (up to a maximum employee contribution of $2,000 per year) and were an employee to contribute the maximum $2,000, the employer would then contribute an additional $1,000 for a total account value of $3,000. That is a 50 percent return on the employee's savings before interest!

Employers offering such plans occasionally provide several savings and investment options from which the employee may choose. For example, the company in the above scenario may allow its employees to contribute to a fund of different common stocks, a regular interest-bearing account with rates competitive to those offered by commercial banks, or a fund of the company's stock. Besides limiting the amount of the contribution, most firms also require that the employee keep the money on deposit for a minimum period of time (perhaps three to five years) before being permitted to withdraw his and the employer's portions of the contribution. Without such restrictions employees could make contributions and withdraw their funds immediately after the employer made his contribution. Such action would seriously limit any benefit the company could derive from managing the fund and would reduce the incentive for the company to contribute.

CLAIM FEWER EXEMPTIONS

When a person begins working for an employer, the government requires the employee to complete a W-4 form for the Internal Revenue Service (IRS). On the W-4, he declares the number of dependents for whom he is responsible; and on the basis of this number, the government calculates the amount of income tax it will withhold from his paycheck. If, at the end of the year, the government has not withheld enough tax, the employee

ELECTRONIC MONEY

Imagine a world in which you no longer carry cash, coins, or even checks. Computers make this futuristic vision technically possible. By using an **electronic funds transfer system (EFTS)**, Americans find themselves making more and more financial transactions without ever seeing their money.

For example, an EFTS enables banks to deposit payroll and social security checks directly into a bank account. Banks can also pay loan installments, mortgages, insurance premiums, electric bills, and even credit card bills for you automatically. You simply give the bank a signed authorization slip, and the bank does the rest. Automatic bill payment saves time, money, and the embarrassment of late payments. You can receive a warning statement prior to the transaction, and you can revoke your authorization at any time.

Many transactions that once required a visit to the bank (or an ATM) can now be done with a home banking system. By linking to their banks through home computers or phones with Internet access, customers can analyze their accounts, pay bills, request investment advice, and purchase products from online retailers.

Other common applications of an EFTS include wire transfers, ATMs, and point-of-sale systems. Financial institutions have long used **wire transfers** to transfer more than half a billion dollars each day between banks. Although ATMs are still popular places for private electronic funds transfers, customers now use debit cards at retail stores and gas stations to transfer money from their personal accounts to the merchants' accounts through what is called a **point-of-sale (POS) system**.

One drawback of an EFTS is the possibility of privacy violations. An account holder's financial transactions are open to anyone who can tap into the computer system. Electronic money also does not prevent bank robberies. In one famous case, thieves claiming to be from the Central Bank of Nigeria requested a wire transfer from a New York bank for $21 million. The money went to overseas accounts from which the thieves withdrew it before the bank knew what was happening. In another case, a programmer working at a bank altered its computer software to siphon off over half a million dollars. The legal system is gaining understanding of and confronting these forms of crime. One new method to thwart thieves is a special thumbprint pad that will allow only the account holder to withdraw money from the account.

must send the IRS a check for the balance due. If the government has withheld too much tax, however, the IRS will refund the overpayment. The more dependents a person claims, the less tax the government will withhold; and the fewer dependents the taxpayer claims, the greater the amount the IRS will deduct. By claiming fewer exemptions than he rightfully could and overpaying his taxes, a person can increase the amount of his income tax refund. Thus, some employees deliberately claim fewer dependents than the law allows and use the US Treasury as a personal savings account.

From an economic perspective, however, this is a poor way to save money. The government is actually getting interest-free use of the person's money for an entire year. Had the employee retained that money and invested it wisely, he could have increased the amount such that he could pay any taxes owed and still have saved some money. Unfortunately, there are those who use this method to force themselves to save because they would not likely invest the money themselves, but their lack of self-discipline still costs them money.

AUTOMATIC TRANSFERS FROM CHECKING TO SAVINGS

For those with checking and savings accounts in the same institution, another simple way of saving is to use an automatic transfer service. This service works from an agreement between a depositor and the bank whereby on a specific day each month the bank transfers a prearranged amount of money from the depositor's checking account to his savings account. As long as the depositor carefully specifies a day of the month when there will be sufficient funds in his account, such as the day after each payday, this can be a useful way of saving. Those using automatic transfer services must also remember to deduct the amount of the withdrawal from their checking accounts to prevent accidentally overdrawing their accounts.

SAVE UNEXPECTED WINDFALLS

During the apple harvest, growers traditionally paid workers to go into the orchards and handpick each apple. Occasionally they were fortunate to have a strong gust of wind blow down a substantial portion of their crop, thus reducing their expenses and increasing their profits. Today, when any unexpected profit comes someone's way, we say he is enjoying a "windfall." Rather than spending the entirety of a financial windfall, such as an inheritance, work bonus, cash gift, or rebate, financial advisors suggest that the recipient spend only 25 percent of it and save the other 75 percent. Following this policy provides a potentially significant savings while at the same time allowing for current use of some of the funds. By saving all windfalls over a relatively short period of time, a person could possibly accumulate a substantial savings account.

ADOPT A "FRUGAL MONTH"

Just as a runner sees the finish line and puts on a last-minute burst of speed, some people can accumulate extra savings by putting on one burst of savings each year in the form of a "frugal month." During the frugal month people reduce every expense as much as possible. For example, during the month family members can take their lunches to work or school and agree to spend no money on clothing, furniture, or entertainment. However, rather than having the frugal month simply become a month of lean living, participants can have some fun and turn it into a challenge. Each family member can work to come up with the best money saving tips. Be prepared, though, because suggestions might include ideas like watering the lawn or washing the cars with bath water and burning candles instead of light bulbs—even living on bread and water! Advisors suggest that the frugal month be either in the spring or fall when utility bills are lower and when no significant holidays will interfere with expenses.

CONTINUE INSTALLMENT PAYMENTS WHEN A DEBT IS PAID

If a person has been making installment payments on a debt over a long period of time, he has adjusted his lifestyle to living on the lower consumption spending. A golden opportunity for savings, therefore, presents itself when he finally pays off the loan. Rather than increasing spending because of having a little extra income each month, he could continue to write a check for what was the installment payment but deposit it into a savings account instead.

SAVE YOUR RAISE

As they become more experienced and productive in their work or as their cost of living increases, employees often receive raises from their employers. Since these workers have been living on their pre-raise income, it might be possible for them to "bank" most if not all of the raise.

STASH YOUR CASH

One final method of saving money is the actual hoarding of cash. Some people keep a jar into which they toss all loose change at the end of the day. Another useful, but sometimes dangerous, method of stashing cash is collecting high denomination pieces of currency. For example, one man had a habit of accumulating $100 bills. Whenever he accumulated enough small bills, he went to the bank and had them converted to hundreds. Within two years he had accumulated twenty-one $100 bills. Granted, his money was not earning interest during those years, but at least he had $2,100 in savings that he may not have had otherwise.

Individuals need to be careful when saving money in this manner. The saver can easily lose or forget where he placed the money, and if others hear of significant stashes of cash, the home may become a target for thieves. Also, since the money sits without earning interest, this method of saving is not good stewardship and has merit only if the collector frequently adds his collected cash to some interest-bearing investment.

You may not presently have a regular source of income; consequently, you may think that you do not have enough money to save or have a need to save. However, having read this article, you should now be aware of sources of income that if managed properly could provide you with funds to save. You may not be able to match funds with your employer or utilize withholdings on your W-4, but you may have occasional windfalls (Grandma's birthday money or an unexpected cash gift for help rendered to a neighbor). You could also participate in a family frugal month and perhaps reconsider what you do with your allowance. Saving is a part of good stewardship. Christians should want to do their best with whatever money God gives them, and often the best thing to do in the intermediate period is to save.

REVIEW QUESTIONS

1. What are the two aspects of saving?
2. What percentage of your income do financial planners advocate saving?
3. Why is claiming fewer dependents not a good way to save?

TERMS

electronic funds transfer system (EFTS)	229
wire transfers	229
point-of-sale (POS) system	229

UNIT FIVE

UNIT FIVE

ECONOMICS OF THE GOVERNMENT

CHAPTER 12
MEASURING THE WEALTH OF THE NATION — 234

Personal Finance: Understanding How Interest Works — 252

CHAPTER 13
THE BUSINESS CYCLE AND UNEMPLOYMENT — 256

Personal Finance: Savings Instruments — 274

CHAPTER 14
INFLATION — 278

Personal Finance: Estate Planning — 294

CHAPTER 15
FISCAL POLICY — 300

Personal Finance: Retirement Planning — 318

CHAPTER TWELVE
MEASURING THE WEALTH OF THE NATION

12A GROSS DOMESTIC PRODUCT — 234

12B FOREIGN TRADE — 243

Business firms take an annual accounting of how much they have produced and sold during the past year to determine if they have met their production and sales goals, how they are faring in their market, and how they compare to their competitors. In similar fashion, nations account for their productivity by determining the total output of the goods and services their various industries have produced. Economists utilize the annual accountings of these production levels to determine their nation's economic progress relative to past years, the overall health of the economy, and the degree to which their nation is competing successfully in international markets as compared with other nations. To make these determinations, economists use the nation's GDP.

12A GROSS DOMESTIC PRODUCT

GDP is one of the most prevalent initialisms found in economics. It stands for **gross domestic product**—the total dollar value of all final goods and services a nation's industries produce within its borders in one year.

To understand gross domestic product, you must grasp four basic concepts economists use to determine it. The first concept is that to calculate a country's GDP for a given year, you multiply the quantity of goods produced in the country that year by their prices. For example, if US manufacturers produce one million washing machines in a year and the price of each machine is $800, the production of washing machines will have contributed $800 million to the US GDP for that year. Of course, to get a complete measure of the GDP, you would have to add up the contributions of *all* the goods and services produced in the United States in a year. Because you would have made your calculation using current, or "nominal," dollar values, you would refer to the result of your work as the **nominal GDP**. Nominal GDP is how the government reports the basic GDP figure. In the first quarter of 2015, the nominal GDP, or total dollar value of all goods and services produced in the United States, was $17,693.3 billion.

The second important concept is that the GDP includes the sale of only **final goods and services**, goods and services that producers sold to ultimate users. Nonfinal goods, or **intermediate goods**, are those that someone purchased either to resell immediately or to incorporate into other goods. For example, economists consider a tire that a car owner buys to be a final good and include it in the GDP. If, however, an automobile manufacturer purchased that tire, its status would be an intermediate good. If the GDP included intermediate goods and services as well as final goods, it would significantly overreport the nation's production for the year. Economists would be counting the same good twice, once when a business purchased it and again when the firm sold it to the final consumer.

Another issue related to separating final from intermediate goods and services is tabulating the value of unsold inventories. For instance, what happens when a car dealership purchases a new car to resell but does not sell the car during the year? Well, as the one left holding the spud in a game of hot potato is out, so the business firm holding unsold inventory at the end of the year is out in the sense that it becomes the final consumer of that inventory. So, in our car dealership example, those determining the GDP would consider the dealership to be the final purchaser of that unsold new car. If you combine this fact with possible taxes owed on final purchases, you can understand why automobile dealerships and other retail businesses hold year-end inventory sales.

Washing machines, an example of a final good, are part of the GDP.

The third concept in determining the GDP is that it includes only those goods and services that manufacturers produced during the past calendar year. This keeps used goods, such as antiques, used cars, and secondhand clothing, from being part of the GDP year after year. If economists were to include the sale of used goods in the GDP, a nation could be experiencing a decline in production without knowing it because the used goods would keep the GDP above the level of the nation's true productivity.

The fourth and final concept for determining the GDP is that it seeks to measure only domestic production. That is, it measures the production of goods and services within a nation's borders. Thus, the production of a Toyota automobile in the United States counts as part of the US GDP, while production of a Ford automobile in Canada does not. The reason for this characteristic of GDP measurement is

Furniture is an example of a final good, while wood and fabric are examples of intermediate goods.

that policymakers want a measuring tool that reflects changes in US employment. Thus, if Toyota has an increase in production in the United States, it would likely translate into an increase in employment at the US Toyota assembly facility.

HOW TO MEASURE GDP

Totaling the dollar value of everything that a nation produces is not an easy task. The government cannot hire workers each year to go out and physically count every good and service the country's manufacturers have produced. Economists have found, however, that they can arrive at a good estimate for the GDP by adding up all the purchases of the four basic economic groups: households, businesses, the government, and foreign buyers. Figure 12-1 shows an overview of the components of nominal GDP for the United States in 2014.

SIMON KUZNETS AND THE ORIGIN OF GDP

During the Great Depression, governmental economic policymakers were having trouble determining a course of action to offset the effects of the economic downturn, and they determined that the primary obstacle to their identifying a proper policy was the lack of coherent data on the overall performance of the economy. Until that time, economic data were small, isolated bits of information that different private and public organizations produced. These groups used differing definitions and took considerable time to develop their results. For these reasons, Congress passed a resolution in 1932 that required the Department of Commerce to assemble and report statistics on economy-wide income.

In January 1933 Simon Kuznets of the National Bureau of Economic Research (NBER) was given responsibility for developing a set of economic statistics that would serve the purposes of the government. Kuznets was a Russian immigrant who had led a section of the bureau of labor statistics for the Soviet Union. At twenty-one he began studying at Columbia University, and in five years he completed three degrees: a BA (1923), an MA (1924), and a PhD (1927). Kuznets and his team completed their initial set of statistics in 1937 and entitled their report *National Income and Capital Formation, 1919–1935*. In this report Kuznets outlined a new concept called national income, which he defined as the sum of all incomes of all individuals in the United States. He also divided this measure into various subcategories, which would help in estimating the effect of the Depression in various sectors of the economy and different geographic regions of the country.

Throughout the ensuing decades, other economists would further refine national income, often responding to specific needs resulting from events such as World War II and the accelerating inflation of the late 1960s and 1970s. Today, economists and policymakers use GDP, national income, and a host of other related economic measures to support economic research and policymaking. These statistics have allowed greater understanding of the business cycle and insight into potential policy choices to resolve economic problems.

The success of this work is due in no small measure to the expertise and insight of Simon Kuznets. He is well-known not only for his contribution to measuring national income but also for his pioneering research into the effect of population growth on the economic development of a country. In 1971, for all his research, Simon Kuznets was awarded the third Nobel Prize in Economics.

Simon Kuznets

Fig. 12-1 Nominal GDP by Type of Expenditure, 2014 (dollars in billions)

Personal consumption expenditures		
durable goods	$1,329.0	
nondurable goods	2,679.0	
services	8,112.3	
		$12,120.2
Plus gross private domestic investment		
fixed investment	$2,850.0	
change in business inventories	93.3	
		$2,943.3
Plus governmental purchases of goods and services		
federal	$1,216.7	
state and local	1,972.6	
		$3,189.3
Plus net exports of goods and services		
exports	$2,352.3	
less imports	2,901.5	
		-$549.2
Equals nominal gross domestic product		$17,703.7

Source: Bureau of Economic Analysis (www.bea.gov)
Note: Components may not add to total due to rounding.

Household Consumption

By far, household expenditures for consumer goods and services account for the greatest portion of the nation's total purchases. In 2014, households spent a total of $12,120.2 billion on consumer durable goods, nondurable goods, and services. This amount is four times what the government spent in the same period and over four times what private businesses spent.

In 2014, American households spent $1,329.0 billion on **consumer durable goods**. These are goods that have a life expectancy of more than one year. Consumer durable goods include vehicles, furniture, and major appliances.

Consumer nondurable goods are items that consumers expect to wear out or use up within one year, such as shoes, soap, and gasoline. Households spent $2,679.0 billion in 2014 on nondurable goods.

The last of the three household consumption categories, consumer services, is the largest. In 2014, consumers spent $8,112.3 billion on services. **Consumer services** include purchases such as haircuts, income tax preparation, and education. The reason for the great size of this category is that nearly every good sold requires some kind of accompanying economic service.

Figure 12-2 illustrates how consumption spending as a percentage of total spending in the United States has changed. Notice how the percentage declined during World War II. During this period the

Washing machines and other major appliances are consumer durable goods.

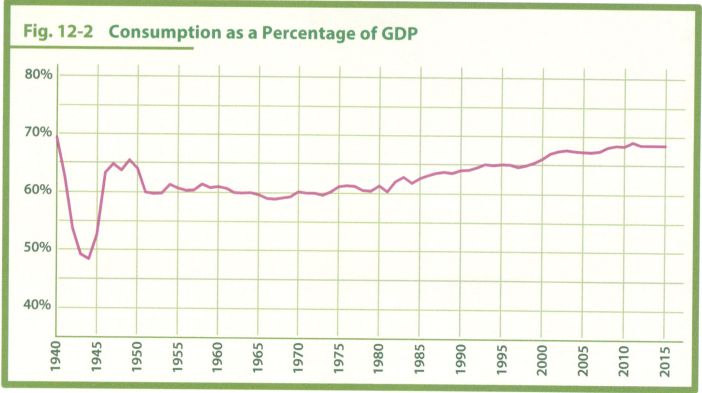

Fig. 12-2 Consumption as a Percentage of GDP

Source: Bureau of Economic Analysis (www.bea.gov)

The work of a mechanic on your car is an example of a consumer service.

US government rationed many consumer goods and channeled a vast quantity of goods to military use.

Business Investment

The second spending category that economists consider when calculating the GDP is **gross private domestic investment (GPDI)**. GPDI, or **business investment** as it is frequently called, is the sum of all business spending on capital investment and unplanned inventories. In 2014, business firms spent $2,850.0 billion on capital investment—purchases of factories and equipment. The second category within GPDI is investment in inventories that businesses purchased but were unable to resell by the end of the year. In 2014, unplanned inventory build-ups added $93.3 billion to GPDI, bringing it to a total of $2,943.3 billion.

During World War II, business investment, like consumer spending, fell dramatically from a prewar level of 14.6 percent of the GDP to a low of 3.2 percent. This drop resulted from several factors. First, rationing limited consumer spending; thus, business investment in new factories and equipment became unnecessary. Second, the government soaked up much of the nation's savings through wartime borrowing and crowded business firms out of the financial market. After the war, producers sought to satisfy consumers' pent-up demands for previously rationed consumer goods, and business investment immediately increased until 1951, when it reached an average of over 16 percent of the GDP. Figure 12-3 illustrates how investment spending as a percentage of total spending in the United States has changed.

> Curiously, the amount spent on capital investment also includes purchases of newly constructed houses. Rather than include new houses under consumer durables, economists have chosen to consider such purchases as investments.

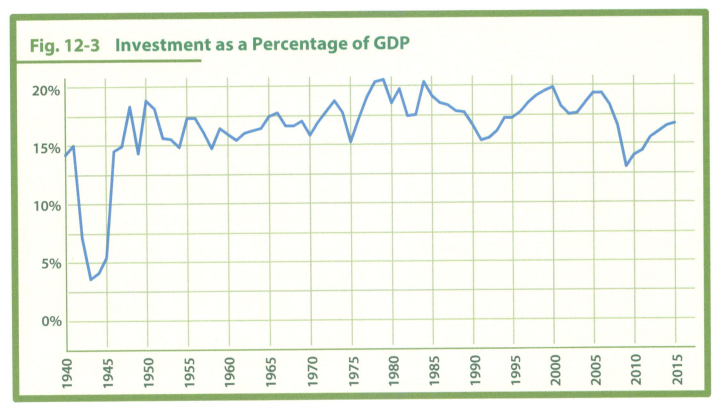

Source: Bureau of Economic Analysis (www.bea.gov)

Governmental Spending

Local, state, and national governments purchase much of the goods and services produced in our country. Indeed, in 2014, the government's purchases of goods and services accounted for $3,189.3 billion, or about one-fifth (20%) of the gross domestic product. In other words, federal, state, and local governments currently purchase about one of every five dollars' worth of products and services made in this country.

Historically, governmental purchases were rather small until the twentieth century. They reached an all-time high in 1943 (during World War II), when they accounted for 46 percent of the GDP. Since the end of the war, they have maintained a fairly consistent rate (fluctuating slightly above or below 20% of GDP), seeing only a slight increase even after the terrorist attacks of September 11, 2001.

Governmental spending, part of the GDP, includes spending for programs such as school lunches.

Net Exports

The final component needed to tabulate the GDP is the amount of goods a nation sells to other countries. **Net exports** are the difference between the dollar amount a nation takes in from the sale of exports and the dollars remaining for the nation to purchase imports. If GDP calculations did not take net exports into account, the GDP would show money flowing into the United States from its sales to other nations but would fail to show money flowing out for the goods it purchases from them. In 2014, the United States experienced a negative trade balance of -$549.2 billion; that is, it purchased $549.2 billion more in goods from other nations than it sold abroad.

Net exports (NX) added to household consumption (C), business investment (I), and governmental spending (G) account for all spending in a nation. Thus, to add all these together is to calculate the GDP. In 2014, the GDP totaled $17,703.7 billion.

$$GDP = C + I + G + NX$$

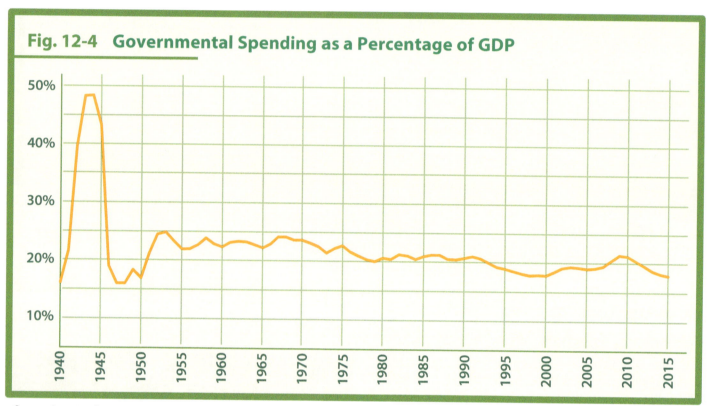

Fig. 12-4 Governmental Spending as a Percentage of GDP

Source: Bureau of Economic Analysis (www.bea.gov)

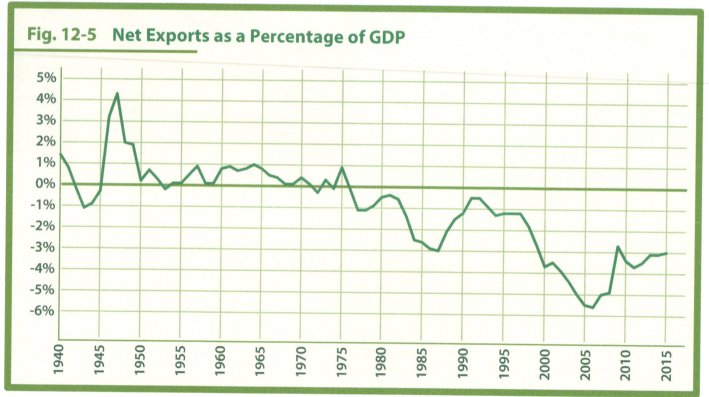

Fig. 12-5 Net Exports as a Percentage of GDP

Source: Bureau of Economic Analysis (www.bea.gov)

PROBLEMS WITH GDP MEASUREMENT

GDP figures are supposed to tell economists and governmental officials how productive the economy has been at any given time. That information helps them make decisions concerning national economic policy. Economists have found, however, that the GDP is not as precise a measuring tool as they would like it to be.

Unrecorded Transactions

One of the reasons the GDP does not perfectly measure a nation's total production is that, contrary to its definition, it does not account for all final goods and services produced in the nation during a year. Many goods and services produced in the country are not recorded because they are not sold for money. Instead their transaction involves barter. A barter transaction is one in which one producer trades his goods or services for the goods or services of another producer. If producers trade goods, there is no record of either the price or the exchange. Since there is no final purchaser of the goods or services, it is, in terms of GDP calculations, as if no goods or services had been produced. No official measure of production will contain the value of these goods.

Transactions at yard sales and flea markets are not included in the GDP.

Other transactions go unrecorded because they are do-it-yourself activities. Obviously, the service a lawn-care business provides to homeowners counts as part of the GDP, but when a homeowner cuts his own grass rather than paying someone else to do it, his work is not a part of the GDP. The homeowner's service is just as real as that of the professional, but since no market transaction took place and no money changed hands, the service is not part of the national figures. Each year millions of productive home activities, such as cutting hair, cleaning and painting houses, washing cars, and raising vegetables in a family garden, go unrecorded in the GDP figures.

For obvious reasons, other unrecorded transactions include the production and sale of illegal goods and services. Suppliers of contraband, counterfeit, or stolen items obviously leave their transactions out of GDP figures because to report them would be to invite arrest and imprisonment.

Mowing the lawn and washing the car, when done by family members, are not counted as part of the GDP.

Counterproductive Items

Besides the many productive transactions, or "goods," that economists do not add to the GDP, there are also counterproductive items, or "bads," that they do not subtract from the GDP. Bads are undesirable products or services, such as water pollution, air pollution, and noise pollution that producers create in the process of making goods. Many economists believe that when a firm produces a $100 good at the expense of $200 in damages to the environment, the nation should reduce its GDP by $100. The problem with subtracting bads from the GDP, however, is how to accurately measure such environmental damages.

Air pollution produced by industries is not a "good" but a "bad."

Inflation

Another source of GDP distortion is inflation. It causes the GDP to not reflect the true dollar value of the nation's production. Inflation indicates that the general level of all prices is rising. Suppose you lived in a very small country that produced only shoes. Last year your nation produced and sold one million pairs at $50 per pair. The GDP therefore totaled $50 million. This year your country again produced one million pairs, but inflation drove the price up to $100 per pair. As a result, your country reported its GDP as $100 million. The casual observer would likely believe that your country's GDP had doubled and conclude that employment had increased and that the economy in your country was doing very well. To the economist, however, your country's GDP did not grow at all since it produced no more actual goods this year than it did last year. In this way, inflation makes actual production less clear in nominal GDP data.

Economists have developed a way to factor inflation out of the GDP to determine an economy's true production. They divide the nominal gross domestic product (GDP in today's dollars) by a factor called the **GDP implicit price deflator (GDP deflator)**. The GDP deflator is a price index that rises as the price of all goods and services rises. The result of this adjustment is a figure that economists call **real GDP**. To calculate the GDP deflator, governmental economists begin by choosing a base year in which they look to see how much of that year's goods a dollar bought. After setting the base year, the government sends out surveyors to check the prices of all goods and services to see if prices have generally risen or fallen. For example, if you were to take 2009 as the base year, you would assign the GDP deflator a value of 100 for that year. If surveys for the first quarter of 2015 then determined that the GDP deflator was 109.099, you would know that prices had risen by 9.099 percent between 2009 and the first quarter of 2015.

$$\text{GDP deflator} = \frac{\text{Nominal GDP}}{\text{Real GDP}} \times 100$$

Changes in Population

By calculating the real GDP, economists have developed a more accurate measure of the wealth of a nation, but the true measure of a nation's wealth is its wealth per person, or **per capita real GDP**. Suppose there are two countries with the same real GDP but with very different populations. It is easy to see that the citizens of the less populated country would generally be better off than those of the more heavily populated country because the GDP would be distributed among fewer people in the less populated country. Suppose

that the US economy produced 2.9 percent more goods and services in 2015 than in 2014 but that the American population increased by 4 percent. The nation's wealth per person, or per capita real GDP, would actually have fallen. Economists determine per capita real GDP by dividing the nation's real gross domestic product by its total population. In 2014 the per capita real GDP of the United States was over $49,600.

SECTION REVIEW 12A

1. Name the four concepts that are part of the definition of GDP.
2. What is the difference between a final and an intermediate good?
3. What four economic groups determine a nation's GDP?
4. Why is the nominal GDP not as useful as the real GDP?

12B FOREIGN TRADE

In 2014 the United States exported $2,352.3 billion in domestically produced goods and services but imported $2,901.5 billion in goods and services produced in foreign nations. The resulting negative $549.2 billion difference carries on the US accounting books as a **trade deficit**, or a *negative balance of trade*. Had the United States sold $2,901.5 billion in goods and services while purchasing goods totaling $2,352.3 billion, it would have achieved a *positive balance of trade* in the form of a $549.2 billion **trade surplus**.

From 1929 until the early 1970s, the United States had only a few years of trade deficits (see Fig. 12-5 on page 240). Since 1976, however, the United States has experienced continually increasing trade deficits. Though net exports currently account for a relatively low drain

The United States imports and exports billions of dollars' worth of goods.

on total GDP, news headlines have featured the trade deficit for at least three reasons. First, dollars flowing out of the United States due to trade deficits generally produce an increase in foreign jobs at the expense of American jobs. Second, the deficits tend to coincide with a decline in US manufacturing and indicate a shift to the nation's being more of a consumer than a producer. Third, American prestige as the world's foremost manufacturer suffers by recognizing that other nations are able to produce a better or less costly product. For years Americans had accepted the belief that the United States would dominate all meaningful markets. However, other nations of the world have progressed economically, and they are now able to produce some goods more cheaply and of better quality than those made in the United States. Many Americans, therefore, have become concerned by their country's response to the increasing international competition and the continuing trade deficits.

REASONS FOR TRADE DEFICITS

Foreign trade is a very sensitive issue in the United States. Some Americans argue that trade deficits hurt the nation, while others believe that a negative trade balance helps the economy. Before you examine philosophies of trade, it will help you to look at the reasons that trade imbalances exist. What exactly causes positive or negative balances of trade? In other words, what causes someone to buy more from his neighbor than he sells to him? There are six main causes of trade imbalances:

1. Domestic inability to produce some goods
   A country's inability to produce some goods in any meaningful quantity will force it to import those products. For example, since American businesses cannot profitably produce sufficient quantities of bananas, coffee, and teakwood, we must import these goods.

2. Better quality of some foreign goods
   Although domestic firms may be able to manufacture an acceptable product, buyers may believe that, dollar for dollar, the competing foreign good is of higher quality. Consumers' shunning the domestic good and demanding the foreign product will, therefore, drive up imports.

3. Cheaper foreign materials
   Some foreign producers have sources of less expensive, readily available raw materials and, consequently, are able to manufacture and sell a product for a lower price than domestic competitors.

4. Lower foreign wages
   Foreign competitors may be able to sell their products at lower prices because their nation's workers receive lower wages than American workers. Though the products themselves may be comparable, the foreign firms can sell theirs at a lower price because of lower production costs.

5. Lower foreign capital costs
   Some foreign governments may attempt to foster the growth of certain industries in their nations by providing low-interest-rate loans and tax breaks to firms in those industries. When a government engages in such a national industrial policy, it enables some businesses to purchase capital equipment at an overall lower cost, ultimately resulting in a lower-priced product that can compete more effectively in the world market.

6. Foreign subsidies
   Finally, some foreign competitors are able to sell their products at lower prices because their governments tax their citizens and pay the companies subsidies. A **subsidy** is a government's payment to a producer to help with manufacturing costs. Lower production costs allow the manufacturer to charge a lower price. For example, suppose France wants one of its products to have a lower price than its American counterpart; and to make that happen, its producers charge a price in America lower than their manufacturing costs. To make up the difference, the French government gives those manufacturers a subsidy; and to supply that subsidy, the government adds a tax on its people. Consequently, the nation's taxpayers

The US imports some items because of its inability to produce those items in a profitable quantity and quality.

ultimately make up for their domestic business firm's lost profits.

TRADE POLICY: PROTECTIONISM VS. FREE TRADE

Two distinct groups have appeared on the American scene espousing opposing views regarding trade policies. Each believes its position to be beneficial to the US economy and its opponent's to be harmful. One group, the **protectionists**, claims its policies will protect domestic manufacturing and jobs, while its counterpart, the advocates of **free trade**, views its program as the best one to move the American economy forward.

Protectionists believe that trade deficits lead to a decrease in the number of American jobs; therefore, they wish to protect those jobs through trade legislation. First, they support **trade quotas**, limitations on the quantities of certain goods that foreign nations may import into the United States. To use a simple example, if Americans purchased one million motorcycles per year and if American motorcycle manufacturers were able to produce only one hundred thousand, then protectionists would support legislation to limit the number of imported motorcycles to nine hundred thousand. Protectionists believe that limiting the number of imported motorcycles would save jobs at American manufacturing plants and would keep the American unemployment rate from rising. Second, many protectionists support using a tariff to limit the desirability of imports.

DAVID RICARDO (1772–1823)
The Apostle of Free Trade

David Ricardo was a British entrepreneur who made a large fortune in stocks and lending at a very young age. Due to his financial success, he retired from business at the age of forty-one and thereafter was able to devote his time to intellectual pursuits. Ricardo had read Adam Smith's *The Wealth of Nations*, and upon his retirement he devoted himself to a study of economics, a study that lasted the remainder of his life. He wrote tracts discussing ideas that would ultimately become part of the quantity theory of money as espoused by modern monetarist economists. He also wrote responses to the work of Robert Malthus in respect to the possibility of overproduction in an economy. Ricardo recognized that free markets would automatically adjust prices and production so as to prevent great shortages or surpluses.

Among Ricardo's most influential writings were those incorporated in his *Principles of Political Economy and Taxation* (1817). In this work he articulated the now familiar principle of comparative advantage, which went contrary to the view of foreign trade prevalent at the time. British trade policy had customarily protected domestic industry with high protective tariffs. Ricardo argued that a country is always better off when it focuses its efforts on producing those goods and services that it can produce at relatively low cost and purchasing the goods and services that it cannot from other countries.

Ricardo was elected a member of the British Parliament in 1819 and served there until his death.

A **tariff** is a tax on an imported product that makes a comparable domestic product more price-competitive. For example, if an American motorcycle costs $16,000, while a foreign model of equal quality costs $14,000, many protectionists would support a tariff greater than $2,000 on each imported unit. The American product, which was formerly undesirable because of its higher price, would become the lesser-priced good and could therefore potentially become the purchaser's first choice.

Those who support free trade, on the other hand, believe that the consumer, not the producer, is of paramount importance and that trade deficits do not automatically lead to higher levels of unemployment. Proponents of free trade believe that protectionism is a return to the mercantilist policies of the seventeenth and eighteenth centuries. Under mercantilism, a nation believed it increased its wealth if it sold more goods than it purchased. Free traders agree that protectionist legislation would, in our example, increase employment in the American motorcycle manufacturing industry. However, they argue that a decrease in the overall American unemployment rate would not necessarily follow. For example, advocates of free trade point out that if Congress passed laws to limit the quantity of imported foreign motorcycles, many American dock workers could become unemployed, since fewer motorcycles would need to be unloaded from foreign ships. American salesmen and service technicians who sell and service the foreign motorcycles could lose their jobs as well. Moreover, any trade quota ultimately results in higher prices for consumers. In addition, if Americans cease buying foreign goods, foreigners will not acquire the dollars they need to purchase American goods, and these purchases increase employment in the United States.

Free traders believe that increasing tariffs on imports, the protectionists' second policy action, will have the same effect. To use the previous example, when Americans purchased the less expensive foreign motorcycles, they had more money left over to purchase other products. Making the foreign product more expensive to encourage Americans to buy the American motorcycles would only eliminate those leftover dollars and possibly the jobs supported by them. Free traders believe that in the long run, protectionist legislation passed by Congress has a tendency to save jobs in targeted industries only by redistributing the unemployment to other industries.

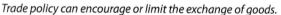
Trade policy can encourage or limit the exchange of goods.

The issue of foreign trade is and will likely always be one that stirs up great emotion, for it strikes at the pride of a nation. Whether, therefore, a nation should undertake protectionist trade policies or allow the free market to rule will be a subject of ongoing debate. What, then, is the correct policy? As you recall, the science of economics is the science of making choices, so it is important for you to make the wisest choice regarding which trade policy to support. As regards the trade policy debate, you should keep before you these basic economic considerations:

1. Under free trade, domestic industries that are not competitive with foreign rivals will experience unemployment.

NAFTA: A FREE-TRADE PACT

The North American Free Trade Agreement (NAFTA) brought together Canada, Mexico, and the United States to create a free-trade zone. These countries crafted the agreement to promote international investments and to increase trade through fair competition. NAFTA went into effect on January 1, 1994, and gradually removed all tariff and nontariff trade barriers until its full implementation on January 1, 2008.

Since its passage, NAFTA has had its greatest impact on two major US industries: agriculture and manufacturing. Critics blame the agreement for the loss of well-paying US manufacturing jobs, and many in the South blame NAFTA for the demise of the textile industry. Proponents of the agreement, however, believe it will create jobs in the long term because increased trade tends to increase the employment rate. Trade among the member nations increased from $297 billion in 1993 to $930 billion in 2007 to over $1 trillion in 2011; and according to the Office of the United States Trade Representative, NAFTA is the major cause of the increase.

While NAFTA does not overrule national laws, it does provide a system for resolving trade-related conflicts between member nations, companies, and individuals. The NAFTA Free Trade Commission oversees a panel that, upon request, reviews rulings made by each country's international trade courts. The panel consists of experts on international trade law from NAFTA countries.

Trade statistics from "The North American Free Trade Agreement (NAFTA)" by the Congressional Research Service (April 6, 2015)

US President Bill Clinton signs the North American Free Trade Agreement in 1993.

A PETITION

Frederic Bastiat (1801–50) was a Frenchman whose writings attacked the growth of socialistic thought in nineteenth-century France. As an economist and statesman, he argued against protectionist policies that discouraged the purchase of foreign goods and against other increased governmental controls of the economy. In the following excerpt, Bastiat satirizes the protectionist–free-trade debate in a way that proves to be still relevant today.

From the Manufacturers of Candles, Tapers, Lanterns, Candlesticks, Street Lamps, Snuffers, and Extinguishers, and from the Producers of Tallow, Oil, Resin, Alcohol, and Generally of Everything Connected with Lighting.

To the Honorable Members of the Chamber of Deputies....

We are suffering from the ruinous competition of a foreign rival who apparently works under conditions so far superior to our own for the production of light that he is flooding the domestic market with it at an incredibly low price; for the moment he appears, our sales cease, all the consumers turn to him, and a branch of French industry whose ramifications are innumerable is all at once reduced to complete stagnation. This rival, which is none other than the sun, is waging war on us so mercilessly that we suspect he is being stirred up against us....

We ask you to be so good as to pass a law requiring the closing of all windows, dormers, skylights, inside and outside shutters, curtains, casements, bull's-eyes, deadlights, and blinds—in short, all openings, holes, chinks, and fissures through which the light of the sun is wont to enter houses, to the detriment of the fair industries with which, we are proud to say, we have endowed the country, a country that cannot, without betraying ingratitude, abandon us today to so unequal a combat....

...When a product—coal, iron, wheat, or textiles—comes to us from abroad, and when we can acquire it for less labor than if we produced it ourselves, the difference is a gratuitous gift that is conferred upon us. The size of this gift is proportionate to the extent of this difference. It is a quarter, a half, or three-quarters of the value of the product if the foreigner asks of us only three-quarters, one-half, or one-quarter as high a price. It is as complete as it can be when the donor, like the sun in providing us with light, asks nothing from us. The question, and we pose it formally, is whether what you desire for France is the benefit of consumption free of charge or the alleged advantages of onerous production. Make your choice, but be logical; for as long as you ban, as you do, foreign coal, iron, wheat, and textiles, in proportion as their price approaches zero, how inconsistent it would be to admit the light of the sun, whose price is zero all day long!

(Frederic Bastiat, *Economic Sophisms*, trans. and ed. Arthur Goddard [Irvington-on-Hudson, NY: The Foundation for Economic Education Inc., 1964], 56–57, 60)

2. Under protectionism, domestic industries and jobs will be protected from foreign competition.
3. Under free trade, consumers will pay less for foreign goods.
4. Under protectionism, foreign goods will be more expensive in order to protect American jobs and industry.

MEASURING THE WEALTH OF THE NATION 249

CALVIN AND HOBBES © 1993 Watterson. Reprinted with permission of UNIVERSAL UCLICK. All rights reserved.

The ultimate question is whether the government should get involved in the economy to protect jobs even if prices might be raised for consumers.

Which side of the trade policy debate you decide to support will likely require prayerful consideration. You will no doubt be influenced by your local economy as well as church and family sentiments. In making decisions on trade policies, Christians should apply the commandment to love one's neighbor as oneself. The challenge, however, is how best to show love (e.g., getting low prices for American consumers, safeguarding American manufacturing, creating employment opportunities for people in foreign countries). Christians must thoughtfully examine and evaluate each new trade agreement or policy. They should seek to demonstrate a Christ-like love for all their neighbors—those in their own country as well as those who live abroad. Consequently, they should favor a trade policy that produces the greatest benefits for all.

GDP—before reading this chapter, you may have seen those letters in magazine or newspaper articles, and you may have even known what they stood for: gross domestic product. However, you may not have known what that was or why it was important. Now you know. Now you should be able to explain the basics about what goes into determining the GDP, how it is calculated, the difference between nominal and real GDP, and how to adjust it for inflation and population changes. More importantly, you should have some understanding of the value of this measure and how economic policymakers rely on it to understand their nation's economic health and to know what policies they should adopt as corrective measures. One such corrective policy may focus on trade. As you now know, trade deficits have several causes; but regardless of their cause, they lower the GDP. Consequently, significant or prolonged trade deficits stir policymakers to consider solutions, and the search for solutions will likely stir the protectionism versus free trade debate. Now when you read editorials or articles in favor of or opposed to some new trade agreement, you will be better prepared to understand and evaluate the arguments presented. As to which side you choose, that may depend on whether you, family members, or close friends are a part of the industry seeking protection or simply more concerned with overall lower prices. To choose rightly is to choose wisely. To do that, you need to be well-informed and to remember that wisdom comes from God, who promises to give it to those who ask (James 1:5).

SECTION REVIEW 12B

1. Does the United States currently have a trade surplus or a trade deficit? Define terms, and explain your answer using data from the text.
2. What are six possible reasons for a trade deficit?
3. What are the two main groups of differing opinion on the subject of international trade?
4. What two methods do protectionists propose to accomplish their economic goals?
5. What economic philosophy did David Ricardo and Frederic Bastiat hold in common?

CHAPTER REVIEW

CONTENT QUESTIONS

1. What are the four basic concepts economists use to determine the GDP?
2. Why is the sale of used goods not included in the GDP?
3. The purchases of what four economic groups are used in figuring the GDP?
4. Household consumption includes what three kinds of purchases?
5. In 2014, governmental spending was what percentage of the American GDP?
6. What are the four complications that lead to inaccuracies in GDP figures?
7. What kinds of transactions are not recorded in the GDP?
8. What two methods do protectionists advocate for reducing trade deficits?
9. Why do those who advocate free trade believe protectionism to be ineffective or harmful to the economy?

APPLICATION QUESTIONS

1. Give some reasons that the GDP tends to increase each year.
2. What might be some ways in which the government or business firms could use GDP information?
3. Given the following figures from the first quarter of 2013, compute the per capita real GDP for the year. (Monetary amounts are in billions of dollars.)

Purchases of consumer durables	$1,237.8
Purchases of consumer nondurables	$2,594.4
Purchases of consumer services	$7,518.9
Capital investment	$2,499.1
Inventory investment	$44.2
Governmental purchases	$3,135.9
Exports	$2,219.4
Imports	$2,747.4
GDP deflator	106.4
US population	316,129,000 (0.316,129 billion)

4. What Christian concern should have major influence on the foreign trade policy you support?
5. If you worked for an American car company, how would you react to news that Congress was passing protectionist legislation in behalf of American automobile manufacturers? What would you expect the ramifications of this action to be? Explain your answers.

TERMS

gross domestic product	234
nominal GDP	234
final goods and services	234
intermediate goods	235
consumer durable goods	237
consumer nondurable goods	237
consumer services	237
gross private domestic investment (GPDI)	238
business investment	238
net exports	239
GDP implicit price deflator (GDP deflator)	242
real GDP	242
per capita real GDP	242
trade deficit	243
trade surplus	243
subsidy	244
protectionists	245
free trade	245
trade quotas	245
tariff	246

PERSONAL FINANCE

UNDERSTANDING HOW INTEREST WORKS

One of the most important principles of money management is "Never let your money sit idle." If a person has capital he is not using, he ought to lend it to others who are willing to pay interest for its use. In Matthew 25, Jesus presents a parable that supports this principle. A master gave to each servant a sum of money to manage in his absence. Upon his return, he commended the servants who earned a profit but condemned the servant who let his money sit idle.

> His lord answered and said unto him, Thou wicked and slothful servant, thou knewest that I reap where I sowed not, and gather where I have not strawed: Thou oughtest therefore to have put my money to the exchangers, and then at my coming I should have received mine own with usury. Take therefore the talent from him, and give it unto him which hath ten talents (Matt. 25:26–28).

The master's words about receiving his money with usury refer to earning interest.

When you are saving money, it is important to consider the rate of interest a deposit will earn. The following example is one that financial analysts frequently cite to emphasize the importance of interest. According to tradition, the Native Americans received a mere $24 for Manhattan Island in 1626. That money deposited into a savings account at 6 percent interest would have rendered an account balance in 2005 of $88 billion! That is the effect of compound interest.

Compound interest is the calculation of interest on reinvested interest compounded with the original principal. For example, assume that on January 1 you deposit $100 in a savings account that is paying 5 percent interest. At the end of the year your account balance would be $105.00, an increase of $5 (5% of your original $100). At the end of the next year, your account would increase by an additional $5.25 to a new total of $110.25. The bank is now paying the 5 percent interest not on the original $100 but on the $105 that had the previous year's interest added. Therefore, the next year the account would earn 5 percent on $110.25, and so on. The amount a deposit grows, or is compounded, is a result of three factors: the nominal rate of interest, the frequency of compounding, and the length of time the funds remain on deposit.

NOMINAL INTEREST RATE

The first factor to consider when saving is the nominal rate of interest. The **nominal interest rate** is the interest rate financial institutions will pay for your deposit, and they normally express this rate in annual terms. The nominal interest rate an institution will pay depends on the size of the deposit and the length of time for which you are willing to commit your funds. As you are willing to deposit greater amounts of money, institutions are willing to pay a higher nominal rate of interest. The reason is simple: as borrowers seek larger loans, the pool of funds becomes smaller, so they become willing

Peter Minuit oversaw the purchase of Manhattan for the Dutch colony in America.

UNDERSTANDING HOW INTEREST WORKS

FOXTROT © 1999 Bill Amend. Reprinted with permission of UNIVERSAL UCLICK. All rights reserved.

to pay a higher rate of interest. Thus, to attract sizable deposits, financial institutions offer a higher nominal interest rate.

Financial institutions also pay a higher nominal interest rate on savings that depositors commit for longer periods of time. Statistically speaking, a borrower who signs a note to repay a loan in thirty days has a lower chance of defaulting than someone who signs a note for thirty years. Because the risk of default is greater on long-term loans, financial institutions are reluctant to make them at the same interest rate that they charge on short-term loans. Borrowers who wish to secure long-term loans, therefore, must be willing to pay a higher rate of interest. In a similar fashion, lenders must offer savers a higher nominal rate of interest for committing their funds for longer periods of time.

FREQUENCY OF COMPOUNDING

As a Christmas gift from their parents, two brothers, Andrew and Alex, each received $1,000 with instructions that they were to save it for college. They devised a little savings contest, and on January 1 each set out to earn the greatest possible one-year return. Andrew, who had never taken an economics class, did not realize that he ought to pay attention to the type of interest rate a savings institution offers. He thought simply that a higher rate was always better. When he saw the big blue sign in a window of First National Bank promising 5.80 percent interest, he immediately went in and made his deposit. Alex secretly laughed at his sibling's ignorance as he deposited his $1,000 in an account at Second National Bank advertising a 5.75 percent interest rate. At the end of the year when the two brothers withdrew their funds, Andrew was confident of winning as he pocketed his $1,058 in principal and interest. His self-satisfaction turned to shock and confusion, however, as his brother withdrew $1,059.18. How could this be possible? With a wry little smile, Alex simply said, "You chose the higher nominal interest rate; I chose the higher effective interest rate."

The **effective interest rate** is the true rate of interest an account earns taking into account the frequency of compounding. Previously, you read that $100 at 5 percent interest will earn $5 over a one-year period. The unspoken assumption in that example was that the bank compounded the interest annually, meaning the institution calculated the interest once at the end of the year. Economists refer to such interest as **simple interest**. What would happen if the bank calculated the interest semiannually, or twice each year? Instead of calculating 5 percent interest at the end of the year, the bank would add 2.5 percent to the account in the middle of the year and add the other 2.5 percent at the year's end. If the bank adds one-half of the interest to the account in the middle of the year, then the account balance would be $102.50 by the end of June. At the end of the year, when the bank compounds the second half of the interest, it would calculate the 2.5 percent interest on $102.50, bringing the end-of-the-year balance to $105.06. Financial institutions may compound interest as many times per year as they choose and may do so annually, semiannually, quarterly, monthly, weekly, or even daily. In the case of the two brothers, Second National Bank compounded its interest every day. Second National calculated 1/365 of 5.75 percent each day and added it to the previous day's balance.

The effective interest rate on a deposit is the actual one-year percentage gain the deposit earns. As Figure A illustrates, a deposit will see the year-end balance rise as the frequency of compounding increases. Note the balance of the final month. The effective interest rate of 5% compounded annually is 5%; if it is compounded semiannually, it is 5.06%; quarterly, 5.10%; and monthly,

Fig. A   Simple and Compound Interest ($100 at 5%)

Month	Balance at End of Each Compounding Period			
	Annually	Semi-annually	Quarterly	Monthly
1	—	—	—	$100.42
2	—	—	—	100.84
3	—	—	$101.25	101.26
4	—	—	—	101.68
5	—	—	—	102.10
6	—	$102.50	102.52	102.53
7	—	—	—	102.95
8	—	—	—	103.38
9	—	—	103.80	103.81
10	—	—	—	104.25
11	—	—	—	104.68
12	$105.00	105.06	105.10	105.12

HOW TO CALCULATE THE EFFECTIVE RATE OF INTEREST

The effective rate of interest on a deposit is a combination of the nominal interest rate and the frequency of compounding. The formula for calculating the effective interest rate is

$$Y = 100 \times \{[1 + (i/n)]^n - 1\},$$

where Y = the effective rate of interest,
i = the nominal rate of interest, and
n = the number of times interest is compounded per year.

Here is a simple example: What would be the effective interest rate on a deposit at 6% interest compounded semiannually?

$$Y = 100 \times \{[1 + (0.06/2)]^2 - 1\}$$
$$= 100 \times [(1 + 0.03)^2 - 1]$$
$$= 100 \times (1.0609 - 1)$$
$$= 100 \times 0.0609 = 6.09\%$$

The calculations become difficult as the number of times the account is compounded each year increases. For example, if the deposit at 6% were compounded each minute, the formula would be

$$Y = 100 \times \{[1 + (0.06/525{,}600)]^{525{,}600} - 1\}.$$

To work this kind of formula, you would need a calculator that calculates powers. In this case the effective interest rate would be 6.183919326%.

5.12%. Thus the effective interest rate of a deposit increases as the frequency of compounding increases.

As noted earlier, had the native people of Manhattan Island taken the $24 they received in 1626 and invested it at 6 percent interest, their descendants would have had $88 billion by 2005. This amount is what they would have earned with just simple interest compounded annually; however, if the bank had compounded their account monthly, the total in 2005 would have been $158 billion! As the first principle of money management is "Never let your money sit idle," so the second builds upon that foundation: "Have your money compounding as frequently as possible."

There are, though, two important considerations to compounding. First, when you save money, you need to realize that financial institutions do not necessarily compound interest and post it to savers' accounts at the same time. That is, for the bank's bookkeeping purposes, it may compound interest monthly, but it might not post that interest to a saver's account until later. For example, assume that the bank compounds the interest monthly on the deposit in Figure A but posts it semiannually. If a depositor withdrew his money in the month of November, he would receive only $102.50 since that was the amount in his account at the last semiannual posting. Theoretically, a bank could compound interest each minute, but if it posts the interest annually, the saver would receive no interest were he to withdraw his funds the day before the bank posted his interest. Therefore, in addition to looking for high effective rates and frequent compounding, you should also find out when the bank posts interest.

The second consideration has to do with the length of time you may keep idle money on deposit. To prevent financial institutions from having to pay interest on money that someone has deposited and apparently forgotten, each state has passed laws of escheat. **Escheat laws** dictate that if depositors leave accounts dormant for lengthy periods of time (usually around five years), then the financial institution must turn the funds over to the state. An account holder can usually keep his money from going into escheat by conducting some account activity every few years, such as making a deposit or a withdrawal. Before opening an account, savers should consult with the financial institution about their particular state's escheat laws.

DURATION OF THE DEPOSIT

Whereas the effective interest rate is a result of combining the nominal interest rate and the frequency of compounding, the ultimate dollar amount a person earns is a result of the effective interest rate and the length of time he keeps his money on deposit. It is important for savers to resist the constant temptation to withdraw from their savings accounts to pay for current consumption. Setting a specific dollar goal for your savings account is one way to discourage you from taking money out of that account. For example, a couple may have the goal of purchasing a house. If they are looking at a house in the $90,000 price range and if their lender requires a 20 percent down payment, the couple should not withdraw any funds from their savings until the account reaches at least $18,000.

Rather than having a specific dollar goal, some savers might have the goal to keep their money on deposit until it doubles. Financial analysts use a rule of thumb called the Rule of 72 to determine approximately how long money must stay on deposit to double. The **Rule of 72** states that the product of the approximate number of years required for doubling a deposit with accruing interest multiplied by the interest rate should equal 72. For example, approximately how long will it take to double a $1,000 deposit earning 6 percent interest? The formula works like this:

Number of years × Interest rate = 72

$N \times 6 = 72$

$N = 72/6$

$N = 12$ years

A person could also use the Rule of 72 to calculate the approximate rate of interest he must receive to have his money double over a specific number of years. For example, if a saver wants to double his money over a three-year period, he would need to receive an approximate rate of interest of 24 percent (72/3 years).

Having read of ways to set aside some of your earnings, you have now seen that, if invested properly, even small amounts can grow substantially to provide funds for future expenses. Perhaps you can think of some money you could set aside now on a regular basis. That amount may be small and perhaps you can save it only once a month. But at least you have a plan. Now you also understand the importance of having that money not sit idle and having it earn the best interest available. You have learned how interest rates work and the differences in rates and compounding schedules. You can use this knowledge to make choices that will best serve your overall financial plan and help you to be a good steward. Recognize that the money you have, like athletic, artistic, or academic ability, is a gift from God that you are to manage well, like the servants in Christ's parable. Learn these principles now, make them your habitual practice, and you will be rewarded as your savings grow.

REVIEW
QUESTIONS

1. What are two important principles of money management?
2. List two important considerations as regards compounding.
3. What is the formula for calculating the effective rate of interest being paid on a deposit?
4. Why is it important to determine when a bank posts interest to a savings account?

TERMS

compound interest	252
nominal interest rate	252
effective interest rate	253
simple interest	253
escheat laws	254
Rule of 72	255

CHAPTER THIRTEEN

THE BUSINESS CYCLE AND UNEMPLOYMENT

13A   THE BUSINESS CYCLE — 256

13B   UNEMPLOYMENT — 262

Many people tend to assume that the US economy is relatively stable—until it takes a notable downturn. In actuality, however, our economy is consistently volatile. If you were to talk about our nation's economy with a grandparent or great-grandparent, he or she could probably tell you of numerous times when businesses were booming, jobs were plentiful, prices were low, and folks seemed to be prospering. However, you would also likely hear of equally numerous hard times when businesses were failing, jobs were hard to find, prices were high, and many struggled to make ends meet. What causes our economy to fluctuate as it does? Why does it often seem more like a roller coaster ride than a flat, unbroken interstate cruise? These are questions many have asked and still ask. Economists are still seeking ways to lessen the gaps between the ups and downs of the economy. A key reason for their work is the impact these ups and downs have on people's lives. The link between the ups and low unemployment and the downs and high unemployment means the economic cycle has implications beyond just the world of business.

13A THE BUSINESS CYCLE

The US economy experiences the periodic upswings and downturns that are characteristic of business activity in a market economy. This **business cycle**, as economists call it, consists of alternating periods or phases when the real gross domestic product (GDP) rises and falls. Economists identify four phases of the business cycle: expansion, peak, recession, and trough.

PHASES OF THE BUSINESS CYCLE

During the **expansion phase** of the business cycle, the nation's GDP rises, the number of available jobs grows, the unemployment rate falls, and national income expands.

Another characteristic of the expansion phase is that people increase their credit purchases because they feel more financially secure and self-satisfied. A danger, though, in financial security and being self-satisfied is viewing finances as the source of your security and yourself as the one who provided the finances. In Deuteronomy, God gave a warning to the children of Israel that still applies to us today: during times of economic expansion and prosperity, we should be careful not to trust in our financial success or to act as though we are responsible for it, but rather we should give thanks and glory to God.

> Lest when thou hast eaten and art full, and hast built goodly houses, and dwelt therein; And when thy herds and thy flocks multiply, and thy silver and thy gold is multiplied, and all that thou hast is multiplied; Then thine heart be lifted up, and thou forget the Lord thy God, which brought thee forth out of the land of Egypt, from the house of bondage. . . . And thou say in thine heart, My power and the might of mine hand hath gotten me this wealth. (Deut. 8:12–14, 17)

Eventually, after running its expansionary course, the economy will reach the **peak phase**, which signals a halt to rapid expansion. A nation's economy cannot continually grow. While it is possible for a particular country's GDP to increase year after year, it is not possible for that country's economy to sustain the rapid rate of growth of its expansion phase. Three factors act as a ceiling that prevents further rapid growth: limited raw materials, limited labor, and limited financial capital.

As the economy expands so does the number of available jobs.

First, as the economy expands, sales of almost all goods hit record levels. To replenish their inventories, stores flood manufacturers with more orders than their factories can fill. Suppliers then seek to ration their limited materials by raising their prices, and this, in turn, causes stores to pass along these higher prices to their customers.

Second, the expanding economy causes the price of labor to rise. To meet the demand for additional products, firms must enter the labor market to hire more employees. However, because the prior economic expansion lowered the unemployment rate, businesses find that they must promise larger paychecks to lure workers from competing companies. Yet, for the firms to keep those promises and pay the higher wages, they must push the price of their goods even higher.

Third, businesses must pay more to borrow money in a time of expansion. As the demand for goods and services continues to rise, banks receive numerous applications for business loans. Fast-food restaurants need new equipment; steel companies desperately need new factories; and retail firms look to renovate, lease, or build to increase their store space. As banks face increased pressure on the

Both cash and credit purchases increase as economic activity rises.

> Economists formally define a recession as two consecutive quarters (a total of six months) of declining real GDP.

limited amount of assets that they can lend, they react by charging a higher interest rate to ration their scarce funds.

The converging of these three factors results in shortages of natural resources, high wages, and rising interest rates—all of which combine to create higher prices for consumers. This situation is characteristic of the peak of the business cycle.

Eventually, prices of goods and services rise to a point that consumers are no longer willing to purchase them in greater and greater quantities. This change in consumer attitude marks the turning point in the economy and begins the **recession phase**. During a recession consumers gradually adjust their spending habits.

The first type of purchase to decline is that of "big-ticket" consumer durable goods, such as new homes, automobiles, and major appliances. Consumers typically purchase these items on credit. The demand for these more expensive goods decreases because when buyers become uncertain of their future ability to pay off their credit debts, more of them delay purchasing until they have greater confidence in their personal financial situations. As sales of such items decline, suppliers cut their prices to sell excess inventory. Factory owners, experiencing a drop in new orders and finding their warehouses filling up with unwanted inventory, see little need to continue their production rates. Decreasing production requires fewer workers; consequently, manufacturers begin to lay off employees.

As the suction created by a large sinking ship pulls under smaller vessels floating nearby, so the whirlpool caused by a declining durable-goods market draws in numerous smaller, related businesses. Because purchases of new homes are declining, the sales of items connected to the housing market—furniture, carpet, lumber, glass, paint, cookware, entertainment systems, and even light bulbs—also decline. This decreased demand eventually causes even more people to become unemployed. A downward spiral develops: the newly

The purchase of a major appliance is a big-ticket purchase.

When the bottom of the recession phase is severe, as it was in the 1930s, it is referred to as a depression.

unemployed reduce their spending, thereby further decreasing demand and causing even greater unemployment.

Eventually the business cycle reaches the bottom or **trough phase**, characterized by low prices, a high unemployment rate, and depressed incomes. If economic conditions are especially bad and remain so for an extended time, the trough phase will become an economic **depression**.

Christians who understand the business cycle should take advantage of the peak phases to prepare for the coming downturns. The prudent man anticipates problems and makes preparation (Prov. 22:3). He learns from the ant, which works through summer and fall to prepare for the winter (Prov. 6:6–8). Though he may not be able to prevent the coming of economic downturns, like Joseph (Gen. 41–45) he can be used of God to take care of his family in times of economic hardship.

An economic decline can result in the abandonment of factories and industrial sites.

CAUSES OF THE BUSINESS CYCLE

Economists know that the economy moves in cycles, but they do not fully understand why. Many believe that if they could determine why the cycles exist, they might be able to smooth them out by eliminating the frantic peaks and miserable troughs.

Sunspot Theory

One of the first and most bizarre explanations of the business cycle was put forth by William Stanley Jevons. (You should recall reading about him and the principle of diminishing marginal utility in Chapter 2.) In 1875, after years of observations, Jevons became convinced

In an age when America's economy was more agrarian, the Dust Bowl had a significant impact.

SPIRITUAL GOOD FROM AN ECONOMIC BAD

No nation wants to experience an economic depression, yet God may use such a tool for the spiritual benefit of His children in that nation. Christians, like their unbelieving neighbors, can fall into the trap of trusting in their wealth (Ps. 49:6) and even glorying in it (Jer. 9:23). By doing so, they violate the first commandment: to have no other god before Jehovah (Exod. 20:3). When this happens, God may see fit to remove their wealth to show them that their security and their joy were misplaced. It is God alone in whom Christians are to trust for all things and in whom they are to glory.

that sunspots had a significant impact on the business activity of England. He noted that with remarkable regularity, shortly after sunspots appeared, business activity tended to fall. While at first Jevons's sunspot theory seemed laughable, it actually had some logical basis. Jevons reasoned that sunspots, which are violent nuclear explosions on the surface of the sun, altered the earth's weather patterns. These alterations would cause changes in agricultural yields, which would dramatically affect national economies that are predominantly agrarian.

Psychological Theory

As time progressed and business cycles continued in spite of the reduced economic impact of a less predominantly agricultural industry, economists sought a better explanation for business cycles. They abandoned the search for physical causes and chose instead to look for psychological reasons. You know what it is like to have a bad day on the basketball court, in the classroom, on the job, or with your friends. Once a person loses confidence in his abilities—athletic, academic, or social—problems begin to compound, often causing a further decline in performance. Likewise, the psychological theory of business cycles attributes cyclical economic behavior to the degree of confidence people have in their economy.

According to this theory, the business cycle is tied to human emotions. When a nation's economy is reaching its peak, the people will begin to feel that prosperity cannot continue indefinitely; so at the first hint of economic decline, they will postpone major purchases out of fear for their future economic security. This action will cause sales, profits, and incomes to drop and will set in motion a downward economic spiral as unstoppable as a roller coaster in its first plunge. When incomes and prices finally hit bottom, consumers will decide that things cannot worsen; and at this point they will begin to

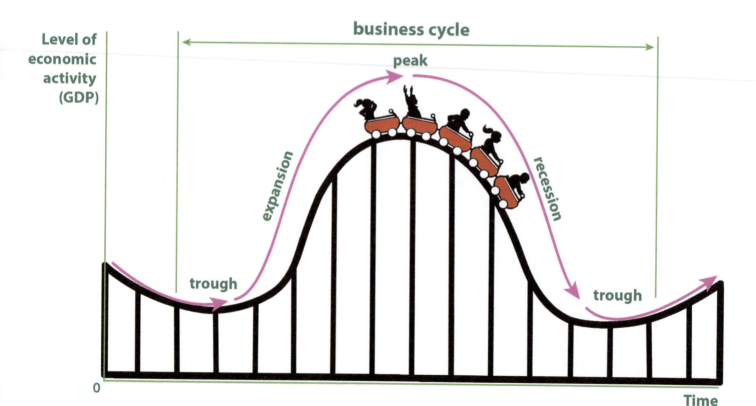

HEART OF THE CITY © 2008 Mark Tatulli. Dist. By UNIVERSAL UCLICK. Reprinted with permission. All rights reserved.

make purchases again, which in turn will raise national income and employment. The roller coaster begins to climb again.

Monetary Theory

A third and possibly the most logical explanation for the business cycle examines the effect that changes in the money supply have on prices and interest rates. According to the monetary theory, increases in the money supply fuel the expansion phase. As the Federal Reserve increases the money supply in the economy, the demand for goods and services increases, and firms seek to expand production to meet that demand. The competition for resources, such as labor and capital, drives the costs of production up, and the prices of products rise. Furthermore, the expanding of the money supply pushes interest rates downward, and lower interest rates encourage business firms to borrow money to increase production through building new factories and stores. As a result the economy tends to expand. Eventually the explosive growth in the money supply halts, leaving prices high. Unable to sell the higher-priced goods, the economy begins to stall and then to slide into the recessionary spiral.

SERVING GOD AS AN ECONOMIST

From the variety of theories proposed in this section, you can conclude that a single, precise explanation of the cause of business cycles has not yet been discovered. More than likely, several of the factors discussed interact to create them. However, which of those factors react with which others and in what proportions has yet to be determined. More work needs to be done to demonstrate that one of these theories is better than all the others or that it is the primary catalyst that activates a change in the cycle. Or perhaps another theory waits to be formulated.

Discovering the cause of business cycles and determining how to reduce their negative economic impact is part of managing God's world, part of the mandate God gave humans in Genesis 1:26–28. The world is so complex, however, that no single person can manage all of it; consequently, different people specialize in different areas of "earth management." Perhaps God has given you an ability to understand and apply economics. If He has, consider praying about whether God would have you serve Him as a Christian economist who examines and seeks to apply economic theories and policies from a biblical perspective.

Technological innovations can produce increases in the business cycle.

When the Federal Reserve reduces the growth of the money supply, the process reverses itself. Less money in the economy causes people to demand fewer goods and services. Producers cut back on production, and profits and incomes fall.

The most well-known proponents of the monetary explanation of business cycles are Milton Friedman (see p. 199) and Anna Schwartz. They present their case for the monetary theory in their classic book entitled *A Monetary History of the United States, 1867–1960*. They persuasively explain the business cycles of the US economy from after the Civil War until the beginning of the 1960s. They cite detailed data on how restrictions in the money supply explain severe recessions in the economy, such as the panics of 1837 and 1857, the recession of the 1870s, and the Great Depression of the 1930s. They also link the periods of expansion with money-supply growth and show a strong connection between the business cycle and the money supply.

Technology and Political Theories

Two other theories economists have proposed to explain the business cycle focus on technological innovations and the political party in power. The technology theory holds that bursts of inventiveness give rise to greater investment spending, which leads to recovery. Lapses in inventiveness and subsequent investment spending lead to recession. The political theory purports that liberal politicians tend to overspend, stimulating the economy into recovery and eventually into an inflationary peak, and that conservative politicians tend to reduce governmental spending, reducing economic stimulation and prompting a recessionary downturn.

> With all the potential for the economy to go bad, what comfort can a Christian draw from Psalms 66 and 146:3–9? What other Bible verses can you think of that can provide comfort during low economic times?

SECTION REVIEW 13A

1. What are the four phases of the business cycle?
2. Describe two characteristics of each of the four phases of the business cycle.
3. What five theories attempt to explain the business cycle?

13B UNEMPLOYMENT

Historically, economists associate the two predominant swings in the business cycle with two major economic problems. Recessionary downswings are linked to growing unemployment, while upswings are linked to inflation. The remainder of this chapter examines the problem of unemployment, and Chapter 14 takes a closer look at inflation.

The foremost problem connected with the downside of the business cycle is an increase in unemployment. The following passage, taken from a letter written by an unemployed worker to the governor of Pennsylvania during the Depression, clearly and poignantly illustrates the heartache of unemployment.

During a depression, jobs are few and unemployment lines are long.

I have six little children to take care of. I have been out of work for over a year and a half. Am back almost thirteen months and the landlord says if I don't pay up before the 1 of 1932 out I must go, and where am I to go in the cold winter with my children? If you can help me please for . . . the children's sakes . . . please do what you can and send me some help, will you, I cannot find any work. I am willing to take any kind of work if I could get it now. Thanksgiving dinner was black coffee and bread and was very glad to get it. My wife is in the hospital now. We have no shoes to were [sic]; no clothes hardly. Oh what will I do I sure will thank you. (Milton Meltzer, *Brother, Can You Spare a Dime? The Great Depression 1929–1933*)

Perhaps one of the greatest blessings God gave mankind was the ability to work. In Ecclesiastes 5:19, Solomon spoke of work as a gift: "Every man also to whom God hath given riches and wealth, and hath given him power to eat thereof, and to take his portion, and to rejoice in his labour; this is the gift of God." When a person is not able to take advantage of God's gift of labor, the effects on his

Employment is a blessing and is fundamental to a growing economy.

ROBERT LUCAS (1937–)

Expositor of the Rational Expectation Hypothesis

Born in Yakima, Washington, Robert Lucas initially planned to attend MIT but ended up at the University of Chicago. There he earned an undergraduate degree in history and a PhD in economics. He taught for several years at Carnegie Mellon in Pittsburgh before returning to his alma mater. He is known primarily for his work on various aspects of monetary policy, for which he won the Nobel Prize in Economics in 1995.

Lucas, a professor at the University of Chicago, takes a different approach to economic theory from the monetarists at that school, such as Milton Friedman. Lucas has advanced the rational expectation hypothesis, which says that people act rationally when they foresee economic changes and their actions in turn affect the results of the changes.

Lucas put forward what became known as the *Lucas critique*. He claims that predicted results of changes in monetary policy may not occur because those predictions are often based on insufficient study. For example, if the government announces that it will increase the money supply in an attempt to solve an unemployment problem, the people recognize that the increase will probably bring inflation. Therefore, they take precautions to minimize their losses and seek wage increases to compensate for the expected inflation. When this occurs, the money that the government intended to be used by businesses hiring new workers instead must go for higher wages and costs. The unemployment problem is left unsolved because the people's "rational expectations" naturally led them to divert the money from its intended purpose.

Lucas contends that publicly announced measures to change the money supply or alter other economic features will often result in failure. People are concerned about the impact of national economic adjustments on their personal finances, and their reaction to discretionary measures tends to shift the outcome of any governmental economic action away from its desired end.

Lucas also studied monetary policy as it relates to the flow of money between nations. He developed the *Lucas paradox*, which considers why the flow of money from economically advanced nations to economically underdeveloped nations does not occur as economists expect it would.

finances and family can be tragic, and the longer a person remains unemployed, the greater his loss of future productivity. His skills deteriorate, further reducing his employability.

When an entire nation experiences high levels of unemployment for an extended period, the consequences can be truly devastating. Economists have noted sharp increases in spousal and child abuse, suicides, heart attacks, divorces, homicides, and psychological disorders in nations experiencing long periods of joblessness. As unemployment continues, a generation of senior citizens faces the specter of hunger and deprivation in their old age. The savings accounts they set up for retirement become needed for present consumption.

To avoid these tragic effects, economists seek methods to lower the unemployment rate. For Christian economists and policymakers, finding ways to lower unemployment is part of their responsibility to love their neighbors. They know that policies that reduce the unemployment rate are as much a way of showing love as offering clothing, food, and shelter to the unemployed.

THE UNEMPLOYMENT RATE

Before economists can hope to control the unemployment rate, they must be able to measure it. The **unemployment rate** is the percentage of the labor force that is not employed but is looking for work. To calculate the unemployment rate, the United States Bureau of Labor Statistics separates the population into two groups. The first one consists of three subgroups: those who are under sixteen or over sixty-four years of age; those who are in the armed forces; and those who are institutionalized in schools, prisons, or asylums. Labor statisticians do not count these people in unemployment data.

The second group comprises the majority of the US population and commands the attention of economists. It consists of those between sixteen and sixty-four years of age who are neither in the armed forces nor institutionalized. Labor statisticians divide this major segment of the population into two subgroups: those in and those not in the labor force.

The **labor force** includes the employed and the unemployed who are actively looking for a job. There are two reasons economists consider people to be not in the labor force. First, some are not there by choice, such as homemakers who choose not to work outside the

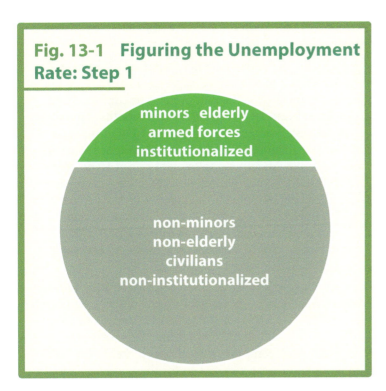

Fig. 13-1 Figuring the Unemployment Rate: Step 1

Fig. 13-2 Figuring the Unemployment Rate: Step 2

Fig. 13-3 Figuring the Unemployment Rate: Step 3

home. Second, some people have been out of work for an extended period and no longer appear to be actively looking for a job. When a person has been unemployed for many months and is no longer actively looking for a job, the government assumes that person has stopped looking for work. Statisticians refer to these chronically unemployed people as **discouraged workers**.

To determine the unemployment rate, therefore, economists divide the number of unemployed people by the total number of those in the labor force. According to the data from the early 2000s, the average unemployment rate has remained at roughly 5 percent of the labor force. The unemployment rate is a very important number to economists and politicians. Increases in the unemployment rate create concern that the United States is slipping into recession, while declines in the unemployment rate may indicate a rising economy.

WEAKNESSES IN UNEMPLOYMENT STATISTICS

We are aware that in a nation the size of the United States, statistics such as the unemployment rate will not be completely accurate. Gathering data on the unemployed is difficult, and unemployment statistics do not always give an accurate picture of the reality of the unemployed. Because the government bases its spending policies on the unemployment information provided by the Bureau of Labor Statistics, these figures are very important, but the following considerations must be remembered when discussing the unemployment rate.

1. *Many people who work are not counted as being employed.* Those determining the unemployment rate do not count in the employment statistics homemakers, those in the armed forces,

Industrial plant workers laid off during an economic downturn are listed among the unemployed.

> While unemployment statistics may not be as accurate as they should be, economists find the changes in the unemployment rate useful. These changes give them a good idea as to the direction the economy is going in a business cycle.

Many people who work are not counted as being employed.

students in work-study programs, or prisoners on work-release programs.

2. *Some people who do not work are not included in the unemployment statistics.* Even though discouraged workers are not working, economists do not count them as unemployed because they have been out of work for many months. This omission gives the casual observer a false impression of the state of the economy (see Figure 13-4). For example, suppose that we have an economy with an unemployment rate of 10 percent and that all those who are unemployed lost their jobs on January 1. Let us further assume that all those unemployed persons are unsuccessful in finding jobs. On July 1 they will receive the label "discouraged workers." This new labeling causes the unemployment rate to fall to a deceptively low 0 percent, since all those now in the labor force are working.

3. *Some people who are counted as being employed are actually underemployed.* The government considers someone employed even if he works only part-time. People who would like to work full-time but can get only part-time work are underemployed. The **underemployed** are those workers who have a job but earn an income insufficient for them to be able to provide a living for themselves. For example, someone earning $7.00 per hour but working only five hours per week would be counted as employed. However, assuming that person worked fifty-two weeks in a year, his annual income would be only $1,820 (before taxes).

4. *Some people who have jobs are counted as unemployed.* If a person has been laid off his job for a very short period of time or has signed a contract to go to work but has not yet begun, he is still counted as being unemployed. Anyone who works jobs only irregularly or for cash (and as such is unlikely to report those earnings as income to the IRS) is also officially unemployed.

Returning now to the original question of what unemployment is, you can see that the government narrowly defines unemployment as something that happens only to persons between the ages of sixteen and sixty-four who are neither in the armed forces nor institutionalized in schools, prisons, or asylums; who have been without work for only a few months; and who are actively looking for work.

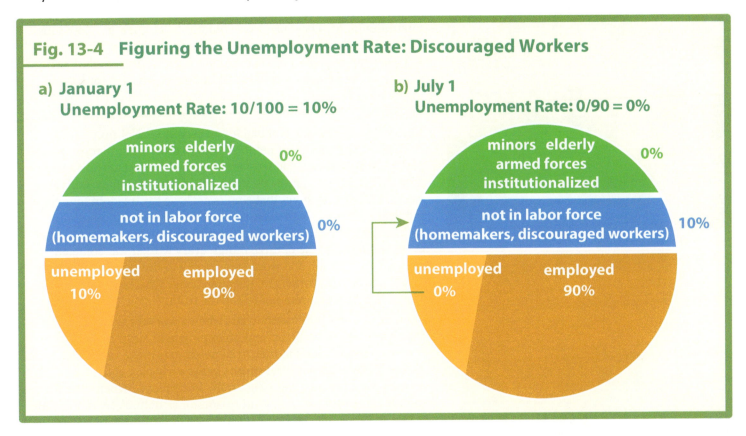

Fig. 13-4 Figuring the Unemployment Rate: Discouraged Workers

a) January 1 Unemployment Rate: 10/100 = 10%

b) July 1 Unemployment Rate: 0/90 = 0%

UNEMPLOYMENT ERROR

As an example of a problem caused by unemployment statistics, economists note that governmental policymakers misspent billions of dollars trying to counteract high unemployment during the recession of 1973–75. Economists saw too late that the huge governmental expenditures were not truly necessary because the unemployment rate really had not changed significantly in light of other data. The unemployment rate increased, they noted, not because workers lost their jobs but because there was a significant increase in the number of women and teenagers unsuccessfully entering the labor force. Whereas they were "not working" before and not counted as unemployed, now they were "not working" but counted as unemployed.

Some economists note that this sort of error could be prevented if policymakers would use the *employment rate* rather than the unemployment rate. The employment rate is simply the number of those employed divided by the noninstitutionalized civilian adult population. With this in mind, look again at Figure 13-4. While the unemployment rate suggests that unemployment declines, the employment rate would have remained constant. Since the number of those who were employed stayed the same and the non-labor-force population did not change, the employment rate would likewise remain unchanged.

People who relocate can experience frictional unemployment.

Certain employment markets fluctuate with the changing of seasons.

TYPES OF UNEMPLOYMENT

Why are people unemployed? Economists have sought to answer this question in the hope of finding some solution to the problem of unemployment and the economic woes that accompany joblessness.

Many are unemployed simply because they are temporarily between jobs. These people experience what economists identify as **frictional unemployment**. They may have voluntarily left their previous jobs to seek ones that pay more money, better fit their talents, or better suit their future goals. Others may have been victims of downsizing and layoffs or perhaps were fired. Whatever the reason for leaving the first job, it takes time to locate another one, and during that time the person is unemployed.

Is frictional unemployment bad for an economy? Not necessarily. Frictional unemployment demonstrates that the labor market is competitive. It is evidence that workers have the freedom to leave a job if they think their employers are not paying them what their skills are worth. Likewise, it shows that employers have the freedom to replace indolent employees with more productive workers. Some socialist nations have boasted of having a 0 percent unemployment rate. That claim could mean one of three things: every worker was completely satisfied with his job and would not leave it to find another, the law would not permit workers to quit and change jobs, or those who reported the statistics were not telling the truth.

Structural unemployment occurs when a worker's skills do not match available jobs. Structural unemployment exists for at least two reasons. First, changes in industrial needs may make certain job skills obsolete. For example, blacksmiths in the early part of the twentieth century found themselves structurally unemployed when the automobile came into use. A second reason for structural unemployment is that some people have never developed the skills necessary for existing jobs. This group includes individuals such as high-school dropouts with no work experience. Of course, some employers provide training for new unskilled personnel; however, in many cases the cost of training new workers exceeds the revenue those employees could bring into the firm. Consequently, hiring them becomes financially difficult for the employer.

A certain number of those in the unemployment lines of America are out of jobs because of seasonal factors. As its name suggests, **seasonal unemployment** occurs because changes in the seasons create some jobs and eliminate others. While the construction industry experiences job losses at the onset of winter, the number of jobs linked to the sales of winter products, such as snow tires, Christmas decorations, and winter clothing, increases. When students over sixteen years of age leave the workforce after the summer to return to school, it results in a seasonal decrease in the labor force and creates another type of seasonal unemployment. Seasonal unemployment in one sector tends to balance seasonal employment in another so that overall seasonal unemployment tends to be negligible.

The downside of the business cycle causes **cyclical unemployment**, and it is this type of unemployment with which you, members of your family, and your friends are probably most familiar. When the economy is strong, new businesses appear and existing ones often expand their workforce. However, when the economy slides into a recession, the opposite occurs. As demand, sales, and spending all decline, many of the start-up businesses cannot survive financially. They cease operations and dismiss their employees. Existing businesses soon recognize that their operating expenses now exceed their income, and they have to enact cost-cutting measures. They may encourage older employees to take early retirement or ask all employees to take unpaid time off, pay cuts, or fewer hours. If these measures prove insufficient, the company will likely need to lay off a certain percentage of its workers. Often this means the employees with the least experience or seniority with that firm find themselves unemployed.

> Since the economy always experiences a certain amount of frictional, structural, and seasonal unemployment, economists refer to the sum of these three as the *natural level of unemployment*.

UNEMPLOYMENT AND THE GOVERNMENT

The United States Congress, noting that recessions followed previous wartime expansions and fearing that soldiers returning from combat in World War II would come home to unemployment, passed the Employment Act of 1946. This legislation declared that it

> is the continuing policy and responsibility of the Federal Government to use all practicable means consistent with its needs and obligations and other essential considerations of national policy with the assistance and cooperation of industry, agriculture, labor, and State and local governments, to coordinate and utilize all its plans, functions, and resources for the purpose of creating and maintaining, in a manner calculated to foster and promote free competitive enterprise and the general welfare, conditions under which there will be afforded useful employment, for those able, willing, and seeking to work, and to promote maximum employment, production, and purchasing power.

In other words, Congress declared that the federal government's number one priority was maximum employment. The Employment Act of 1946 lacked clear goals; therefore, three decades later, Congress, fearing another recession, passed the Full Employment and Balanced Growth Act of 1978 as an amendment to its previous legislation. The Humphrey-Hawkins Act, as Congress later called it, proposed specific goals for governmental control of unemployment and inflation. For example, Congress decreed that by 1983 the unemployment rate should be 4% of the labor force, and the inflation rate should be 3%. (They were actually 9.6 % and 3.8%, respectively, that year.) Congress further declared that the inflation rate should be 0% by 1988. You know that both national and local governments desire to prevent joblessness, but you might wonder what the government can actually do to reduce the rate of unemployment. The answer, unfortunately, is not much.

The development of more efficient procedures for bringing job seekers and employers together could, theoretically, reduce frictional unemployment. Attempts have been made to do this through the establishment of local employment security commission offices, which act as central clearinghouses for job information and financial assistance. Though such programs may be helpful, the unemployed locate most jobs by themselves without governmental assistance. Perhaps the most effective tool for reducing frictional unemployment is not a product of the government. Internet job-search sites have reduced the time and cost of job searches and have made the average duration of unemployment times shorter.

MINIMUM-WAGE LAWS AND UNEMPLOYMENT

When Americans hear that Congress has approved an increase in the minimum wage, the general reaction seems to be one of rejoicing. While workers in low-paying jobs have visions of higher paychecks, economists recognize that the effects of such mandatory increases in the cost of labor are not totally beneficial. In fact, one negative impact is that such increases actually encourage unemployment. The following example may help you understand how this effect occurs.

Suppose that a business firm has a demand curve for workers like the one in Figure A. Given the demand curve for labor, the company will hire one hundred workers at $20 per hour, two thousand workers at $1 per hour, or a number of workers in between for the corresponding wage as shown. Now, assume that there are five hundred workers available to work for this firm. The graph clearly shows that, in a situation in which wages are the only consideration, the market would be in equilibrium if the business paid the workers $7.50 per hour. At that price all five hundred workers would have jobs, and the firm would have the number of employees it needs.

What would happen if Congress enacted a minimum-wage law that set wages at $12.50 per hour? Figure A shows that at that level, there would still be five hundred workers available, but the firm would demand only two hundred employees. Therefore, three hundred of the workers would be unemployed. Such are the laws of supply and demand. Whenever the price of anything—shoes, cars, or workers—is higher than its equilibrium price, there will always be a surplus. A surplus of employees in the labor market means higher unemployment.

Another problem economists find with minimum-wage laws is that they tend to hurt the people they are intended to help. Because most jobs requiring skilled workers pay well above the minimum wage, the law has little effect on them. However, unskilled workers with low incomes have the most to lose from a minimum wage that is higher than the market level. Many of them will be in danger of losing their jobs because employers will not consider their work to be worth the increased wages. Fast-food restaurants and other businesses that hire unskilled employees will keep their most valuable help in the face of the increased wage costs and will lay off those that they can no longer afford to pay. Thus many teenagers, who suffer significantly higher unemployment than the general population, high-school dropouts, and other hard-to-employ individuals will be left without jobs entirely.

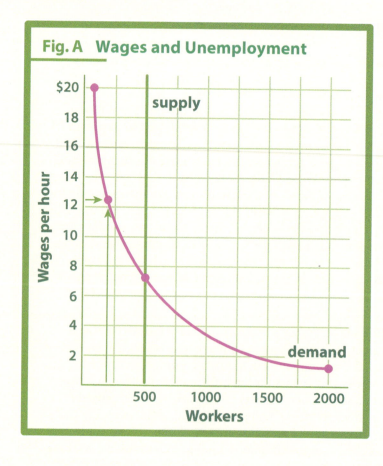

Fig. A Wages and Unemployment

The government has attacked structural unemployment by providing job training and creating programs that pay all or part of an employee's salary during the unproductive phase of his training in a private business. Two major economic problems, however, plague governmental job training programs. First, the government can spend only the money that it taxes away or borrows from its citizens. In setting up job training programs or paying salaries of trainees while they are learning a skill, the government must appropriate taxpayers' money, much of which they would otherwise spend on consumer goods. When the government taxes its citizens to set up job training programs, it decreases the taxpayers' ability to buy things, such as cars, houses, appliances, and thousands of other products and services. This decrease in spending causes unemployment in the manufacturing, sales, and service divisions of the economy. Therefore, the jobs gained through governmental job training programs are partially, if not totally, offset by jobs lost in other sectors of the economy. A second problem with governmental job training programs is a sluggish response time. In many cases by the time the government perceives a need, recruits trainees, and provides the training, the need for those specific skills has disappeared, rendering the training program of little effect. According to the US Department of Labor, fewer than 40 percent of the young people receiving training under the Job Training Partnership Act receive a job, even for one day.

The government can do little or nothing about seasonal unemployment except to suggest that companies that produce seasonal goods spread their work over the course of the year. For some firms, however, nonseasonal production can be very expensive because it means producing goods that will sit idle until their big selling period begins.

Statistics show that cyclical unemployment relates to the economy's position in the business cycle. To reduce this form of unemployment, the government would need to control the business cycle itself. Though in a market economy it will not seek such control, the government often does try to combat this problem by penalizing firms with a higher incidence of cyclical unemployment. It may require that businesses hit hardest by downturns in the business cycle make higher contributions to unemployment compensation programs as their layoffs increase. The intended result of such a policy is that the financial loss incurred by keeping unneeded workers becomes somewhat less painful than the financial loss resulting from paying higher unemployment compensation insurance. However, one undesired effect of these graduated contributions is that when business finally picks up, employers may not hire new workers out of a fear that later they may have to lay them off and incur the financial penalties.

Governmental employment offices seek to reduce frictional unemployment.

UNEMPLOYMENT AND THE MARKET

Earlier in this chapter you learned that there are four types of unemployment: frictional, structural, seasonal, and cyclical. Free-market economics holds that the latter three are related to a single cause—a difference between the price that sellers of labor are asking and the price that buyers of labor are willing to pay. Chapter 4, you will remember, reveals that the laws of supply and demand are the basis for all economic decisions. A buildup of the inventory of a certain product is not due to the unwillingness of irrational people to pay an obviously just price, but rather it results from rational buyers' realizing that the benefits they would enjoy would be overshadowed by the price they would have to pay. The same principle holds true with labor. If the price the suppliers of labor (the workers) charge for their services exceeds what the buyers (the employers) are willing to pay, there will be a buildup of unused labor, and unemployment will result. Therefore, the market's solution to unemployment is to allow wages to adjust to supply-and-demand conditions; thus, workers may need to allow wages to decline as the nation's economy turns downward.

Having read this chapter, you should be able to analyze business news articles from several months and determine with a fair measure of accuracy the current phase of the economy's business cycle. You should also understand how that phase may have ramifications on your job market, potential wages, and the interest rates on possible business loans your employer may seek. You may have also found an interest in what causes this cycle and desire to study more of a particular theory. You have seen the relationship between the business cycle and employment: the former has a direct and inverse impact on the latter. Since the two are interconnected—downturns in the business cycle cause high unemployment, and high unemployment has harmful effects on society—you can understand why economists and policymakers seek to lessen the volatility of the business cycle. They continue to study the cycle and its causes in an effort to reduce its highs and lows and its effect on prices and unemployment. You can also understand why they aggressively study unemployment. They need accurate data on its causes and the numbers of people affected to develop possible solutions. You should also recognize that the government is not the cause nor can it be the cure for many unemployment problems.

Christians should look at unemployment through the commands to do good to all men (Gal. 6:10) and to love their neighbors as themselves (Matt. 22:39). The Christian economist sees in these commands an extra motivation for finding solutions to the problems of the business cycle and unemployment. And for all Christians, downturns in the business cycle and the corresponding rise in unemployment present opportunities to show the love of Christ by extending aid to those in need, even if offering that help means making personal sacrifices. If Christ delays His coming, you will more than likely experience several phases of the business cycle, including one or more declines. Keep in mind what you have learned of this cycle and its effects and always look for opportunities to use what you have learned to help others.

SECTION REVIEW 13B

1. What two major economic problems are associated with downturns and upswings in the business cycle?
2. When statisticians tabulate the unemployment rate, why are some people who are not working not counted as unemployed?
3. Name the four kinds of unemployment.
4. What is the free-market solution to unemployment?

CHAPTER REVIEW

CONTENT QUESTIONS

1. Describe the expansion and recession phases of the business cycle.
2. When the economy reaches the peak of its business cycle, what three factors prevent further growth?
3. Briefly describe the five theories that attempt to explain the existence of business cycles.
4. Is frictional unemployment undesirable in a nation's economy? Explain your answer.
5. What has the government done to try to eliminate structural unemployment? What is the hidden cost of its efforts?
6. How does the free market explain the existence of unemployment? (Be sure to consider all four types.)

APPLICATION QUESTIONS

1. Describe why some business firms actually do well in periods of recession and depression.
2. What do you think would be the short- and long-term results if the government, in its effort to reduce structural unemployment, simply required businesses to hire a certain percentage of unskilled workers?
3. Suppose there is an announcement on the evening news that the unemployment rate is 6 percent. Does this number accurately reflect the number of people out of work? Why or why not?

TERMS

business cycle	256
expansion phase	256
peak phase	257
recession phase	258
trough phase	259
depression	259
unemployment rate	264
labor force	264
discouraged workers	265
underemployed	266
frictional unemployment	268
structural unemployment	268
seasonal unemployment	268
cyclical unemployment	268

PERSONAL FINANCE
SAVINGS INSTRUMENTS

From reading previous Personal Finance articles, you have seen how to accumulate money to save and how to evaluate the interest rates of different savings instruments. Now you need to look at how those savings instruments operate. Generally speaking, there are three types: floating-rate accounts, time deposits, and governmental securities.

FLOATING-RATE ACCOUNTS

As the name implies, a **floating-rate account** is a short-term savings instrument for which the interest rate may fluctuate as economic conditions change. You have read about one popular floating-rate account, the NOW account. This federally insured account provides a floating rate of interest competitive with regular savings accounts and offers the saver the opportunity to write an unlimited number of checks.

Another popular floating-rate account is the money market account. Commercial banks and thrift institutions offer insured accounts, known as **money market deposit accounts (MMDAs)**, that pay interest based on the market's demand for short-term loans. Account holders can usually make as many deposits into MMDAs as they wish but are limited as to the number of withdrawals they can make. Most institutions require a minimum initial dollar investment of $500–$1,000 to open a money market account. Stock brokerage firms offer similar accounts called **money market mutual funds (MMMFs)**. These accounts pay the same rate of interest as financial institutions, if not slightly higher; however, brokerage firms' accounts are not insured by the federal government.

TIME DEPOSITS

Unlike the accounts that have fluctuating interest rates, **time deposits** are savings accounts that earn fixed rates of interest as they remain on deposit. Time deposits are so called because either they require a specific amount of time between the request for a withdrawal and the actual withdrawal of the funds or they carry a specific maturity date. Time deposits that require notification of withdrawal include passbook accounts, club accounts, and restricted passbook accounts. Time deposits with fixed maturity dates are called certificates of deposit.

A **passbook account** is a time deposit that commercial banks and thrift institutions offer to savers with relatively small amounts of money (usually less than $2,500) or to those who need to have ready access to their money. Passbook accounts received their name because many years ago, when they opened small savings accounts, customers received actual passbooks—booklets in which bank tellers would record all deposits, withdrawals, and interest payments. Today, however, most banks no longer rely on passbooks. They became inconvenient, and customers often misplaced them or had them stolen. Consequently, most institutions now allow their customers to make

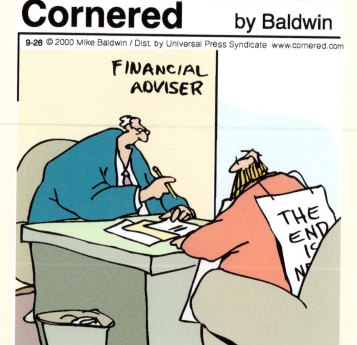

CORNERED © 2000 Mike Baldwin. Reprinted with permission of UNIVERSAL UCLICK. All rights reserved.

IS YOUR MONEY SAFE?

When more than eight thousand banks failed during the Great Depression, Americans became wary about depositing their savings in financial institutions. The failures resulted in heavy losses for some depositors and created a fear that depositors might lose their life savings in future bank failures. To restore the reputation of the nation's banks, Congress created the *Federal Deposit Insurance Corporation (FDIC)* in 1933. This federal agency began insuring the nation's bank deposits in return for a flat fee collected from all participating banks. Originally the FDIC insured each account for $5,000, but through the years that amount has increased to $100,000. Depositors can increase that amount by dividing larger sums into a mixture of individual, joint, and trust accounts. In addition to the FDIC, similar insurance programs came into being for S & Ls and credit unions: the Federal Savings and Loan Insurance Corporation (FSLIC) and the National Credit Union Administration (NCUA).

The trust inspired by insured deposits stabilized the banking industry for several decades, but underlying weaknesses began to surface in the 1980s. Large numbers of S & Ls began to turn up insolvent, and many banks were also in serious trouble. The FSLIC's resources were soon depleted from the many failures, and the FDIC was in danger of a similar plight. This crisis prompted Congress to provide over $100 billion to bail out, at taxpayers' expense, the failed S & Ls. It also dissolved the FSLIC and placed the remaining insured S & Ls under the FDIC's protection. However, the potential for future problems remained high because Congress left the basic insurance system intact.

Unfortunately, the protection provided by deposit insurance also creates some unhealthy incentives for banks and depositors. Since the FDIC now guarantees that the depositor will not lose his money, both bank managers and depositors have less concern about how well the bank operates. The failure of S & Ls usually resulted from their willingness to make many risky high-interest loans that they would not otherwise have made. When those loans went into default in the 1980s, the S & Ls lost the assets that were tied up in them. With their assets depleted, the thrifts were soon insolvent, and taxpayers were left to make good on the government's promise.

The FDIC tries to examine banks and keep them out of serious financial troubles, but governmental regulation is difficult. Many institutions are able to portray themselves as sound and responsible, yet they have too many assets tied up in risky ventures or have managers who use deceit to cover their own mismanagement or graft.

There are some alternatives to the present system, but not all are feasible. One is to abolish the deposit insurance altogether and "let the depositor beware." Another is to step up governmental regulation of financial institutions, but that would increase governmental bureaucracy and hamper the operation of good financial institutions. A third is to allow private deposit insurance companies to replace the FDIC. Private companies would naturally demand that the institutions they insure were worthy of their backing, and the amounts they charged for insurance could increase with the risks presented by each bank or thrift. The financial institutions would have an incentive to manage their assets wisely in order to maintain their own reputations and lower their insurance rates. If they did not act responsibly, they would lose their insurance and with it their depositors. None of these options is without drawbacks, but if no action is taken, more S & L and bank failures will undoubtedly result in a mounting need for further bailouts.

deposits and withdrawals without them. Instead of using a passbook to itemize deposits, withdrawals, and interest payments, account holders can access their accounts online or use the statements, mailed monthly or quarterly from the bank, that detail their account transactions.

People do not usually identify passbook accounts with time deposits because they are able to access their money immediately. What they are not aware of, however, is that most financial institutions reserve the right to require prior notice (usually ten days) before account holders may withdraw their funds. Because passbook accounts tend to be small with nearly immediate availability of funds, they pay a relatively low rate of interest.

One of the biggest cash drains on the average family is the expense of holidays and vacations. Instead of preparing for these events by saving, many people incur sizable debts that last months into the next year. To help customers avoid turning their holiday or vacation spending into debt, some financial institutions offer holiday and vacation club accounts as a means for orderly saving. Perhaps the best example of a club account is a Christmas club account. Club account deposits are typically quite small—$5 to $10 per week—and the rate of interest is usually the same or less than that offered on passbook accounts.

Offering 0.25–0.5 percent greater interest is the restricted passbook account. Virtually identical to the passbook account, the restricted passbook account limits the number of withdrawals. For example, some accounts permit withdrawals only during the first ten days of each calendar quarter, while others require ninety days' notice before an account holder can make a penalty-free withdrawal.

Certificates of deposit (CDs) are time deposits that have a specific maturity date and that yield a higher rate of interest than passbook or club accounts. Financial institutions usually offer an assortment of CDs with maturity dates varying from just seven days to as long as five years. Certificates of deposit with longer maturity dates usually pay higher rates of interest.

Depositors who choose the longer maturity CDs must be willing to leave their money on deposit, for the penalties for early withdrawal can be substantial. For example, the penalty for early redemption of a CD with a maturity greater than one year can be six months' worth of interest. If a depositor purchases a two-year CD today and tomorrow changes his mind and redeems the CD, he will receive his principal minus the equivalent of six months' worth of interest. Savers should purchase CDs only if they are willing to hold them to maturity, but they can plan ahead for emergencies. For example, suppose you had $10,000 and you wished to purchase a two-year CD. Instead of purchasing one large CD, you might consider purchasing ten $1,000 CDs. That way, were you to need some of your money, you could redeem just one CD without penalizing your entire principal.

Though most institutions sell CDs for a minimum of $500, depositors can usually purchase CDs in any odd amount as long as it is greater than the required minimum. When shopping for a CD, be sure to determine if the institution compounds its interest or if it pays simple interest. If a one-year $10,000 CD is paying 8 percent interest, the depositor will receive $800 in interest if simple interest is paid. If, on the other hand, interest is compounded quarterly, the depositor will earn $24.32 more.

GOVERNMENTAL SECURITIES

In its need to finance the national debt, the federal government provides some of the safest and most profitable savings instruments available today. The most popular types of short-term governmental securities are US savings bonds and US Treasury securities.

Financial advisors consider **US savings bonds** to be risk-free investments because they are backed by the full faith and credit of the United States government. They come in two versions—Series EE and Series HH.

Most people think of **Series EE bonds** when they hear the term savings bonds. A person can purchase EE bonds in denominations ranging from $50 to $10,000 and purchase them at a discount, that is, at one-half of their face value. As interest accrues, the value of the bond approaches the amount stated on the front of the bond. As a result of the interest's being the difference between the value of the bond and its purchase price, the bondholder receives no periodic interest

directly. Savers purchase EE bonds directly from the Treasury Department or often through payroll deduction plans set up by their employers. Purchasers can redeem the EE bonds beginning six months after purchase. Bonds held less than five years pay a guaranteed fixed rate of interest compounded semiannually. If a person holds an EE bond longer than five years, his rate of interest is the fixed rate given for the latest six-month average rate paid on five-year US Treasury securities. A person can hold EE bonds for up to thirty years, after which time interest will stop accruing.

Not only is the interest rate on Series EE bonds attractive, but savers should consider other benefits as well. First, the IRS does not consider interest on EE bonds to be taxable income until the bonds are redeemed. In contrast, the person who purchases a five-year CD might not receive his interest until the end of the five-year period; however, he must pay income tax on the interest as it accrues each year. Second, interest on EE bonds is not subject to state and local income taxes. Third, for those with incomes under $60,000, the federal government will not tax the interest as income at all if it will be used to pay for educational expenses of the bondholder or his dependents.

Series HH bonds are similar to Series EE bonds, but they differ in three ways. First, savers purchase Series HH bonds for full face value. Second, a person cannot buy Series HH bonds with cash; he can purchase them only by "rolling over" (redeeming) Series EE bonds. Third, the government pays interest on HH bonds with Treasury checks to the bondholders. Just like EE bonds, the interest on HH bonds is exempt from state and local taxes. Federal income tax on HH interest is not due until the bond matures.

The final type of governmental savings instrument discussed here is US Treasury securities. Whereas US savings bonds finance a relatively small portion of the enormous national debt, the sales of Treasury bills (T-bills), Treasury notes (T-notes), and Treasury bonds (T-bonds) fund most of the budget deficit, with Treasury bills financing the majority of it.

Treasury bills are available with maturities as short as ninety days or as long as one year and may be purchased in one of two ways. First, people can purchase T-bills directly from the US Treasury through any main office or branch of the Federal Reserve Bank. Second, for a fee one may purchase a Treasury bill through a commercial bank or stockbrokerage firm. Interest rates on T-bills are low relative to other investments, but they are among the most secure investments, having nearly zero probability of default.

You now have at your disposal an understanding of savings instruments—passbook accounts, CDs, mutual funds, governmental savings bonds, T-bills, and others. You can take your scheduled savings, examine what instruments and interest rates are currently available to you, and use this understanding to make choices that will best serve your financial plan and show good biblical stewardship of your God-given assets.

REVIEW QUESTIONS

1. What are the two main types of floating-rate accounts?
2. How did time deposits earn that name?
3. What investment do financial advisors consider to be risk free, and why?

TERMS

floating-rate account	274
money market deposit accounts (MMDAs)	274
money market mutual funds (MMMFs)	274
time deposits	274
passbook account	274
certificates of deposit (CDs)	276
US savings bonds	276
Series EE bonds	276
Series HH bonds	277
Treasury bills	277

CHAPTER FOURTEEN
INFLATION

14A IMPACT AND MEASUREMENT — 278

14B CAUSES AND CURES — 285

Were you to ask the average worker what he would change about his job if he had the power to make changes, you would probably receive a variety of answers. You would likely hear about improving working conditions, increasing employee benefits, adding vacation days, and perhaps changing supervisors. However, you would probably find that the majority of the answers would be about increasing salary or raising the hourly wage.

Some of these responses are verification of the biblical truth that the eyes of man are never satisfied (Prov. 27:20). Human nature being as it is, were those workers to receive the greater pay they desire, they would likely soon find themselves again wishing they could grant themselves another increase. No matter how much we have, it seems we always want just a little more.

However, the answer may also reflect that as the worker's pay increases, so do the prices he has to pay for the necessities of life—food, clothing, fuel, utilities, and so forth. In fact, some workers might be tempted to believe that an unwritten law exists somewhere that states whenever their employers do give them salary increases, prices must go up by an equal or greater percentage, thus leaving them in the same or worse financial state than they were before their raises.

Though no such law exists, it is a fact that prices have been going up almost every year for several decades, and it appears that price increases will continue for many years to come. While it is probably true that you could identify certain products whose prices have actually declined during your high-school years, the overall trend is typically toward fairly steady price increases.

14A IMPACT AND MEASUREMENT

Inflation is the term economists use to describe a sustained rise in the average price level. The existence of inflation does not necessarily mean that the price of every good is rising. Even when most prices are rising, some prices fall. For example, the general price level rose between 1967 and 2004, yet the price of electronic calculators and computers actually declined. However, during that same period, the price of energy rose faster than the general price level.

Though some prices may fall during an inflationary period, the key is that prices increase overall. To be sure, the inflation experienced in the United States has been burdensome, but it seems insignificant when compared to the very rapid inflation, or hyperinflation, experienced by other nations. For example, in 2002 Zimbabwe's currency lost its value rapidly. According to the *International Herald Tribune*, in April 2002 Zimbabwe's currency could be traded on the black market at Z$120 to the US dollar. But the following December it went for Z$6,200 to the US dollar. In 2005 the American dollar bought as many as Z$25,000, and the inflation was continuing to rise.

How much does a cup of coffee cost today?

One indication of inflation has been an ongoing rise in the price of postage stamps.

LOSERS AND WINNERS

Inflation takes a toll on many people, but those hardest hit are persons living on fixed incomes, such as the elderly. There are senior citizens who depend on retirement pensions that provide fixed monthly payments. The amounts are fixed in that they do not adjust automatically to the rate of inflation. They remain the same every month, every year regardless of what is happening in the current economy. Consequently, for those living on these fixed amounts, it is increasingly difficult to survive repeated years of inflation. As prices go up and their dollars purchase fewer and fewer goods, those with fixed incomes find that they must dig deeper into their savings. Currently many employers take future inflation into consideration when developing their pension plans. These plans include a **cost of living adjustment (COLA)**, which adjusts payments upward as inflation causes prices to rise. The Social Security Administration annually adjusts its payments according to changes in the cost of living.

Those most affected by inflation are the elderly living on fixed incomes.

Inflation also hurts creditors. Those who have lent money to others stand to lose money during periods when the fixed repayments on their outstanding loans no longer keep pace with their rising operating costs. They suffer financially because the dollars they receive in repayment are worth less (in terms of their purchasing power) than the dollars they lent originally. To illustrate, let us say that you lend a friend $100 today to be repaid in one year without interest. If prices rise by 5 percent over the course of that year, the $100 dollars your friend repays will have the purchasing power of only $95. If inflation becomes too severe, credit markets may collapse entirely, making it impossible for businesses or consumers to receive loans. No creditor would want to lend money to someone for the purchase of a luxury car, only to have the money he received in future loan repayment equal the value of a compact car.

To remedy this inflationary problem, many lenders incorporate inflation-fighting clauses into their loan contracts. They tie the interest rate of the loan to the

Technological advances can cause the price of some goods to fall, even during times of inflation.

inflation rate. Such floating-rate loans require higher payments as the general price level rises and lower payments should deflation or a fall in prices occur. If inflation occurs very rapidly, it becomes impossible for creditors to adjust their records as lenders suffer from a kind of information overload.

A third group hurt by inflation is savers, those wanting to put their money in banks. Rising prices seriously discourage saving. If prices increase at a rate greater than the interest rate offered on savings, it becomes economically unwise to save money. For example, imagine that you have the money to purchase a $10,000 car. However, you decide that you can drive your old car for one more year and save that money at a 6 percent interest rate. You reason that at the end of the year you can purchase the $10,000 car and pocket $600 interest. If the nation is experiencing a 10 percent inflation rate, however, you stand to lose money by saving. The car's price next year will be $11,000 ($10,000 + 10%), while your savings account would grow to only $10,600 ($10,000 + 6%). Obviously, in this case it would not be prudent for you to save your money. In general, whenever the inflation rate exceeds the rate of interest on a savings account, the money a person saves is actually losing its purchasing power. A logical outworking then of inflation is that it prompts consumers to spend their money to stay ahead of future price increases.

Lenders can be hurt by inflation as the money they lend buys less when it is repaid.

Inflation also causes an almost uncontrollable fear of lost savings. As a result, the economy suffers two major blows. First, inflation contributes to a rise in consumer spending that places a heavier burden on the nation's factories, equipment, and personnel. However, many of the factories and equipment may be inadequate and in need of repair or replacement; consequently, without sufficient renovations, they will be unable to produce at a rate that matches the increased demand. That leads to the second blow.

When personal savings decline, business firms find less money available to borrow from the financial market. This decline in available funds results in businesses' being unable to borrow sufficient capital to repair old factories or to buy new ones; therefore, they are unable to produce goods for tomorrow's needs.

The fourth and perhaps most obvious group hurt by inflation is consumers. Some economists believe that a little inflation, around 2–3 percent per year, can be a good stimulant to the nation's "economic bloodstream." They claim that the rising prices that accompany inflation act like the proverbial carrot on a stick, encouraging business firms to invest more money in factories, equipment, and employees. However, such is not the case. Over long periods of time, consumers' incomes tend to rise, but so do the prices of goods and services. Whenever the average consumer's income does not rise as fast as prices, inflation robs him of the purchasing power he has earned and acts like a hidden tax on his income. Consider the following illustration. A man entering the labor force in the 1930s as a factory worker earning 25¢ per hour could purchase a loaf of bread for 5¢. Upon his retirement in the

Inflation discourages saving.

1980s, that worker earned $5.00 per hour for the same job, but to purchase a loaf of bread cost him $1.00. Economists would say that in terms of the bread he purchased, his real income did not change.

Are there any winners during inflation? Actually, for almost every loser there is a corresponding winner. In the case of those living on fixed pensions, the winner is the former employer or fund holder. By virtue of its massive size, the pension fund is not subject to the inflationary plight of the small savings account. By investing in governmental securities, fund managers are able to earn a return greater than the inflation rate. While gathering substantial profits from those investments, the fund manager pays out only the required low fixed pension amounts to the retirees.

While creditors lose to inflation, borrowers tend to be the winners. As inflation progresses, the incomes of borrowers rise, but payments on fixed-rate loans remain the same.

Finally, while savers lose by keeping their money in low-yielding bank accounts, financial institutions, like managers of big pension funds, are able to use the capital on which they are paying relatively low interest for investments that garner them greater profits.

Now it may appear that inflation would not really be a problem if a person could ensure that he is always on the winning side of business transactions. In reality, however, even the apparent winners are part of a general loss; for when inflation envelops a country, the entire nation loses confidence in its economic system. As inflation takes hold, the nation's citizens lose confidence in their governmental leadership, lose their desire to maintain their work ethic, and disregard thrift and saving. Instead, current consumption becomes paramount, and each person takes on an attitude of "every man for himself."

A HIDDEN TAX

During the Revolutionary War, the Continental Congress had the power to levy taxes on each of the colonies, but since each colony was a sovereign state, any one of them had the right to refuse payment. As a result, revenues to finance the war dried up. The Continental Congress immediately used the only available means it had for paying for the war—printing currency without gold backing. As the Continental Congress printed more continentals, the currency already in the hands of the colonists decreased in value and purchasing power. The reduction of the people's purchasing ability was just as real as if the Continental Congress had been able to tax away their dollars. Thus, the inflating of the nation's currency acted as a hidden tax. Incidentally, out of this situation came a phrase to describe something that was worthless—*not worth a continental*.

HYPERINFLATION

After World War I, Germany's economic troubles led to one of the worst cases of hyperinflation in history. The reparation payments imposed on Germany by the Allied victors fueled inflation. The German government, known as the Weimar Republic, desperately tried to meet these payments but quickly found itself unable to do so. Germany's defeat in the war had almost completely crippled its industries and trade. The government printed more and more deutsche marks, Germany's basic unit of currency, to meet expenses. The result of the increase in the money supply was that the German people soon lost all confidence in the mark and its value plummeted. The inflation devastated life savings and created a panic that helped pave the way for the rise of Adolf Hitler.

Although the most famous case of hyperinflation was that in post–World War I Germany, an even worse case occurred in Hungary during World War II. Prior to the war, it took about 6 Hungarian pengos to purchase a dollar's worth of goods. By the end of the war, it required nearly 4,600,000,000,000,000,000,000 (4.6 sextillion) to make the same purchase.

The worst case of modern inflation occured in Zimbabwe in the early 2000s (see p. 279).

Date	Number of marks equal to $1 (monthly average)
July 1914	4.2 DM
Nov. 1923	4,200,000,000,000.0

During the post–World War I period, the German marks became virtually worthless. Marks lost so much value that people burned them for fuel.

During periods of high inflation, borrowers may find it easier to make their loan payments.

MEASURING INFLATION

Because of the harmful effects of inflation, economists must have some device to detect its existence, measure its growth, and make adjustments to dampen its effects. Economists have developed two tools for this purpose: the gross domestic product implicit price deflator (GDP deflator) and the consumer price index (CPI).

GDP Deflator

Chapter 12 introduced you to the ultimate inflation-measuring device: the GDP deflator. Calculated by comparing the prices of all goods and services from year to year, the GDP deflator is able to measure the changes in prices of everything from hot dogs to battleships. Once economists have an idea of the rise in general prices, adjusting loan contracts and wages is a simple task. The problem with using the GDP deflator as a COLA factor is that it measures changes in the prices of all goods in the nation. If the price of military hardware rises while prices on everything else remain level, the GDP deflator will still rise. However, it would obviously not be an economically sound decision to increase wages paid to construction workers because the GDP deflator rose as a result of increased military costs. Economists recognized this problem and developed a way to measure changes in the prices that household consumers pay. They call this improved measure the consumer price index.

Consumer Price Index

Governmental economists use the **consumer price index (CPI)** to measure the changes in the prices that affect a selected market basket of goods and services. To calculate the CPI, economists repeatedly measure the prices of approximately four hundred goods and services that an average urban household purchases. The prices of these goods and services in the initial period of the survey, or **base period**, serve as a benchmark against which to compare future prices. In Figure 14-1 the base period is that of the years 1982–84. This table lists CPI figures and inflation rates for the years 1980–2014. The price indices in the table indicate that a basket of goods that cost the average urban household $100 during the base period cost $82.40 in 1980 and $236.74 in 2014.

Uses of the CPI. One of the major uses of the CPI is for determining inflation rates. It is possible to calculate the rate of inflation for the interval between any two CPI figures by using the following formula:

$$\frac{(\text{Recent CPI} - \text{Earlier CPI})}{\text{Earlier CPI}} \times 100 = \text{Rate of inflation.}$$

For example, let us calculate the inflation rate that occurred between 2006 and 2007:

$$\frac{(207.3 - 201.6)}{201.6} \times 100 = 2.827\%$$

Based on these calculations, the inflation rate for 2007 was 2.827 percent. That is, a good that cost $100 in 2006 cost $102.83 in 2007 (see Fig. 14-1).

In addition to being useful for determining the rate of inflation, the CPI also allows economists to determine an individual's purchasing power. Using the CPI to compare current and past purchasing power is quite easy. For example, assume that someone earned $12,500 in 1990, $24,000 in 1995, and $37,000 in 2000. Obviously, his nominal income went up, but was he able to purchase more with those added dollars? To determine his real purchasing power relative to the CPI, you must divide nominal earnings by the CPI for that year. As you can see, between 1990 and 1995 our example's purchasing power relative to the CPI's market basket of goods rose but did not double. Between 1995 and 2000

ZIGGY © 1994 ZIGGY AND FRIENDS, INC. Reprinted with permission of UNIVERSAL UCLICK. All rights reserved.

> The *market basket of goods and services* is a selected group of four hundred goods and services that a typical urban household of four might purchase during any given month.

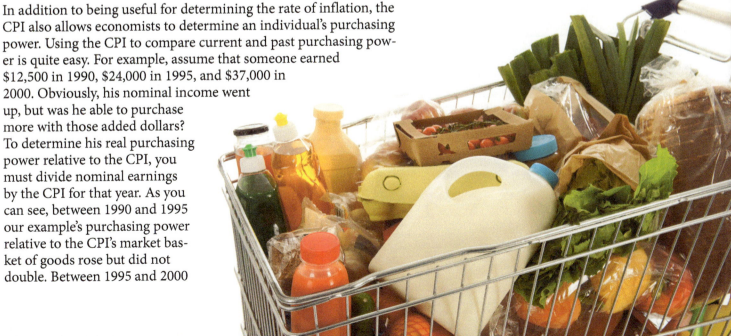

Fig. 14-1 Consumer Price Index, 1980–2014

Year	CPI	Inflation rate
1980	82.4	%13.5
1981	90.9	10.3
1982	96.5	6.2
1983	99.6	3.2
1984	103.9	4.3
1985	107.6	3.6
1986	109.6	1.9
1987	113.6	3.6
1988	118.3	4.1
1989	124.0	4.8
1990	130.7	5.4
1991	136.2	4.2
1992	140.3	3.0
1993	144.5	3.0
1994	148.2	2.6
1995	152.4	2.8
1996	156.9	3.0
1997	160.5	2.3
1998	163.0	1.6
1999	166.6	2.2
2000	172.2	3.4
2001	177.1	2.8
2002	179.9	1.6
2003	184.0	2.3
2004	188.9	2.7
2005	195.3	3.4
2006	201.6	3.2
2007	207.3	2.8
2008	215.303	3.8
2009	214.537	-0.4
2010	218.056	1.6
2011	224.939	3.2
2012	229.594	2.1
2013	232.957	1.5
2014	236.736	1.6

$(96.5 + 99.6 + 103.9)/3 = 100$

Source: U.S. Department of Labor Bureau of Labor Statistic
*This table of CPI data is based upon a 1982 base of 100. What does this mean? A CPI of 195.3, as an example from 2005, indicates 95.3% inflation since 1982.
**CPI data as of June 2015.

For this calculation, you must use a decimal form of the CPI. CPI figures are not percentages, but in this type of problem, they should look like percentages to get the right answer. One hundred becomes 1.00, and 130.7 becomes 1.307.

his purchasing power rose only about half of his salary increase.

1990: $12,500/1.307 = $9,563.89

1995: $24,000/1.524 = $15,748.03

2000: $37,000/1.722 = $21,486.64

Many individuals and business firms have recognized the eroding influence of inflation on purchasing power and have, therefore, accepted the CPI as the primary tool to index or adjust wages, prices, and interest rates. **Indexing** is a process of tying present wages and prices to some adjustment figure to maintain a balance between real wages and real prices. A building contractor may include an inflation clause in his bid that would tie his price to the CPI and allow him to raise his price to keep pace with the rising costs he must pay. Workers, realizing how the purchasing power of fixed wages and pensions can be eroded by inflation, often include COLA clauses in their job contracts and pension plans. They want their wages and retirement benefits tied to the CPI. The federal government indexes social security payments using a cost-of-living index based in the CPI.

Limitations of the CPI. For all its benefits, the CPI is not a perfect measure of changes in living costs but only a good approximation. There are at least three major reasons that the CPl does not provide exact information on changes in the cost of living.

First, the CPI assumes that all urban households consistently purchase, month after month, the same market basket of goods and services, while in reality buying preferences change.

A second limitation of the CPI is the problem of adjusting price changes to quality changes. We are fond of thinking that the quality of goods manufactured in the past was significantly better than the quality of today's products. While the durability and perhaps even reliability of some older items may have been better, many of today's goods are more efficient and productive. Hence, today's products may be considered more valuable, but economists do not adjust the higher prices of today's goods with respect to their higher quality. For example, if a washing machine that cost $250 ten years ago costs $500 today, the CPI would report that the price has doubled. However, what if the quality of today's washing machine has improved so that it will last four times longer? Would it not be correct to say that the new machine actually costs $125 (500/4)? Because the CPI does not take quality into account, it tends to overstate the rate of inflation.

A third problem with the CPI is that it tends to ignore the law of demand. As the price of a good rises, other things being held constant, people will tend to demand less of the good and will purchase a less

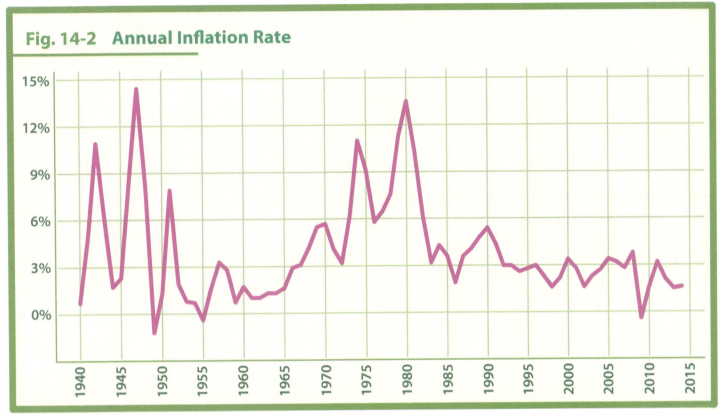

Fig. 14-2 Annual Inflation Rate

CoinNews Media Group LLC; US Inflation Calculator. COPYRIGHT © 2008-2015 COINNEWS MEDIA GROUP LLC (COIN NEWS). ALL RIGHTS RESERVED.

expensive substitute. As the price of housing rises, people tend to rent rather than buy. As new automobiles become too expensive, consumers tend to hold on to their old cars longer, choosing to repair rather than replace them. The CPI, however, assumes that no matter how high the price a good in the market basket rises, consumers will continually purchase the same quantity. To allow a true picture of the cost of living, the CPI's market basket should constantly reflect change in the quantities consumers buy as prices change.

SECTION REVIEW 14A

1. What is a COLA, and how does it work?
2. Who is generally hurt by inflation?
3. Who receives some benefits from inflation?
4. What are the two tools used to measure inflation?
5. How is the consumer price index calculated?
6. Describe the limitations involved in the CPI.

Many of today's manufactured items offer better-quality features.

14B CAUSES AND CURES

One of the most disturbing problems with inflation is its tendency to worsen rapidly. The inflationary experiences of many South American and African nations have demonstrated this sad fact. A nation's inflation rate may begin at a modest 2 or 3 percent per year, but it has a frightening tendency to accelerate to the point that

> The total demand and total supply curves are often referred to as aggregate supply and demand curves.

prices double or triple on a daily basis. When this occurs, a nation's financial system grinds to a halt, panic becomes commonplace, industries shut down as workers strike for higher and higher wages, and there is a serious threat to national security.

CAUSES OF INFLATION

To better understand the causes of inflation, recall your introduction to the concept of price. Remember that the two key variables in determining the price of every good and service are supply and demand. As Figure 14-3 illustrates, the intersection of a good's supply and demand curves determines its price.

Since the intersection of the supply and demand curves determines the price of a good, only two situations can cause a price increase: 1) a shift of the supply curve to the left (see Fig. 14-4a) or 2) a shift of the demand curve to the right (see Fig. 14-4b). A leftward shift of a supply curve indicates that the producer is producing less of the good, while a rightward shift of the demand curve indicates that buyers are suddenly demanding more.

Likewise, the intersection of what we might call the total demand and total supply curves determines the overall price level in the country (see Fig. 14-5). Instead of a graph showing the price of a single good relative to its quantity, the total supply and demand curves use a graph with the price level on one axis and the gross domestic product on the other. Why the GDP? Because the GDP is the total quantity of all goods sold in the country.

Since the intersection of the total supply and the total demand curves determines the nation's price level, there can be only two possible explanations for inflation: 1) a decrease in the nation's supply of goods and services (represented by a

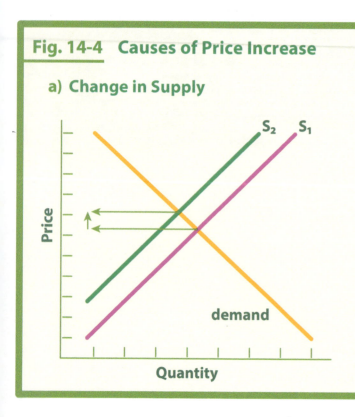

Fig. 14-3 Market Price

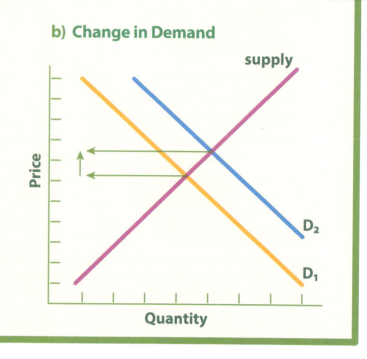

Fig. 14-4 Causes of Price Increase

a) Change in Supply

b) Change in Demand

leftward shift in the total supply curve) or 2) an increase in the nation's demand for goods and services (represented by a rightward shift in the total demand curve). Economists have labeled these two explanations cost-push inflation and demand-pull inflation respectively.

Cost-Push Inflation

Many economists believe that one trigger for inflation is the raising of prices by the nation's businesses, either to accumulate higher profits or to pass along higher costs of materials or labor. Consumers, unable to pay the higher prices, demand higher wages from their employers. It is from this cycle of higher costs' pushing up prices, causing an increase in wages, and further pushing up prices that the name **cost-push inflation** originates. According to the cost-push theory, business firms begin the inflationary process by charging higher prices, an action that shifts the total supply curve to the left (see Fig. 14-6).

As prices soar, consumers become unhappy because they are unable to buy as many goods and services with their normal incomes. They complain, petition, strike, or engage in other forms of persuasion to prompt their employers to grant them pay increases. Employers, either out of sympathy to their employees' plight or out of fear of a strike, grant their employees larger paychecks. As employees receive larger paychecks, consumer income rises, causing the total demand curve to shift to the right.

As a result of these two shifts, the GDP is right back where it was before, but notice that the price level has risen. The story does not end here, however. Where will the businesses that agreed to the wage increases get the money to pay their workers higher salaries? They will get it by increasing prices and shifting the supply curve to the left again, prompting workers to again demand higher wages. Thus, the cost-push inflationary spiral continues: rising prices lead to rising wages, which again lead to rising prices, and so forth.

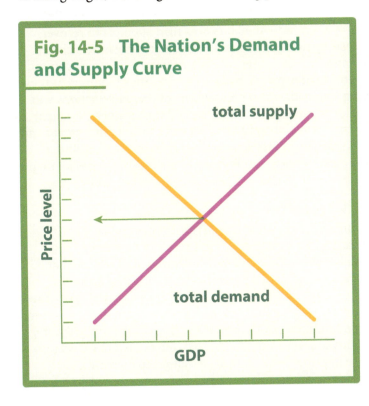

Fig. 14-5 The Nation's Demand and Supply Curve

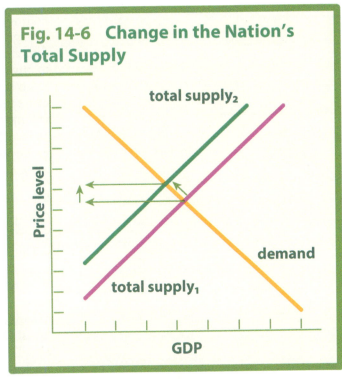

Fig. 14-6 Change in the Nation's Total Supply

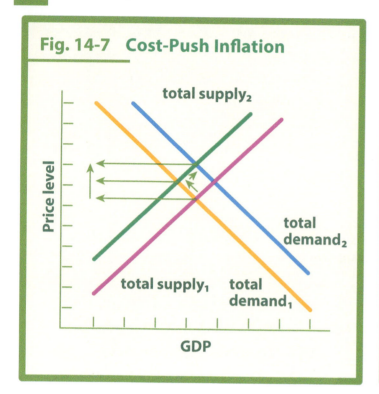

Fig. 14-7 Cost-Push Inflation

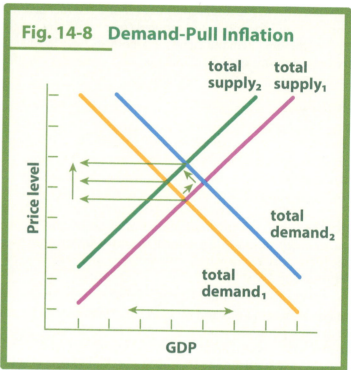

Fig. 14-8 Demand-Pull Inflation

This cost-push inflation theory is attractive to both business firms and labor unions. Big business firms claim that the demands of labor unions for higher wages trigger the cost-push spiral, while union leaders argue that business firms' raising their prices to glean higher profits plants the seeds of inflation. As appealing as the cost-push theory may be, it fails to explain the cause of sustained inflation. There is one basic variable in the inflationary spiral for which the cost-push believers do not account: money.

If the prices of all goods and services are rising and the paychecks of all workers are increasing as well, the supply of dollars must also increase; otherwise, inflation could not continue its upward spiral.

Follow this logic: an individual business firm attempts to recover its higher costs by hiking its prices. Consumers now have a choice. Either they may buy less expensive substitutes, or they may continue to buy the now higher-priced good. The latter may require that they forgo buying some other good. Either one of these two actions will cause the sales of some goods to suffer, and higher unemployment will likely result. The only way all firms can charge higher prices and pay workers more is if there is more money to do so. If additional money does not circulate, employers will not be able to pay all their workers higher salaries and will need to reduce their workforces.

Demand-Pull Inflation

Cost-push inflation holds that the inflationary spiral begins with a shift leftward in the supply curve as a result of businesses' passing along higher costs. **Demand-pull inflation**, on the other hand, maintains that the inflationary trend begins with an increase in demand. According to demand-pull inflation, consumers, for some reason, begin demanding more of everything: cars, houses, washing machines, and millions of other products. According to the theory, this shift rightward in the demand curve causes the price level to rise. The rise in prices forces businesses either to increase their workers' wages or else to risk watching their employees depart for higher-paying jobs. When business firms pass on to consumers their higher payroll costs in the form of higher prices, the total supply curve shifts to the left. Consumers now unable to buy the more expensive goods demand still higher wages, and when companies pay the higher wages, the consumers' total demand curve shifts to the right. On and on the spiral continues, much like cost-push inflation.

Money Growth: The Root Cause of Inflation

The argument between the proponents of cost-push and demand-pull inflation is purely academic. It really does not matter what triggered the inflationary episode. The important thing is recognizing that a continual increase in the money supply keeps the price level going up.

Though it is in keeping with the official definition, the definition of inflation given at the beginning of this chapter is still somewhat inaccurate. Traditionally, economists have defined inflation as a situation in which prices of virtually everything in the nation are rising. In reality, however, a rising price level is merely a symptom of inflation. Consider the following illustration. If you were to fill a car's tires with air, you would see the car rise. In the strictest sense of the word, the action of the car rising is not inflation. Inflation is actually that which caused the car to rise—specifically the addition of more air into the tires. The lifting of the car is merely a logical result. Likewise, price increases are but a logical result of the infusion of more money into the economy. If new money is not injected into the economy, business firms would be unable to pay higher wages and consumers would be unable to pay higher prices.

CURES FOR INFLATION

How people try to cure inflation depends on what they view as causing it. Depending on their view, people try to stem inflation by implementing wage-price controls or limiting the creation of money.

Wage-Price Controls

Those who view inflation as a price phenomenon have a rather simple solution: make it illegal for business firms to raise the prices of their products or the wages of their workers. In a sense they advocate freezing in place the total supply and total demand curves.

The problem with wage and price controls is that they cannot work if the government continues inflating the money supply. Imagine the foolishness of inflating a car's tires but putting a barrier above the car that will not allow it to rise. If the inflation continues for too long, the car will suffer damage and the tires will explode. Likewise, if the government imposes wage and price controls while continuing to inflate the money supply, demand for goods and services will continue to grow, but business firms will have neither the ability to produce more nor the power to increase the prices of

PRICE CONTROL: AN OLD IDEA

Wage and price controls are not a new idea. Attempts to artificially hold down prices and wages date back to around 1800 BC, when a Babylonian ruler threatened death by drowning to anyone who violated his wage and price freeze. The Roman emperor Diocletian issued an edict in AD 301 called *commanded cheapness*, in which he set a maximum price on beef, clothing, and other commodities. In addition he set maximum wage rates for doctors, lawyers, and other workers. (Those who violated the edict were to be slain.) In AD 314 Lactantius, a Christian author and apologist, wrote of the harmful effects of such price controls, lamenting that there was "much bloodshed upon very slight and trifling accounts; and the people brought provisions no more to market, since they could not get a reasonable price for them; and this increased the dearth [famine] so much that after many had died by it, the law itself was laid aside."

existing products. The store shelves of law-abiding merchants will be picked clean as buyers snatch up scarce goods at bargain prices. Afterward, the producers of those goods will be unable and unwilling to supply more because to continue to sell goods may mean incurring losses. Elsewhere, other producers will continue to produce, selling their products on the black market at the profitable but illegal market price.

The problem with wage and price controls is that they do not address the underlying causes of a rise in prices. Unless the supply of a product increases or the demand for the product falls, there will still be pressure for the price to rise. Price controls create artificial shortages of products because the quantity demanded for goods exceeds the quantity supplied. Under free-market conditions, the increased demand would prompt higher prices and increased production to meet the demand. However, since price controls created the shortage, there is little motivation for manufacturers to increase supply because they cannot increase the price to pay for their increased production costs.

Limitation of Money Creation

If one believes that increases in the money supply create an excessive demand for goods and services that causes inflation, then the obvious solution is to limit the quantity of money being created. In 1985 Bolivia was experiencing an annual inflation rate of over 25,000 percent: prices were changing by the minute, workers were taking managers hostage, and the nation's third biggest import was currency. In August of 1985 Bolivia's president announced that the government would stop creating money to pay its bills and would spend only money that it received in tax revenues. Up to that point the government was creating 85¢ of each dollar spent. Within two months, inflation was down to an annual rate of 20 percent.

Perhaps you have heard someone make the statement, "Just when I thought I could make ends meet, someone moved the ends." Though somewhat humorous, this statement summarizes the feeling of many workers who face the struggle of trying to match income with inflated prices. As you saw in this chapter, the push to

A. W. PHILLIPS (1914–75)
Creator of the Phillips Curve

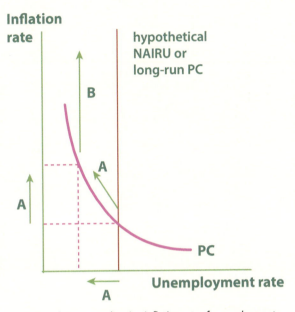

NAIRU is the non-accelerating inflation rate of unemployment.

Alban William Phillips was born and spent his early years in New Zealand. At sixteen he began working at an Australian mine, where he learned electrical engineering. In 1937 at age twenty-three, he left Australia for England. Shortly thereafter, he served as a soldier in World War II and became a Japanese prisoner of war. He was freed at the close of hostilities.

After the war, in spite of being significantly older than many other students, Phillips enrolled at the London School of Economics. His life experiences had made him interested in social issues, so he began studying sociology. His interest in sociology was short-lived, however, and he replaced it with an interest in economics. For one of his first projects in economics, he utilized his engineering skills to construct a machine that used liquids to illustrate the economic concepts of stocks and flows as applied to a macroeconomic model of John Maynard Keynes's. The presentation of the machine and its economic application in a 1950 paper earned him a position teaching statistics at LSE, where he remained for seventeen years.

Phillips spent his entire career at LSE studying the dynamics of national economy and ways to stabilize it. In this context Phillips made his most famous contribution to economic theory—the Phillips Curve. In preparing data for use in a project, he discovered an extremely significant statistical relationship between changes in wages and the prevailing rate of unemployment in an economy. In the 1958 paper in which he published these findings, he noted that the relationship indicated that there is a kind of economic policy tradeoff between the rate of inflation and the level of unemployment. Other economists since that time have refined and applied the Phillips Curve to modern macroeconomics, but Phillips's discovery remains important in the development of our understanding of how national economies work and what policy options are available for governments.

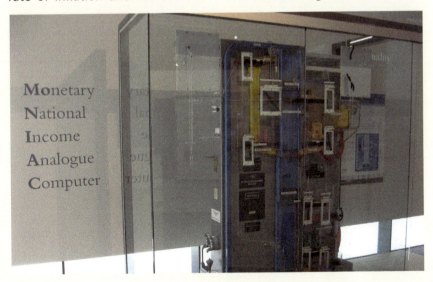

raise income to the level of inflation often succeeds in also increasing inflation. Consequently, it may seem impossible to make ends meet. Perhaps you, too, have been in the workforce and have had personal experience with seeing your paycheck lose some of its purchasing power. Having read this chapter, you should now have a better understanding of why it seems this way. You understand better what inflation is and what causes it, and you are aware of its harmful effects. Because of the hurt caused by rising prices, particularly to those on fixed incomes, Christians should support policies that curb inflation. Yet, which of those policies is best is not always easy to discern because some policies do not always produce their intended result. Christians should work to promote policies that will prove beneficial.

Having studied demand and supply curves earlier in this text should have helped you understand the cost-push and demand-pull inflation theories. Also having studied how countries create money and regulate the money supply should have aided your understanding of how increasing the money supply contributes to inflation. Perhaps you also noticed how something you learned at the beginning of this study, the unlimited wants versus limited goods conflict, also contributes to inflation. People always seem to want more—more income, more goods and services. However, that demand for more often drives prices ever upward, leading only to renewed demands for more. You should be seeing how so many of the economic principles you have studied in separate chapters work simultaneously and together in our economy.

SECTION REVIEW 14B

1. What is the difference between cost-push and demand-pull inflation?
2. What is the root cause of inflation?
3. Why are wage and price controls usually ineffective?

CHAPTER REVIEW

CONTENT QUESTIONS

1. What is the official or traditional definition of inflation?
2. What is hyperinflation?
3. Why is it unprofitable for people to save during periods when the inflation rate is high?
4. How is the consumer price index different from the GDP deflator?
5. What are the two possible means of curing inflation? Which is better? Why?

APPLICATION QUESTIONS

1. A worker's income in 1997 was $24,000. In 2003 his income was $30,800.
   a. If these figures were adjusted for inflation (according to the CPI statistics in Figure 14-1), would his income have increased or decreased during the seven-year period?
   b. If his earnings of $24,000 in 1997 were strictly tied to the CPI, what would have been his equivalent earnings in 2003?
2. Given the CPI data found in Figure 14-1, calculate the rate of inflation between 1998 and 2004.

TERMS

inflation	278
cost of living adjustment (COLA)	279
consumer price index (CPI)	283
base period	283
indexing	284
cost-push inflation	287
demand-pull inflation	288

PERSONAL FINANCE
ESTATE PLANNING

Financial planning is the process of developing and implementing plans to achieve financial objectives. Typical financial objectives have both short-term and long-term perspectives. The first area in a Christian's short-term financial plan is preparation for events that could occur at any time, especially death and disability. Some precautions for dealing with both death and disability are discussed in the Personal Finance article "Insuring Your Home, Auto, and Life" (see p. 58). Part of being a prudent person who foresees evil and hides himself (Prov. 27:12) is anticipating what could happen and making preparations for it. Unless the Lord returns, Christians, like the unsaved, can anticipate that they will die. Therefore, they ought to prepare for death by providing life insurance to meet the financial needs of dependents that may be left behind and by establishing a last will and testament.

THE NECESSITY OF A WILL

Many people make no effort to create a will because of its close association with death, and others believe that only the wealthy need a will. However, each adult Christian needs to establish a **last will and testament** as his opportunity to ensure that what he leaves behind will be disposed of according to his wishes and in a manner that glorifies God. By completing a will, a Christian fulfills this essential part of his role as a Christian steward.

What a person leaves behind is known as his **estate** and includes both assets and liabilities. For example, on the asset side, a person's estate may consist of all his cash (including his portion of joint accounts that have right of survivorship), jewelry, stocks, bonds, other investments, life insurance, his portion of jointly held real estate, and any other possessions that would be considered valuable. On the other hand, a person's estate also includes his liabilities, that is, what he owes. Though a person has died, his debts still must be paid, and a will provides for an orderly payment of all obligations.

While any person who is over eighteen years of age and of sound mind may write a will, a recent survey showed that over 50 percent of the adult population of the United States does not have a will. If a person dies without a will, the state in which he lived will use a predetermined formula to divide his property among his relatives. State laws do not consider what the deceased "would have wanted," nor do they provide for charitable contributions to ministries that the deceased supported. Likewise, the courts care nothing about how the relatives will spend the money once it is distributed. In many cases the formula for dividing an estate is so strict that surviving members must sell family heirlooms at a public auction to provide that each recipient receives an equal share. In addition, a will also allows a person to avoid the high fees that come

when the state appoints a stranger to administer his estate.

Perhaps the most compelling reason for a Christian to execute a will is to ensure biblically proper care for his children. If a couple with young children were to die without a will, the court would appoint **guardians** for the children. The court would first look for potential guardians from the ranks of immediate relatives. However, if it could not locate a suitable guardian, it might place the children in foster homes pending adoption. In cases of families of three or more children, the court may find it extremely difficult to locate guardians willing to care for all the children together, thus necessitating that it break up the family. By executing a will, a Christian couple can locate born-again relatives or friends who would be willing to assume the care of their children in the event that both die at the same time. By locating potential Christian guardians, parents are seeking to fulfill their spiritual responsibility to bring up their children "in the nurture and admonition of the Lord" (Eph. 6:4).

TYPES OF WILLS

There are three ways to complete a will. First is the do-it-yourself will. Many financial advisers discourage using this type of will for two reasons: disgruntled beneficiaries may successfully challenge it in court, and the court may rule it invalid if it fails to conform to technicalities in the law.

The second type of will is a **statutory will**. Statutory wills are simple forms, often written in a multiple-choice format. Those executing statutory wills can be confident that they have a valid will because it is a document authored by the state. States designed statutory wills for people with small, uncomplicated estates. Because the forms come in a prewritten, multiple-choice format, they tend to be inflexible. Generally speaking, statutory wills are for married couples who want to leave everything to the surviving spouse and make routine provisions for their young children.

The third type of will utilizes the services of a lawyer. People who deem it best to avoid a do-it-yourself will and who do not live in a state where a statutory will is available should have a lawyer draw up a will.

MAJOR PROVISIONS OF WILLS

Because lawyers usually charge expensive hourly fees, persons who retain lawyers to complete their wills should thoroughly acquaint themselves with the major provisions of wills and should decide beforehand how they want these provisions to read.

1. Provide a personal testimony. Christians should realize that the reading of their last will and testament may be a final opportunity to share the gospel of Jesus Christ with unsaved relatives and loved ones. Therefore, those who are born again should consider including a clear and concise testimony of their salvation. Relatives and friends have accepted Christ after hearing the gospel presented in a will.

2. Appoint an executor. The **executor** of the estate is the person entrusted with the responsibility of carrying out the provisions of the will. Should a person die without a will, the court will appoint an **administrator** to perform the same functions. Before naming an executor, the person creating the will should make sure that his choice is willing and able to carry out the job. He should ask only persons that he believes can handle the complicated tasks of dealing with potentially quarrelsome heirs, a slow court system, and demanding creditors. He should also ask someone to serve as an alternate executor in case his first choice is unable or unwilling to do the job.

3. Appoint a guardian for dependent children. As in the case of the executor, those whom couples ask to serve as guardians for their children should be willing and able to serve as substitute parents. Husbands and wives should pray specifically and choose carefully. The responsibility for their children may fall on the guardians, and if so, they will be the ones instilling values and character traits into the children. In addition to naming guardians for their children, couples should list one or two

A major purpose of writing a will is to appoint a guardian for children who are minors.

alternates. At the time of death, the persons the couple previously selected may be unwilling to serve, they may have moved and cannot be located, or they may have died. Couples should stay informed about the lives of their children's potential guardians. Situations and values change over time, and some of these changes may require rewriting a will.

4. List specific gifts. If a person wishes to leave certain items of property to specific heirs, it is important to describe the gift, also known as a **bequest** or **legacy**, in such a way that there is no confusion regarding the item. The person may also wish to provide for a substitute gift in the event the item has been lost, stolen, or destroyed. For example, "I leave my gold ring with the one carat ruby encircled with six diamonds to my grandson Bradley Allen Parker, son of Jeffrey and Sandra Parker. If for some reason the ring cannot be given, Bradley Allen shall receive the value of the ring in cash." The will should always include a provision to cover the eventuality that the beneficiary may die first. For example, "Should Bradley Allen Parker die before I do or at the same time, the ring shall be considered part of my residuary estate."

5. List other gifts. Out of the money provided by the estate, a person may wish to make some general gifts of cash. Funds from the estate pay for these gifts. However, since these same estate funds must be used by the family to pay any outstanding bills, the writer of the will should be careful not to make the gifts too large, otherwise the court may reduce the amount of the gifts to ensure that creditors receive payments owed them. Again, the person should make a provision to cover the possibility that the beneficiary may precede him in death. For example, "To my niece Kimberly Ann Parker, I leave the sum of ten thousand dollars ($10,000). Should Kimberly Ann Parker die before I do or at the same time, the money shall be given to Trinity Bible Church of Kennesaw, Georgia."

6. Provide instructions for paying taxes and administrative expenses. It is in this portion of a will that the writer instructs the executor as regards paying taxes and other expenses. If, for example, a person does not want his heirs to sell his 1964 vintage red Ford Mustang convertible to pay the estate's taxes, then he makes that wish known in this section.

7. Provide full authority to the executor. The will should give the executor full power and authority to carry out the provisions of the will including the authority to sell or lease assets, distribute specific and general gifts, and pay the estate's taxes.

FORM AND DETAIL

As concerns form, when a person writes out the rough draft of his will, he should avoid the temptation to use legal-sounding words and leave such wording to an attorney. If the will is more than one page long, each page should bear a page number and the sequence (e.g., "page 3 of 4"). This format makes it difficult for unscrupulous potential beneficiaries to add pages after the fact. The writer of the will should also initial or sign each page and write all numbers in numerals and in words (e.g., "I leave to my son Kenneth one hundred dollars [$100]"). The person creating the will should sign it just after the bottom line of text to make it nearly impossible for someone to add extra lines or paragraphs. The person should sign the will in the presence of at least three others who are not beneficiaries of the will and who are willing to sign as witnesses.

If a person changes his mind about any provision in his will, he must not simply scratch through the appropriate portion and write a new entry. To do so

> Because the state may seal a person's safe-deposit box for several days or weeks upon his death, it is not a wise place to store a will. Rather, a person should keep a will on file with his lawyer or executor.

LAST WILL AND TESTAMENT OF ALAN JOSEPH DOE

Believing that faithful stewardship to my Lord and Savior Jesus Christ is as necessary in death as it is in life, I, Alan Joseph Doe, of 211 Griffin Drive, Bedford Falls, Tennessee, state that this is my last will and testament, revoking all previous wills. On April 24, 1964, after reading Romans 3:23, "For all have sinned, and come short of the glory of God," I realized that I was a sinner. Further realizing that "the wages of sin is death; but the gift of God is eternal life through Jesus Christ our Lord" (Rom. 6:23), I accepted Jesus Christ as my personal Savior in accordance with Romans 10:13: "For whosoever shall call upon the name of the Lord shall be saved." I urge all readers and hearers of this will to claim Jesus Christ as their Savior that they may know the forgiveness of their sins and the gift of eternal life in heaven.

1. EXECUTORS: I appoint my wife, Jonna Doe, executor of this will. I also appoint my friend and business associate Blake Spencer to serve as a substitute in the event that Jonna is unable or unwilling to do so or ceases to do so.

2. GUARDIANS: If Jonna dies before I do or at the same time, I appoint my friends Ken and Janice Jones to serve as guardians of the persons and property of my children until they are eighteen (18) years of age. I also appoint my brother and his wife, Bradley and Rachel Doe, substitute guardians in the event that Ken and Janice are unable or unwilling to act as guardians or cease to do so.

3. SPECIFIC GIFTS: I leave all my tools to my son, Alan Joshua Doe. If the tools no longer exist at the time of my death, Alan shall receive five thousand dollars ($5,000) in cash. To my daughter Ashleigh Janine Doe, I leave all my stock in the IBM Corporation. If the stock no longer exists at the time of my death, Ashleigh shall receive five thousand dollars ($5,000) in cash. To my daughter Bethany Lynn Doe, I leave all my stock in the Mylan Pharmaceuticals Inc. If the stock no longer exists at the time of my death, Bethany shall receive five thousand dollars ($5,000) in cash. Should any recipient of any specific gifts die before I do or at the same time, the specific gifts shall be counted part of my residuary estate.

4. GENERAL GIFTS: I leave to my church, Faith Baptist Church of Bedford Falls, Tennessee, the sum of fifteen thousand dollars ($15,000). Should this gift not be accepted, it shall become part of the residuary estate.

5. RESIDUARY ESTATE: I give all the rest of my property to my wife, Jonna. If she dies before I do or at the same time, I give all this property in equal parts to my children. If my wife and my children die before I do or at the same time, I leave all this property to my brother, Bradley Doe.

6. TAXES AND ADMINISTRATIVE EXPENSES: All taxes and expenses related to my estate are to be paid out of the residuary estate.

7. EXECUTOR'S OPTIONS: To expeditiously carry out the distribution of my estate, I give my executor full power to sell, lease, mortgage, reinvest, or otherwise dispose of the assets in my estate.

Signed _____ Date Signed _____

WITNESSES: At Alan Doe's request, we met on the date inserted above to witness his signing of this will. With all of us present at the same time, he signed it and stated that it was his last will.

Signed _____ Address _____

Signed _____ Address _____

Signed _____ Address _____

TRUSTS

Establishing a trust is a common method for people to reserve portions of their estates (usually large amounts of cash, securities, or property) for relatives or charities. A trust is an arrangement that gives a person control of the property involved and a charge to manage it for the good of the intended beneficiary. The one responsible for managing a trust is called the trustee. The benefactor (or grantor) may choose a responsible and capable relative, friend, or associate to serve as trustee for the beneficiary, or banks often serve in this position. A trustee accepts a legal obligation to manage the trust and may be held liable for financial losses due to mismanagement.

Testamentary trusts are those established by the dictates of a person's will after death. The grantor may also establish trusts and see that they become operational before his death, in which case they are *inter vivos*, or living trusts.

The most common purpose of a trust is to make provision for dependent children, who as minors cannot receive a bequest directly from the estate. The grantor may then specify the time and other conditions for paying trust funds to the beneficiary. A grantor may also set up trusts for beneficiaries who are incapable of handling money properly or wisely themselves. In addition, a grantor may establish a trust to support a charitable organization. Usually in this situation, the trust manager periodically distributes earnings from the trust fund to the organization, thereby ensuring that the gifts of the grantor continue long after his death.

may make the entire will invalid. Instead, he would need to file a **codicil**, or an amendment to the original will. Because codicils have virtually the same requirements as an original will, it would be better to draw up an entirely new will.

Because situations such as financial holdings, number of children, names, and the like change from time to time, it is wise to periodically review one's will and rewrite it as necessary.

For married couples it is wise to draw up *three* separate wills—one for the husband, one for the wife, and one for them jointly should they die at the same time. Under laws of **dower**, state courts may legally override a will if the share of the estate left to the spouse is less than the minimum amount the state requires. For example, if a man attempted to leave his wife only $1 of his $1 million estate and if he were living in a state that required the spouse to receive 40 percent of a decedent's estate, the state would declare his spouse legally entitled to $400,000 and would likely award that sum. Almost every state, however, permits parents to disinherit their children.

As Hebrews 9:27 states, "It is appointed unto men once to die." Unless Christ returns to call out His own, Christians, like everyone else, will die. Though it is most important that you be prepared spiritually for that eventuality, you should also be prepared financially. You have learned the types and parts of a will, how to create one, and why it is important that you do. One of the lessons this book endeavors to teach is that life is not about you—and neither is death. You write a will, in part, because you understand this. Your assets belong to God, and you want them distributed as He would see fit. You want your loved ones to be cared for properly. You want certain funds to go to ministries or causes you supported. In many ways a will is a final statement of the Christian's desire to please God and love others.

REVIEW
QUESTIONS

1. Why is the writing of a will the first step in a comprehensive financial plan?
2. What are three ways in which a will may be completed?
3. List the major provisions of a will.

TERMS

last will and testament	294
estate	294
guardians	295
statutory will	295
executor	295
administrator	295
bequest	296
legacy	296
codicil	298
dower	298

CHAPTER FIFTEEN
FISCAL POLICY

15A GOVERNMENTAL SPENDING — 301

15B TAXATION — 308

15C GOVERNMENTAL BORROWING — 313

A revolution of sorts occurred in the United States in the early 1930s. It was a quiet revolution, not consisting of violent conflicts and nightly news headlines. This revolution was one of attitude, and the battlefield was within the minds of the American people. Though having once believed that the only responsibilities of their government were to maintain military and police forces and to provide a limited number of public goods, Americans began to demand that their government pull the nation out of its economic morass.

This outcry, born of the deepest economic depression ever experienced in the United States, precipitated the extensive use of fiscal policy. **Fiscal policy** refers to the ability of the government to affect output (gross domestic product) and employment through the way it spends, taxes, and borrows.

To understand fiscal policy, you must understand the business cycle, the perpetual increase and decrease in real GDP (see Ch. 13). Obviously, periods of economic decline are undesirable because they include reductions in national income, increases in unemployment, and declines in standards of living. Likewise, periods of economic prosperity can be equally harmful. If real GDP grows too quickly, the economy may "overheat." That is, the nation's ability to purchase goods and services may outstrip its ability to produce them, resulting in growing inflation. Fiscal policy attempts to keep this cycle of economic decline and prosperity in check.

Keynes (KANEZ)

In 1936 British economist John Maynard Keynes developed the basic idea of fiscal policy in his book *The General Theory of Employment, Interest, and Money*. Keynes's ideas, later dubbed **Keynesian economics**, hinge on the premise that alternating periods of excessive and insufficient demand for the nation's production cause the peaks and troughs in the business cycle. Therefore, according to Keynes, the government should intervene in the economy to regulate demand.

During periods of economic expansion (periods of heavy demand for goods), the government should seek to lessen national demand by reducing its own purchases of goods and services. It also should increase taxes, thereby decreasing consumers' purchasing power and weakening their demand for more and more goods. The reduction of governmental spending combined with an increase in taxes would lead to a federal budget surplus, which the government should hold in reserve against the day of economic decline. Then,

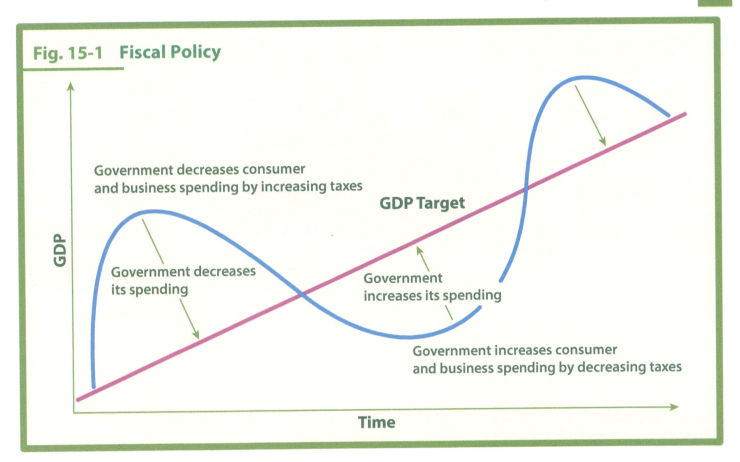

Fig. 15-1 Fiscal Policy

according to Keynes, during the periods of economic decline the government should "reverse gears" by increasing its spending while reducing taxes to encourage consumer spending and boost demand for goods and services.

15A GOVERNMENTAL SPENDING

> It is the highest impertinence and presumption, therefore, in kings and ministers to pretend to watch over the economy of private people, and to restrain their expense, either by sumptuary laws, or by prohibiting the importation of foreign luxuries. They are themselves always, and without any exception, the greatest spendthrifts in the society. Let them look well after their own expense, and they may safely trust private people with theirs. If their own extravagance does not ruin the state, that of the subject never will.
>
> Adam Smith, *An Inquiry into the Nature and Causes of the Wealth of Nations*

The first tool the government can use in its effort to control the economy is to manage its own spending, but how exactly does the government spend its money? An obvious answer is that it purchases the goods and services it needs to operate. Congress buys everything from paper clips to space shuttles, and it pays for the services of its employees. Its payroll reaches down to the lowest-level congressional staff member and extends as high as the White House.

In addition to purchasing goods and services, the government makes transfer payments—payments of money for which the government receives nothing in exchange. Transfer payments include

Maintaining the national park system is one of the government's expenses.

Governmental daycare programs are included in governmental spending.

FRANK & ERNEST © 2010 Thaves. Used By permission of UNIVERSAL UCLICK for UFS. All rights reserved.

food stamps and other income maintenance programs, social security benefits, unemployment compensation, and farm subsidies.

Whenever a discussion about governmental spending arises, three issues invariably dominate the conversation: the size of the national budget, the programs that the government supports, and the way dollars flow through the economy after they leave the government's hands.

THE NATIONAL BUDGET

In 2015 the federal government spent a total of $3.8 trillion on goods and services. While amounts this large are difficult to comprehend, the $3.8 trillion represents only about 20 percent of the total spending in the United States. Figure 15-2 shows the various categories of spending by the federal government and the percentage of the total each category represents. The largest portion (33%) of federal spending goes to the Social security, unemployment & labor category.

Another important item in the federal budget is interest on the national debt. Just as consumers pay interest on money they borrow from banks, so the government

Fig. 15-2 Federal Governmental Spending, 2015

	$ Spent (in billions)	% of total budget
Social Security, Unemployment & Labor	$1,275.7	33%
Medicare & Health	1,051.8	27
Military	609.3	16
Interest on Debt	229.2	6
Veterans' Benefits	160.6	4
Food & Agriculture	135.7	4
Education	102.3	3
Transportation	85	2
Housing & Community	61.5	2
International Affairs	50.2	1
Energy & Environment	44.8	1
Science	29.8	1
Total	3,835.9	100

Source: OMB, National Priorities Project, www.nationalpriorities.org
Note: Components may not add to total due to rounding.

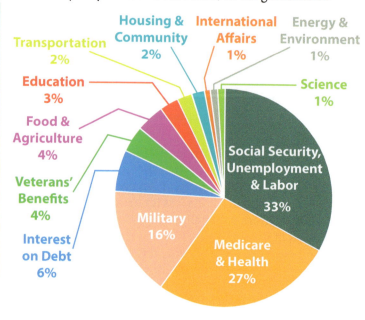

must pay interest on the capital it borrows. In 2015 the federal government paid out over $229 billion in interest. This item is important because it is payment for goods and services the government has already received and is therefore money it cannot use for current needs (like paying off a credit card balance). Economists and policymakers have expressed concern about the growth of this figure because it represents an expenditure that the government must pay without receiving anything tangible in return.

THE EXPENDITURE MULTIPLIER

You have learned how the money multiplier acts in such a way that dollars deposited into financial institutions are constantly lent and redeposited, with each round increasing the money supply a little more. A similar situation occurs with spending on goods and services. A dollar spent has a tendency to become more than a dollar's worth of income in the overall economy. After receiving their paychecks, people tend to save a little of their income and spend the rest. Merchants who subsequently receive consumers' money tend to do the same, saving a little and spending the rest. On and on the process continues, providing income and jobs.

The portion of each dollar that the average person spends is called the **marginal propensity to consume (MPC)**. If the average person spends 85¢ of each dollar he earns (85% of his income), the MPC is 0.85. On the other hand, the percentage of each dollar that the average consumer saves is known as the **marginal propensity to save (MPS)**. The MPS will always be 1 minus the MPC. If the average person spends 85 percent of his income, then by definition he is saving 1 − 0.85, or 15 percent. The MPC makes the income multiplication process possible. Let us assume, for example, that the nation's MPC

Fig. 15-3 The Expenditure Multiplier in Action

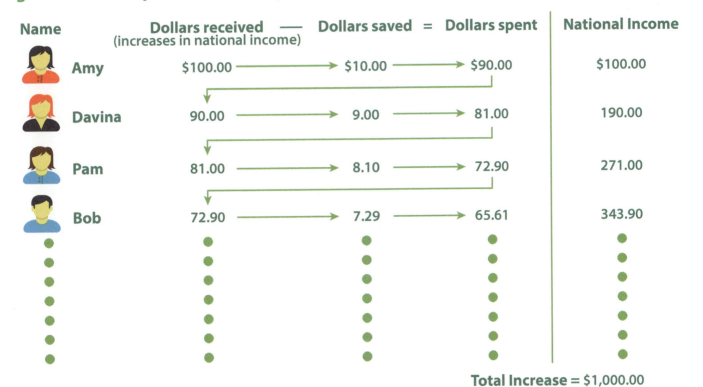

Total Increase = $1,000.00

is 0.90. Amy, a bright high-school senior, wins an essay contest and receives a $100 prize. Figure 15-3 illustrates how Amy's prize check initially increases the nation's income by $100. In keeping with the national MPC of 0.90, Amy purchases $90 in goods from Davina, the owner of a clothing store. After the sale, Davina's income goes up by $90; hence, national income rises by an additional $90. Davina later spends $81 (90% of $90) and saves $9. Eventually this process creates income for many people. This is the cycle that economists know as the **expenditure multiplier**.

Notice how Amy's $100 prize actually turned into $1,000 of income for the nation as a whole. If you wanted to find out how a given amount would affect national income without having to go through each cycle, you could use the expenditure multiplier formula:

$$\text{amount initially received} \times \frac{1}{(1 - \text{MPC})} = \text{total change in national income.}$$

In Amy's case,

$$\$100 \times \frac{1}{(1 - .90)} = \$100 \times \frac{1}{(.10)}$$

$$\$100 \times \frac{1}{(.10)} = \$100 \times 10$$

$$\$100 \times 10 = \$1,000$$

The expenditure multiplier is of great importance to the government in its attempts to level out the business cycle. By increasing or decreasing its own spending, the government may either pull the nation out of a recession or cool down an overheating economy.

Consider the following scenario of a government's fighting recession. Governmental economists notice that the nation's GDP is $100 billion lower than they think it should be. If the nation's MPC is 0.90, Congress would need to spend only $10 billion to raise the GDP by the desired $100 billion, but how should the government

Congress uses its spending power both to control the economy and to provide necessary goods and services.

spend that money? Since the purpose of the spending is to boost national income and GDP by $100 billion, it would not really matter how the $10 billion enters the system. Some policymakers would want the funds spent on social programs, while others would advocate earmarking the money for additional defense spending or business incentives.

Conversely, if an economy is heading toward higher inflation, the government would attempt to use the expenditure multiplier process in reverse. Policymakers, responding to estimates that national income needed to decline by $100 billion, would decrease governmental spending by $10 billion.

PROBLEMS WITH GOVERNMENTAL SPENDING AS A TOOL OF FISCAL POLICY

During the early 1930s, Keynesian economic theory seemed to be a refreshing change from Adam Smith's free-market principles. During periods of national economic distress, free-market capitalism promised that the economy would stabilize itself if given enough time. However, with Keynes's ideas it appeared that the nation had found a quick cure to the economic downturns in the business cycle. If the economy began sliding into a recession, Congress would need only to increase its spending slightly and let the expenditure multiplier work its magic. If, on the other hand, Congress got too carried away and overexpanded the economy, it would need only to reduce spending.

When Keynesian policies failed to pull the nation out of the Great Depression and later were unable to cure even mild recessions and inflations, it was clear that something was wrong with Keynes's "new economics." Economists have identified four critical problems that make it difficult for the government to control the economy.

Depression refugees on a New Mexican highway in the 1930s

Problem #1: Time Lags

Congress frequently puts off fiscal policy issues and then delays further by spending an exorbitant amount of time debating possible solutions. By the time its members finally agree on a solution, that solution no longer matches the problem. Time lags caused by debate, political maneuvering, and compromise often render many decisions on fiscal policy useless.

Problem #2: An Uncertain Multiplier

According to Keynesian theory the expenditure multiplier enables Congress to stimulate the economy to a greater degree than its original spending would do. Likewise, if Congress wished to slow down a rapidly accelerating economy, it would need only to reduce its spending to a fraction of the total decrease deemed necessary. Keynesian theory fails, however, because it is not possible for governmental economists to gauge the multiplier with any great precision, and without that knowledge it is impossible to predict with any degree of accuracy the full effect of an increase or reduction in governmental spending.

Problem #3: Politics

Theoretically, the cure for recession is for the government to reduce taxes and increase spending, while its inflationary counterpart calls for an increase in taxes and a cut in governmental expenditures. Such theory works well on paper but fails miserably in political reality. Whereas most politicians are happy to cut taxes and boost spending on governmental programs to battle recession, they are extremely reluctant to take the opposite actions during inflationary periods. Many view raising taxes and cutting governmental spending as political suicide. On the contrary, political success requires

FLEECING THE NATION

The growing national debt stifles business expansion and greatly concerns many American taxpayers. The budget deficit seems out of control. Why? Senator William Proxmire of Wisconsin pointed to one major culprit in 1975 when he began issuing what he called Golden Fleece Awards, monthly recognitions of ridiculous governmental expenditures. The first award went to the National Science Foundation for using $84,000 in federal funds for a study of why people fall in love. One obvious way to help fight national debt is to eliminate governmental waste and inefficiency. While this method of reducing the debt may be naturally appealing, a further examination reveals that it is not easy to accomplish.

In the 1980s Americans watched as governmental expenditures doubled to over $1 trillion per year and budget deficits skyrocketed. The Reagan administration began an attempt to cut waste in 1982 by appointing a group of private businessmen to study federal finances and find ways to save money. The group, known as the Grace Commission (because of its chairman, J. Peter Grace), reported two years later that "the government is run horribly." They cited examples such as the Pentagon's paying $91 for screws that could have been bought at any hardware store for a few cents as well as spending enormous sums for inexpensive spare parts. They noted many instances of inefficiency, including the processing of a letter in one cabinet department that took forty-seven days and fifty-five to sixty people to produce. Also, they pointed out many cases of continuing unneeded expenses. These included funds for maintaining obsolete military bases, post offices in very small towns, and Veterans Administration's health facilities that cost two to three times as much as similar private facilities. A final major recommendation was that pensions for retired governmental employees, which are often far more generous than those in the private sector, be pared down to reasonable levels.

Action to eliminate such abundant governmental waste should be swift, but it is not. For one thing, governmental bureaucracy makes corrective measures, such as streamlining slowly produced, labor intensive letters, difficult. For another, members of Congress rarely refuse to support legislation that offers federal funding to their constituents. For example, they regularly block military base closings in their states or districts, and they regularly supply funds for ridiculous programs in order to win votes. Such programs, often termed "pork barrel" legislation, have included a Massachusetts congressman's seeking to appropriate $60,000 for the Belgian Endive Research Center at the University of Massachusetts and a North Dakota senator's supporting a provision to require the government to buy $10 million worth of sunflower oil. Members of Congress often engage in political favor swapping and back scratching to pass these absurd requests, which become law by being attached as riders to important bills. The president must either pass the entire bill or veto the important legislation along with the riders.

Although some policies could possibly prevent bureaucratic waste and create greater efficiency and accountability, there seems to be little hope of significant improvement. One option that offered a possible remedy became law on January 1, 1997. It allowed the president to veto individual line items of bills that carried too many riders; however, in February 1998, the Supreme Court ruled that law unconstitutional. Another possible solution would be to require Congress to pass all appropriations as separate bills, thus eliminating the "lard-filled" riders. Again, however, it is unlikely that Congress would pass such self-limiting legislation.

that politicians constantly increase spending and reduce taxes regardless of the economic conditions.

Problem #4: The Source of Additional Spending

At first a person might believe governmental spending is a good way to level out the business cycle. However, it is important to recall one of the central lessons of economics: every choice has a cost. When considering governmental spending as a fiscal tool, a person must ask, Who is paying for it, and, more specifically, from where does the government get the money to spend? Though many Americans seemingly believe that the government can spend money, create jobs, and expand the economy at no cost, the truth is that Congress can spend only the money that it borrows, receives in taxes, or creates through its monetary policies. Because excessive use of monetary policy causes inflation, taxation and borrowing become Congress's chief sources of revenue.

Politicians are quick to support heavy governmental spending, such as that for Johnson's Great Society programs in the 1960s, even though the spending fuels inflation.

Let us assume that the MPC is 0.90 and that the government attempts to expand the economy by spending $10 billion. According to the expenditure multiplier, this should become $100 billion. Such a move should create millions of jobs. Without a doubt the government would be praised for its action, but what about the opportunity cost? The government cannot create jobs cost free. Where did it get the job-creating money? If the government had to increase personal taxes by $10 billion, then consumers would become $10 billion poorer, and the economy as a whole would have $100 billion less in income. The two actions of taxing and spending would offset each other. Therefore, in reality, the government created no new employment; it merely redistributed it.

If Congress taxes business firms, instead of the public, for the $10 billion, then firms will have that much less money with which to pay employees and purchase new machines, inventory, and buildings. Again, the increase in the GDP caused by governmental spending will be offset by a decrease in business investment. In short, Congress may be able to create some jobs, but it will eliminate others in the process. Taxation, then, cannot create more jobs for the economy as a whole without destroying other jobs in the process. Borrowing, the alternative to taxation, has detrimental effects as well; you will examine those later in this chapter.

SECTION REVIEW 15A

1. Who was the British economist that developed the concept of fiscal policy?
2. According to the proponents of fiscal policy, what two steps should be taken in periods of economic decline?
3. What economic term refers to the portion of each dollar that the average person chooses to spend?
4. What four problems are associated with using governmental spending as a tool of fiscal policy?

15B TAXATION

There is no art which one government sooner learns of another, than that of draining money from the pockets of the people.

Adam Smith, *An Inquiry into the Nature and Causes of the Wealth of Nations*

Immediately after a people establishes its governing authority, that government establishes a system of taxation to cover the expenses it incurs in fulfilling its role. Since the 1930s, however, the US government has used its powers of taxation as a tool of fiscal policy.

SOURCES OF TAX REVENUES

In 2014 the US government received over $3,000 billion in tax receipts. Figure 15-4 illustrates the size and importance of various sources. Personal income taxes constitute the greatest source of tax revenue for the federal government. The government deducts most personal income taxes from workers' incomes before they receive their paychecks.

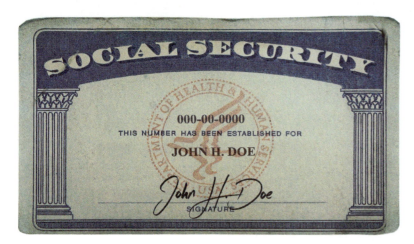

The **Federal Insurance Contribution Act (FICA)** requires social security taxes, and the government also deducts these from paychecks before workers receive them, but on a slightly different basis. Employees pay a percentage of their income (up to a certain maximum income) that the employer then matches and sends to the government. Although not designed to be a complete retirement program, social security taxes provide retirement benefits for older Americans and disability income for survivors of employees who have contributed to the system.

Corporations must also pay taxes on their income, but these taxes come out of the firms' profits after all other expenses have been paid. Many business firms are able to minimize their tax burden by planning expenses in such a way as to reduce reported profits. In 2006, business firms paid out over $370.2 billion in corporate taxes.

A final source of revenue is excise taxes. An **excise tax** is a tax the government levies on the sale of certain targeted consumer goods, such as gasoline, alcoholic beverages, and cigarettes.

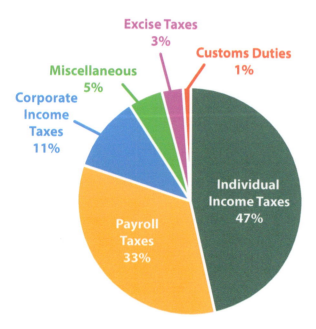

Fig. 15-4	Federal Tax Revenue Sources, 2015	
	Total (in billions)	% of receipts
Individual Income Taxes	$1,480.0	47%
Payroll Taxes	1,070.0	33
Corporate Income Taxes	341.7	11
Miscellaneous	158.6	5
Excise Taxes	95.9	3
Customs Duties	36.8	1
Total	3,183.0	100

Source: OMB, National Priorities Project, www.nationalpriorities.org
Note: Components may not add to total due to rounding.

FRANK & ERNEST © 2006 Thaves. Used By permission of UNIVERSAL UCLICK for UFS. All rights reserved.

TYPES OF TAXES

Not all taxes are meant to apply equally to all people. The current US tax system classifies taxes by what proportion of a person's or a business firm's income the government takes, which changes as that income rises.

Proportional Taxes

A **proportional tax** is one in which all people, no matter how great or small their income, pay the same percentage of their earnings. For example, if the government were to bill income taxes at a rate of 10 percent, a person would have to pay $1,000 on an income of $10,000 or $1 million on an income of $10 million. The most common example of a proportional tax is a flat tax, which taxes everyone's income at the same percentage rate.

Progressive Taxes

A **progressive tax** is one that takes a greater percentage of a person's income as his income increases. A tax would be progressive if one person had to pay $1,000 on an income of $10,000 (10%) while another paid $3 million on an income of $10 million (30%). The personal income tax in the United States is an example of a progressive tax. It arises from a philosophy called the ability-to-pay principle. The **ability-to-pay principle** defines a tax as being fair if the taxing authority levies it on those who have the ability to pay, whether or not benefits received are proportionate to the amount paid.

As you read earlier, Keynesian economic theory holds that the government can smooth the business cycle by reducing its spending during periods of economic overexpansion and increasing its spending when the economy slips into recession. Another tool of the government is its ability to tax. According to Keynes the government should tax away consumers' greater purchasing power during periods of economic expansion. Conversely, as consumers' incomes decline during periods of recession, the government should decrease the tax rate.

It is in this regard that some economists view the personal income tax as an "automatic stabilizer." As the economy expands and prices rise, increasing paychecks cause additional upward pressure on prices. To relieve this pressure, the progressive feature of the personal income tax allows the government to take a higher percentage of each additional dollar consumers receive. On the other hand, as

The IRS (logo above) is responsible for collecting taxes.

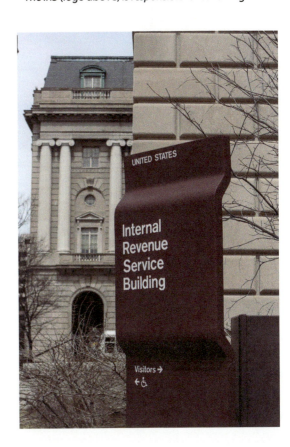

LAFFER CURVE

It seems logical that as the government increases its tax rates, its tax revenues would also increase. While that is the case for a given range of tax increases, there comes a point at which the government's revenues actually begin to fall. Why? Because of the disincentive effects of taxes. To illustrate this, Dr. Arthur Laffer of the University of Southern California developed the Laffer Curve.

To construct the Laffer Curve, an economist labels a graph with the heading "Government Revenue" on the vertical axis and "Tax Rate" (ranging from 0% to 100%) on the horizontal axis. The Laffer Curve is an inverted U with one end touching the 0% tax rate and the other touching the 100%. This illustrates the obvious conclusion that if the government has a 0% tax rate, it will receive $0 in revenues. Likewise, at a 100% tax rate, the government's revenues will be $0 because no one will bother working. As the tax rate increases from 0%, tax revenues increase up to a point. After this point, its revenues decline. At what point is the peak reached? No one is sure because each person has his own Laffer Curve.

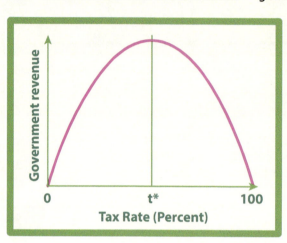

incomes decline during recession, the government allows people to keep more of their incomes through the lower personal tax rates.

Regressive Taxes

A **regressive tax** is one that takes a smaller percentage of a person's income as his income rises. For example, the tax on gasoline is a regressive tax. While at first glance it looks like a proportional tax—with everyone, regardless of income, paying the same amount of tax per gallon—it actually takes a smaller percentage of a buyer's income as his income rises. Why? People do not increase their purchase of gasoline to the same degree that their incomes rise. Figure 15-5 shows typical results if the gasoline tax were 10¢ per gallon. The principle upon which policymakers base a regressive tax is the **benefit principle**, which says that a tax should be paid by those who receive the benefits of the tax revenue.

PROBLEMS WITH TAXATION AS A TOOL OF FISCAL POLICY

Obviously, the use of taxation as a means of altering the economy presents many of the same problems that plague governmental spending. While it also suffers from the problems of time lags, politics, and the effects of an uncertain multiplier, taxation poses two additional, unique problems.

Problem #1: Effect on the National Work Ethic

The traditional work ethic in the United States holds that work is morally good and that if one works hard enough, is frugal in his spending habits, and saves his money, he can enjoy a progressively

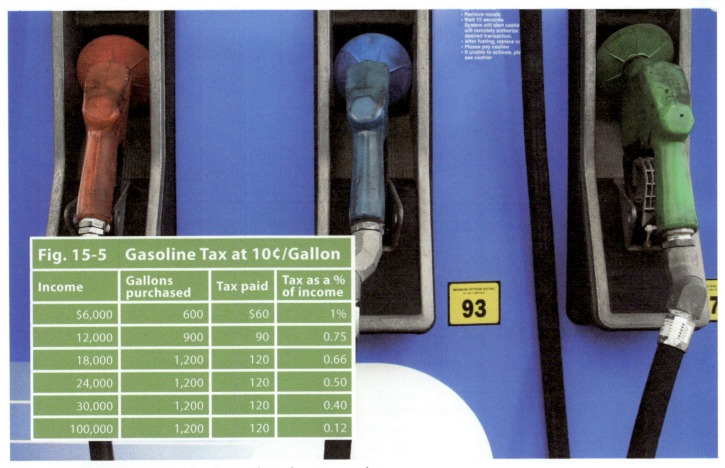

Fig. 15-5	Gasoline Tax at 10¢/Gallon		
Income	Gallons purchased	Tax paid	Tax as a % of income
$6,000	600	$60	1%
12,000	900	90	0.75
18,000	1,200	120	0.66
24,000	1,200	120	0.50
30,000	1,200	120	0.40
100,000	1,200	120	0.12

higher standard of living. Fiscal policy, with its short-term solutions, may have the undesired effect of undermining this belief. There exists an obvious disincentive to work harder and produce more when the laborer realizes that he will receive a progressively lower percentage of his earnings. If his increased earnings will simply move him into a higher tax bracket, in which he will have to pay out more of his earnings and not really see a net gain in his income, the typical laborer sees little reason to increase his productivity. The decrease in the work-ethic incentive increases part-time employment, decreases productivity, and increases the use of barter to avoid reporting income-producing transactions.

Problem #2: Confusion in the Marketplace

A business firm bases many financial decisions on the effect the decision will have on the firm's tax burden. In the 1970s, farmland values were high. Tax incentives, coupled with low-interest governmental loans, influenced farmers to borrow heavily to purchase agricultural equipment. After a few years, farmers who were ready to trade in their used equipment found that it commanded an attractive price. While they could have used the income from the sale of their old equipment to pay for a majority of their new higher-priced equipment, tax incentives made it more attractive for them to borrow the money again. Then, 1981 saw an end to these tax incentives. Between 1981 and 1984 exports of grain and soybeans plummeted, commodity prices fell, interest rates escalated, and land values declined by 25 percent. Maturing debts forced many farmers to refinance their loans at higher interest rates. Other farmers, whose land value had declined,

Tax incentives in the 1970s encouraged farmers to buy too much equipment on credit.

JOHN MAYNARD KEYNES (1883–1946)
Proponent of Fiscal Policy

Coming from a well-educated family and receiving his advanced instruction at Eton and King's College, Cambridge, the British economist John Maynard Keynes developed a quick, analytical mind and a sharp tongue. He was swift to condemn economists and politicians for actions that he believed would hurt the economy. One such open criticism appeared in 1919 when he wrote *The Economic Consequences of the Peace*, an attack on the reparations agreements made at Versailles at the end of World War I. Though Keynes was chided for his rebuke of eminent world leaders on this matter, his economic views soon gained prominence as many of his insights proved correct.

In contrast to the economists of the past who had maintained that, in the long run, the basic principles of economics would lead the market to adjust naturally to an equilibrium point, Keynes was concerned with making immediate economic progress during times of economic imbalance. Keynes observed that "in the long run we are all dead," and therefore something should be done to improve the situation now.

The economic problems of the Great Depression gave Keynes the opportunity to advance his new approach. He set forth a macroeconomic view of the situation, noting that the major problem of the economy at that time was that manufacturers were producing more than consumers were buying. The key to solving the problem, then, would be increasing spending to a level at which demand would rise to meet the supply. Keynes then prescribed ways in which the government could increase the flow of spending by increasing governmental expenditures and encouraging consumers to spend their money. Keynes's work *The General Theory of Employment, Interest, and Money*, published in 1936, elaborated on his view.

The idea that the government should try to fine-tune the economy flew in the face of traditional laissez-faire thought. Nonetheless, the hardships and despair of the Depression brought popular support for measures that might help alleviate the economic difficulties. Thus many of the New Deal measures introduced by Franklin D. Roosevelt grew out of Keynesian thought. Since the Depression era, several flaws and shortcomings have been revealed in Keynesian economics; however, the basic idea of the government's taking an active role in the economy has remained.

could not obtain refinancing because they now lacked sufficient collateral, and many were forced into bankruptcy.

Taxes on gains from savings and investment also confuse the market. In its attempt to boost the nation's MPC, the government has systematically penalized investing in capital assets, such as stocks, bonds, and homes, through high taxes. Capital-gains taxes are taxes imposed on the profit investors realize on the sale of such assets. In reality, however, the "profit" may be only an increase in the selling price caused by inflation, such as the sale of a home after several years of inflation. Though the homeowner sold the home for more than he paid for it, he did not earn a profit in terms of purchasing power; the home's price only reflected the rate of inflation. When the tax penalty for such a sale is greater than the reward, households shift their dollars from investing to buying consumer goods, thereby reducing the pool of funds available for businesses to borrow for expansion.

Taxes on investment such as stock can cause investors to reduce saving for the future.

SECTION REVIEW 15B

1. What is the greatest source of tax revenue for the federal government?
2. Under which type of tax does everyone pay the same percentage of his earnings? Give an example of this type of tax.
3. Under which type of tax is a greater percentage taken from those with a higher income? Give an example of this type of tax.
4. Under which type of tax is a smaller percentage taken as a person's income rises? Give an example of this type of tax.
5. What are the two distinct problems with using taxation as a tool of fiscal policy?

15C GOVERNMENTAL BORROWING

It seems almost impossible to stimulate the economy without slowing it to the same degree. If the government wants to spend more, taxpayers will have to spend less, offsetting in the long run any gains the additional governmental spending brought about. Keynesian economists developed what they thought to be the answer to this problem by forging the third link in the fiscal policy chain, governmental borrowing. They reasoned that through borrowing, the government could increase its spending without taxing consumers or businesses.

"PUMP PRIMING"

Keynesians believe that during a recession the government could borrow money and spend it. The expenditure would boost national income via the expenditure multiplier, and the economic momentum would keep the GDP rising. Then when the economy became prosperous again, the government would raise taxes and use the increased revenue to retire the debt.

Thus, according to a famous Keynesian analogy, the government would use debt to "prime" the economy, much as the old-time farmer primed a water pump with a bucket of water. After the pump began working, the farmer refilled the bucket and set it aside. In a similar fashion Keynesians expected the government's priming to cause the economy to expand and prosper, and the government could then tap into that prosperity to repay the debt.

Old-fashioned hand pumps worked by creating a vacuum that pulled water out of a well. When the pump had not been used for some time, its inner workings would become dry. The pump then needed water to help seal air out of its chamber. This seal allowed the pump to create the vacuum. Thus the water used to prime the pump helped to get the device to work on its own. In the economic analogy, the government pours some spare money into the economy to help get the economy to function better on its own.

PROBLEMS WITH GOVERNMENTAL BORROWING AS A TOOL OF FISCAL POLICY

The analogy of governmental borrowing to priming an antique hand pump may be attractive and nostalgic, but it has serious flaws.

Problem #1: There Is No Reserve "Bucket" of Idle Money

According to Keynesian economic thought, the idle funds waiting to prime the economic pump are those dollars that households save. Keynesians believe that savings are wasted money because they do not purchase job-creating goods and services. By borrowing the funds from the financial market, the government becomes the liberator of those captive, idle dollars and puts them back into service.

However, banks and other financial intermediaries do not accept deposits only to let them sit idle. Rather, they use deposited funds to make loans to business firms to purchase capital that will later generate enough income to pay off the loans and provide a profit. If the government channels these funds to itself, it will stimulate the economy to a certain extent through increased governmental spending; however, it will also slow the economy to the same degree by the reduction in business investment.

Problem #2: Governmental Borrowing Becomes Addictive

Keynesian theory states that the government should borrow to level out declines in the business cycle and pull the economy out of recession. The government can then retire the debt later when the economy has expanded. Politicians, on the other hand, desire to stimulate the economy constantly to produce jobs for the voting public. This attitude has led to more borrowing than debt reduction. In fact, the US federal budget has been in deficit all but one of the last forty years. Occasionally, a presidential candidate will suggest that it is necessary to increase taxes to retire the tremendous governmental debt. He may argue that the economy has recovered sufficiently from any recession and that it is time to pay the debt. However, such suggestions generally do not result in an electoral victory. Sadly, governmental borrowing is no longer reserved for economic emergencies; it has become a way of life.

Problem #3: Governmental Borrowing Destroys a Nation's Future Productivity

Chapter 1 emphasizes that every decision provides both an opportunity benefit and an opportunity cost. The opportunity benefits of governmental borrowing are immediate and obvious: jobs for the unemployed, food for the poor, shelter for the homeless, and clothing for the destitute. Less obvious but far more important is the opportunity cost. What does a nation forgo when it chooses to borrow from the financial market? For what would the money have otherwise been used? Business firms would have borrowed the funds to build larger factories and purchase more-efficient equipment. They too would have created jobs and income for the hungry, homeless, and destitute; however, the result would be less immediate since it requires time to build new factories.

The short-term benefits of governmental borrowing are deceptively attractive, but the long-term effects are truly debilitating. When the borrowed money runs out, the government must terminate civil service jobs. Consequently, the food, shelter, and clothing supported by those jobs disappear. Business firms, on the other hand, use the funds to create long-term jobs. By building new or renovating old factories and equipment, they create products that generate revenues sufficient to pay off loans and provide employment for years into the future. By borrowing from the financial market, the government succumbs to short-term opportunity benefits that are eventually overshadowed by a far greater opportunity cost—the loss of future national productivity.

The biblical economist cannot embrace economic policies that will benefit him at the expense of following generations. Christians need to be prudent and foresee problems (Prov. 22:3), pursuing and advocating fiscal policies that do not produce immediate gain at the expense of future difficulties. The believer, far better than the unregenerate person, understands the consequences of the tradeoff between a short-term gain and a long-term consequence. He knows that it does not profit a man to gain the world only to lose his soul (Matt. 16:26).

You may have found much in this chapter informative but also much that prompted thought, often strongly for or against a particular aspect of fiscal policy. Now you understand better why fiscal policy is often a contentious topic amongst politicians and the voting public. This chapter introduced you to John Maynard Keynes, whose economic principles have become a driving force in American governmental economic policymaking. His emphasis on short-term gains influenced policy during the Great Depression and has

PAYING DOWN THE DEBT

Since the late 1930s when President Roosevelt implemented Keynesian economics to lift the United States out of the Great Depression, Americans have increasingly looked to their government for solutions when the economy declines. This dependence on the government for economic support necessitates governmental spending, but the government cannot spend money it does not have. Hence, it must increase its revenues through either increased taxes or borrowed funds. Politicians know that approving tax increases will likely damage their careers, so they seldom pursue that option. As a result, the government has borrowed more and more money and has subsequently increased the national debt to an alarming level.

Keynesian economics is attractive because it provides nearly immediate short-term gains. You recall that Keynes disparaged traditional economic principles with his retort, "In the long run we are all dead." However, while those making policy decisions may not live to see the long-term effects of Keynesian practices, someone else will. For the government to pay its enormous debt, either the tax rate would have to rise sharply or the government would have to limit its spending severely. Neither option is attractive though both will likely become a necessity. The real question is which generation will surrender the short-term gains to pay the long-term debt?

President George W. Bush and his administration desired to cut taxes during his terms in office. While he was able to push a tax-cut initiative through Congress, it failed to stimulate the economy enough for increased tax revenues to allow the government to pay down the debt. Why? Part of the answer lies in the inability of the government to rein in its spending. Knowing the tax cuts would decrease revenues in the short term, Congress would have had to curtail its spending in equal proportion until the long-term effects of the tax cuts began. However, no such decline in spending took place. In addition, President Bush faced unexpected and overwhelming tragedies, such as Hurricane Katrina, 9/11, and the ensuing war on terror. To cover the financial needs of those emergencies, President Bush called for spending that exceeded the levels of any previous president.

continued well beyond that era. You should now have a better understanding of the pros and cons of such an emphasis. Having read how the tools of fiscal policy can alter the nation's business cycle, you should be able to list ways that such altering is profitable but also ways in which it is harmful. Now you know that governmental spending, taxing, and borrowing policies can have beneficial results, yet you now also understand the limits and problems of each. You can see that a constant emphasis on short-term gains and constant policy changes that endeavor to maintain those gains do not eliminate the long-term consequences. They only delay them.

A believer who desires to exercise good stewardship and who wants to love others as himself should look at fiscal policy and all of economics through a biblical lens. He should recognize that the fundamental problems in the world are not economic but spiritual (Gen. 3) and that the only solution to these problems is the return of Jesus Christ (Isa. 11).

SECTION REVIEW 15C

1. How did Keynesians expect governmental borrowing to stimulate the economy?
2. What are the three problems associated with using governmental borrowing as a tool of fiscal policy?

CHAPTER REVIEW

CONTENT QUESTIONS

1. What group is responsible for fiscal policy?
2. What are the three tools of fiscal policy?
3. List the three largest expenditures in the federal budget.
4. Explain the expenditure multiplier. Include terms and definitions.
5. What are the three largest sources of federal tax revenues?
6. What are excise taxes? Give several examples.
7. How do proportional taxes, progressive taxes, and regressive taxes relate to a person's income?
8. Name the two principles on which taxes are based. With which type of tax is each associated?
9. Explain how the metaphor of pump priming relates to Keynesian economics.

APPLICATION QUESTIONS

1. Analyze the current economic climate in the nation. What conditions suggest that the government is following Keynesian economic policies? Note any examples of laissez-faire policies.
2. Discuss how a flat income tax might change an individual's thinking about the individual income tax. Include definitions, examples, and the principles on which the tax would be based.

TERMS

Term	Page
fiscal policy	300
Keynesian economics	300
marginal propensity to consume (MPC)	303
marginal propensity to save (MPS)	303
expenditure multiplier	304
Federal Insurance Contribution Act (FICA)	308
excise tax	308
proportional tax	309
progressive tax	309
ability-to-pay principle	309
regressive tax	310
benefit principle	310

PERSONAL FINANCE

RETIREMENT PLANNING

Many people neglect retirement planning, as they do other aspects of financial planning, until it is too late. A common reason people fail to plan for retirement is uncertainty. After all, how many people in their twenties know how large their families will be, the amount of social security income they can expect to receive, the standard of living they will achieve, and the age at which they will retire? Because of these and other uncertainties, many Americans do not have a systematic retirement plan, and that omission can have tragic results. Consider the following statistics:

- The median income of people aged sixty-five and older is below that of all other age groups.
- Even after adding social security income, many elderly people live below or near the poverty level.
- Those who retire at age sixty-five have a life expectancy of sixteen additional years.

People often wait too long to start building a nest egg for retirement.

To enjoy a financially secure retirement and to avoid becoming a burden upon others, it is imperative to develop a comprehensive retirement plan. A total retirement plan includes an estimation of needs at retirement, such as spending and housing costs, and a determination of an adequate retirement income.

PHASE ONE: ESTIMATION OF NEEDS

Obviously, it is impossible to predict the exact amount of money a person will need for living expenses forty to fifty years from now. However, analysts have observed certain spending trends among the elderly. According to the Bureau of Labor Statistics, in 2011 the average annual expenditures of households aged sixty-five and older equaled $39,173.

Within the categories listed by the Bureau of Labor Statistics, certain trends are evident:

- Expenses for clothing and personal care usually decline because retirees no longer need to pay for work wardrobes, which often consist of higher priced clothing.
- Medical expenses generally tend to increase with age, and health-care costs can become a significant part of the average retiree's budget, especially if the care includes multiple prescription medications.
- Payments for health and life insurance tend to rise as a person ages because of the increased probability of filing claims and the elimination of employer contributions. For some, however, these increases are offset by Medicare.
- As their incomes decline, those retirees who choose to keep their gifts and contributions to churches and other organizations at the same dollar level find that their giving takes up a higher percentage of their total income.
- Paying off a mortgage before retirement reduces the cost of housing; however, increases in property taxes may cause this figure to rise.

As a person ages, his housing needs change. With a growing family and an increased need for space, a larger home is necessary; however, as couples age and their children leave the home, other needs take priority. As their income declines and maintenance and house-cleaning chores become more troublesome, smaller homes or homes in communities offering maintenance services become more desirable. After retirement, the location of housing also becomes

RETIREMENT PLANNING

important. Easy access to church, shopping centers, transportation, and medical facilities becomes a primary consideration for retirees.

The image of the elderly American living out the balance of his days in a rest home has changed. Older Americans are asserting their independence, and their housing preference is one of the biggest reflections of this tendency. Over 90 percent of five thousand Americans surveyed indicate that they want to live in their own homes during retirement.

PHASE TWO: SOURCES OF INCOME

Having estimated his needs at retirement, the person planning for retirement next turns his attention to his sources of income to meet those needs. Many workers have several investment and retirement savings options available. However, once they retire, most of them ultimately rely on the two most common sources of retirement income: government-sponsored social security and private pension plans provided either by the employee himself or by his employer.

Social Security

When most Americans consider postretirement income, the first source that often comes to their minds is social security. **Social security** is a government-mandated, employer/employee-financed retirement and disability plan. Although social security provides a minimal "safety net" of income for elderly Americans, no one should ever consider it the primary source of retirement income.

The government uses a complex formula to determine the amount of each person's social security benefits. The formula enters a person's average earnings over his wage-earning career, the age at which he retired, and the rate of inflation. In addition to the benefits formula, the government may make certain adjustments. For example, there is a reduction in payments before age sixty-seven; therefore, if a person retires at age sixty-two, he permanently reduces his monthly payments by 30 percent of what they would be if he delayed retirement to age sixty-seven. The person who chooses to retire later than age sixty-seven increases his benefits for each month past age sixty-seven. To receive a history of earnings and an estimation of future social security benefits, wage earners may visit their local Social Security Administration office and fill out form SSA-7004. Within approximately one month, a statement will arrive that will show the amount of their benefits, in current dollars, if they were to retire at age sixty-two, sixty-seven, or seventy. If inflation has caused the cost of living to rise from the previous year, social security benefits rise automatically in January.

Many Americans are justifiably concerned about the reliability of social security as part of their retirement income. The social security program is not really a "trust fund" in which, for each American paying into the system, an amount of money is set aside to earn interest until it is needed upon retirement. It is rather a "pay-as-you-go" system, in which employee contributions provide retiree benefits. So, as the number of Americans reaching retirement increases and as retirees live longer, the amount of money needed to pay retirement benefits continues to increase. One study estimated that when the program began in 1945, there were forty-two workers making contributions for every one person drawing benefits. Today, there are just over four workers per recipient. Clearly, the program is becoming less able to cover the retirement benefits that many Americans are expecting, and unless Congress passes a plan to reform the program, there is some question as to how much longer funds will be available. Therefore, it may be best to make plans for retirement without relying on the availability of social security.

Employer-Sponsored Pension Plans

Because the benefits the Social Security Administration pays are minimal and may be subject to political forces, it would be wise for the financial planner to consider personal pension plans. One of the first of such plans to examine is the employer-sponsored pension plan. As they are with life and health insurance, more and more employers are providing retirement funds for their employees. As a person's employer contributes to the fund, the benefits accrue to the employee tax-free.

To ensure that an employee has a long-term interest in his job, employer-sponsored retirement plans have what is known as a **vesting period**; that is, a specified number of years is necessary for the employee to be fully enrolled in the plan and eligible to withdraw from his account upon termination of employment. For most firms, full vesting occurs after seven years at the latest.

Most employer-sponsored retirement plans are **defined-contribution plans**, which provide an individual account for each employee. Each employee receives a document specifying the amount of the employer's contribution to the plan. When the employee retires, he may withdraw the amount in his account, and it is considered taxable at the time of withdrawal. Four specific types of defined-contribution plans exist:

1. Money purchase plan: Each year your employer promises to deposit for you a specific amount, usually a percentage of your wages.

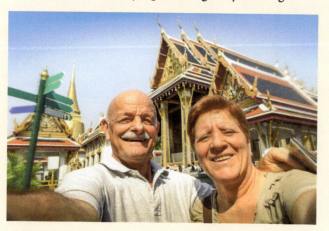

2. Stock plan: As a variation of the money purchase plan, your employer uses the specific contribution to purchase stock in the company under your name. The company holds the shares for you until you choose to retire, at which time you may hold them or sell them at the current market price.

3. Profit-sharing plan: The amount that your employer contributes is dependent upon the profits of the firm.

4. 401(k): Under a **401(k)** an employer makes a contribution to the retirement plan and matches the amount of the contribution with a contribution from the employee's paycheck. The employee does not pay taxes on his contribution until he withdraws the money at retirement, and at that time his taxable income may be lower.

Personal Pension Plans

Besides employer-sponsored pension plans, there exist two popular do-it-yourself pension plans: the individual retirement account (IRA) and the Keogh plan.

An **individual retirement account (IRA)** is a retirement account that individuals open at banks or other financial institutions. The amount that an individual can contribute to an IRA and receive a tax benefit for varies from year to year and according to the person's age and level of income.

A **Keogh plan** is a retirement plan for self-employed people. As with the employer-sponsored 401(k), payments to Keogh accounts are taken as deductions from taxable income.

Keogh (KEE oh)

As a high-school student, you may be tempted to look back at what you have just read and dismiss it as irrelevant. Though it may be difficult to see how social security and IRAs have anything to do with your present life, the reality is that your exposure to this information is important. From the outset, this text has sought to emphasize your need to be a good steward of what God entrusts to you—be that athletic, academic, or artistic talent or sums of money. Part of being a good financial steward is understanding financial planning, which includes comprehending the differences between having a comprehensive financial plan and simply taking a "live one day at a time and see what comes" approach. Perhaps you have read or heard of social security and 401(k)s, but now you have a better understanding of them. Simply because you may not have immediate use for what you have learned from this article is no reason to disregard it. See beyond today and recognize that if Christ does not come and if God allows you to grow old upon this earth, you will have need then for what you are learning now.

REVIEW QUESTIONS

1. Why is retirement planning necessary?
2. What are the four types of employer-sponsored retirement plans?
3. What is the difference between a 401(k) and a Keogh plan?

TERMS

social security	319
vesting period	320
defined-contribution plans	320
401(k)	320
individual retirement account (IRA)	320
Keogh plan	320

Glossary

A

ability-to-pay principle policy that declares a tax to be fair if it is levied on those who have the ability to pay, regardless of the benefits they receive

administrator a court-appointed person entrusted with the disposition of the estate of someone who died without a will

American Stock Exchange (Amex) a lesser-known but still reputable American stock market

amortization schedule a chart displaying the monthly interest costs of a loan at a given rate of interest

anticompetitive takeover a situation in which business firms buy out other firms in their industry to eliminate or reduce competition

appreciating assets goods that increase in value over time

artificial barrier to entry the prevention of a new firm from entering an industry because of governmental regulations

assignment of savings account a loan for which the borrower's savings account serves as collateral

Austrian economics the school of economic thought that advocates a return to Adam Smith's concept of classic liberalism and promotes private ownership of a majority of the nation's factors of production while permitting only minimal governmental intervention

B

bait-and-switch a deceptive advertising technique that draws customers into the business for an advertised product that is unavailable or unsuitable, thereby providing an opportunity to sell a more expensive product

barrier to entry a condition that prevents a new firm from entering an industry and competing on an equal basis with established firms

barter the exchange of one person's goods or services for another's goods or services

base period the initial period of a survey, such as that for consumer prices, against which changes over time are compared

beneficiary the person named on a life insurance policy to receive the proceeds upon the death of the policyholder; the recipient of a trust or legacy

benefit principle policy that says that a tax should be paid by those who receive the benefits of the tax revenue

bequest a gift left by a deceased person to an heir

Better Business Bureau an organization providing information about businesses and their products to consumers and helping consumers gain redress for unjust treatment from businesses

Board of Governors a group selected by the president and confirmed by Congress to guide the actions of the Federal Reserve System

budget a tabulation of income and planned expenditures

budget deficit a situation in which a government, business firm, or individual receives less income than is paid out in expenses

budget surplus a situation in which a government, business firm, or individual receives more income than is paid out in expenses

business cycle an economic condition consisting of alternating periods of rising and falling real GDP, characterized by four phases: expansion, peak, recession, and trough

business investment another name for gross private domestic investment (GPDI)

C

capital *See* real capital

capital goods items that are used to produce consumer goods; also called real capital

capital intensive describes a business firm that uses more automated equipment than human labor

capitalism an economic system in which private individuals own most of the factors of production and make most economic decisions

cartel a group of producers who cooperate to control the price of their goods

cash advance a feature of a bank card that enables the holder to obtain cash from a bank on request while increasing his bank card account debt by that amount

cashier's check a guaranteed check bought by a customer and drawn on the bank itself

cash management the activity of accounting for cash inflows, storing short-term cash balances in the most profitable ways, and the timely payment of one's financial obligations

cash value the amount accumulated in the savings component of a whole life insurance policy

caveat emptor Latin expression meaning "Let the buyer beware!"

cease and desist order a legal order prohibiting a party from continuing a harmful practice

central bank a bank that the government uses to control and accommodate the nation's finances by providing an elastic national currency, serving as the nation's fiscal agent, regulating the nation's private banks, providing a national check-clearing mechanism, serving as a bank to the nation's private banks, and creating money

centralized socialism a form of socialism in which the government is both the central owner and the decision maker in all economic affairs of the state

certificates of deposit (CDs) time deposits that carry a specific maturity date and yield a high rate of interest

certified check a personal check for which the bank guarantees payment

change in demand the shifting of a demand curve experienced when demand for an item increases or decreases regardless of price

change in quantity demanded a situation in which the change in the price of an item causes a change in the number demanded

change in quantity supplied a situation in which the change in the price of an item causes a change in the number supplied

change in supply the shifting of a supply curve that occurs when suppliers are willing to produce more or less of an item regardless of price

charter an authorization for a bank to exist, issued either by the federal government or by the state government

checking account a non-interest-bearing transaction account offered by commercial banks

circular flow model a model depicting the flow of economic goods and services between households, business firms, the government, and financial markets

classic liberal capitalism the form of capitalism allowing the government only minimal ownership of resources and decision-making power

clearinghouse an operation organized to settle accounts between banks and to clear checks or send them to the banks from which they were drawn

codicil an amendment to a will

collateral valuable goods that may be taken by a lender and resold if the borrower does not repay his loan

collision insurance insurance that pays to repair or replace the policyholder's car

collusion agreement among a small number of producers to reduce their output and increase prices

commercial bank a financial institution that accepts deposits and makes commercial and private loans

commission the fee paid for a stockbroker's services

commodity money a commonly used or valued good that serves as a medium of exchange

common stock the most prevalent type of stock that companies offer, represents true ownership of the firm

communism in the economic sense, the most extreme form of socialism, in which all individuals voluntarily contribute their labor for the good of the society while taking from the economy only the goods and services that they truly need

complementary goods items that are usually purchased or used together

compound interest the calculation of interest on reinvested interest as well as on the original principal

comprehensive insurance insurance that protects the homeowner from heavy loss due to misfortunes that generally include fire, theft, windstorms, hail, and lightning damage

consumer durable goods items that have a life expectancy of more than one year

consumer finance companies finance companies that make secured and unsecured personal loans and debt consolidation loans to the general public

consumer goods items that are purchased for personal use

consumer goods/capital goods tradeoff the allocation of limited resources to produce either consumer goods or capital goods

consumerism political action in behalf of consumer rights

consumer nondurable goods items that are expected to be worn out or used up within one year

consumer price index (CPI) a group of figures measuring changes in prices that household consumers pay for their purchases

consumer services intangible products purchased by consumers

consumption borrowing the use of debt to purchase goods that will be consumed almost immediately

consumption expenditures the total expenditures made by all households

contingency an uncertain or unexpected event that may result in unplanned expense

corporation a business entity recognized by the government as separate from its owners or stockholders

correspondent banking an arrangement in which two banks have numerous regular transactions between them and, therefore, hold deposits with one another to aid the check-clearing process

cosigning agreeing to pay the debt of another person if he does not pay it

cost of living adjustment (COLA) an adjustment of wages, payments, and other sums according to inflation levels

cost-push inflation inflation believed to be triggered when a nation's businesses raise their prices, resulting in new demands by consumers for higher wages from their employers

counteradvertising advertising that a firm must produce at its own expense for the purpose of correcting prior false claims in its advertising

credit bureau an organization that keeps consumers' credit records for credit-extending companies to use

credit limit the maximum amount a borrower may draw from an open-end credit account

creditor a lender to whom a debt is owed

credit union a cooperative institution that pools the savings of its members and makes consumer loans available to them

crowding out a situation in which governmental borrowing reduces the financial capital available to business firms

cyclical unemployment unemployment caused by the downside of the business cycle

D

debt consolidation loan a loan used to pay all the borrower's outstanding debts so that his monthly payments may be reduced to that of one loan payment

debtor a borrower who is in debt for the credit he has received

decrease in demand a leftward shift in the demand curve representing a decrease in the willingness of buyers to demand an item at any price

decrease in supply a leftward shift of the supply curve indicating a decrease in the quantity suppliers are willing to produce at any price

deductible an amount that must be paid by a policyholder before his insurance will begin to cover claims

default failure to pay money when it is due

defined-contribution plans employer-sponsored retirement plans that provide an individual account for each employee

demand the number of units of a product that will be bought at a given price

demand curve a graph illustrating the various quantities of an item that are demanded at various prices

demand-pull inflation inflation believed to be triggered when consumers demand more products and the rising demand results in rising prices and wages

demand schedule a tabular model listing various quantities demanded at various prices

depression a severe and prolonged trough phase of the business cycle

diamond-water paradox the riddle that asks which is more valuable, a handful of diamonds or a glass of water, solved by Carl Menger in 1871 when he proposed that value is not inherent in an object but rather is determined by the buyer (*See subjective value*)

differentiated products products that are different from one firm to another

disability income insurance insurance that provides one's family with weekly or monthly payments to replace the income of someone unemployed because of illness or injury

discounting the lending of money to banks by the Federal Reserve System

discount rate the interest rate charged by the Federal Reserve to banks for borrowed money

discouraged workers chronically unemployed people who have been out of work for six months or more

dissaving the action of withdrawing money from an account or borrowing money

dividends a distribution of a portion of the corporation's profits

double coincidence of wants both parties involved in a trade of goods or services wanting what the other has to trade

dower the part of a deceased person's estate that the law requires to be given to his or her spouse

Dow Jones Industrial Average (DJIA) the most well-known American stock index

duopoly an oligopoly composed of two business firms

E

economic cost the value people place on a good or service

economic Darwinism another name for the libertarian view of economic fairness allowing for a "survival of the fittest" in the accumulation of wealth

economic goods items that bear a positive economic cost

economic growth an increase in the quantity of goods and services a nation can produce

economic leveling an equal distribution of the nation's income regardless of each person's ability to contribute to its pool of wealth

economics the science of how and why people, businesses, and governments make the choices that they do

economic services services that bear a positive economic cost

effective interest rate the true rate of interest, derived from compounding interest at the nominal interest rate

egalitarian fairness a viewpoint maintaining that each person in the nation has a right to a part of the nation's wealth simply because he is a part of the human race

elastic currency a money supply that can be expanded or contracted

electronic funds transfer system (EFTS) financial transactions conducted electronically via the Internet

endorse to sign the back of a check to acknowledge its receipt by the payee

entrepreneurship the factor of production denoting the activity of creatively combining natural resources, human labor, and financial capital in unique ways to develop new and useful products and services

equity the increased value of a home (because of inflation or improvements) beyond the amount owed on any outstanding mortgage

escheat laws laws that allow a state to confiscate money from a dormant account

escrow account a sum of money collected by a lender in addition to loan repayments for the purpose of paying for taxes and insurance to protect the mortgaged property

estate the assets and liabilities left by a deceased person

excise tax a tax the government levies on the sale of certain targeted consumer goods

executor a person named in a will to oversee the disposition of an estate according to the provisions of the will

expansion phase that part of the business cycle in which the nation's GDP is on the rise, the number of available jobs is growing, the unemployment rate is falling, and the national income is expanding

expenditure multiplier the means by which any given change in expenditures causes a greater change in national income, found by the formula $1/(1 - MPC)$

extensive growth the production of more goods and services because business firms are using more land, labor, or financial capital

F

factor costs the payments business firms make in exchange for the four factors of production

factors of production the resources used in producing the nation's GDP: land, labor, financial capital, and entrepreneurship

favorable balance of trade the condition experienced when a nation sells more goods abroad than it purchases from foreign nations

Federal Insurance Contribution Act (FICA) legislation requiring the deduction of social security taxes from workers' paychecks

Federal Open Market Committee (FOMC) the agency of the Federal Reserve System that is responsible for buying and selling governmental securities

Federal Reserve System the governmental institution that serves as the central bank of the United States

fiat money money that is not backed by anything of value but serves as money because of governmental decree

final goods and services goods and services that are sold to ultimate users

financial capital the factor of production denoting all money lent directly to business firms from the household sector

financial market the vast collection of financial institutions that receive deposits of excess funds from households and that lend to business firms; includes commercial banks, savings and loan associations, credit unions, insurance companies, finance companies, and stockbrokerage firms

financial plan a strategy for achieving financial objectives

first mortgage a home loan in which the property serves as collateral

fiscal agent an entity, such as a bank, that handles financial matters for another party

fiscal policy the ability of the government to affect GDP and employment through the way it spends its money, taxes its citizens, and borrows

fixed expenses expenses that do not rise or fall as the family's income changes in the short run

floating-rate account a short-term savings instrument for which the interest rate may fluctuate as economic conditions change

floor traders stock traders physically present on the trading floor to execute requested trades

401(k) an employer-sponsored retirement plan that is formed by both employer contributions and matching contributions withdrawn from the employee's paychecks

fractional reserve banking a system in which a banker lends out more paper money than he can back

free goods items provided freely by God in nature

free services services provided freely by God in nature

free trade a condition in which governments do not impose trade legislation and people are free to buy and sell products regardless of the nation that produced them

frictional unemployment unemployment that results merely because people are temporarily between jobs

full-bodied coin a coin that contains an amount of gold or silver of equal worth to its face value

G

garnish to legally withhold a portion of a debtor's wages in payment for a loan in default

general partnership a business firm owned by two or more people

good any tangible thing that has a measurable life span

gross domestic product (GDP) the total dollar value of all final goods and services produced by a nation in one year

gross domestic product implicit price deflator (GDP deflator) a price index that rises as the prices of all goods and services rise

gross private domestic investment (GPDI) the sum of all business spending on capital investment and unplanned inventories

group health insurance a health-care policy that provides coverage for a large group of people, usually the employees of a certain employer

guaranteed check a check that is affirmed by a bank or other reputable backer to be cashable by the payee

guardians persons legally appointed to care for orphaned children

H

hospitalization insurance insurance that pays for the costs associated with staying in a hospital

I

imperfect competition the condition of a market in which there are many sellers of slightly differentiated goods, sellers and buyers are reasonably aware of conditions that may affect the market, each seller has some control over his good's price, and sellers find it relatively easy to enter and exit the market

impulse buying making unplanned nonessential purchases

increase in demand a rightward shift in the demand curve representing a willingness on the part of buyers to demand more of a good or service at any price

increase in supply a rightward shift in the supply curve indicating a willingness of business firms to produce more of an item at any given price

indexing tying present wages and prices to some adjustment figure so that real wages and real prices are maintained

individual retirement account (IRA) a retirement account held in a financial institution and to which tax-deductible deposits of up to $4,000 annually may be made by qualified account holders

industry a family of common concerns, a group of businesses that sells a similar product, sells to a certain group of customers, or produces its products in a similar way

inferior good an item that typically experiences a decrease in demand as buyers' incomes increase

inflation the situation in which overexpansion of the nation's money supply leads to a sustained rise in the average price level

initial public offering (IPO) the initial sale of a company's stock through an investment bank

installment credit the ability to pay for a purchase with periodic payments according to a loan contract

intensive growth the production of more goods or services by using existing factors of production with greater efficiency

interest an additional charge that a creditor demands from a borrower to cover the expense of the loan and to provide a profit; the factor cost involving the payments made on borrowed money

interlocking directorate a situation that reduces competition in an industry by placing one or more directors on the boards of competing firms

intermediate goods items that are purchased either to be resold immediately or to be incorporated into other goods

intrinsic value value ascribed to a good or service because of its nature

investment borrowing the use of debt to purchase goods that will increase in value, produce income in the future, or reduce expenses

J

joint account an account shared by two or more people

K

Keogh plan a retirement plan for self-employed people who wish to make tax-deductible contributions to a retirement account

Keynesian economics economic policies based upon the ideas of John Maynard Keynes, who believed that governments could eliminate severe conditions of the business cycle by using fiscal policy

L

labor the factor of production denoting all human effort that goes into the creation of goods and services

labor force those persons who are working (the employed) and those who are actively looking for a job (the unemployed)

labor intensive describes a business firm that uses a great deal of human labor relative to real capital

laissez-faire the idea that the government should generally leave the economy of a nation alone and allow the people to seek their own profit

land the factor of production denoting all the natural resources that go into the production of goods

last will and testament a legal document left by a person to indicate his desires for the disposition of his possessions after his death

law of demand a law stating that, everything else being held constant, the lower the price charged for a good or service, the greater the quantity people will demand and vice versa

law of supply a law stating that the higher the price buyers are willing to pay, other things being held constant, the greater the quantity of the product a supplier will produce and vice versa

legacy a gift left by a deceased person to an heir

legal monopoly a monopoly in which the government allows one firm an exclusive right to provide a good or service

legal tender a form of money that a government declares must be accepted by creditors if it is tendered (offered) by a debtor

lender of last resort an agency able to lend money to banks when a greater than expected number of depositors wants to receive cash from their accounts

liability insurance insurance that pays for property damage and bodily injury incurred by any visitor on the insured person's property

libertarian fairness a viewpoint maintaining that the only economic right to which citizens are entitled is the right to own and use property free of governmental interference and that the accumulation of wealth is the sole responsibility of each individual

limited liability company (LLC) a form of business organization that combines the benefits of a corporation with those of a partnership

limited partner a partner in a limited partnership who has no management responsibilities and no liabilities in the firm other than his total investment

limited partnership a partnership in which there is at least one general partner who has unlimited personal financial liability and decision-making responsibility and at least one limited partner

line graph a graph formed by the plotting of data involving two variables and the connecting of the resulting points to form a line of infinite information from the data

loose monetary policy the use by the Federal Reserve System of one or more of its policy tools to increase the money supply

loose oligopoly an oligopoly in which the top four firms account for 50–75 percent of the industry's total sales

M

M-1 a measure of the nation's money supply that is available for immediate spending and includes currency, traveler's checks, and checking accounts

M-2 a measure of the nation's money supply that includes all M-1 money plus all money that is available to spend after a short delay, such as savings accounts, small-time deposits, and other short-notice deposits

macroeconomics the level of economic study that is concerned with large-scale economic choices and issues

major medical insurance health-care insurance that provides benefits for virtually all types of medical expenses resulting from accidents or illnesses

marginal propensity to consume (MPC) the percentage of each dollar that the average person chooses to spend

marginal propensity to save (MPS) the percentage of each dollar that the average person chooses to save

marginal utility curve a graphic representation of observations of utility received from some good or service

marginal utility schedule a tabular model displaying observations of utility received from some good or service

market arrangements people have developed for trading with one another

market equilibrium point the point at which the demand curve and the supply curve for an item intersect

market equilibrium price the price corresponding to the intersection of an item's supply and demand curves; the price at which consumers are willing to buy the same quantity that suppliers are willing to produce

mercantilism an economic philosophy commonly held in Europe from the sixteenth to the eighteenth centuries that advocated the accumulation of gold and silver as national wealth

microeconomics the level of economic study that is concerned with choices made by individual units

monetary policy the increasing or decreasing of the money supply to influence the economy

money anything that is commonly used and generally accepted in payment for goods and services; a medium of exchange

money market deposit accounts (MMDAs) insured accounts offered by commercial banks and thrift institutions that pay a rate of interest based on the market's demand for short-term loans

money market mutual funds (MMMFs) accounts offered by stock brokerage firms

money multiplier the factor that represents the number of times a deposit may be multiplied as it experiences the money multiplier effect

money multiplier effect the expansion of the money supply as a result of commercial banks' lending their depositors' money to others

money order a small guaranteed check bought at a bank, post office, or other business

monopoly a form of market organization in which there is only one supplier in the industry selling an undifferentiated product

mutual funds privately managed stock portfolios

mutual savings bank a financial institution that exists almost exclusively in the northeastern United States and resembles a savings and loan except for some technicalities concerning its organization

N

NASDAQ the National Association of Securities Dealers Automated Quotations, the largest exchange that does not have a trading floor

nationalization the government's acquisition of the ownership of major industries

natural barrier to entry the situation in which new firms are prevented from entering an industry because other firms already own all a vital natural resource necessary for the business

natural monopoly a monopoly that exists because one firm owns or controls 100 percent of some resource vital to the industry

negotiable order of withdrawal (NOW) account an interest-bearing transaction account offered by banks and S & L's

net exports the difference between the dollar amount a nation takes in from the sale of exports and the dollar amount it pays for imports

net worth the value of what a debtor owns minus the amount he owes

New York Stock Exchange (NYSE) the most well-known and reputable stock market in the world

nominal GDP the gross domestic product reported in current or nominal dollar values

nominal interest rate the stated rate of interest paid by a financial institution

normal good an item for which demand typically increases when the buyers' incomes increase

normative economics the approach to economic study involving value judgments about existing and proposed economic policies

nuisance goods items that bear a negative economic cost

O

oligopoly a market in which only a handful of firms are selling either highly differentiated or undifferentiated products, sellers and buyers are not fully aware of all market information, each seller has a great deal of control over the price, and sellers find it relatively difficult to enter and exit the industry

open-end credit credit from which a debtor may continually draw more money (e.g., credit-card credit)

open market operations the purchase or sale of governmental securities by the Federal Reserve System to inject or withdraw money from the money supply

opportunity benefit the satisfaction a person receives from a choice

opportunity cost the satisfaction one gives up or the regret one experiences for not choosing a desirable alternative

overdraft protection a financial institution's provision to extend credit (up to a predetermined limit) to cover an overdrawn checking account

P

partnership a business firm that is owned by two or more people

passbook account a time deposit offered by banks and thrift institutions for savers with relatively small amounts of money

pawnbroker a person who makes small loans at high rates of interest, taking valuable merchandise as collateral

payee the person or organization receiving a check

peak phase that part of the business cycle in which rapid expansion comes to a halt as shortages in natural resources, high wages, low unemployment, and rising interest rates combine to create higher prices for consumers

per capita real GDP the nation's real gross domestic product divided by its total population

perfect competition the condition of a market when there is a very large number of sellers who are selling an identical product, each seller and buyer is perfectly aware of all information about the market, no seller can affect the price, and sellers find it relatively easy to enter and to exit the market

personal loan a loan considered as consumption borrowing for personal wants or needs

point-of-sale (POS) system a system through which customers use debit cards at retail stores and gas stations to transfer money from their personal accounts to the merchant's account

positive economics the approach to economic study involving the observation of economic choices and the prediction of economic events

postdated describes a check given a future date in an attempt to withhold payment until that time

preferred stock stock that carries less risk of loss because preferred shareholders have claim to the company's assets before the common shareholders if business losses force the corporation to close

premium a regular payment for insurance

price ceiling a barrier preventing the price of an item from rising above a certain price

price discrimination the selling of the same goods or services by a business firm to different buyers at different prices

price floor a barrier preventing the price of an item from falling lower than a certain price

principal the original amount of a loan received by the borrower

principle of diminishing marginal utility the tendency of people to receive less and less additional satisfaction from any good or service as they obtain more and more of it during a specific amount of time

private corporation a corporation owned by private citizens

privatization the government's selling of nationalized businesses back to private owners

production possibilities curve (PPC) a model that enables an economist to see the maximum feasible amounts of two commodities that a business can produce when those items are competing for that business's limited resources

profits factor costs involving the rewards entrepreneurs receive for successful risk taking

progressive tax a tax that takes a greater percentage of a person's income as his income increases

proportional tax a tax in which all people pay the same percentage of their earnings

protectionists people who believe that trade deficits lead to a decrease in the number of domestic jobs and wish to protect those jobs through trade legislation

public corporation a corporation owned by the general public and managed by the government

public goods and services needed goods and services that private firms cannot create at a profit

R

radical capitalism the most extreme form of capitalism in which private citizens own all factors of production and make all economic decisions

real capital the tools business firms use to produce goods and services

real GDP the gross domestic product adjusted for inflation

recession two consecutive quarters (six months) of declining real GDP

recessionary phase that part of the business cycle in which consumer purchases decline and unemployment increases

reconciling adjusting the account holder's check register record to balance with periodic bank statements of account activities

recycling turning nuisance goods into economic goods

redress to compensate or make amends for a wrong

regressive tax a tax that takes a smaller percentage of a person's income as his income rises

rent payment for the use of an owner's property

representative money money that represents a commodity held in store

reserve requirement a specified percentage of depositors' money that must be kept on hand by banks

right of survivorship the right of a person sharing a joint account to claim the whole account balance upon the death of the other account holder

Rule of 72 a rule that states that the approximate number of years required for interest to double a deposit multiplied by the interest rate should equal 72

run on the bank a rush of depositors to the bank seeking to withdraw all their money

S

sales finance companies subsidiary companies created by large corporations to provide credit for the purchase of the corporation's products

savings and loan association (S & L) a financial institution designed to collect savings and use that capital to make loans

scarcity the condition of a good or service being finite or limited in quantity

schedule a table or chart explaining the relationships between pairs of variables; also called a tabular model

seasonal unemployment unemployment occurring when the labor force needed for certain industries or businesses expands and contracts seasonally

second mortgage a loan secured on a home (that already has a first mortgage) with the equity of the house serving as collateral

secured loan a loan with collateral

Securities and Exchange Commission (SEC) a governmental agency founded to ensure that corporations provide accurate and current information to the public about their financial situations and their business dealings

Series EE bonds US savings bonds worth $50–$10,000 that are purchased at a fraction of their face value

Series HH bonds US savings bonds purchased at full face value by rolling over Series EE bonds with interest paid by Treasury checks

service an intangible function produced by useful labor

shortage an insufficient supply of an item as a result of a price below the market equilibrium price

simple interest interest compounded annually

single-payment loans loans that, according to contract, must be repaid completely in one payment

social democracy a transitional economic system bridging the gap between capitalism and socialism with the predominant characteristic of the state's taking possession of those industries that are the cornerstones of the economy

socialism an economic system in which a central authority, committee, or the people in common generally own the factors of production and make economic decisions

social security a retirement and disability plan mandated by the government but financed by employers and employees

sole proprietorship a business firm that is owned by one person

speculation actively buying and selling stocks for the purpose of taking advantage of short-term price changes

speculative bubble stock prices rising in an industry or across the entire market simply because of expectations and rising in excess of the corporations' true value

stale dated describes a check bearing a date more than six months old

Standard and Poor's 500 (S&P 500) a commonly reported investment index that includes five hundred stocks and is intended to give an even broader perspective on business in the United States than the DJIA

state capitalism a form of capitalism in which the vast majority of the factors of production are owned by private citizens but the government intervenes widely in economic decisions to ensure that egalitarian goals are carried out

statutory will a valid will written in a standard form by the state and completed by simple indications of a person's desires for his estate

stock shares or portions of ownership in a corporation

stockbroker a person who generally works for a brokerage company and who specializes in buying and selling stocks on behalf of his clients

stock exchange a location at which stock is traded

stock index a group of stocks that analysts use to help identify stock trends in specific industries

stock portfolio a collection of stocks from different individual corporations

stop payment order a request by an account holder that his bank stop payment on a check that he has written, thus prohibiting it from being cashed

structural unemployment unemployment that occurs when workers' skills do not match available jobs

subchapter S corporation a corporate status for small businesses that allows them to continue being taxed at the lower personal income tax rates

subjective value the worth of a good or service as determined by its usefulness to the buyer

subsidy a government's payment to a producer to help with manufacturing costs

substitute goods items that resemble one another and that may be used in place of each other

supply the amount of goods and services business firms are willing and able to provide at different prices

supply curve a graph illustrating the quantities of an item that suppliers are willing to produce at various prices

supply schedule a tabular model noting the quantities of an item that suppliers are willing to produce at various prices

surety one who obligates himself to pay the debts of another; a cosigner

surplus an excess of unsold products resulting from a price above the market equilibrium price

synergy interaction in which the total is greater than the sum of the parts

T

tabular model a table or chart explaining the relationships between pairs of variables; also called a schedule

tape an electronic message board used to indicate stock prices and transactions

tariff a tax on an imported product

tenants in common two or more holders of a joint account without the right of survivorship

term the period of time in which a debtor must repay his loan according to the contract

term insurance life insurance providing only death protection during the period covered by the policy

tight monetary policy the use by the Federal Reserve System of one or more of the policy tools to reduce the money supply

tight oligopoly an oligopoly in which the top four firms account for at least 75 percent of the market sales

time deposits savings accounts that earn fixed rates of interest and have a specific maturity date or a delay period for account withdrawals

token coin a coin that contains a quantity of metal worth less than its face value

trade deficit a negative balance of trade experienced when a nation imports more than it exports

trade quotas limitations on the quantities of certain goods that foreign nations may import

trade surplus a positive balance of trade experienced when a nation exports more than it imports

transaction account an account at a financial institution against which one may write a note ordering the institution to pay a specific sum of money to the one named on the note

transfer payments payments of money or goods from the government to individuals for which no specific economic repayment is expected

traveler's checks guaranteed checks bought through banks from various financial institutions as a means of safekeeping cash during travel

Treasury bills (T-bills) governmental savings instruments that mature from ninety days to one year

trough phase that part of the business cycle in which the recessionary phase has bottomed out and the unemployment rate is high while prices and incomes are low

trust a business combination in which a group of companies in the same industry eliminate their competition by putting their stock into a single account and allowing a manager to look after the affairs of the group and distribute the profits; an arrangement that gives a person control of property and a charge to manage it for the good of an intended beneficiary

tying contracts contracts forced upon smaller companies by a supplier to give exclusive rights to the supplier and thus reduce competition

U

underemployed those workers who have a job but earn insufficient income for them to be able to provide a living for themselves

undifferentiated products products that are exactly alike from firm to firm

unemployment the state in which a person who wishes to work cannot find a job

unemployment rate the percentage of the labor force that is not employed but is looking for work

unit pricing the price per measure of the product

universal life insurance flexible life insurance that combines some of the benefits of both term and whole life insurance policies

unsecured loan a loan without collateral

US savings bonds bonds offered by the federal government bearing a high rate of interest and carrying the backing of the full faith and credit of the government

util an imaginary unit of satisfaction

utility usefulness

V

variable expenses expenses that may rise and fall as the family's income changes

vesting period the length of employment required before an employee is fully enrolled in and entitled to benefits from an employer-sponsored pension plan

W

wages factor costs involving all payments for labor used to produce goods or services

welfare state a nation under extreme state capitalism in which high taxes are used to provide wide social programs

whole life insurance life insurance providing both death protection and a means for saving

wire transfer an electronic process financial institutions use to transfer money between banks

Index

A

ability-to-pay principle, 309
acceleration clause, 123
accountability, 118, 119, 120
add-on clause, 123
administrator, 295
American Revolution, 77, 103, 281
American Stock Exchange (Amex), 152, 153
amortization schedule, 122–23
anticompetitive takeovers, 177
Antimerger Act. See Celler-Kefauver Act
antitrust legislation, 175–78
appreciating assets, 105
artificial barriers to entry, 167
assignment of savings account, 142
AT&T, 177
Austrian economics, 13, 35
automatic payroll deductions, 228
automatic teller machine (ATM), 143, 182, 203, 229
automatic transfers, 230
automobile insurance, 59, 103

B

bads, 242
bait-and-switch, 39
balance, 123, 124, 125
balloon clause, 123
bank failures, 275
bankruptcy, 81, 195
banks. See commercial banks
barrier to entry, 167, 175
barter, 187–88, 208, 241
base period, 283
Bastiat, Frederic, 248
bear market, 154
beneficiary, 61, 298
benefit principle, 310
bequest, 296
Better Business Bureau (BBB), 38, 42
black market, 116
board of directors, 136, 139, 140, 147, 210
Board of Governors (Fed), 210–14, 216, 218
bonds, 30–31, 34, 138
borrowing, 80–83, 102–5, 122–24, 125, 142–45
Bradford, William, 119
brand loyalty, 171
budget, 16–21
budget deficit, 33, 35
budget surplus, 33
bull market, 154
Bureau of Labor Statistics, US, 264
business cycle, 307
  causes, 259–62
  phases, 256–59
business investment, 238

C

capacity, 160
capital (financial), 29, 31, 113, 138, 139, 170
  from sale of stock, 146, 149, 154
  sources for creditors, 144
capital (net worth), 161, 162
capital (real), 29, 31
capital goods, 29, 89–90. See also real capital
capital intensive, 93, 94
capitalism, 35, 96, 109, 111, 114–15
  contrast with socialism, 117–20
  forms of, 111–13
  opposition to communism, 116
Carnegie, Andrew, 166
cartel, 173
cash advance, 143
cashier's check, 198, 203
cash management, 180–83
cash value (insurance), 61
caveat emptor, 39, 41
cease and desist order, 41, 178
Celler-Kefauver Act, 178
central bank, 209–14
centralized socialism, 111, 114–16
certificates of deposit (CDs), 274, 276
certified check, 198, 203
Chamberlin, Edward H., 170
change in demand, 52–56, 69
change in quantity demanded, 51
change in quantity supplied, 67
change in supply, 67–68, 69, 71
charter (bank), 196
check cashing, 204
check clearing, 215, 216–17
checking account, 142, 143, 182, 206–7
  as part of M-1, 193, 218
  deposits, 144
  in commercial banks, 196
  overdrawn, 143
checks, 142, 194
Chicago school, 199
chief executive officer, 136
circular flow model, 26–36, 187
classic liberal capitalism, 111, 112–13
Clayton Act, 176–78
clearinghouse, 216–17
club accounts, 276
codicil, 298
collateral 124, 131, 142, 145
  home equity as, 143
  in creditworthiness, 161
collision insurance, 59
collusion, 173
command economy, 90–91, 93, 95–97
commercial banks, 33, 114, 142–43, 182
  relation to Board of Governors, 211
  relation to district banks, 209
  role in creating money, 193, 195, 208, 218
  role in financial market, 195–98
commission, 148
commodity money, 191
common stock, 147
communism, 70, 91, 96, 111, 116, 120
Communist Manifesto, 96, 114
competition, 164–78
complementary goods, 54
composite index, 153
compound interest, 252, 253–54
comprehensive insurance, 58, 59
Comptroller of the Currency, 196
consumer credit, 102, 105, 122–25
Consumer Credit Protection Act. See Truth in Lending Act
consumer demands, 110
consumer durable goods, 237, 258
consumer finance companies, 144
consumer goods, 89–93
consumer goods/capital goods trade-off, 89–90, 92
consumerism, 41
consumer loan clauses, 123
consumer nondurable goods, 237
consumer price index (CPI), 283–85
Consumer Product Safety Act, 41
Consumer Product Safety Commission (CPSC), 41
consumer rights, 41
consumer services. See services
Consumers Union, 42
consumption borrowing, 102–4, 105, 122
consumption expenditures, 27
contentment, 4, 5
contingency, 20
contractual savings institutions, 199
copyright, 169

corporate spying, 172
corporation, 135–40, 157
correspondent, 216–17
cosigning, 135
cost of living adjustment (COLA), 279, 282–84
cost-push inflation, 287–88
counteradvertising, 41
counterfeit, 192, 196
covetousness, 102–3, 105, 155, 186
credit, 80–83, 102–5, 135, 160
    sources, 142–45
    types, 122–25
credit application, 160
credit bureau, 160
credit card, 80, 81, 104, 125
    bank-issued, 143, 198
    compared with debit cards, 143
    debt, 144
    fraud, 124
    relation to credit score, 162
credit limit, 144
creditor, 80–81, 131
    hurt by inflation, 279
    in determining creditworthiness, 160–63
    relation with partnerships, 132
    role in loans, 122, 123, 124, 125
credit records, 135, 162
credit report, 162, 163
credit score, 160, 162, 163
credit unions, 33, 144, 199, 208
creditworthiness, 160–63
crowding out, 35
cyclical unemployment, 268

D

Dartmouth College v. Woodward, 135
Darwin, Charles, 70, 98
Das Kapital, 96
debit cards, 143, 198, 229
debt, 80–83, 102–5, 125
    cause of garnishment, 123
    in corporations, 138
    in partnerships, 133
    in sole proprietorships, 131
    relation to creditworthiness, 160–62
    surety for, 135
debt consolidation loan, 144
debtor, 80–82, 124
deception, 39
decrease in demand, 52–56, 76, 94
decrease in supply, 67, 71, 73
deductible, 20, 59
default, 81, 123, 138
    in savings account, 142
    of loans, 144, 162
defined-contribution plans, 320
deflation, 87
demand, 50–56, 69–78, 110
    in inflation, 288
    in labor intensive business, 94
    in market economy, 91, 167
    relation to stock shares, 151
demand curve, 50–56, 67, 70, 72–73, 75
    for money, 223
    in inflation, 286–89
demand-pull inflation, 288
demand schedule, 51
Department of Health and Human Services, US, 42
Department of the Treasury. *See* Treasury, US
deposits, 80, 82, 142, 196, 198
depression, 259
diamond-water paradox, 8, 13
differentiated products, 165, 170, 171, 172, 174
diminishing marginal utility, 45–47, 48, 56
Diocletian, 290
disability income insurance, 62, 181
discounting, 220
discount rate, 220, 221
discouraged workers, 265
dismal science, 11
dissaving, 33
distribution of wealth, 95–100, 117
dividends, 138, 147, 148, 149
double coincidence of wants, 188
Dow, Charles, 152, 153
dower, laws of, 298
Dow Jones Industrial Average (DJIA), 152, 153, 154
Dow theory, 152
dual banking system, 196
duopoly, 172

E

economic choices, 3
economic cost, 7
economic Darwinism, 98
economic goals, 86–88
economic goods, 7, 8
economic growth, 87
economic leveling, 97, 99
economic model, 22
economic questions, 88, 98
economics, 2, 6, 17
economic services, 7
economic value, 8
educational loan company, 145
effective interest rate, 253–54
egalitarian fairness, 96, 97, 117
egalitarianism, 97–98, 118
elastic currency, 215
Electronic Funds Transfer Act, 143
electronic funds transfer system (EFTS), 229
electronic money, 229
employer savings plans, 228–29
Employment Act of 1946, 269
endorsement, 206
energy index, 153
Engel, Ernst, 18
Engels, Friedrich, 70, 96
Engel's law, 18
entrepreneurship, 29, 30, 31, 128
    in centralized socialism, 115
    in monopolies, 174
Environmental Protection Agency, 42
Equifax, 162
equilibrium, 71
equity, 143, 144
escheat laws, 254
escrow account, 19
estate, 294
estate taxes, 60, 296
excise tax, 308
executor, 295, 296
expansion phase, 256–57
expenditure multiplier, 303–5
Experian, 162
extensive growth, 87

F

factor costs, 29–31. *See also specific factor costs*
factors of production, 28–29, 106, 110, 116, 128
fad items, 55
Fair Isaac Corporation (FICO), 162
favorable balance of trade, 106. *See also* trade
federal budget, 302–3
Federal Communication Commission (FCC), 173
Federal Deposit Insurance Corporation (FDIC), 196, 275
Federal Insurance Contribution Act (FICA), 308
Federal Open Market Committee (FOMC), 212, 218
Federal Reserve Act, 212, 213, 214
Federal Reserve Bank of New York, 212
Federal Reserve district banks, 196, 209–10, 215, 216–17
Federal Reserve System (FRS), 196, 208,

209–11, 218–22
Federal Savings and Loan Insurance Corporation (FSLIC), 275
Federal Trade Commission, (FTC), 41, 104, 178
fiat money, 192
final goods and services, 234
finance companies, 33, 114, 142, 144–45
financial index, 153
financial liability
    in corporations, 136, 138
    in partnerships, 133, 134
    in sole proprietorships, 130, 131
financial market, 33–36, 91, 92, 114, 195–200
financial planning, 16
first mortgage, 143, 144
fiscal agent, 215
fiscal policy, 300–316
    relation to governmental spending, 305–7
fixed expenses, 18
floating-rate account, 274
floor traders, 148
Food and Drug Administration (FDA), 41
food stamps, 97
foreign trade, 243–49
401(k) plan, 320
fractional reserve banking, 193, 195
fraud, 39, 41, 124
free banking, 195
free goods and services, 7–8
free market. *See* market economy
free trade, 245–49
frictional unemployment, 268
Friedman, Milton, 199, 262
full-bodied coin, 192
Full Employment and Balanced Growth Act. *See* Humphrey-Hawkins Act

G

gambling, 155, 156, 166
garnishment, 81, 123
GDP deflator, 242, 282–83
general partnership. *See* partnership
Germany, 282
Golden Fleece Awards, 306
goldsmiths, 193, 195, 208, 211
goods, 7–8, 27–29, 31–33, 65, 241
    availability, 116
    in centralized socialism, 115
    in economic growth, 87–88
    in legal monopolies, 174, 176–77
    in market economy, 95, 110
    in mercantilism, 106

relation to supply of money, 223
role in economic questions, 88–89, 93, 95
See also specific types of goods
government, 31, 35, 65, 73, 74–75
    as artificial barrier to entry, 167
    bank regulation, 196
    distribution of wealth, 88, 95–100, 116
    in capitalism, 111–13
    in command economy, 91, 97
    in corporations, 135, 136, 138–39, 158
    in laissez-faire economy, 107–10
    in monopolies, 173–74, 175–78
    in socialism, 114–20
    relation to sole proprietorship, 129
    relation to stock market, 154, 157–58
    unemployment efforts, 99, 269–71
governmental borrowing, 313–16
governmental securities, 276–77
governmental spending, 239, 301–7, 312
Grace Commission, 306
Great Depression, 154, 157, 158, 173
    cause, 225–26
Greenspan, Alan, 213
gross domestic product (GDP), 27, 28, 31, 234–43
gross private domestic investment (GPDI), 238
group health insurance, 62
guaranteed check, 203
guardians, 295

H

Hazlitt, Henry, 10
health care, 114, 117
health insurance, 20, 59, 62–63
Hitler, Adolf, 282
homeowner's insurance, 19, 58
hospitalization insurance, 20, 62
Humphrey-Hawkins Act, 269
Hungary, 282
hyperinflation, 282

I

imperfect competition, 168, 170–71
impulse buying, 16
income, 82, 118, 139
income taxes, 33, 138, 139
incorporation. *See* corporation
increase in demand, 52–56, 69, 73, 77–78, 94
increase in supply, 67, 76
indexing, 284
individual retirement account (IRA), 198, 320
industries, 165, 167

inferior goods, 53–54
inflation, 76, 87, 181, 191–92, 278
    causes, 199, 222–23, 286–89
    cures, 289–92
    distortion to GDP, 242
    effect on purchasing value, 188
    impact and measurement, 278–85
initial public offering (IPO), 149
installment credit, 122–24
installment loan, 122, 142, 144
insurance, 58–63, 94
insurance companies, 33, 59, 61, 114, 199
intensive growth, 87
interest, 30–31, 102, 252–55
    charges with credit, 80, 82, 104, 122–23
    interest-free loans, 104
    with cash advances, 143
    with debt consolidation loans, 144
    with savings, 82
interest rates, 81, 92, 104, 131
    affected by supply of money, 223–24
    in unsecured loans, 124, 142
    of banks, 142, 144, 198
    of credit cards, 125, 143
    of credit unions, 144
    of finance companies, 144, 200
    of installment loans, 122
    of pawnbrokers, 145
    of S & Ls, 144
interlocking directorates, 176
intermediate goods, 235
Internal Revenue Service (IRS), 139, 215, 218, 229–30
intrinsic value, 8
investment bank, 149
investment borrowing, 104–5, 122
investment companies, 200
investments, 102, 154

J

Jevons, William Stanley, 45, 47, 48, 56, 259
job training, 271
joint account, 202
Jones, Edward, 152

K

Kennedy, John, 41
Keogh plan, 320
Keynesian economics, 300, 305, 309, 313–15
Keynes, John Maynard, 35, 170, 291, 300–301, 312
Kuznets, Simon, 236

L

labor, 29, 31, 87, 93–95, 113
labor force, 264
labor intensive, 93–94
Laffer Curve, 310
laissez faire, 107–9, 110, 199
land, 28–29, 31
last will and testament, 294. *See also* wills
law of demand, 50, 65
law of increasing marginal costs of production, 26
law of supply, 65–67
legacy, 296
legal barriers to entry, 175
legal monopoly, 174
legal tender, 187, 192
lender of last resort, 218
lending, 80–83, 131, 160–63
liability, 139, 143, 146
    in estates, 294
    in personal financial statement, 161
    insurance, 58
    See also financial liability
liberalism, 109, 111
libertarian fairness, 97–98, 117
life insurance, 20, 58, 59–63, 145
limited liability company (LLC), 139
limited partnership, 134
line graph, 24, 26, 51
loans. *See* credit
loose monetary policy, 223
loose oligopoly, 172
Lucas, Robert, 263

M

M-1, 193
M-2, 193
macroeconomics, 12
major medical insurance, 62
marginal propensity to consume (MPC), 303
marginal propensity to save (MPS), 303
marginal utility curve, 46
marginal utility schedule, 46
market, 111, 165–78
market basket of goods and services, 283–84, 285
market economy, 65, 70, 110, 111
    competition in, 172
    government's role in, 111, 112–13
    monopoly in, 174
    solution to distribution question, 95–97
    solution to output question, 89–93
market equilibrium level, 76
market equilibrium point, 71, 73, 76, 77
market equilibrium price, 71, 72, 74, 77
market interest rate, 91, 92
market price, 65, 70–78, 91, 115, 168
Marshall, Alfred, 70
Marshall, John, 135
Marx, Karl, 70, 96, 115, 116, 117, 170
Medicaid, 97
Medicare, 97
Menger, Carl, 8–9, 13, 35, 45, 47, 56
mercantilism, 106–10, 120, 246
merger, 171
microeconomics, 12
Microsoft, 177
minimum-wage laws, 113, 270
Mises, Ludwig von, 35
model
    purposes, 23–24
    types, 24–36. *See also specific models*
monetarist, 199
Monetary Control Act, 215
monetary policy, 222
monetary system, 112, 187, 188
monetary theory, 261–62
money, 4, 107–8, 186–95
    characteristics of, 188
    Christian view, 155, 257
    creation of, 193
    functions of, 187
    See also money supply
money management. *See* cash management
money market deposit accounts (MMDAs), 198, 274
money market mutual funds (MMMFs), 274
money multiplier, 219, 221
money multiplier effect, 218–20
money order, 203
money supply, 209, 210, 212, 223–26
    change in, 218–22
    in inflation, 289
    limitation of, 290, 292
monopoly, 168, 170, 173–75, 176–77, 178
Morgan, J. P., 166, 211
Morris, Robert, 103
mortgages, 143
mutual funds, 154
mutual interdependence, 171
mutual savings banks, 198

N

Nader, Ralph, 42
NASDAQ, 151, 153
National Banking Act, 195
National Credit Union Administration (NCUA), 275
national debt, 302–3
nationalization, 114
natural barriers to entry, 167, 175
natural monopoly, 174
natural resources, 167, 171, 174
negative balance of trade. *See* trade deficit
negotiable order of withdrawal (NOW) account, 182, 274
net exports, 239–40
net worth, 161
New York Stock Exchange (NYSE), 149, 150, 151, 153, 157
nominal GDP, 234
nominal interest rate, 252–53
nomos, 6
normal goods, 53–54
normative economics, 12–13
North American Free Trade Agreement (NAFTA), 247
nuisance goods, 7

O

Office of Thrift Supervision (OTS), 198
oikos, 6
oligopoly, 168, 171–73
open-end credit, 122, 124–25
open-end loan, 142–43
open market operation, 221
operating agreement, 139
opportunity benefit, 9–11
opportunity cost, 9–11
Organization of the Petroleum Exporting Countries (OPEC), 173
overdraft charge, 142
overdraft protection, 142, 144
overdrawing, 206
"over-the-counter" trading, 151

P

partnership, 132–35, 155
passbook account, 274, 276
pawnbrokers, 145
payee, 202, 203, 206
peak phase, 257–58
Penney, J. C., 137
penny, 191
pension plans, 198, 320–21
per capita real GDP, 242–43
perfect competition, 168–70
personal identification number (PIN), 182
personal loan, 144
Phillips, Alban William, 291

Phillips Curve, 291
planned economy, 91
point-of-sale (POS) system, 229
population growth, 33
Porter, Sylvia, 161
positive balance of trade. *See* trade surplus
positive economics, 12
postdated check, 202
preferred stock, 147
premium, 61
prepayment penalty, 123
price, 24, 64–65
    affected by supply of money, 223
    changes of, 50–56, 65–66, 70, 71, 104. *See also* inflation
    control of, 116, 138, 209, 290. *See also* price ceilings, price floor, *and specific types of competition*
    determining, 71–78
    function of, 47–50
    setting, 138, 165, 173
    takers, 167
price ceiling, 75, 77, 78
price discrimination, 178
price floor, 73, 78
principal, 122–24, 142
private corporation, 135
private ownership, 117, 120
private sector, 34
privatization, 114
production costs, 68, 70, 78, 87
    as natural barrier to entry, 167
    in foreign competition, 244
    in market economy, 95
production possibility curve (PPC), 24–26, 90, 92
profits, 31, 105, 109, 173
    from interest, 122
    from stock, 149–50
    in dividends, 147
    in entrepreneurship, 128
    in LLCs, 139
    in monopolies, 174
    in trusts, 175–76
    of corporations, 138
    relation to competition, 165, 171
progressive tax, 309
property ownership, 117
property taxes, 33, 103
proportional tax, 309
proprietor, 129, 130, 131, 146
protectionism, 245–49
Proxmire, William, 306
psychological theory, 260–61
Public Citizen Inc., 42

public corporation, 136
public goods, 112–13
public sector, 34
pump priming, 313
purchasing, 38–40

R

radical capitalism, 111–12, 116
rational expectation hypothesis, 263
real capital, 29, 35, 89–93. *See also* capital goods
real estate, 198, 104–5, 162
real GDP, 242
real income, 117
recession, 199, 223, 258–59
reconciling, 206
recycling, 7
redress, 41
regressive tax, 310
regulatory barriers to entry, 175
relative ease, 171
rent, 29, 31, 75
repossession, 123
representative money, 192
reserve requirement, 211, 220
retirement, 81, 154, 318–21
revolving credit. *See* open-end credit
Ricardo, David, 245
Robinson, Joan, 170
Robinson-Patman Act, 178
Rule of 72, 255
Rule of 78s, 123
run on the bank, 218, 220

S

sales finance companies, 144
sales taxes, 33
savings, 18, 33, 104, 228–31
    in command economy, 91
    in market economy, 92
    instruments, 274–77
savings accounts, 82, 92, 142, 193, 198
savings and loan associations (S & Ls), 33, 143–44, 198, 208, 275
savings assignment. *See* assignment of savings account
savings bonds, 34, 276–77
savings deposits, 144
scarcity, 4–6, 7, 8, 9, 14, 16
schedule. See tabular model
Schwartz, Anna, 262
seasonal unemployment, 268
second mortgage, 143, 144
secured loan, 124, 142
Securities and Exchange Commission (SEC), 157–58

self-employment, 130
Series EE bonds, 276–77
Series HH bonds, 277
services, 7, 27, 32, 65
    consumer, 90, 237
    distribution question, 95
    in entrepreneurship, 29, 128
    in legal monopolies, 174
    in market economy, 110, 117
    output question, 89
    relation to economic growth, 87–88
    relation to money supply, 223
    See also public goods
share certificates. *See* stock
shareholders, 136, 138, 139, 147–48, 200
shares, 136, 144, 146, 147, 154, 155
Sherman Antitrust Act, 175–76
shortage, 74–78, 116
simple interest, 253
single-payment loans, 122
Smith, Adam, 107–10, 112, 117
social democracy, 111, 114
socialism, 35, 70, 110
    contrast with capitalism, 117–20
    forms of, 114–16
social security, 33, 94, 97, 319–20
Social Security Act, 13
Social Security Administration, 60
sole proprietorship, 129–31
Soviet Union, 115, 116
Sowell, Thomas, 205
speculation, 156–58, 166
stale dated check, 202
Standard and Poor's 500 (S & P 500), 153, 154
standard of living, 117
state banking authorities, 215
state capitalism, 110, 111, 112, 113
statutory will, 295
stewardship, 6, 7, 104, 155, 158
    financial, 180, 183
    saving, 228–31
stock, 136, 138, 146–58, 177
stockbroker, 33, 136, 148, 158
stock certificates, 147
stock exchange, 150–52, 154, 158
stockholder, 136, 138, 140
stock index, 153, 154
stock market, 136, 146–58
    contrast to gambling, 155
    crash of 1929, 154, 156–57, 161
    indicator of economic conditions, 154, 156–58
stock portfolio, 154
stock trading, 148, 150–53, 157
stop payment order, 206

structural unemployment, 268
subchapter S corporation, 138, 139
subjective value, 8–9, 45, 51, 56
subsidy, 244
substitute goods, 54, 73, 78
sunspot theory, 259
supply, 50, 65–68, 70–74, 77–78
    in market economy, 167
    relation to stock shares, 151
supply curve, 66–70, 73, 77–78
    for money, 224
    in inflation, 286–87
supply schedule, 66
surety, 134
surplus, 72–74, 77–78
survivorship, right of, 202
synergy, 171

T

tabular model, 24–25, 26
tape, 148, 149
tariff, 246–47
taxes, 33, 34
    in command economy, 96–97
    in fiscal policy, 308–13
    in state capitalism, 113
    of corporations, 138
    of LLC, 139
tax rates, 138
technology, 67–69, 76, 78, 154
    relation to stock market, 157
    theory of business cycle, 262
tenants in common, 202
Tennessee Valley Authority (TVA), 136
term, 122, 145
term insurance, 61
thrift institutions, 142, 143–44, 198, 200
tight monetary policy, 222
tight oligopoly, 172

time deposits, 274, 276
token coin, 192
trade, 86, 106
    of stocks, 148, 150–53, 158
    See also foreign trade
trade deficit, 243–45
trademarks, 169
trade quota, 245
trade surplus, 243
Traffic and Motor Vehicle Safety Act, 42
transaction account, 182–83, 202–7
transfer payments, 33, 301–2
transportation index, 153
TransUnion, 162
traveler's checks, 182, 198, 203
Treasury, US, 198, 208, 215
    as savings account, 229–30
    relation to FRS, 215, 218
Treasury bills, 34, 277
Treasury bonds, 277
Treasury notes, 34, 277
trough phase, 259
trust, 175, 298
Truth in Lending Act, 104
tying contracts, 176–77

U

underemployed, 266
undifferentiated products, 165, 168, 169
unemployment, 35, 86–87, 100, 262–64
    compensation, 94, 97
    natural level, 269
    rate, 94, 117, 264–65
    relation to government, 209, 269–71
    relation to interest rates, 224
    relation to market, 271–72
    relation to minimum-wage laws, 270
    relation to monetary policy, 223
    relation to trade policy, 246, 247

    statistics, weaknesses in, 265–67
    types, 268–69
unit pricing, 40
universal life insurance, 61
unsecured loan, 124, 142
util, 11, 46
utilities index, 153
utility, 9, 11, 13, 46, 47
    relation to public goods, 112–13
    relation to wealth, 107

V

value, 44–50, 56, 187, 188
variable expenses, 18
vesting period, 320

W

wage-price controls, 289
wages, 29–30, 123
Wall Street, 150, 152, 157
Wall Street Journal, 152, 153
wampum, 192
wealth, 234–50
Wealth of Nations, The, 107–10, 112
welfare, 116
welfare state, 113
whole life insurance, 61
wills, 198, 294–98
windfall, 230
wire transfers, 198, 229
withdrawal, 143
workfare, 100

Y

Yap, 189

Z

Zimbabwe, 279

Photo Credits

Key: (t) top; (c) center; (b) bottom; (l) left; (r) right (fg) foreground; (bg) background; (i) insert

Cover
(front) vetkit/Shutterstock.com; (back) © iStock.com/splain2me

Unit Openers
xiv Jeff Sheldon/Public Domain; 84 © iStock.com/traveler1116; 126 © iStock.com/mbbirdy; 184 © Fotoeye75 | Dreamstime.com; 232 © Tanarch | Dreamstime.com

Chapter 1
2 © iStock.com/97; 4 © iStock.com/Guenter Guni; 7t Sascha Burkard/Bigstock.com; 7bl © iStock.com/StrahilDimitrov; 7br © iStock.com/Steve Debenport; 8l © JupiterImages Corporation; 8r © iStock.com/Shannon Long; 9bg Jeff Sheldon/Public Domain; 13 DeAgostini/Getty Images; 17 © iStock.com/Yin Yang; 18, 20l, 20c © 2009 JupiterImages Corporation; 19 John Trever, The Albuquerque Journal ©Copyright 2005 John Trever – All Rights Reserved.; 20r © iStock.com/chrisboy2004

Chapter 2
22 © iStock.com/EricFerguson; 25 © iStock.com/Pleasureofart; 27l © iStock.com/onfilm; 27r © iStock.com/trekandshoot; 28tl © iStock.com/Robert Ellis; 28bl © iStock.com/Sherwin McGehee; 28tr All rights reserved by Digital Vision; 28br Public Domain; 33t Erkan Avci/Anadolu Agency/Getty Images; 33b vedrich/Bigstock.com; 35 "Ludwig von Mises"/Ludwig von Mises Institute/Wikimedia Commons/CC BY-SA 3.0; 38l Courtesy of Better Business Bureau; 38r, 41b, 43 © 2009 JuperImages Corporation; 41t "Logo"/U.S. Food and Drug Administration/Wikimedia Commons/Public Domain

Chapter 3
44bg © iStock.com/mladn61; 44fg © iStock.com/rolandtopor; 47 Hulton Archive/Getty Images; 53 © 2008 JupiterImages Corporation; 55 C Squared Studios/Media Bakery; 58 © iStock.com/BanksPhotos; 59 © iStock.com/Michael Krinke; 60t, 62, 63 © 2009 JupiterImages Corporation; 60bl, 60br Frank Schwere/Getty Images; 61 Jozef Polc / 123RF

Chapter 4
64 Ralf Hirschberger/picture-alliance/dpa/AP Images; 65 AP Photo/Steven Senne; 66l © iStock.com/travenian; 66r © iStock.com/fadhilkamarudin; 68l © iStock.com/karma_pema; 68r © iStock.com/mbbirdy; 69tl © iStock.com/t-woo; 69cl House of Digital/Bigstock.com; 69bl © iStock.com/Mark Evans; 69tr BigKnell/Bigstock.com; 69tcr UserSam2007/Bigstock.com; 69bcr © iStock.com/mgkaya; 69br © iStock.com/Todor Tsvetkov; 70l Stock Montage/Getty Images; 70r "Principles of Economics" by Alfred Marshall/Public Domain; 72t © iStock.com/sturti; 72b © 2008 JupiterImages Corporation; 74 © iStock.com/zhudifeng; 75t steve_byland / 123RF; 75b © iStock.com/mihricat; 77 Private Collection / Photo © Christie's Images / Bridgeman Images; 81t © 2009 JupiterImages Corporation; 81b © samlocke – Fotolia.com; 82 © iStock.com/Jrcasas; 83 Courtesy of Roger Harvell, Greenville News (SC)

Chapter 5
86 © iStock.com/Grafissimo; 87 © Southwest Productions/PhotoDisc/Getty Images; 88bg Courtesy of wildtextures.com; 88tl, 88bl Courtesy of pixedin.com; 88tr, 88br Courtesy of zippypixels.com; 89l © iStock.com/İhsan Eroğlu; 89r © iStock.com/Lightguard; 92l Stocktrek Images/Media Bakery; 92r © Jeff Gilbert / Alamy; 93t ©Copyright 2009 Paresh Nath – All Rights Reserved.; 93b © iStock.com/leezsnow; 94t © iStock.com/Ricardo Azoury; 94b, 96 © 2008 JupiterImages Corporation; 95 © K.L. Howard / Alamy; 97l © iStock.com/Onfokus; 97r © iStock.com/FrankvandenBergh; 98 AP Photo/Marcio Jose Sanchez; 102 © Philippe-Olivier Contant – Fotolia.com; 103 Stock Montage/Getty Images; 104 milwifekmd/Bigstock.com; 105 lightkeeper / 123RF

Chapter 6
106 © 2008 JupiterImages Corporation; 107t © iStock.com/James Brey; 107b "Wealth of Nations" by Adam Smith/Wikimedia Commons/Public Domain; 108l "AdamSmith" created by Cadell and Davies, John Horsburgh, or R.C. Bell/Wikimedia Commons/Public Domain; 108r "Adam Smith" by Duncan Harris/Flickr/CC BY 2.0; 113 © iStock.com/ispyfriend; 114 © iStock.com/Jerry Moorman; 115t AP Photo/Lucas Flory; 115b © iStock.com/jos mata; 116 © iStock.com/Mordolff; 117l © iStock.com/Ben-Schonewille; 117r hikrcn / 123RF; 118 © iStock.com/Justin Horrocks; 119 © Massachusetts Institute of Technology, Courtesy of MIT Libraries, Rotch Visual Collections; Photograph by G. E. Kidder Smith; 122, 125 © 2009 JupiterImages Corporation; 124 © iStock.com/ewg3D

Chapter 7
128 © iStock.com/devteev; 129 © iStock.com/YinYang; 130 © iStock.com/AzmanL; 132 © 2008 JupiterImages Corporation; 136t © iStock.com/joshuaraineyphotography; 136c © iStock.com/EdStock; 136b © iStock.com/Johnny Grieg; 137l Underwood Archives/SuperStock; 137r Pictorial Parade/Getty Images; 139 Kristoffer Tripplaar/Sipa USA/AP Images; 140 © iStock.com/OJO_Images; 142 © corbis_fancy – Fotolia.com; 143t © iStock.com/GeorgePeters; 143b © iStock.com/andresr; 144 "Federal Credit Union" by Consumerist Dot Com/Flickr/CC BY 2.0; 145 © iStock.com/Joe_Potato

Chapter 8
146 kasto / 123RF; 147 Robert Brown Stock/Shutterstock.com; 148 Joe Corrigan/Getty Images; 149tl "Western Union Universal 3-A stock ticker (5900034065)" by Don DeBold/Wikimedia Commons/CC BY 2.0; 149tc National Archives; 149tr "Morgan Stanley ticker, Times Square" by Jiahui Huang/Flickr/CC BY-SA 2.0; 149bl "Chicago Welcomes the Apollo 11 Astronauts – GPN-2002-000035" by NASA/Wikimedia Commons/Public Domain; 149br JEWEL SAMAD/AFP/Getty Images; 150t © iStock.com/Songquan Deng; 150bl, 152l, 152r Library of Congress; 150br FPG/Getty Images; 151t "NY NYSE (2)" by Arnoldius/Wikimedia Commons/CC BY-SA 3.0; 151bl 4X5 Collection/Superstock; 151br Spencer Platt/Getty Images News via Getty Images; 153t © iStock.com/EdStock; 153bl © iStock.com/gmutlu; 153br Public Domain; 154t, 160b © 2009 JupiterImages Corporation; 154b Investment Company Institute. 2015. 2015 Investment Company Fact Book: A Review of Trends and Activity in the Investment Company Industry. Washington, DC: Investment Company Institute. Available at www.icifactbook.org; 156 Library of Congress, LC-USZ62-662; 157t © iStock.com/Olha Rohulya; 157b ullstein bild/ullstein bild via Getty Images; 158 "US-SecuritiesAndExchange Commission-Seal" by US Government/Wikimedia Commons/Public Domain; 160t Jean-Philippe WALLET/Shutterstock.com; 161 Library of Congress, LC-USZ62-109683; 162t queensoft/Bigstock.com; 162b © iStock.com/danielfela

Chapter 9
164 © iStock.com/Popartic; 165t © iStock.com/Susan Chiang; 165bl © iStock.com/fotoVoyager; 165br © iStock.com/pagadesign; 166t "Andrew Carnegie"/Library of Congress/Wikimedia Commons/Public Domain; 166b © Boscophotos1 | Dreamstime.com; 169tr © iStock.com/hauged; 169tl © iStock.com/YinYang; 169b © rimglow – Fotolia.com; 170l, 170r Ramsey and Muspratt, (Cambridge); 171t Mrs Butterworth® is a registered trademark of Pinnacle Foods Group LLC; 171b © iStock.com/EllenMoran; 173t © iStock.com/EdStock; 173b © iStock.com/slobo; 174 © iStock.com/kai zhang; 176t Library of Congress, LC-USZCN4-122; 176b © iStock.com/Aldo Murillo; 177 ©Copyright 2014 Paresh Nath – All Rights Reserved.; 178 "Seal of the United States Federal Trade Commission"/US Government/Wikimedia Commons/Public Domain; 180 © iStock.com/18percentgray; 181l © iStock.com/BartCo; 181r © 2009 JupiterImages Corporation; 182 Dasha Petrenko/Bigstock.com; 183 © iStock.com/Timurpix

Chapter 10
186 Matthias Kulka/The Image Bank RF/Getty Images; 187t © iStock.com/Janka Dharmasena; 187c © iStock.com/RyanJLane; 187b © Patrimonio | Dreamstime.com; 188 © iStock.com/dehooks; 189 imageBROKER/Frank Schneider/Getty Images; 190t Hoberman Collection/Hoberman Collection/SuperStock; 190bl "Pieces of Eight" by USFWSmidwest/Flickr/CC BY 2.0; 190bcl "1976S Eisenhower

Obverse" by Brandon Grossardt/Wikimedia Commons/GFDL, CC BY-SA 3.0; **190bcr** Department of Treasury, US Mint; **190br** Public Domain; **191t** © iStock.com/Jodi Jacobson; **191c, 191b** United States Mint image; **192t** Newberry Library/Newberry Library/SuperStock; **192b** Courtesy of the National Numismatic Collection, National Museum of American History; **193l** © iStock.com/NoDerog; **193c** © iStock.com/PeopleImages; **193r** © iStock.com/Deejpilot; **194** "Miss Myrtle Berheim"/US National Archives and Records Administration/Wikimedia Commons/Public Domain; **196t** © iStock.com/Maher; **196c** © iStock.com/jenjen42; **196b** "US-FDIC-Logo" by US Government/Wikimedia Commons/Public Domain; **198** SuperStock/SuperStock; **199** "Milton Friedman"/Wikimedia Commons/Public Domain; **200** Reprinted with permission of The Wall Street Journal, Copyright © 2013 Dow Jones & Company, Inc. All Rights Reserved Worldwide. License numbers 3677710807642 and 3677711141523.; **202** © iStock.com/Sean Locke; **203t** Don Murray/Getty Images; **203b** "Well's fargo counterfit cashier's check" by Kalmia/Wikimedia Commons/GFDL, CC BY-SA 3.0; **205** Stanford Visual Art Services; **206t** Comstock/Media Bakery; **206b** © iStock.com/MBPHOTO.

Chapter 11
208 Karl Gehring/The Denver Post via Getty Images; **209t** Federal Reserve System; **209c** jiawangkun / 123RF; **209b** Courtesy of the Woodrow Wilson Presidential Library, Staunton, Virginia; **210** "The Federal Reserve Bank of San Francisco" by Michele Ursino/Flickr/CC BY-SA 2.0; **211, 218** Everett Collection Inc / Alamy Stock Photo; **212tl** "US-FederalReserveBoard-Seal" by U.S. Government/Wikimedia Commons/Public Domain; **212bl** "Janet Yellen official Federal Reserve portrait" by United States Federal Reserve/Wikimedia Commons/Public Domain; **212r** "Federal Open Market Committee Meeting"/Federal Reserve Bank of Philadelphia/Wikimedia Commons/Public Domain; **213l** "Alan Greenspan color photo portrait"/Federal Reserve/Wikimedia Commons/Public Domain; **213r** Mark Wilson/Getty Images; **214t** Xinhua / Alamy Stock Photo; **214b** www.doverpublications.com/cd; **215t** strick9/Bigstock.com; **215b** "US-BureauOfEngravingAndPrinting-Seal" by U.S. Government/Wikimedia Commons/Public Domain; **220** Scott Eells/Bloomberg via Getty Images; **222l** © iStock.com/simazoran; **222r** © iStock.com/EdStock; **225** CARLSON © 2001 Milwaukee Journal Sentinel. Reprint with permission of UNIVERSAL UCLICK. All rights reserved.; **228t, 230l** © 2009 JupiterImages Corporation; **228b** Peter Dazeley/Stone/Getty Images; **229** © iStock.com/BraunS; **230r** © iStock.com/ryasick; **231** Robert Byron / 123RF.

Chapter 12
234 © iStock.com/Aenyeth; **235t** bdstudio – Fotolia.com; **235bl** © iStock.com/mihalis_a; **235br** © iStock.com/doodah_stock; **236** AP Photo/Frank C. Curtin; **237** © iStock.com/RakicN; **238** © iStock.com/Gary Douglas-Beet; **239** AP Photo/Hans Pennink; **241t** © iStock.com/hsvrs; **241bl** © iStock.com/morozena; **241br** © iStock.com/Pamela Moore; **242** © iStock.com/acilo; **243** © iStock.com/Roberto A Sanchez; **245** Universal History Archive/Getty Images; **246l** © iStock.com/unkas_photo; **246r** © iStock.com/Daniel Barnes; **247l** AP Photo/Doug Mills; **247r** "NAFTA logo" by Nicoguaro/Wikimedia Commons/CC BY 3.0; **248** The Warren J. Samuels Portrait Collection; **249** CALVIN AND HOBBES © 1993 Watterson. Reprinted with permission of UNIVERSAL UCLICK. All rights reserved.; **252t, 255** © 2009 JupiterImages Corporation; **252b** © North Wind Picture Archives; **253** FOXTROT © 1999 Bill Amend. Reprinted with permission of UNIVERSAL UCLICK. All rights reserved.

Chapter 13
256 © iStock.com/GeorgeStanden; **257t** © iStock.com/Rob Belknap; **257bl** © iStock.com/Steve Debenport; **257br** canadapanda / 123RF; **258l** © iStock.com/wynnter; **258r** Library of Congress, LC-USZ62-55376; **259t** © iStock.com/pawel.gaul; **259b** Library of Congress; **261** HEART OF THE CITY © 2008 Mark Tatulli. Dist. By UNIVERSAL UCLICK. Reprinted with permission. All rights reserved.; **262t** © iStock.com/vgajic; **262b** Franklin D. Roosevelt Library; **263t** catcha/Bigstock.com; **263b** Ralf-Finn Hestoft/Contributor/Corbis Historical/Getty Images; **264t** "Bureau of labor statistics logo"/US Dept of Labor/Wikimedia Commons/Public Domain; **264bl** © iStock.com/skynesher; **264br** © iStock.com/Squaredpixels; **266t** © iStock.com/hanhanpeggy; **266bl** © iStock.com/SolStock; **266bc** © iStock.com/MivPiv; **266br** © iStock.com/chrisjo; **268t** © iStock.com/Vesna Andjic; **268b** © iStock.com/MarioGuti; **270** Gideon Mendel/Corbis Historical/Getty Images; **271** Spencer Platt/Staff/ Getty Images News; **274** CORNERED © 2000 Mike Baldwin. Reprinted with permission of UNIVERSAL UCLICK. All rights reserved. **275** Patrick Fallon/Bloomberg via Getty Images; **276** © 2009 JupiterImages Corporation

Chapter 14
278, 278i, 279tl, 282t © 2008 JupiterImages Corporation; **279tr** Tony Baggett/Bigstock.com; **279c** michaeljung/Bigstock.com; **279i** "US-SocialSecurityAdmin-Seal" by U.S. Government/Wikimedia Commons/Public Domain; **279b, 285** Scanrail/Bigstock.com; **280t** Library of Congress, LC-USZ62-B4079; **280c** Imagesbavaria/Bigstock.com; **280b** gemenacom/Bigstock.com; **281t** stokkete/Bigstock.com; **281b** "Continental Currency One-Third-Dollar 17-Feb-76 obv" by Benjamin Franklin/Wikimedia Commons/Public Domain; **282c** Library of Congress; **282b** Ariel Skelley/Digital Vision/Getty Images; **283t** ZIGGY © 1994 ZIGGY AND FRIENDS, INC. Reprinted with permission of UNIVERSAL UCLICK. All rights reserved.; **283b** Ivonnewierink/Bigstock.com; **291tl** Courtesy of Carol Somervell; **291tr** Giuseppe Vittucci/Wikipedia; **291b** "MONIAC Computer" by Kaihsu Tai/Wikimedia Commons/Public Domain; **294l** zimmytws/Bigstock.com; **294r, 295** © 2009 JupiterImages Corporation; **296** Lilun/Bigstock.com; **298** alexraths/Bigstock.com

Chapter 15
300 Orhan/Bigstock.com; **301t** tab62/Bigstock.com; **301b** CQ Roll Call via AP Images; **302** FRANK & ERNEST © 2010 Thaves. Used By permission of UNIVERSAL UCLICK for UFS. All rights reserved.; **304** REUTERS / Kevin Lamarque - stock.adobe.com; **305** Library of Congress, LC-DIG-fsa-8b29797; **307** "Ceremony for National Head Start Day"/NARA/Flickr/CC BY 2.0; **308** zimmytws/Bigstock.com; **309t** FRANK & ERNEST © 2006 Thaves. Used By permission of UNIVERSAL UCLICK for UFS. All rights reserved.; **309c** Internal Revenue Service; **309b** Kevin Grant/Bigstock.com; **311t** cjpix/Bigstock.com; **311b** Makaule/Bigstock.com; **312l** Bettmann Archive/Getty Images; **312r** Hulton Deutsch/Corbis Historical/Getty Images; **313t** Russell Kord / Alamy Stock Photo; **313b** rob_lan/Bigstock.com; **318** Paul Brady/Bigstock.com; **319t** monkeybusinessimages/Bigstock.com; **319b** © iStock.com/William Mahar; **320t** AndreyPopov/Bigstock.com; **320b** viewapart/Bigstock.com